THE STRATEGY CONCEPT
AND PROCESS

Second Edition

THE STRATEGY CONCEPT AND PROCESS

A Pragmatic Approach

Arnoldo C. Hax
Massachusetts Institute of Technology

Nicolas S. Majluf
Catholic University of Chile

PRENTICE HALL, Upper Saddle River, New Jersey 07458

Library of Congress Cataloging-in-Publication Data

HAX, ARNOLDO C.
  The strategy concept and process : a pragmatic approach / ARNOLDO
C. HAX, NICOLAS S. MAJLUF,—2nd ed.
    p. cm.
  Includes bibliographical references and index.
  ISBN 0-13-458894-0
  1. Strategic planning.   I. Majluf, Nicolas S., [date].
II. Title
HD30.28.H3885   1996
658.4'012—dc20   95-25156

Acquisitions editor: *David Shafer*
Project manager: *Edie Riker*
Cover design: *Wendy Alling Judy*
Marketing manager: *Jo-Ann DeLuca*
Buyer: *Ken Clinton*
Editorial assistant: *Nancy Kaplan*

 © 1996, 1991 by Prentice-Hall, Inc.
A Simon & Schuster Company
Upper Saddle River, New Jersey 07458

Printed in the United States of America

20   19   18   17   16   15

ISBN 0-13-458894-0

Prentice-Hall International (UK) Limited, *London*
Prentice-Hall of Australia Pty. Limited, *Sydney*
Prentice-Hall Canada Inc., *Toronto*
Prentice-Hall Hispanoamericana, S.A., *Mexico*
Prentice-Hall of India Private Limited, *New Delhi*
Prentice-Hall of Japan, Inc., *Tokyo*
Simon & Schuster Asia Pte. Ltd., *Singapore*
Editora Prentice-Hall do Brasil, Ltda., *Rio de Janeiro*

Dedication

To our families, the sources of much joy, encouragement, and support.

The Haxes: *Neva Sr., Neva Jr., and Andrés.*

The Majlufs: *Lichy Sr., Lichy Jr., Nicolás, Javier Cristóbal, and María Paz.*

And, especially, to Ignacio Majluf, who brought our families together.

Contents

PART IV FUNCTIONAL STRATEGY

Preface

As this century comes to an end, managers are facing challenges of enormous dimensions. The trend toward globalization, which is present in all significant business activities, has resulted in a dramatic increase in the intensity and diversity of competition. A manager today has to understand not only the familiar domestic markets, but also the subtleties of doing business in foreign markets against unfamiliar competitors. The increasing trend toward globalization stems from the pervasive forces of technology, which are reshaping industries and deeply affecting the ways to compete. These two forces of globalization and technology are demanding a new form of leadership. It is essential now that executives feel comfortable with managing changes in a highly dynamic environment and have the capacity to provide a sense of strategic direction to guide the organization constructively into the future.

Paramount to accomplishing this demanding task is for a manager to be able to articulate a vision of the firm with charismatic zeal. This is the essence of leadership: managing strategically by imprinting the vision of the firm throughout the organization.

The central objective of this book is to help managers to bring the vision into a concrete reality. Rather than philosophizing in the abstract about the attributes of leadership, we have adopted a pragmatic approach to strategic management. Our hope is to offer practicing managers and business students a disciplined process that facilitates the formulation and implementation of strategy to allow this demanding task of identifying and imprinting the vision of the firm to become a meaningful reality.

We believe this book, which is the result of years of research work, teaching, and consulting experience, offers the following unique attributes:

- *There is a bias toward pragmatism.*
  It is our intent to provide carefully crafted methodologies that facilitate the applications of relevant concepts and tools into strategy development.

- *It proposes an effective process to facilitate communication.*
  At the heart of strategy resides a willingness to change, to adapt the organization, to improve its competitive position. That change can only be realized if there is a basic consensus among key managers about the central strategic direction of the firm. We believe the strategic process we recommend constitutes a powerful instrument to address all the essential managerial tasks and eventually reach that quality of consensus. Incidentally, consensus does not mean that dissenting views are not tolerated; quite the contrary, a proper strategic planning process will stimulate controversy and the expression of different points of view. But it will also recognize that there is a time to confront and disagree, and a time where differences must be put aside with the emergence of a shared vision agreed upon by all of its key architects.

- *It represents the state of the art of the practice of strategic management.*
  We have made a conscious effort to recognize all key advances in the vast field of strategic management that can assist business executives in addressing the totality of the tasks required to bring a strategic vision to the firm.

- *There is an integrative and comprehensive approach to strategic management.*
  There is no book on strategy, to our knowledge, that has as broad a scope as this book. The essential frameworks that are treated in reasonable depth are: the concept of strategy and the strategy formation process (Part I); the tasks pertaining to the development of business strategy (Part II); the tasks required for the formulation of corporate strategy (Part III); and the tasks associated with the development of functional strategy (Part IV).

- *Practical illustrations are offered throughout.*
  In every chapter of the book we have made a constant effort to exemplify with relevant and real-life applications the concept and tools that are described. Cases of particular importance are: Procter and Gamble, that we use to illustrate the development of corporate and business strategies; NKK Materials Sector, that is used in the corporate strategy part of the book; and Merck, that is discussed in Chapter 8 to evaluate the merits of a strategy. In the part of the book dedicated to functional strategies, Citibank is used as the example for human resources strategy; Packard Electric, a component division of General Motors, is the illustration of manufacturing strategy; and a massive parallel computer company is used to discuss technology strategy.

Reflecting more specifically about the contributions in each of the book's four parts, we can say the following:

PART I - STRATEGY AND PROCESS. It provides a unified definition of the concept of strategy, as well as suggesting a disciplined step-by-step approach to formalize the development of a strategic plan. Chapter 1 serves to provide an integrative view of the major schools of thought that have contributed to the development of the concept and process of strategy. In Chapter 2 we present the five basic frameworks that we propose to advance strategic thinking in a business organization: corporate strategy, business strategy, functional strategy, strategic planning process, and strategic management. The fundamental tasks that are needed to develop these frameworks are summarized in that chapter. They constitute the underlying disciplines of this book.

PART II - BUSINESS STRATEGY. It covers the core concepts of business strategy: strategic business unit (SBU), mission of the business, industry analysis, competitive positioning, and the tasks required to put together a comprehensive business strategy. This part integrates the two conceptual frameworks proposed by Michael Porter—industry and competitive analysis, and the value chain—as the fundamental constructs to support a business strategy. This part concludes with Chapter 8 where we present a methodology to evaluate the merits of a strategy.

PART III - CORPORATE STRATEGY. Although corporate strategy is vital in defining the vision of the firm, there is no book that has treated in detail the nature of the strategic tasks to be conducted at the corporate level. We recognize ten fundamental activities linked to the development of corporate strategy: the environmental scan at the corporate level, the mission of the firm, business segmentation, horizontal strategy, vertical integration, corporate philosophy, strategic posture of the firm, portfolio management, managerial infrastructure, and human resources management of key personnel. Each of these tasks is treated in significant detail and illustrated accordingly to provide managers with a full understanding of what is needed to construct a corporate strategy and to make it a reality.

PART IV - FUNCTIONAL STRATEGY. In this part, we cover an immense amount of information to facilitate the development of strategy for all of the key functions of the firm: finance, human resources management, technology, procurement, manufacturing, and marketing. Chapter 18, in a very compact way, lists the major categories of strategic decisions and the associated measures of performance related to each one of the functional strategies. Chapters 19, 20, and 21 illustrate how to develop human resources, technology, and manufacturing strategies, respectively.

This second edition of our book has represented a major rewrite. About 60 percent of its content is completely new. Two major changes have materialized. First, we needed to incorporate recent developments that have impacted strategic thinking since we published the first edition. Primarily among them are the concepts of core competencies and strategic intent espoused by C. K. Prahalad and Gary Hamel; the positioning-sustainability-flexibility framework of Pankaj Ghemawat; and the resource-based view of the firm. We have integrated these concepts into the framework we propose to support the formal strategic planning process in a business firm. Second, we have largely updated most of the illustrations we have used. Finally, our methodology is presented in a much more explicit way which will greatly facilitate the ability of the reader to implement it. This, to a great extent, is due to the support that we have gotten through the availability of two softwares that have jointly been developed by Arnoldo Hax and Electronic Data Systems.*

We owe a great deal to our colleagues at MIT and elsewhere who have established the solid foundations of strategic management. Their contributions are acknowledged throughout the book. We also have benefited greatly from the work of many of our students at MIT who wrote masters theses and working papers under our supervision. We would especially like to recognize Scott Beardsley, Alain Boutboul, David Burgner, Dexter Charles, Chin-Tain Chiu, Daniel DiSano, John Gray, Lynnet Koh, Marianne Kunschak, Lily Lai, Kung-Shih Lee, Emmanuel Maceda, Manuel No, Luis Ortega, Kenji Sakagami, Masayuki Tada, Luis Tena-Ramirez, Mark Webster, and Antoinette Williams.

We would like to express our most sincere thanks for the support that the Sloan School of Management at MIT and the School of Engineering at the Catholic University of Chile have provided for our work.

In the production of this book we owe our deepest thanks to Deborah Cohen for an outstanding job of typing, editing, and proofreading the many versions of the original manuscript.

---

* EDS Corporate Strategic Planner and EDS Business Strategic Planner.

Software that supports the methodology described in this book has been developed by EDS in collaboration with Professor Arnoldo Hax. Business Planner supports the development of business strategy described in Chapters 3 through 7. Corporate Planner supports the development of corporate strategy described in Chapters 9 through 16. If you are interested in learning more about this software, please call EDS at 214-605-5846 or fax your request to 214-605-0520.

CHAPTER 1

The Concept of Strategy and the Strategy Formation Process

What is strategy? The challenge to provide a definition of strategy is not straight-forward because there are some elements of strategy that have universal validity and can be applied to any institution, regardless of its nature. Others seem to be heavily dependent not only on the nature of the firm but also on its constituencies, its structure, and its culture. To break this impasse, we find it useful to separate the concept of strategy from the process of strategy formation.

By the concept of strategy, we mean its content and substance. This subject has received a great deal of attention by various authors in the last few decades. Most of them, however, seem to have emphasized a different and unique perspective, providing only a single dimension of this fairly complex concept.

We start this book by revisiting the central definitions that have been proposed, and by suggesting an integrative view that, we believe, captures more comprehensively the various dimensions of the concept of strategy. We have reviewed the work of some of the most salient contributors to the strategy field. Whenever possible, we have attempted to discuss their work in a chronological order. What emerges is more than a series of isolated definitions of strategy, but a change in what has been emphasized as the essence of strategy through time.

Some of these dimensions and emphases, particularly those proposed in the last decade, have generated a great deal of controversy. We will attempt to harmonize these seemingly contradictory views and provide a unified definition of strategy that integrates, in a constructive and pragmatic way, all of the different contributions to the field.[1]

The process of strategy formation is much more elusive and difficult to grasp. The first step is to define the key players in charge of formulating and implementing the strategy. Are they supposed to act as a team, or are they going to be divided into independent groups; and if so, how is the information going to flow from one to another? Second, what tasks are those teams going to accomplish, and in which sequence? Is there a calendar that will be driving these efforts, with constant regularity, or will they be acting in a more flexible and ad hoc capacity? To what extent will the process of strategy formation be explicitly stated and communicated to the various constituencies both inside and outside the firm? How disciplined and rational will the resultant process be? Will the process be heavily dependent on formal-analytical tools, or will it be more the result of unorganized deals where bargaining becomes the guiding force? All of these issues are part of the process of strategy formation. Later in this chapter we begin its development, and in Chapter 2 we propose a working framework to support a formal strategic planning process. How to put this process to work is really what this book is all about.

Although it is useful to separate these two elements of strategy in order to gain a better understanding of them, it is essential that substance and process are not decoupled, because they are intrinsically integrated. The substance of strategy is to achieve superior financial performance by differentiating the firm from its competitors; the process of strategy provides the discipline that allows all the key managers to participate actively in the definition of strategy.[2]

The Various Dimensions of the Concept of Strategy

Strategy can be seen as a multidimensional concept that embraces all the critical activities of the firm, providing it with a sense of unity, direction, and purpose, as well as facilitating the necessary changes induced by its environment. Reviewing some of the most important works in the field of strategy, we have identified the following critical dimensions that contribute to a unified definition of the concept of strategy.

1. Strategy as a means of establishing the organizational purpose in terms of its long-term objectives, action programs, and resource allocation priorities.

This is one of the oldest and most classical views of the concept of strategy. Strategy is a way of explicitly shaping the long term goals and objectives of the organization, defining the major action programs needed to achieve those objectives, and deploying the necessary resources.[3]

We are presented with a pragmatic and useful definition of the nature of strategic actions. First, we need to define the long-term objectives of the firm. These objectives should have a certain sense of permanence, and are not modified unless external conditions or internal changes call for a reexamination of the long-term commitments of the firm. Nothing could be more destructive and distracting than an erratic reorientation of the firm's objectives, without substantive reasons other than hesitations on the part of the top managers of the organization. Continuous strategic redirection of the firm will end up confusing all its stakeholders, most importantly, its customers and employees.

The desired stability of long-term objectives does not, however, preclude continuous steering and readaptations of the firm's programs. This is accomplished by a reexamination of the strategic action programs, which are more short-term oriented in character, while seeking congruency with long-term objectives .

Finally, this dimension of strategy points to the relevance of resource allocation as the most critical strategic implementation step. The alignment between strategic objectives and programs on the one hand, and the allocation of the human, financial, technological, and physical resources of the firm on the other hand, are required in order to assure strategic consistency.

2. Strategy as a definition of the competitive domain of the firm.

It has long been recognized that one of the central concerns of strategy is defining the businesses the firm is in or intends to be in. This places strategy as the basic force that addresses issues of growth, diversification, and divestment .[4]

The key first step in defining a formal strategic planning process is an effective business *segmentation*. This concept occupies a great deal of attention throughout the book. At this point it is enough to say that most of the strategic attention, both in terms of the formulation and implementation of strategy, resides at the business unit of the firm. Therefore, the basic question to be addressed is "What businesses are we in?"; a question that also carries with it two additional corollaries: "What businesses are we in but we should not be in?", which leads to the hard decision of divestment; and "What businesses we are not in but should be in?", which leads into the decisions of entry and diversification.

If you have never attempted to respond seriously to these questions, you might find them trivial. But we have repeatedly faced great difficulties in extracting clear-cut answers containing full consensus from an experienced group of managers when these questions are addressed for the first time. There seem to be discrepancies in the criteria defining businesses, in the desired degree of aggregation of the business units, and even in the identification of the responsibilities of those in charge. The issues are further complicated because business segmentation ultimately has enormous impact in defining the organizational structure of the firm. Consciously or unconsciously, issues of turf and executive responsibilities tend to have a major input in the way those questions are addressed.

Segmentation is the key for business analysis, strategic positioning, resource allocation, and portfolio management. Segmentation is more an art than a science, because there are no clear guidelines to be provided that assure a proper outcome for this task. The essence of segmentation consists of selecting the customers the business units will be serving, and consequently, the competitors that they will be facing. In today's rapidly changing environment, there is a continuous transformation affecting businesses and competitors which makes this selection process a moving target.

Adding to this incessant change is the fact that most businesses are competing in global markets making competitor's benchmarking an exceedingly difficult task. This is due to the fact that simultaneously the business is confronted with global, regional and local competitors.

Endproducts, which have been the classical dimensions of segmentation, might no longer constitute the most relevant ones. Instead, core products, which are recipients of core competencies of the firm, are signaled as more appropriate platforms to respond to the dynamics of change. Core products are the basis for the fast development of end products serving fast changing end-markets, as well as achieving economies of scale and scope.[5]

As we have indicated before, there is a close interrelationship between business segmentation and the existing organizational structure of the firm. As new organizational forms are introduced, resulting in more compact, less hierarchical, and more horizontally driven structures, additional dimensions for segmentation are emerging. These include business processes, as well as core competencies and capabilities.

3. Strategy as a response to external opportunities and threats, and internal strengths and weaknesses, in order to achieve a sustainable competitive advantage.

According to this perspective, the central thrust in strategy is to achieve a long-term sustainable advantage over the key competitors of the firm in every business in which it participates. This dimension of strategy is behind many of the approaches used to support the search for a favorable competitive position. It recognizes that competitive advantage results from a thorough understanding of the external and internal forces that impact the organization. Externally, we have to identify the industry attractiveness and trends, as well as the characteristics of the major competitors. This generates opportunities and threats to be reckoned with. Internally, we have to assess the firm's competitive capabilities, which produce strengths and weaknesses that have to be further developed and corrected.

Strategy is needed in order for organizations to obtain a viable match between their external environment and their internal capabilities. The role of strategy is not viewed as just passively responding to the opportunities and threats presented by the external environment, but as continuously and actively adapting the organization to meet the demands of a changing environment.

From this perspective emerges the fundamental framework of business strategy with three areas of attention: the business unit, as the central subject of analysis; the industry structure, which determines the key environmental trends; and the internal competencies, which define the ways to compete. Figure 1–1 illustrates how these three areas of attention provide the framing of the strategic issues for a business; and how they become the key forces determining strategy formulation and implementation. The long-term objectives,

FIGURE 1–1. The Basic Framework for Explaining the Profitability of a Business

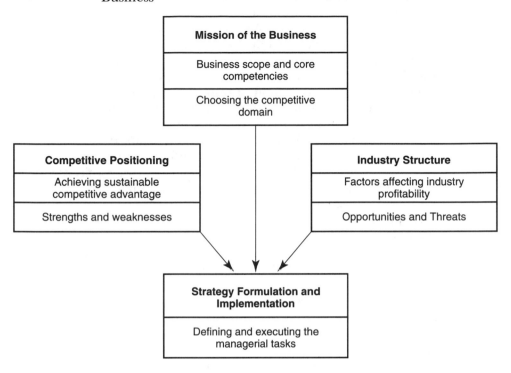

strategic action programs, and resource allocation priorities thus become conditioned to the role that the business unit intends to play within the portfolio of businesses of the firm, the favorable or unfavorable trends of its industry structure, and the internal capabilities needed to be deployed in order to achieve the desired competitive position.

Michael Porter[6] unarguably has been the dominant figure in shaping and communicating this framework of business strategy. He proposed his now famous Five-Forces model to explain the different level of profitability among industries, and the celebrated Value Chain model, that allows firms competing in the same industry to be differentiated. According to Porter, industry structure explains the sustainability of profits against bargaining and against direct and indirect competitors. Profit difference vis-à-vis direct rivals, however, depend on competitive positioning. From this perspective, a business is identified as a discrete but interrelated set of activities. Competitive advantage results from the firm's ability to perform the required activities, either at lower costs than their rivals, or in differentiated ways that create buyer value and allow the firm to command a premium price.[7]

4. Strategy as a way to define managerial tasks with corporate, business, and functional perspectives.

There are three distinct perspectives—corporate, business, and functional—that are important in defining the strategy of the firm, and which carry on quite different managerial responsibilities. The corporate perspective encompasses those tasks that need the fullest scope to be addressed properly. They deal, primarily, with issues pertaining to the definition of the overall mission of the firm, the validation of proposals emerging from business and functional levels, the identification and exploitation of linkages between distinct but related business units, and the allocation of resources with a sense of strategic priorities. The business perspective includes all the activities necessary to enhance the competitive position of each individual business unit within its own industry. The functional perspective deals with developing the necessary functional competencies in finance, administrative infrastructure, human resources, technology, procurement, logistics, manufacturing, distribution, marketing, sales, and services needed to sustain competitive advantage. Recognizing the differences among of these perspectives and the impact they have on the corresponding managerial roles, and integrating the resultant efforts, is another key dimension of strategy.[8]

Normally, one tends to associate corporate, business, and functional perspectives with three different hierarchical levels in the firm. We have purposely avoided the use of the word *hierarchical*, because it tends to have a misleading connotation, particularly when the current trend is for organizations to flatten their structure rather than depend on rigid hierarchies. We are not necessarily segmenting the strategic tasks according to conventional and orthodox hierarchies. However, regardless of the type of organizational structure adopted by the firm, there continue to exist three highly differentiated strategic concerns. The first addresses the organization as a whole; we refer to this concern as the issues pertaining to corporate strategy. The second concern is inherent to the business unit, regardless of where this responsibility resides in the organization—these are the issues pertaining to business strategy. And the third one involves the development of functional capabilities and corresponds to the issues pertaining to functional strategy.

It is our experience that most companies allocate a lion's share of their strategic thinking and actions to activities dealing with business strategy; but, neglecting corporate and functional strategies can be quite costly. Many organizations that used to enjoy extraordinary performance, and that once were heralded as the most admired corporations in America, have seen dramatic losses, primarily as a result of mistakes being made at the corporate level. At the end of 1993, the companies that were at the bottom among the Fortune 1000, in terms of value created for their stockholders, were IBM, RJR Nabisco, General Motors, Digital Equipment, and Ford Motors. Collectively, they were responsible for destroying $14.2 billion of shareholder value. [9] In 1992 these five companies had been in a much worse position, having destroyed $63.4 billion. One could argue that there was a great recovery from 1992 to 1993. The fact of the matter is, however, that they had dug themselves such a big hole, that the major improvement was insufficient to take them out from the bottom of the list. Obviously, there are many reasons and great controversies surrounding this dismal performance of companies that not too long ago were a model of management; but it is hard not to argue that some of the most critical mistakes were concentrated among their top managers and had, at their roots, corporate strategic issues.

Similarly, it is important to raise a voice of warning about the need to develop effective functional strategies, which are the depositories of the distinctive capabilities of the firm. To a great extent, the decline of U.S. competitiveness during the 1970s was due to lack of strategic attention to manufacturing as a key source of competitive advantage. The recent movement advocating for business-process reengineering has led people to embrace the notion of tasks being defined in terms of processes at the expense of paying careful attention to functional capabilities.[10] Functions seem to be out of fashion, while business processes are in. This is also a dangerous position. It is our view that both dimensions are necessary and must receive a fair share of managerial attention.

5. Strategy as a coherent, unifying, and integrative pattern of decisions

It is quite common to consider strategy as a major force that provides a comprehensive and integrative blueprint for the organization as a whole. From this perspective, strategy gives rise to the plans that assure that the basic objectives of the total enterprise are fulfilled.[11]

By considering strategy as the pattern of decisions of the firm, we recognize that strategy is an unavoidable construct —it just emerges from what the firm does. We can go into an organization and study, from a historical perspective, the nature of its decision making and its resultant performance. Strategic patterns can be discerned when detecting major discontinuities in the firm's direction, stemming either from changes in its top management or triggered by important external events that call for strategic repositioning. The resultant "eras" of a firm can be used to analyze the coherence of strategic patterns. It is up to the managers in charge to make those patterns the result of well-defined visions of the firm, or to resort to improvisation and sheer luck. In any event, strategies will emerge, willingly or not, leaving footprints of the major steps the firm has taken in the past which might also define its future destination.

6. Strategy as a definition of the economic and noneconomic contribution the firm intends to make to its stakeholders.

The notion of stakeholders has gained importance as an element of strategic concern in the past few years. *Stakeholders* is a term designating everybody who directly or indirectly receives the benefits or sustains the costs derived from the action of the firm: shareholders, employees, managers, customers, suppliers, debt-holders, communities, government, and so forth.

This dimension of strategy recognizes the responsibility of the firm in much wider ways than simply maximizing the shareholders' wealth. It views strategy as a means of establishing social contracts—a collection of cooperative agreements entered into by individuals with free will—to produce a process of social interchange that affects a wide variety of constituencies. The final output imprints the kind of economic and human organization the firm is and would like to be. It is a key determinant of both corporate philosophy and organizational culture.

Caring about the stakeholders could be a useful way of putting the central strategic concerns of the firm in a proper perspective. It is obvious that in a profit-making organization, profit becomes an important objective: the proverbial "bottom line." However, it might become a dangerous trap to fall into, if managers look at short-term profitability as the ultimate driving force rather than to the legitimate and deserved reward of a job well done that emanates from being responsible toward the remaining stakeholders of the firm.

A firm has to recognize that if customers are not properly serviced, eventually another firm will dominate the market with the consequent loss of competitiveness and profitability. Similar arguments can be made for the firm's employees and suppliers; if fair and mutually beneficial relationships are established, constructive associations will result that logically should be translated into enhanced profits. Abusive and unjust associations, which might lead to short-lived financial benefits, would not be sustainable in the long run. Finally, behaving as a good citizen in relationship with the communities in which the firm resides as well as with other external agencies, will likely lead to an enhanced corporate image and the fulfillment of sound social responsibilities.

7. Strategy as an expression of strategic intent: stretching the organization.

One of the major concerns that has to be present in any effort leading towards the strategic positioning of the firm has to do with the degree to which the organization is challenged to achieve truly demanding goals. If the strategic planning process only leads to a recording of programs the organization already has in place, it will fail to serve the ultimate objective of any strategic planning effort; that is, to unleash creativity and move the organization towards a new state of excellence. This is characterized as the degree of *stretch* that is implicit in the strategy development. The existing capabilities that reside in the firm and its current resources will not be sufficient. We need to invoke a dramatic challenge to move the organization towards a more ambitious state, perhaps an unimaginable one.

Gary Hamel and C.K. Prahalad coined the term *strategic intent* to address this issue.[12] According to these authors, strategic intent envisions a desired leadership position and establishes the criteria an organization will use to chart its progress. Strategic intent captures the essence of winning. The examples that are given are: the Apollo Program, "Landing a man on the moon"; Komatsu's drive against Caterpillar, "Encircle Caterpillar"; Canon's determination to surpass Xerox, "Beat Xerox"; Honda's aspiration to conquer the American auto industry, "Become a second Ford." These are all examples of successful expressions of strategic intent.

Strategic intent encompasses an active management process that creates a sense of urgency, focuses the organization on the essence of winning, and motivates people through actions such as:

- Developing a competitor focus at every level through widespread use of competitive intelligence.
- Providing employees with the skills they need to work effectively, leaving room for individual and team contribution.
- Guiding resource allocation through the consistent use of intent.
- Giving the organization time to digest one challenge before launching another.
- Establishing clear milestones and review mechanisms to track progress and ensure that internal recognition and reward reinforce desired behavior.

The strategic intent message deviates from the more classical approaches that seek a fit between opportunities presented by the industry and the competitive position sustained by the firm to establish competitive advantage. Strategic intent abandons the business unit as a central focus of strategic analysis and moves the relevant dimension of strategic concern to the corporate level of the firm. Rather than matching industry opportunities with available resources, it encourages members of the firm to seek seemingly unattainable goals. Instead of searching for advantages that are inherently sustainable, it strives to accelerate organizational learning that will enable the firm to develop new rules that eliminate the incumbent's advantages. Instead of allocating resources to product-market units, it fosters investment in core competencies to develop core product capabilities. Finally, rather than seeking strategic fit between the organization and its environment, consistency comes from the allegiance of the organization to its particular strategic intent.

8. Strategy as a means to develop the core competencies of the organization.

Strategic intent moves the central focus of strategy from the business level to the corporate level. Prahalad and Hamel, in their influential article, "The Core Competence of the Corporation," develop an even more frontal and penetrating attack on the use of the Strategic Business Unit (SBU) as the key focus of strategic analysis. They suggest that an excessive dependence on the SBU perspective for strategic analysis has led to unacceptable autonomy at the SBU level. This, in turn, has generated a corporate structure anchored in today's products with businesses related in product-markets terms. The resources are being inappropriately allocated business-by-business thereby ignoring the creation and nurturing of core competencies cutting across business units. The resulting "tyranny of the SBU" has produced underinvestment in core competencies and core products, imprisoned resources at the business-unit level, and bounded innovation. Their answer to this dilemma is to consolidate corporatewide technologies and production skills into core competencies that empower business units to adapt quickly to changing opportunities. A new strategic architecture that allows the building of core competencies has to replace the conventional SBU structure.

The basic notion about core competencies is that they are being nurtured and developed at the corporate level, and that they define the foundation of the competitive strategy for the entire firm. There are three tests that can be used to identify core competencies in a company. One, a core competency provides potential access to a wide variety of markets; two, a core competency should make a significant contribution to the perceived customer benefits of the end product; and three, a core competency should be difficult for competitors to imitate. The core competencies, particularly those involving collective learning, are knowledge based and can be improved as they are applied.

Collectively taken, the concepts of strategic intent and core competencies represent a major challenge to the "industry structure-competitive positioning" paradigm. The major attack is directed at the importance of industry structure as the source of superior financial performance. Industry does not seem to matter any more.[13] What truly distinguishes the performance of different firms competing in a given industry is not explained by the conditions of industry structure conditioners, but rather by the capabilities and internal resources that the firms are deploying to differentiate from each other.

9. Strategy as a means of investing in tangible and intangible resources to develop the capabilities that assure a sustainable advantage.

The notion of core competencies is closely related to the so-called *resource-based view of the firm*,[14] which is the most recent model to understand the mechanisms for achieving competitive advantage. It represents a major departure from a strategic approach based on market-driven considerations, which considers industry conditions to be responsible for creating opportunities for superior profitability. The resource-based view departs significantly from this approach and postulates that the central sources of competitive advantage are factor driven; that is to say, they depend on the development of resources and capabilities on the part of the firm. The basic framework that we have identified in Figure 1-1 tacitly assumes that industry structure and competitive position contributed roughly in equal terms to the profitability performance of a business. The resource-based view drastically switches the explanation of superior performance to the competitive positioning side.

The essence of the resource-based model is depicted in Figure 1–2. It simply states that competitive advantage is created when resources and capabilities that are owned exclusively by the firm are applied to developing unique competencies. Moreover, the resulting advantage can be sustained due to the lack of substitution and imitation capabilities by the firm's competitors. Furthermore, the benefits derived from these advantages are retained inside the firm, not being appropriated by external parties. Finally, the timing of the acquisition of the necessary resources and capabilities is so opportune that their cost will not offset the resulting benefits. If all of these conditions are met, the competitive advantage that is created will generate an incremental economic value of the firm.

The four basic premises of the resource-based view model to achieve competitive advantage are the following:

FIGURE 1–2. The Resource-Based View–Elements of Competitive Advantage

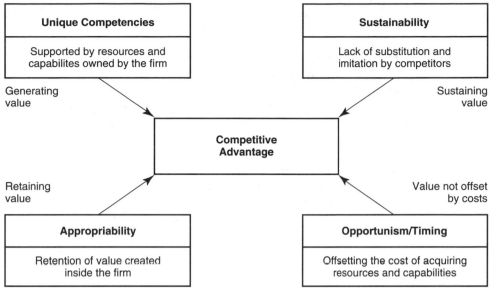

SOURCE: Adapted from Peteraf (1993) and Ghemawat (1991).

1. Unique Competencies.

Resources and capabilities are the sources of the unique competencies of the firm. Resources could be both tangible (such as financial resources and physical assets) and intangible (such as reputation, customer orientation, product innovation, technology superiority, etc.). Resources are converted into capabilities when the firm develops the necessary organizational routines to use them effectively. Often, resources and capabilities are the result of investments in durable, specialized, and untradeable factors. This is what Ghemawat has defined as *commitment*.[15] In his view, commitment explains both the persistence in an organization's performance, as well as the difference in profitability enjoyed by distinct firms competing in the same industry. Commitment represents irreversible decisions supported by significant investments, which shape strategies as a continuous pattern of decision making. These patterns are punctuated by discontinuities due to commitment changes emerging from a significant repositioning of the firm strategy.

2. Sustainability.

For a competitive advantage to be sustainable, the conditions of uniqueness associated with a business unit strategy should be preserved. This means that there should be no threats of either substitution or imitation. From a resource-based point of view, the resources of a firm must have the following attributes to hold the potential for sustainable competitive advantage: they must be valuable, scarce, and difficult to imitate or substitute.

3. Appropriability.

A strategy that is both unique and sustainable would generate a significant economic value. The issue of appropriability addresses the question of who will capture the resulting economic rent. Sometimes, the owners of the business unit do not appropriate the totality of the value created because of the gap that might exist between ownership and control. Nonowners might control complementary and specialized factors that might divert the cash proceeds away from the business. This type of dissipation of value is called *holdup*. A notorious example of holdup in recent business history has taken place in the personal computer industry, where Intel and Microsoft have captured 80 percent of the total market of that industry, leaving the computer manufacturing firms the meager 20 percent remaining.

The second threat for the appropriability of the economic value is referred to as *slack*. It measures the extent to which the economic value realized by the business unit is significantly lower than what potentially could have been created. Slack is often the result of inefficiencies or unwarranted benefits that prevent the accumulation of economic rents in the business. One of the major sources of slack in America has been the dysfunctional and confrontational relationships between managers and labor unions.

While holdup produces a different distribution of the total wealth created, slack reduces the size of this wealth.

4. Opportunism and Timing.

One other condition that is necessary to obtain competitive advantage occurs prior to establishing a superior resource position. It is necessary that the cost-incurred in acquiring the resources are lower than the value created by them. In other words, the cost implicit in implementing the strategy of a business unit should not offset the value generated by it. This condition is what we aspire to capture under this requirement of opportunism and timing in order to secure competitive advantage.

Toward a Unified Concept of Strategy

The concept of strategy embraces the overall purpose of an organization. It is not surprising, therefore, that many dimensions are required for its proper definition. The ones we have just presented simply emphasize the various components of the concept of strategy, one at a time. All of them are meaningful and relevant and contribute to a better understanding of the strategic tasks.

A unified definition of strategy has to address the controversy between the "industry structure-competitive positioning" paradigm and the "resource-based view" of the firm. Figure 1–3 represents a proposal to bring together these seemingly conflicting views. On the right-hand side we represent the industry-structure viewpoint. This corresponds to the market perspective, which requires attending the product-market needs in an effective way. On the left-hand side we see the factor requirements, emphasizing investments in resources and capabilities that will differentiate the firm from its competitors.

What the framework in Figure 1–3 offers is a reconciliation between the market-driven and the factor-driven approaches, the bridge being the mission of the business. The mission captures the two central questions that link these approaches: business scope and unique competencies that determine the key capabilities of the firm.

The business scope is defined in terms of the products the firm is offering, the selection of customers to be served, and the geographical reach the firm aspires to have. In this way, it establishes the competitive domain of the business. The business scope specifies where the firm is competing and how it is serving the dynamic needs of the market in the most effective way. Given the enormous turbulence that is inherent in market dynamics, this concern, by neccssity, has to be flexible and short-term oriented.

The second dimension of the mission of the business is how to compete. This refers to the development of those unique or core competencies that will allow the firm to achieve a sustainable competitive advantage. These compe-

FIGURE 1–3. The Mission of Business: Integration of Factor-and-Product/ Market-Driven Views of Strategy

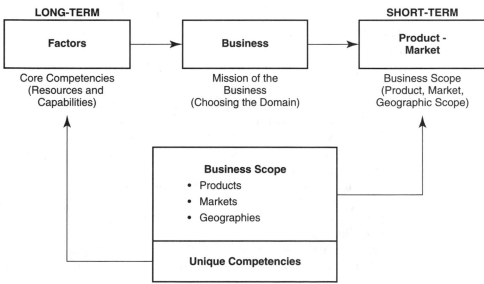

tencies stem from the basic factors of production, as well as the resources and capabilities that belong exclusively to the firm. The core competencies provide the long-term competitive standing of the business.

As a summary, industry and market considerations dictate the dynamics of continuous change, while factors and resource considerations dictate the long-term foundations of the way to compete. In our approach, the bridge is the mission of the business when we are addressing business strategy and the mission of the firm when we are concerned about corporate strategy.

From this standpoint, we could combine all of the various dimensions of strategy that we have presented, and propose an integrative, and comprehensive definition of strategy.

Strategy

1. determines and reveals the organizational purpose in terms of long-term objectives, action programs, and resource allocation priorities;
2. selects the businesses the organization is in, or is to be in;
3. attempts to achieve a long-term, sustainable advantage in each of its businesses by responding appropriately to the opportunities and threats in the firm's environment, and the strengths and weaknesses of the organization;
4. identifies the distinct managerial tasks at the corporate, business, and functional levels.
5. is a coherent, unifying, and integrative pattern of decisions;
6. defines the nature of the economic and noneconomic contributions it intends to make to its stakeholders;
7. is an expression of the strategic intent of the organization;
8. is aimed at developing and nurturing the core competencies of the firm;
9. is a means for investing selectively in tangible and intangible resources to develop the capabilities that assure a sustainable competitive advantage.

From this unifying point of view, strategy becomes a fundamental framework through which an organization can simultaneously assert its vital continuity and facilitate its adaptation to a changing environment. This is the essence of successful management of change. It is aggressive in order to meet head-on the opportunities for enhanced profitability; it is also respectful of the culture, tradition, and history of the firm's approach to doing business. At the heart of strategy there is a purposeful search for the achievement of competitive advantage in every business in which the firm is engaged. Strategy does not just happen; it is made by managerial actions and decisions when opening up new opportunities for a sustained profitability in all the businesses of a firm.

Also, there is a formal recognition that the ultimate objective of strategy should address the stakeholders' benefits, thus providing a base for conducting the host of transactions and social contracts among them and the firm.

The Strategy Formation Process

The substance of strategy can not be separated from the process of strategy making in any actual organizational setting. In fact, the process school of research[16] views strategy as the outcome of three different processes contributing to strategy formation:

- *The cognitive processes of individuals* where the rational understanding of the external environment and internal capabilities of the firm reside.
- *The social and organizational processes* that contribute to internal communication and the development of a consensus of opinion.
- *The political processes* that address the creation, retention, and transfer of power within the organization.

Within this perspective, the task of the chief executive officer (CEO) is viewed as the administration of these three processes. This requires the CEO to develop a broad vision of what to achieve, and to manage a network of organizational forces that lead to the discovery, evolution, and enrichment of that vision.

We will now discuss options that are particularly relevant in designing the strategy formation process, and adapting it to the strategic objectives, management style, organizational culture, and administrative systems of a particular firm.

EXPLICIT VERSUS IMPLICIT STRATEGY

Perhaps the greatest controversy surrounding strategy making centers on how explicitly strategy should be communicated both internally within the organization and externally to relevant constituencies. Edward Wrapp, a noted contributor to the business policy field, suggests four strata for the definition of corporate strategy.[17]

STRATUM I—CORPORATE STRATEGY FOR THE ANNUAL REPORT. This is a statement that is primarily directed toward the shareholders; conveys a general sense of direction in terms of where the company is going, as well as a reflection on its past performance. The statement is highly sanitized, with a bias toward presenting a favorable view of the company, it is heavily edited by the public relations department.

STRATUM II—CORPORATE STRATEGY FOR THE BOARD OF DIRECTORS, FINANCIAL ANALYSTS, AND MIDDLE MANAGERS. This statement is more comprehensive and revealing than Stratum I. It provides information that is more sensitive and addressed to company insiders as well as critical external constituencies that need to be more thoroughly informed. However, the bias still persists in presenting the organization in its best possible standing, intending to assure that intelligent and successful directions are being pursued.

STRATUM III—CORPORATE STRATEGY FOR TOP MANAGEMENT. This version of strategy is intended to go deeply into the key issues facing the firm and is addressed to the top management team which is expected to participate fully in setting up strategic directions and to be responsible for overseeing the implementation efforts. Since the CEO needs the critical support of this group, there is still a positive bias in the way in which issues are framed and information is presented. However, full consideration is given to all of the moves and countermoves needed to strengthen the competitive position.

STRATUM IV—THE CEO'S PRIVATE CORPORATE STRATEGY. The CEO is a critical figure in developing the vision of the firm and carrying this vision to fruitful completion. This stratum recognizes that regardless of how communicative or participative the CEO management style might be, there is always a remnant of his or her innermost thoughts that are unlikely to be shared with anybody.

Wrapp's four levels of strategy point to the enormous influence of the CEO in both shaping and communicating the strategy of the firm, and the various mechanisms that are available to make the process more or less open.

FORMAL-ANALYTICAL PROCESS VERSUS POWER-BEHAVIORAL APPROACHES

Whether the process of strategy formation should be formalized is subject to controversy. On one extreme, there are those who believe in an integrated decision-making process that relies heavily on analytical tools and methodologies to help managers, at all levels, to reach a better quality of strategic thinking. Strategy formation is regarded as a formal and disciplined process leading to a well-defined organization-wide effort aimed at the complete specification of corporate, business, and functional strategies. Those favoring this approach tend to advocate the use of formal planning systems, management control, and consistent reward mechanisms to increase the quality of strategic decision making.[18]

At the other extreme, a second school of management rests on the behavioral theory of the firm and espouses a power-behavioral approach to strategy formation. This school emphasizes multiple goal structures of organizations, the politics of strategic decisions, executive bargaining and negotiation, the role of coalitions in strategic management, and the practice of "muddling through."[19]

These two schools of thought have made significant contributions to increasing our understanding of the central strategic issues. However, neither the formal-analytical nor the power-behavioral paradigms adequately explain the way successful strategy formation processes operate. These taxonomies have been useful in focusing academic research work but neither serves as a normative or descriptive model. To get the best out of strategy making, formal analytic thinking should be combined with the behavioral aspects of management.

STRATEGY AS A PATTERN OF PAST ACTIONS VERSUS A FORWARD-LOOKING PLAN

Another element of controversy in strategy making resides in the amount of attention to be given to events through time. Some authors view strategy as exclusively shaping the future direction of the firm; thus, strategy becomes the collection of objectives and action programs oriented at managing the future change of the organization.

Alternatively, strategy is viewed as a pattern of actions emerging from the past decisions of the firm. A leading proponent of this school of thought is Henry Mintzberg, who defines strategy as "a pattern in a stream of decisions." According to this view, strategy is deciphered as consistency in behavior, whether or not intended, observed in the past actions of the firm.[20]

The emergence of strategy from the operating decisions of the firm is one of the central issues of strategy making. Thousands of decisions are being made every day in large and complex organizations. The only way to make them consistent is to establish a sense of permanent strategic direction to provide a framework within which those decisions can be made.

Nonetheless, interpreting strategy too rigidly as a pattern revealed in the past stream of decisions might lead to an inability to shape new directions for the firm. In a strict sense, strategy could only become known and explicit ex post, when, from a historical perspective, it could be deciphered from the continuum of past events. From a managerial point of view, this notion of strategy is clearly impractical. Indeed, strategy is most important when dealing with intended change. Strategy should be formed in cognizance of the past heritage of the firm, but at the same time, it should be forward looking.

Consequently, strategy making becomes a delicate balance between learning from the past and shaping new courses of action to lead the organization toward a future state that might include a substantial departure from its past conduct.

DELIBERATE VERSUS EMERGENT STRATEGY

A different way to characterize the strategy formation process arises from the definition of deliberate and emergent strategies.[21] A strategy is considered *deliberate* when its realization matches the intended course of action, and *emergent* when the strategy is identified from the patterns or consistencies observed in past behavior despite, or in the absence of, intention.

These two concepts, especially their interplay, form the basis for a typology to characterize various kinds of strategy formation processes. At one end of this continuum falls the purely deliberate strategy, at the other, the purely emergent. Between these two extremes are strategies that combine varying degrees of different dimensions: openness, participation, CEO's involvement and consensus management, formalization, negotiation, continuity with the past, and orientation toward future change. Also, the type of strategy is affected by the nature of the firm's environment, particularly whether it is more or less benign, controllable, and predictable.

This typology is based on the idea that strategy is formed by two critical forces acting simultaneously: one deliberate, the other emergent. Managers need deliberate strategies to provide the organization with a sense of purposeful direction. Emergent strategy implies learning what works—taking one action at a time in search for that viable pattern or consistency. Emergent strategy means no chaos, but unintended order. Emergent strategy does not have to mean that management is out of control—only that it is open, flexible, and responsive—in other words, willing to learn.

A Typology of Strategy Formation

From our previous discussion it is clear that the relevant dimensions that should be considered in delineating a strategy formation process responsive to the firm's needs are:

Explicit versus Implicit Strategy

1. The openness and breadth to communicate strategy, both internally in the organization and to all relevant external constituencies;
2. The degree to which different organizational levels participate;
3. The amount of consensus built around intended courses of action, especially the depth of CEO involvement in this effort.

Formal-Analytical Process versus Power-Behavioral Approach

4. The extent to which formal processes are used to specify corporate, business, and functional strategies;
5. The incentives provided for key players to negotiate a strategy for the firm.

Pattern of Past Actions versus Forward-Looking Plan

6. The linkage of strategy to the pattern of actions in the past; and
7. The use of strategy as a force for change (and as a vehicle for new courses of action).

Deliberate versus Emergent Strategy

8. The degree to which strategy is either purely deliberate or purely emergent.

Profiling and Diagramming the Concept of Strategy and the Strategy Formation Process

We provide in this section a pragmatic way to perform a diagnosis of the quality of the concept of strategy, and of the process of strategy formation. However, it is important to bear in mind the deep differences between these two notions. We have proposed a single unified definition of the concept of strategy that we feel is universally valid and applicable to any firm, regardless of its nature or its management style. This definition of the concept of strategy can therefore be used in a normative way. Figure 1–4 on page 20 gives a simple chart that can be used to obtain the existing and desired profiles of the concept of strategy in a firm. The gap between these two profiles is an indication of the kind and intensity of the managerial work to be allocated to the improvement of the strategic capabilities of the firm. It is our opinion that the attributes listed in that figure can be interpreted in a normative sense, by defining a profile skewed to the left as closer to an idealized model of strategy.

The issue is more complex for strategy formation. An enormous number of different ways exist to reach the ideals imbedded in the concept of strategy. This is simply a manifestation of the huge variety present in any social organization. We can say what strategy is, but we cannot propose a universal formula applicable to any conceivable firm facing any kind of environment that would have a general validity. Figure 1–5 on page 21 provides a chart to facilitate the profiling of the strategy formation process. However, there is no normative paradigm revealed by the profile. The important requirement of the process is that it should be managed consistently in accordance with the overall strategic objectives of the firm, its management style, and its organizational culture. Moreover, the strategy formation process should be integrated with other administrative processes of the firm, particularly management control, information and reward systems, and the organizational structure. Careful integration among managerial processes, structure, and culture is what leads to effective strategic management.

There is a great degree of subjectivity in this profiling of the concept of strategy and the strategy formation process. When different individuals and groups in a firm try to assess the characteristics of strategic thinking in the organization, their varying perceptions on this issue can be used positively to transform the strategy formation process in a way that will help to achieve the ideal of strategy as a unifying pattern for the firm.

FIGURE 1-4. Profile of the Concept of Strategy

	STRONGLY AGREE	AGREE	NEUTRAL	DISAGREE	STRONGLY DISAGREE
1. The purpose of the firm is expressed in terms of:					
• Long-term objectives					
• Action programs					
• Resource allocation priorities					
2. The firm:					
• Segments clearly the business it is currently in					
• Recognizes properly those businesses it considers entering and exiting					
3. The firm:					
• Understands its major competitors					
• Attempts to anticipate intelligent competitors' moves					
• Has a capacity to adapt dynamically its strategy to environmental changes					
• Recognizes its strengths and weaknesses					
• Attempts to achieve a long-term sustainable advantage over its key competitors in every one of its major businesses					
4. The firm clearly recognizes the different managerial tasks to be addressed at:					
• The corporate level					
• The business level					
• The functional level					
5. The decisions of the firm fall into a coherent, unifying, and integrative pattern.					
6. The firm defines the economic and noneconomic contribution it intends to make to its stakeholders.					
7. The firm expresses clearly its strategic intent.					
8. The firm understands, develops, and nurtures its core competencies.					
9. The firm invests selectively in tangible and intangible resources to develop sustainable competitive capabilities.					

FIGURE 1–5. **FIGURE 1–5.** Profile of the Strategy Formation Process

	STRONGLY AGREE	AGREE	NEUTRAL	DISAGREE	STRONGLY DISAGREE

EXPLICIT VERSUS IMPLICIT STRATEGY

1. Strategy is openly and widely communicated:
   - Internally to the organization
   - Externally to all relevant constituencies
2. Strategy is generated through a wide participatory process.
3. The strategic process is managed to build wide consensus around intended courses of action.

FORMAL ANALYTICAL PROCESS VERSUS POWER-BEHAVIORAL APPROACH

4. Strategy is based on a disciplined formal process aimed at the complete specification of corporate, business, and functional strategies.
5. Strategy is based on a negotiation process among all the key players.

PATTERN OF PAST ACTIONS VERSUS FORWARD-LOOKING PLANNING

6. Strategy emerges from the pattern of actions in past decisions.
7. Strategy is mainly a vehicle of change that shapes new courses of action.

DELIBERATE VERSUS EMERGENT

8. Strategy is mostly deliberate.

21

Notes

1. Throughout the text, whenever possible, we will avoid naming all of the authors that have contributed to these various perspectives of strategy. This is simply because, more often than not, various authors have participated in enriching a given perspective. Therefore, to gain information pertaining to individual contributions and the original sources, the reader is referred to a series of footnotes throughout the text.

2. We quite agree with Michael Porter's statement in the paper "Toward a Dynamic Theory of Strategy," *Strategic Management Journal*, 12 (Winter 1991), 95–117. He makes the following brisk assertion referring to the separation of the process and substance of strategy: "The effort by some to dichotomize process and substance is simply incorrect."

3. The most important proponent of this definition of strategy is Alfred D. Chandler, Jr., in his classical work, *Strategy and Structure: Chapters in the History of American Industrial Enterprise* (Cambridge, MA: The MIT Press, 1962).

4. This concept was early espoused by the Harvard Business School policy group and stated in the influential book written by Edmund P. Learned, C. Roland Christensen, Kenneth R. Andrews, and William D. Guth, *Business Policy: Text and Cases* (Homewood, IL: Richard D. Irwin, 1965).

5. The concept of core competence was first advanced by C.K. Prahalad and Gary Hamel in their now classic paper: "The Core Competence of the Corporation," *Harvard Business Review* (May-June 1990), 71–91.

6. Michael E. Porter has championed the quest for competitive advantage as the central thrust of strategy. In his first book, *Competitive Strategy: Techniques for Analyzing Industries and Competitors* (New York: The Free Press, 1980) he defines a framework to assess the attractiveness of an industry, and discusses generic strategies for effectively positioning a firm within that industry. In his second book, *Competitive Advantage: Creating and Sustaining Superior Performance* (New York: The Free Press,

1985), Michael Porter uses the value chain as a powerful conceptual tool to direct the firm's activities toward enhancing its competitive position.

7. For an excellent synthesis of Porter's work, the reader is referred to his paper, "Toward a Dynamic Theory of Strategy."

8. The three levels of strategy have been recognized by many authors in this field, primarily: Kenneth R. Andrews, *The Concept of Strategy* (Homewood, IL: Richard D. Irwin, 1980); H. Igor Ansoff, *Corporate Strategy* (New York: McGraw-Hill, 1965); and George A. Steiner and John B. Miner, *Management Policy and Strategy* (New York: Macmillan, 1977). Richard F. Vancil and Peter Lorange, "Strategic Planning in Diversified Companies," *Harvard Business Review*, 53, no. 1 (January–February 1975), 81–90, were the first to propose a formal planning process to describe the interactions of these three managerial levels. Arnoldo C. Hax and Nicolas S. Majluf, *Strategic Management: An Integrative Perspective* (Englewood Cliffs, NJ: Prentice Hall, 1984a) and "The Corporate Strategic Planning Process," *Interfaces*, 14, no. 1 (January–February 1984b), 47–60, developed a thorough methodology to facilitate the disciplined formulation of strategies at the corporate, business, and functional levels.

9. For a complete analysis of value creation in the Fortune 1000 companies, see: Shawn Tully, "America's Best Wealth Creators," *Fortune* (November 28, 1994) 143–162.

10. For a treatment of the concept and practice of business reengineering, see: Michael Hammer and James Champy, *Reengineering the Corporation* (New York: Harper Business, 1993); and Thomas H. Davenport, *Process Innovation* (Boston, MA: Harvard Business School Press, 1993); James Champy, *Reengineering Management: The Mandate for New Leadership* (New York: Harper Business, 1995); and Michael Hammer and Steven A. Stanton, *The Reengineering Revolution* (New York: Harper Business, 1995).

11. The key initial proponent of strategy as a coherent pattern of decisions is Henry Mintzberg. He voices this point of view in a number of publications. Particularly relevant are: Henry Mintzberg, "Crafting Strategy," *Harvard Business Review*, 65, no. 1 (July–August 1987), 66–75; and Henry Mintzberg, "Patterns in Strategy Formation," *Management Science* (1976), 934–948.

12. Gary Hamel and C.K. Prahalad, "Strategic Intent," *Harvard Business Review* (May–June 1989), 63–76.

13. For a discussion of the importance of the industry in the performance of the firm, see: Richard P. Rumelt, "How Much Does Industry Matter?", *Strategic Management Journal*, 12 (1991), 167–185; Richard Schmalensee, "Do Markets Differ Much?" *The American Economic Review*, 75 (June 1985), 341–351; Birger Wernerfelt and Cynthia Montgomery, "Tobin's q and the Importance of Focus in Firm Performance," *The American Economic Review*, 78, no. 1, 246–250; Richard Nelson, "Recent Writing on Competitiveness: Boxing the Compass," *California Management Review*, 34, no. 2 (Winter 1992), 127–137; Richard Nelson, "Why Do Firms Differ, and How Does It Matter?", in Richard Rumelt, Dan E. Schendel, and David J. Teece (eds.) *Fundamental Issues in Strategy* (Boston, MA: Harvard Business School Press, 1994) 247–269.

14. Some references for the resource-based view: Margaret A. Peteraf, "The Cornerstones of Competitive Advantage: A Resource-Based View," *Strategic Management Journal*, 14, no. 3 (March 1993) 179–192; Jay Barney, "Firm Resources and Sustained Competitive Advantage," *Journal of Management*, 17, no. 1 (1991) 99–120; Birger Wernerfelt, "A Resource-Based View of the Firm," *Strategic Management Journal*, 5 (1984), 171–180.

15. Pankaj Ghemawat, *Commitment: The Dynamics of Strategy* (New York: The Free Press, 1991).

16. For a presentation of the process school of strategic research, see Joseph L. Bower and Yves Doz, "Strategy Formulation: A Social and Political Process," in *Strategic Management: A New View of Business Policy and Planning*, eds. C. W. Hofer and Dan Schendel (Boston, MA: Little Brown and Co., 1979).

17. See H. Edward Wrapp, "Good Managers Don't Make Policy Decisions," *Harvard Business Review*, 62, no. 4 (July–August 1984), 8–21; and Kenneth R. Andrews, "Corporate Strategy As a Vital Function of the Board," *Harvard Business Review*, 59, no. 6 (November–December 1981), 174–184.

18. Primary proponents of the formal-analytical strategy school are: H. Igor Ansoff, *Implanting Strategic Management* (Englewood Cliffs, NJ: Prentice Hall, 1984); Arnoldo C. Hax and Nicolas S. Majluf, 1984a, 1984b; Peter Lorange, *Corporate Planning: An Executive Viewpoint* (Englewood Cliffs, NJ: Prentice Hall, 1980); Michael Porter, 1980, 1985; and Boris Yavitz and William H. Newman, *Strategy in Action: The Execution, Politics and Payoff of Business Planning* (New York: The Free Press, 1982).

19. Major proponents of the power-behavioral strategy school are: Richard M. Cyert and James G. March, A *Behavioral Theory of the Firm* (Englewood Cliffs, NJ: Prentice Hall, 1963); Charles E. Lindblom, "The Science of Muddling Through," *Public Administration Review* (Spring 1959), 79–88; Herbert A. Simon, *Administrative Behavior: A Study of Decision-Making Processes in Administrative Organizations* (New York: The Free Press, 1976); and H. Edward Wrapp, "Good Managers Don't Make Policy Decisions," 1984.

20. For a review of Mintzberg's work, see: Henry Mintzberg and James A. Waters, "Of Strategy Delivered and Emergent," *Strategic Management Journal*, 6, no. 3 (July–September 1985), 257–272.

21. See Mintzberg and Waters, "Of Strategy Delivered and Emergent," 1985.

2

A Formal Strategic Planning Process

The strategic planning process is a disciplined and well-defined organizational effort aimed at the complete specification of a firm's strategy and the assignment of responsibilities for its execution. We concentrate most of the attention in this book on presenting the different components of a formal strategic planning process aimed at improving the overall capabilities of the firm to operate in an intensive and dynamic competitive environment.

It is a complex matter to describe this process in general terms because it depends on the particular characteristics of each firm. The planning process appropriate for a single business firm with a purely functional organizational structure is quite different from one suitable for addressing the strategic tasks of a highly diversified global corporation. There are, however, basic commonalities found in the formal planning process of most business firms: the three perspectives of strategy, and their integration in the planning process. We comment on these subjects now.

The Three Perspectives of Strategy: Corporate, Business, and Functional

A formal planning process should recognize the different roles to be played by the various managers of a firm in the formulation and execution of their firm's strategies. There are three basic perspectives that have always been identified as the essential dimensions of any formal planning process: corporate, business, and functional.

The *corporate strategy* deals with the decisions that, by their nature, should be addressed with the fullest scope encompassing the overall firm. These are decisions that cannot be decentralized without running the risk of committing suboptimization errors. Managers who operate at lower levels of the firm do not have the proper vantage point to make the difficult trade-offs between decisions that maximize the benefits of their own independent units but might affect adversely the corporation as a whole. It should be noted that the decision maker at the corporate level is not necessarily the isolated CEO. Ideally, corporate strategies should be shaped and implemented by incorporating the core team of top executives.

Figure 2–1 on page 26 summarizes the tasks associated with the development of corporate strategy. As the figure indicates, the focus of analysis is the firm as a whole. The first task to be addressed is the corporate environmental scan, which leads to the recognition of opportunities for, and threats to, the firm. This scan analyzes the impacts that external pressures have on the firm's businesses. The corporate internal scrutiny groups five of the most central strategic decisions: the mission of the firm, the segmentation of its businesses, the integration of these businesses through horizontal and vertical strategies, and the definition of corporate philosophy. In conjunction, they help us to assess the strengths and weaknesses of the corporation. The responses to the corporate environmental scan and internal scrutiny are contained in the four remaining corporate tasks: the development of strategic thrusts and corporate performance objectives; the allocation of the firm's resources to satisfy corporate, business, and functional requirements; the design of the managerial infrastructure, which encompasses the organizational structure and the administrative systems of the firm; and the selection, promotion, and motivation of the key personnel.

Business strategy aims at obtaining superior financial performance by seeking a competitive positioning that allows the business to have a sustainable advantage over the firm's competitors. Business managers are supposed to formulate and implement strategic actions congruent with the general corporate directions, constrained by the overall resources assigned to the particular business unit.

Figure 2–2 on page 27 presents the basic framework that we recommend for the development of a business strategy. It starts with a definition of the mission of the business, which includes where to compete (the business scope) and how to compete (the development of the business's unique competencies). The environmental scan deals with the identification of the opportunities and threats in the markets in which the business competes, through the assessment of the current industry structure and its future trends. The internal scrutiny determines the competitive position of the business through a careful examination of key activities of the value chain. This process generates the basic strengths and weaknesses of the business. The responses to the challenges emerging from the mission of the business, the environmental scan and the internal scrutiny define the business strategy, programs, and budgets.

Finally, *functional strategies* not only consolidate the functional requirements demanded by the corporate and business strategies, but also constitute the depositories of the ultimate capabilities needed to develop the unique competencies of the firm.

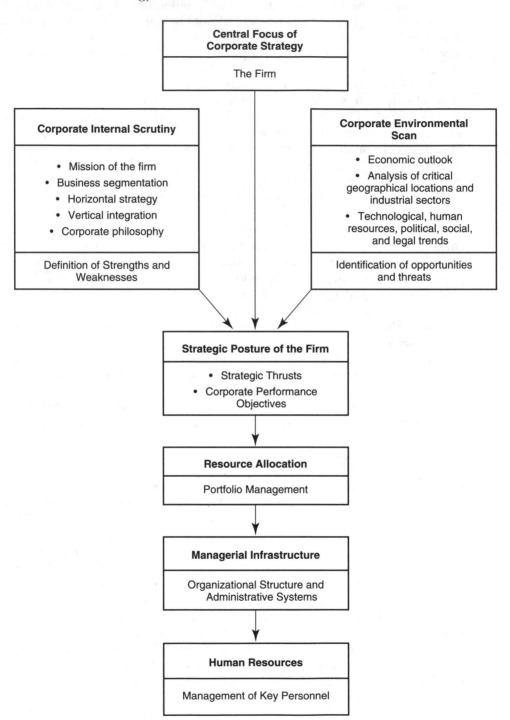

FIGURE 2–2. The Fundamental Elements of the Definition of a Business Strategy

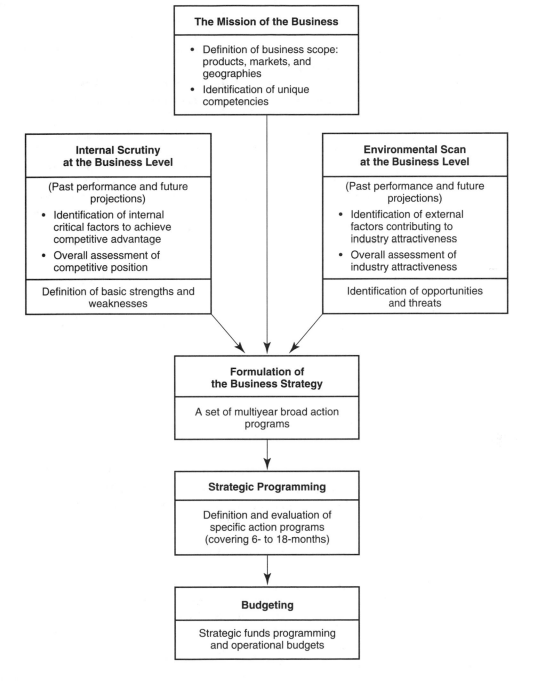

27

Figure 2-3 presents the framework for the definition of the functional strategy. It starts by examining the functional requirements that are originated by corporate and business strategy. It then proceeds, as in the other two frameworks, by conducting an environmental scan and an internal scrutiny. Although we have used the same names to describe these tasks, they are substantially different in each of the three perspectives of strategy. The functional environmental scan produces a benchmarking of the capabilities of the firm against some industry standards; the internal scrutiny leads to the definition and evaluation of key decisions at the functional level. Lastly, functional strategies, programs, and budgets contain the action-oriented responses to the previous analysis.

In the vast majority of American business firms, the strategic attention is almost solely concentrated at the business level. This management practice has severe limitations, which could cause loss of competitiveness in a firm. The lack of a corporate vision deprives the firm of the necessary leadership to consolidate its overall activities, and to facilitate its restructuring whenever needed. Often, corporations fail to adapt to the external environment by remaining anchored in their past successes. Major modifications in the firm portfolio can only be originated from effective corporate strategies. Similarly, treating the key managerial functions strictly with a short-term operational bias weakens the competitiveness of the firm. It is clear that all of the key functions—finance, human resources, technology, procurement, manufacturing, marketing, distribution, and services—need to be dealt with strategically. This means that we ought to have external intelligence to understand how competitors are deploying their functional resources, if we want to be able to respond with the necessary functional skills to enhance our competitive position.

The Strategic Planning Process: Integrating the Three Perspectives

In Figure 2-4 on page 30, we present a model for the formal strategic planning process that recognizes the three essential perspectives of strategy. It also serves to illustrate the different nature of the corresponding planning tasks undertaken by each level, and a recommended sequence for the execution of those tasks. Individual responsibilities have to be assigned at all levels in the organization; for developing, implementing, and controlling the appropriate strategic tasks.[1]

We recognize two major cycles in the planing process. First, *strategy formulation* is intended to frame all of the key strategic issues of the firm through a sequential involvement of the corporate, business, and functional perspectives. The planning tasks associated with each perspective include an environmental scan and an internal scrutiny, and culminate with a suggested competitive positioning. At the corporate level this is expressed in terms of strategic thrusts and

FIGURE 2–3. The Fundamental Elements of the Definition of a Functional Strategy

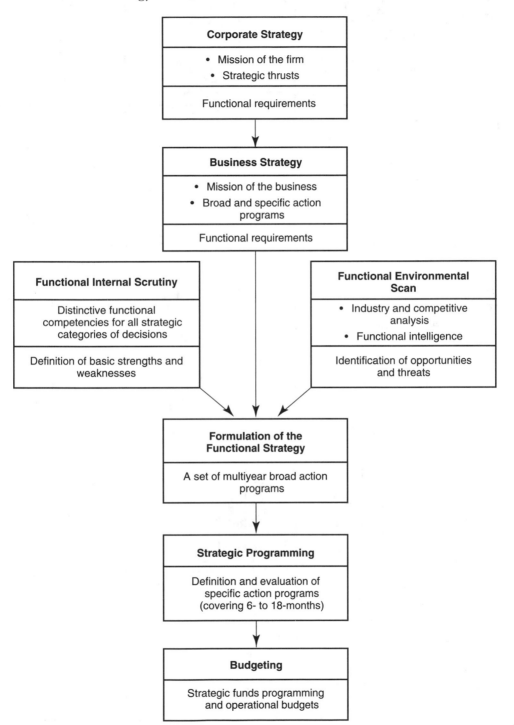

Corporate Strategy
- Mission of the firm
- Strategic thrusts

Functional requirements

Business Strategy
- Mission of the business
- Broad and specific action programs

Functional requirements

Functional Internal Scrutiny

Distinctive functional competencies for all strategic categories of decisions

Definition of basic strengths and weaknesses

Functional Environmental Scan
- Industry and competitive analysis
- Functional intelligence

Identification of opportunities and threats

Formulation of the Functional Strategy

A set of multiyear broad action programs

Strategic Programming

Definition and evaluation of specific action programs (covering 6- to 18-months)

Budgeting

Strategic funds programming and operational budgets

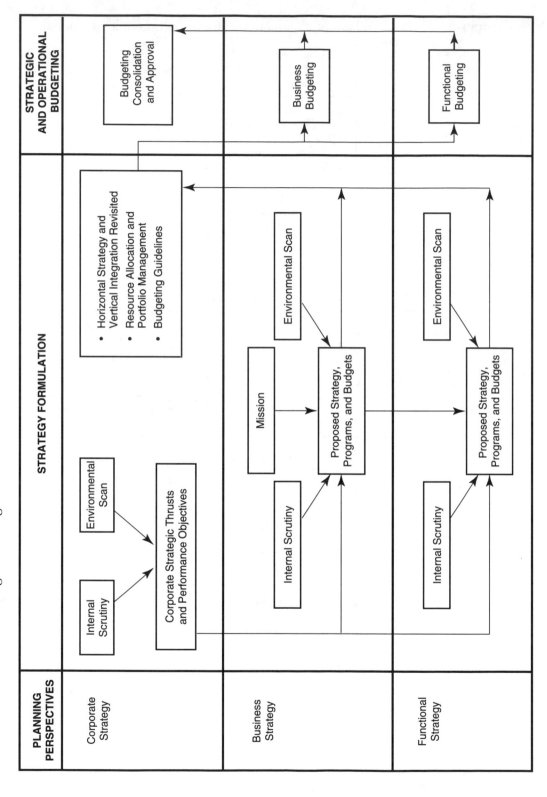

FIGURE 2–4. A Formal Strategic Planning Process

corporate performance objectives; at the business and functional levels, it leads to the proposal of action programs and budgets. These proposals are, in turn, evaluated and consolidated at the corporate level. At this stage, which marks the end of the strategy formulation cycle, we revisit the issues associated with horizontal and vertical integration -primary linking activities across businesses and functions. Moreover, we assign the priorities for resource allocation based upon portfolio management considerations.

The tasks associated with the business level are reviewed in Chapters 3 through 8. Those related to the corporate level are reviewed in Chapters 9 through 17, and functional strategy is presented in Chapters 18 through 21.

The second cycle of the planning process, which we label *strategic and operational budgeting*, deals with the final definition and subsequent consolidation at the corporate level of the budgets for all the businesses and functions of the firm. The budget constitutes the legitimate output of this process, since it represents the commitments for strategy implementation. We believe that these commitments should be defined in such a way as to include explicitly the strategic and operational activities of the firm.

The definition of strategy resulting from this formal planning process evolves from broad guidelines to concrete action plans. Each level and each unit in the organization can find in the definition of strategy a declaration, a piece of information, a goal, or an action plan that appeals directly to them. The explicit definition of a strategy must reflect a widely shared vision of the current potential and future projection of the firm.

With regard to the execution sequence of the planning tasks, the essence of the message portrayed in Figure 2–4 is that planning is neither a top-down nor a bottom-up process. It is a much more complex activity requiring a strong participation of the key managers of the firm. Here objectives are proposed from the top, and specific programmatic alternatives are suggested from business and functional levels. It is a process that, properly conducted, generates a wealth of individual commitments and personal participation from everybody who has a definitive say in sharpening the direction of the firm. It is a rich communication device where the key managers have an opportunity to voice their personal beliefs about the conduct of businesses of the firm and offer a valuable joint experience as well as an educational opportunity to be shared by key participants.

Tom MacAvoy, former president of Corning Glass Works, once said that the most important role of a CEO is to identify, develop, and promote "the one hundred centurions." In the old Roman empire, the centurion was a soldier who received instructions from the Caesar and was sent to remote lands. The Caesar knew that regardless of the number of years he would take for his task, the centurion would always be fighting for the Caesar's interests. If the planning process has any definitive objective and basic influence, it is to develop a strong esprit de corps among the one hundred centurions of the firm.

The Merits of Formal Strategic Planning

Formal strategic planning constitutes a powerful contribution to enhance managerial understanding and decision making. Among the most salient accomplishments we could cite the following:

THE PLANNING PROCESS HELPS TO UNIFY CORPORATE DIRECTIONS. By starting the process with a proper articulation of the vision of the firm, subsequently extended by the mission of each business, and the recognition of functional competencies, the planning process mobilizes all of the key managers in the pursuit of agreed-upon and shared objectives. This unifying thrust could be very hard to accomplish without the formalization and discipline of a systematic process.

THE SEGMENTATION OF THE FIRM IS GREATLY IMPROVED. The formal planning process enriches significantly the firm's segmentation by addressing the recognition of the various strategic focuses of attention—corporate, business, and functional—and their representation in the organizational structure. This process centers on seeking business autonomy that is oriented toward serving external markets, and recognizing horizontal and vertical integration as a means to realize fully the firm's potential by sharing resources across businesses. The business strategy fosters the independence of each business, while the corporate strategy attempts to link them whenever economic value can be added. These two perspectives provide the exact degree of balance between centralization and decentralization.

THE PLANNING PROCESS INTRODUCES A DISCIPLINE FOR LONG-TERM THINKING IN THE FIRM. The nature of the managerial tasks is so heavily dependent on taking care of an extraordinary amount of routine duties that unless a careful discipline is instituted, managerial time could be devoted entirely to operational issues. By enforcing upon the organization a logical process of thinking, with a clearly defined sequence of tasks, planning raises the vision of all key managers, encouraging them to reflect creatively on the strategic direction of the businesses.

THE PLANNING PROCESS IS AN EDUCATIONAL DEVICE AND AN OPPORTUNITY FOR MULTIPLE PERSONAL INTERACTIONS AND NEGOTIATIONS AT ALL LEVELS. Perhaps the most important of the attributes of a formal strategic planning process is that it allows the development of managerial competencies of the key members of the firm by enriching their common understanding of corporate objectives and businesses, and illustrating the way in which those objectives can be transformed into reality. In other words, the most important contribution of the planning process is the process itself. A mere by-product is the final content of the "planning book." The engaging communicational efforts, the multiple interpersonal negotiations generated, the need to understand and articulate the primary factors affecting the business, and the required personal involvement in the pursuit of constructive answers to pressing business questions are what truly make the planning process a most vital experience.

Avoiding the Limitations of Formal Strategic Planning

In spite of its many contributions, the corporate strategic planning process has limitations that, if not properly recognized, could destroy its effectiveness.

RISK OF EXCESSIVE BUREAUCRATIZATION

One of the inherent risks in formalizing any process is to create conditions that impose a bureaucratic burden on an organization, stifling creativity, and losing the sense of the primary objectives intended by that process. Planning could become an end in itself, transformed into a meaningless game of filling in the numbers and impairing the strategic alertness that is the central concern of planning.

It may be difficult to maintain strong vitality and interest in a process that is time consuming and repetitive. Often, the initial stages of introducing a well-conceived planning process in an organization is accompanied by an exhilarating challenge generating a strong personal commitment and enthusiasm. As time goes by, the threat of the planning process becoming a routine bureaucratic activity is very real.

There are several ways to prevent this undesirable situation. One is not to force a revision of all the steps of the planning process outlined in this writing; instead, one might conduct a comprehensive and extensive strategic audit, say, every five years. In the interim, managers should deal simply with minor upgrading of strategies and programs.

Another approach is to identify selectively, each year, the planning units that deserve more careful attention to the planning process, either because of changes in environmental conditions or internal organizational issues. This discriminatory emphasis could help to avoid spending unnecessary effort on businesses that do not require such attention.

A third organizational device to prevent bureaucratization is to select a planning theme each year, which will require the attention of all key managers in their annual planning effort. Possible theme choices are globalization, new manufacturing process technologies, the value of the firm's products to customers, alternative channels of distribution, productivity improvements, information technology questions, and product quality.

PLANNERS DO NOT PLAN: MANAGERS DO

There is an inherent danger in an organization that decides to implement its strategic planning process with a heavy planning department. This is normally a serious pitfall on two accounts. First, planners should not plan. Planning is an inherent managerial responsibility that cannot be delegated to staff units.

Although there are legitimate activities that planning departments could undertake, such as collecting the external information to enlighten managerial decision making; serving as catalysts, inquirers, educators, and synthesizers to guide the planning process in an effective manner; and assuming an educational role to facilitate the understanding of planning methodologies; it is crucial to realize that planning is done by line executives and not by planners. Planners should not plan; this should be done by the line executives.

If you do have a planning department, make it as lean as possible, composed of intelligent and energetic young individuals who could benefit from a brief stay there—a location with a remarkable vantage point in the organization—and be moved later to a more permanent line or staff position. The establishment of heavy planning departments might tend to isolate the planning process from the mainstream of managerial decisions.

The second potential pitfall of having a centralized planning department is that it tends to isolate the planning activity from the remaining administrative systems. This is the sure way of transforming planning into a largely irrelevant activity. No wonder then that, in many instances, planning becomes a yearly ritual, conducted by staff members. This culminates in a thick book that gathers dust on the shelves of those managers who were not involved in the preparations, but whose tasks the book intended to define. Most of the benefits of the planning process, if properly done, accrue in the realization of the process itself. Planning is a decision-making activity, and the planning books are simply subproducts for refreshing our memory and documenting the decisions made. They are certainly not the final aims of the planning process.

GRAND DESIGN VERSUS LOGICAL INCREMENTALISM

An issue that has been raised is whether creative strategic thinking can ever emerge from a formal, disciplined process. Some go even further and question whether it is desirable to commit to a rational grand scheme as a way of projecting the organization forward. A leading scholar who casts a serious doubt on the merits of formal planning is James Brian Quinn.[2] He regards formal planning as an important building block in a continuously evolving structure of analytical and political events that combine to determine overall strategy. He states that the actual process used to arrive at a total strategy, however, is usually fragmented, evolutionary, and largely intuitive. He claims that in well-run organizations, managers proactively guide streams of actions and events incrementally toward a strategy embodying many of the principles of formal strategies. However, top executives rarely design their overall strategy, or even its major segments, in the formal planning cycle of the corporation. Instead they use a series of incremental processes that build strategies largely at more disaggregated levels and then integrate these subsystem strategies step by step for the total corporation. The rationale behind this kind of incremental strategy formulation is so powerful that it, rather than the formal system planning approach, seems to provide an improved normative model for strategic decision making .

We believe that the notion of logical incrementalism is not necessarily contradictory to a well-conceived corporate strategic planning process. By that we mean a process that is supported in the corporate values of the organization, that is participatory in character, that has a sense of vision given from the top but shared by all key managers, and that allows for meaningful negotiations to take place within an organizational framework. This process does not blindly set up long-term objectives, but rather expresses a sense of desired long-term direction. It attempts to adjust its course of action incrementally with a strategic posture in mind.

FORMAL PLANNING VERSUS OPPORTUNISTIC PLANNING

Formal planning systems represent an organized way of identifying and coordinating the major tasks of the organization. If all the planning capabilities were to be dependent entirely on the formal planning structure, the firm would be in a highly vulnerable position, unable to face unexpected events not properly foreseen within the assumptions underlying the strategy formation process. Therefore, coexisting with formal planning, there is another form of planning referred to as *opportunistic planning*. In Figure 2–5 a comparison is presented of the characteristics of formal and opportunistic planning.

FIGURE 2–5. The Characteristics of Formal and Opportunistic Planning

FACTORS	FORMAL PLANNING	OPPORTUNISTIC PLANNING
Timing	Systematic process that follows a prescribed calendar	Responses to unexpected emergencies of opportunities and threats
Scope	Corporate-wide	Usually concentrated on a segment of the corporation
Purpose	Attempts to develop a coordinated and proactive adaptation and anticipation to changes in the external environment, while seeking internal effectiveness and efficiency	It is based on existing capabilities that permit slack and flexibility to respond to unplanned events

Since opportunistic planning is triggered by unexpected events and is usually concentrated in a more narrow segment of the corporate activities, it seems unlikely that the triggering event affects all the businesses of the corporation. The key capability essential for the prompt response to the external event is the existence of *slack*. Often, organizations assign untapped financial resources to be quickly mobilized at the discretion of the corresponding manager to meet the unforeseen emergency. This is a form of financial slack. Even more important is what we might call organizational slack. By that we mean the availability of human resources that are not overly burdened by their program commitments, so that they can absorb additional duties without experiencing a severe organizational constraint.

There is a need to balance the weight of these two coexisting planning processes. Organizations that rely exclusively on formal planning could trap themselves in unbearable rigidities. On the other hand, a firm whose decision-making capability rests entirely on purely opportunistic schemes will be constantly reacting to external forces, without having a clear sense of direction. The answer lies in a good compromise between these two extremes. A proper dose of formal planning provides the broad strategic planning framework without binding every action of the enterprise, while opportunistic planning allows for creative responses to be made within that organized framework.

HIERARCHIES SHOULD NOT BE AN OBSTACLE FOR THE DEVELOPMENT OF STRATEGIC CAPABILITIES

The advent of information technologies is producing enormous impacts in the modern organization, the ultimate implications of which are extremely difficult to grasp at this point. What we now know is that the corporate structure is becoming more compact. The information that was traditionally collected and presented to the company's top managers by its middle managers is now being obtained and presented by computers and communication networks. As a result of this, the middle levels in the management hierarchy are contracting, structure is becoming more compact, and the work force is becoming more diverse and enterprising. Networks are beginning to substitute for the conventional role of the managerial hierarchy. The traditional roles of boss and subordinates, with their associated flow of vertical communications, are being replaced by the notions of networking and group working. Effective coordination across lateral networks is becoming more crucial to understand the firm of the future than the managerial hierarchy, which may become either invisible or irrelevant.[3]

Within this context, one should interpret our strategic tasks at the corporate, business, and functional levels not as a rigid hierarchical sequence of actions, but rather as useful conceptual frameworks that address the different focuses of attention that we believe are central to running a business firm now as well as in the future.

Managing by Strategy

The four frameworks that we have presented in this chapter—dealing with the three perspectives of strategy, and how to formalize the strategic planning process—are all pertinent to the development of an effective strategy for the firm. A final framework that we will present intends to put strategy into a broader context, which integrates strategy in all the managerial decisions and activities of the firm.

What comes after strategic planning? This is a most relevant question that needs to be answered after a firm engages in a rigorous and disciplined strategic planning process that provides us, as an output, an integrated set of corporate, business, and functional strategies. The answer is: strategic management.

There are three overreaching strategic principles related to strategic management:

People Are the Greatest Assets of the Firm

This has been the most important transformation in the management of the 1990s, which has led to identify *people* as the key resource of competitive advantage. Without demeaning the value of other resources, there is an increasing belief that people provide the most lasting and sustainable differentiating capabilities. To some extent, other resources can either be traded, substituted, or imitated, while a skilled, developed, and motivated work force represents a unique asset, that is much more difficult to duplicate.[4]

Integration of Strategy, Structure, Business Processes, Performance, and Culture

Strategy provides the overall foundation from which to develop the managerial capabilities of the firm. However, it is part of a much larger set of managerial constructs that makes strategy alive in the organization. These constructs are the organizational structure, which permits the orderly assignment of the critical tasks of the organization to its work force, the business processes, which allow for a specific ordering of the work activities in an effective manner; the control and motivational systems, which carefully monitor the performance of the firm using relevant and contemporary measures; and the organizational culture, which establishes the set of values and beliefs of the firm, and defines the rules of the organization's individual behavior. The modern term to label these integrating capabilities is organizational architecture, which includes the formal structure, the design of work practices, the nature of the informal organization or operating style, and the process of selection, socialization, and development of people.[5]

The Important Coexistence of Formal and Informal Managerial Processes and Systems

To deal with the increasing complexity that affects the modern corporation, we need the support of some disciplined and formal processes and systems, which we have alluded to already in our previous point. However, these systems should be complemented and reinforced through a host of additional informal mechanisms. Both types of processes and systems are essential for the proper management of the firm. A very important task is to balance their contributions in a productive and integrative way.

Figure 2–6 illustrates the components of the strategic management framework. The figure serves to communicate three issues that are important for strategic management to work effectively. One is the interrelationship that links strategy, structure, processes, performance, and culture. We have expressed this interrelationship in a linear way, although we are conscious of the many interdependencies that exist among them. We believe it is useful to analyze their linkage in a sequential manner. We first define the strategies of the firm; then we design the organizational structure to facilitate their implementation; next we define the business processes that cut across the organizational units that emerge from the organizational structure; fourth, we put in place the performance metrics that will allow for a proper control and reward system; and finally, these performance measurements will impact significantly the culture of the firm. The culture, in turn, impacts the strategy and conditions it. Thus culminates the cycle.

The second point that is revealed from the figure is the different nature of the managerial processes that are supporting these strategic constructs. The planning process is essential for strategy formation. The information and communication processes serve as coordinating media in the organizational structure of the firm. The business processes capture the interdependence of the tasks across the organizational units defined by the organizational structure. The control and reward processes determine the type and quality of the performance measurements used by the organization.

To distinguish the different characteristics of these processes and their impact on the organization, we find useful the taxonomy that is represented in Figure 2–7 on page 40. Often we tend to promote formal systems oriented towards measuring or supporting outcomes in the organization. These include computer-based information systems, well-structured business systems, and formalized control and reward systems. Likewise, the outcomes are fairly unambiguously defined, such as: market share, return on assets, sales margin, etc. Formal systems with an outcome orientation serve a very good purpose, and they are a basic requirement for proper management. At times, they even respond to legal requirements exercised on the firm, such as the observance of well-established accounting rules for financial reporting.

However, what we have come to detect and appreciate is the equally significant role played by informal systems oriented towards processes that address critical activities of the firm. We are referring here to the host of interactions that exist among members of the work force at all levels, casual as well as programmed. These interactions enrich the understanding of the managerial issues and allow management to influence the processes that eventually will generate the desired outcomes of the firm.

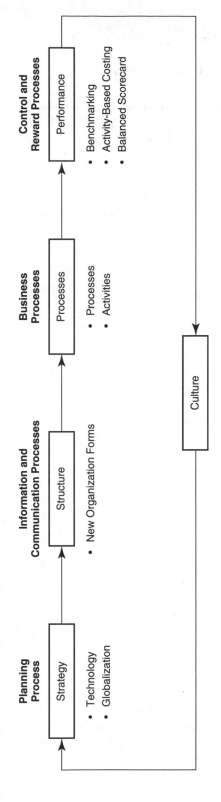

FIGURE 2–6. Strategic Management Framework

39

FIGURE 2–7. Taxonomy of Managerial
Processes

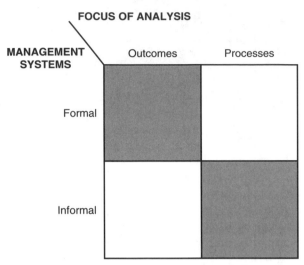

Key: The shadowed area serves to underscore the importance of
formal systems oriented at measuring specific outcomes, and
informal systems concentrating on managerial processes.

The final point to be made has to do with the recognition of the key forces and practices that affect the strategic management constructs identified in our framework. Unarguably, technology and globalization are the forces that are most critical to determining the strategies of the firm. Managing in a global environment with a rapid pace of technological change is a critical challenge that most managers are facing. As a result, new organizational forms have emerged to adapt more quickly to global economic challenges and to enhance the knowledge of the work force. Organizations are becoming flatter, multidisciplinary teams are replacing the individual worker, and horizontal networks are substituting for vertical channels of communication. The emergence of self-managed teams composed of knowledge workers is blurring the conventional distinction between managers and nonmanagers. Creating the conditions that foster a learning organization has become a distinct necessity.

Business process reengineering is, perhaps, the most impacting of all the recent business practices. It offers the promise of dramatic improvements in cost, quality, service, and speed resulting in radical redesign of the business processes. As we have said before, the key is to identify those business processes that cut across the different organizational units within the firm. By their nature, it is quite likely, therefore, that no one is given full responsibility for their effectiveness. Then, particularly through the passage of time, all kinds of inefficiencies could be generated, creating the major opportunities for radical improvements that we alluded to earlier. The processes are broken down into a set of specific activities, and these activities are analyzed to detect whether they are adding value or not. Practitioners of business process reengineering report admirable results. It is not uncommon that more than half of the activities that compose a process are nonvalue added.

Finally, in recent years we have seen an enormous amount of concern about the quality of the performance measures of the firm. These have given rise to some fairly creative new approaches for management control. All of them tend to complement the financial measurements, enrich the strategic nature of the metrics, and correct for deficiencies that are borne in the conventional cost accounting practices being used. Also, they are all quite logical and sensible, which makes their implementation quite appealing. The most important new control practices are benchmarking, activity-based costing, and the balanced scorecard.

The essence of benchmarking is to contrast the firm's performance against some challenging yardsticks. These can be generated by internal-historical comparisons; by comparing ourselves against the key competitors in our industry; or by measuring ourselves against the "best-in-class" performers in every functional activity.[6]

Activity-based costing introduces a simple correction to the allocation of overhead to the various outputs of the firm (e.g., products, services, projects, and the like). The conventional cost accounting practices measure quite exhaustively the direct and variable costs incurred by the firm. In a fairly arbitrary way, conventional cost accounting assigns the overhead to products and services. This was a sound practice when variable costs represented a high percentage of the total costs of the firm and there was not the great proliferation of outputs that exist today. Now, direct costs tend to be a small percentage of the total cost of a high-technology diversified, global corporation. Therefore, the distortions introduced by the old practice are intolerable. Activity-based costing introduces a fairly simple transformation. Rather than allocating overhead directly to outputs, it first defines the activities that the firm is engaged in. Overheads are allocated to these activities, and from there, to the final products and services. (Incidentally, these activities are part of the business processes that we have just discussed, which creates a very strong linkage between business process reengineering and activity-based costing.)

The practitioners of this methodology report outstanding differences in the costs imputed by these two approaches. It seems that most companies have been operating, at best, with very rudimentary information about their costs. At worst, they have been making critical decisions based on misleading cost information.[7]

The balanced scorecard attempts to provide managers with a comprehensive measure of the performance of the businesses. It starts by recognizing that the financial perspective, although essential, only tells you how have you done historically, but offers little, if any, insight on how will you be doing in the future. The financial perspective, which responds to the question "How do we look to our shareholders?", has to be complemented by three additional perspectives that address the following corresponding questions: the customer perspective, How do the customers see us?; the internal business perspective, What should we excel at?; and, finally, the innovation and learning perspective, Can we continue to improve and create value?

The balanced scorecard, pioneered by Robert Kaplan and David Norton, brings in a single management report many of the seemingly disparate elements of the firm's competitive agenda. That is its major strength.[8]

Notes

1. An initial version of a strategic planning process presented in Figure 2-4 was proposed by Richard F. Vancil and Peter Lorange, "Strategic Planning in Diversified Companies," *Harvard Business Review,*. 53, no. 1 (January–February 1975), 81–90. The full specification of the strategic tasks implicit in that process was developed by Arnoldo C. Hax and Nicolas S. Majluf, *Strategic Management: An Integrative Perspective* (Englewood Cliffs, NJ: Prentice Hall, 1984).

2. James Brian Quinn, *Strategy for Changes—Logical Incrementalism* (Homewood, IL: Richard D. Irwin, 1980); James Brian Quinn, "Formulating Strategy One Step at a Time," *The Journal of Business Strategy,* 1, no. 3 (Winter 1981), 42–63; James Brian Quinn, Henry Mintzberg, and Robert M. James, *The Strategy Process: Concepts, Context, and Cases* (Englewood Cliffs, NJ: Prentice Hall, 1988).

3. Tom Malone, a computer scientist and organizational psychologist at MIT is developing a new field, which he refers to as "coordination theory," to study the impact that information is causing in organizations. For a discussion of coordination theory and its implications, the reader is referred to Thomas W. Malone, JoAnne Yates, and Robert I. Benjamin, "Electronic Markets and Electronic Hierarchies," *Communications of the ACM,* 30 (1987), 484–497; Thomas W. Malone and Stephen A. Smith, "Modeling the Performance of Organizational Structures," *Operations Research,* 36, no. 3 (May–June 1988), 421–436; Thomas W. Malone, and John F. Rockart, "Computers, Networks, and the Corporation," *Scientific American,* (September 1991), 121–136.

4. Important references to expand on these points are Edward E. Lawler, III, *The Ultimate Advantage* (San Francisco, CA: Jossey-Bass, 1992); and Jeffrey Pfeffer, *Competitive Advantage through People* (Boston, MA: Harvard Business School Press, 1994).

5. For a discussion of organizational architecture, see: David Nadler, Marc Gerstein, Robert Shaw, and Associates, *Organizational Architecture: Designs for Changing Organizations* (San Francisco, CA: Jossey-Bass, 1992); and Gary Hamel and C.K. Prahalad, *Competing for the Future* (Boston, MA: Harvard Business School Press, 1994).

6. For references in benchmarking see: Robert C. Camp, *Benchmarking: The Search for Industry Best Practices That Lead to Superior Performance* (Milwaukee, WI: Quality Press, 1989); Kathleen H. J. Leibfried and C. J. McNair, *Benchmarking: A Tool for Continuous Improvement* (New York: HarperCollins, 1992).

7. For references in activity-based cost management, see: Robin Cooper, Robert S. Kaplan, Lawrence S. Maisel, Eileen Morrissey, and Ronald M. Oehm, *Implementing Activity-Based Cost Management: Moving from Analysis to Action* (Montvale, NJ: The Institute of Management Accountants, 1992); Robin Cooper and Robert S. Kaplan, "Measure the Costs Right: Make the Right Decisions," *Harvard Business Review,* September–October 1988); Gary Cokins, Alan Stratton, and Jack Helbling, *The ABC Manager's Primer* (Montvale, NJ: The Institute of Management Accountants, 1992).

8. For references on balanced scorecard see: Robert S. Kaplan and David P. Norton, "The Balanced Scorecard—Measures That Drive Performance," *Harvard Business Review,* 70, no. 1 (January–February 1992), 71–79; Robert S. Kaplan and David P. Norton, "Putting the Balanced Scorecard to Work," *Harvard Business Review* (September–October 1993).

3

Business Strategy: The Core Concepts

Out of the three perspectives that we recognize as the central foci for strategic thinking in an organization—corporate, business, and functional capabilities—the business perspective is the core of managerial actions. Business strategy attracts prime executive attention, and many of the concepts and methodologies required to understand the business strategic tasks are also central to the comprehension of corporate and functional strategic issues. Because of these practical as well as pedagogical considerations, we have chosen to start the more in-depth discussion of the content and process of strategy at the level of the business unit.

There are two central concepts essential to achieving a solid understanding of a well-rounded business strategy: the definition of a strategic business unit, and the choice of a competitive business strategy.

The Concept of Strategic Business Unit

A highly demanding and challenging question we need to address at the start of the planning process is: What businesses are we in, and what businesses do we intend to be in? This question of business segmentation normally requires an enormous amount of knowledge and expertise to be answered properly. In order to undertake this task, we have to define the unit of analysis, which is referred to as *the strategic business unit* (SBU).

An SBU is an operating unit or a planning focus that groups a distinct set of products or services sold to a uniform set of customers, while facing a well-defined set of competitors. Notice that the external dimension (that is, customers and markets) is the relevant perspective for the recognition of SBUs.

This stems from the fact that the essence of strategy deals with positioning the business so as to respond effectively to a customer need in a superior way to the competitor's offering. Therefore, a group of products are aggregated into an SBU if they share a common set of customers and competitors.

The concept of a strategic business unit first originated in 1970, when Fred Borch, as Chairman of General Electric (GE), decided to break the GE businesses into a set of autonomous units, following a recommendation made by McKinsey and Company. GE had evolved from a company restricted to the electrical motors and lighting businesses into a conglomerate of activities spanning a wide variety of industries. Complexity increased as size, diversity, international scope, and a spectrum of technologies began to impose an unprecedented challenge to GE's top managers.

Confronted with this formidable task, GE's answer was to break down the businesses of the firm into independent, autonomous units that could be managed as viable and isolated business concerns. Those entities were labeled strategic business units (SBU). The original intent of the business segmentation undertaken by GE was to provide the SBU general manager with complete independence from the rest of the businesses of the firm. The SBU had its own well-defined market segments and the SBU manager had all the resources available to define and carry out a successful strategy with full autonomy.[1]

A similar approach for business segmentation has been proposed by the management consulting firm Arthur D. Little, Inc. (ADL). They define an SBU as a business area with an external marketplace for goods or services, and for which one can determine independent objectives and strategies. To accomplish the business segmentation, ADL suggests the use of a set of clues grounded on conditions in the marketplace rather than on internally shared resources, such as sharing of manufacturing facilities, common technology, or joint distribution channels. Once again, the emphasis on segmentation is articulated in terms of the external environment, attempting to establish the roots of business identification in the behavior of customers and competitors, instead of being driven by internal functional arrangements. The clues that ADL offers to define an SBU are:

1. **Competitors:** The business unit should have a single set of competitors.
2. **Prices:** All products belonging to a business unit should be affected similarly by price changes.
3. **Customers:** Business units should have a single set of well-defined customers.
4. **Quality/Style:** In a properly defined business unit, change in quality and style affects products similarly.
5. **Substitutability:** All products in a business unit should be relatively close substitutes. Also, there should be no clear substitute in different business units, as this would signal the need to unify products in the same unit.
6. **Divestment or Liquidation:** All products belonging to a given business unit should be able to stand alone as an autonomous viable economic entity if divested.

The first four clues indicate that a set of products belongs to a given SBU whenever it faces a single set of competitors and customers, and is similarly affected by price, quality, and style changes. If this is not the case, the set of products might be split into more than one SBU to focus more sharply its strategic actions. Moreover, all products in an SBU should be close substitutes for one another. Finally, an SBU could probably stand alone if divested.[2]

The SBU concept has produced a long-lasting influence in the way companies design, develop, and implement formal strategic planning processes.

Interrelationship across Strategic Business Units

As the previous definitions proposed by GE and ADL testify, the initial concept of an SBU presupposes a sense of autonomy and independence. As the concept began to be more fully recognized, accepted, and implemented in a variety of business firms, the issue of independence began to be seriously contested. There are a number of reasons why breaking businesses into autonomous units is not feasible. First, a firm primarily engaged in a single or dominant business activity with a purely functional organizational structure cannot be broken into totally independent segments. This is a prevalent situation in small enterprises. It is also commonly observed in medium-sized and large organizations in process-oriented industries characterized by high levels of vertical integration.

Our inability to establish autonomous entities in those cases, however, does not preclude the firm from participating in a plurality of external markets, each one possessing distinct opportunities and demanding different competitive efforts. We have to manage a situation in which there is no easy match between the functional organizational structure and the strategic focus for different market segments.

Another important exception to the definition of independent business units is the firm that can be broken into highly distinct businesses, but if those units were to be managed in a totally autonomous way, unacceptable inefficiencies would result. We can identify situations where different units, in order to be run effectively, have to share common resources such as manufacturing facilities, distribution channels, technology, or other functional support. Ignoring these potentials would deprive the organization of significant benefits to be derived from shared experiences and economies of scale. Another form of interrelationship is the existence of shared concerns, such as common geographical areas and key customer accounts.[3]

Consequently, a thorough discussion of business segmentation has to consider the implications of managing the synergy resulting from potential interrelationships across business units. This is the all-important subject of horizontal strategy, which is presented in Chapter 13 as one of the key corporate strategic tasks. In the meantime, the following considerations are important to bear in mind:

1. An SBU is intended to serve an external market, not an internal one. This means that an SBU should have a set of external customers and should not just serve as an internal supplier.
2. An SBU should have a well-defined set of external competitors, with respect to whom it is attempting to obtain a sustainable advantage.
3. The SBU manager should have sufficient independence in deciding the critical strategic actions. This does not mean that the SBU manager could not share resources such as manufacturing facilities, sales force, procurement, services, technologies, and the like with other business units existing in the firm. It simply means that the SBU manager is free to choose where to obtain the necessary resources and how to compete effectively.
4. If the three conditions just stated are met, an SBU becomes a genuine profit center, totally accountable for its profitability as opposed to becoming either a cost center or an artificial profit center where profit is measured through transfer price mechanisms.[4]
5. Finally, an SBU does not have to be a well-defined organizational unit with a line manager in charge to be regarded as a legitimate SBU. In an organization structured along functional lines participating in a variety of markets and facing several distinct sets of competitors, it would not be feasible to match the SBU segmentation with the organizational structure. In those cases, the SBU could still be the central focus for strategic analysis. However, the SBU manager would simply play a coordinating role, seeking the necessary resources from the various organizational units of the firm, none of which might report directly to him or her.

The issue of business segmentation is a key task for the development of a sound strategic planning process. In this chapter, we are simply stating the definition of an SBU, and giving a very introductory treatment to this concept. Since business segmentation resides at the corporate level, we will raise this issue again in Chapter 12, when we address the corporate strategic tasks. Also at that time, we will touch upon recent criticisms on the use of the SBU as a basis of strategic analysis. [5]

The Fundamental Elements of the Definition of a Business Strategy

There are three basic determinants of the profitability of the business unit: the mission of the business, the attractiveness of the industry in which the business belongs, and the competitive position of the business unit within that industry. These are the inputs that determine the strategic agenda of a business and lead to the formulation and implementation of its strategy.

The mission of the business defines the competitive domain in terms of the business scope (products, markets, and geographical locations), as well as the unique competencies that determine the key capabilities of the business. Unique competencies stem from the basic factors of production, and the resources and capabilities the firm has to achieve a competitive advantage. Unique competencies single out the firm from the rest of its competitors. They are genuine expressions of leadership and provide the foundation for superior profitability in this business unit.

The industry attractiveness explains the value generated by the economic activity of the industry participants, as well as their ability to share in the wealth created. The most widely used framework to understand the industry attractiveness is based on Porter's Five-Forces Model,[6] which provides an assessment of the potential for a business to attain a superior profitability by examining the industry structure through the five forces. The five forces are represented by: rivalry among competitors, bargaining power of suppliers, bargaining power of buyers, threat of substitutes, and threat of new entrants. The focus of attention, in this case, is the market for products and services offered by the firm. This element of the planning process is referred to as the *Environmental Scan at the Business Level*, and deals with a set of factors that is normally external to, and uncontrollable by, the firm.

The competitive position establishes the basis for achieving a sustainable advantage, which is the relative standing the firm has against its most relevant competitors. In this case, Porter's Value-Chain Model is the guiding framework to assess the competitive position of the business in all the activities of the value chain. This element of the planning process is referred to as *Internal Scrutiny at the Business Level*, and deals with a set of actions that are essentially controllable by the firm.

The three elements discussed above are the ingredients behind the identification of a business strategy, which is expressed as *broad and specific action programs*. These programs should be comprehensive, insofar as responding to the changes in the mission of the business, the opportunities and threats linked to the industry structure, and the strengths and weaknesses resulting from the evaluation of the business competitive positioning. In addition, they should be expressed with a clear sense of accountability, timing and control capabilities. This will bridge the two inseparable phases of strategy: formulation and implementation. Thus, strategy provides a basis for coordinated action among different people and different units of a business firm and for consistency of action through time.

By putting these four ingredients together—mission, industry structure, competitive position, and strategic action programs—the formula for success can be stated in a fairly straightforward manner: define an action-oriented strategy that selects a business in an attractive industry where you could excel. Figure 3–1 on page 48 provides the essential elements of this basic framework.

Budgeting, the final task of business strategy, simply captures the financial implications of the business programs. The corporation will evaluate those

FIGURE 3–1. The Fundamental Elements of the Definition of a Business Strategy

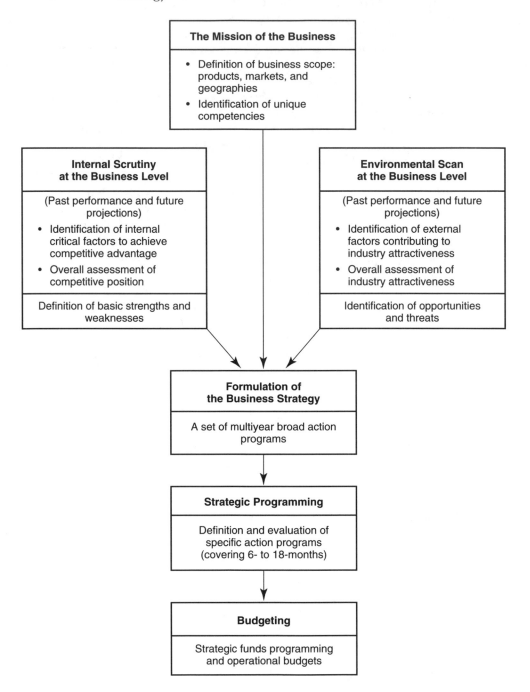

The Mission of the Business

- Definition of business scope: products, markets, and geographies
- Identification of unique competencies

Internal Scrutiny at the Business Level

(Past performance and future projections)
- Identification of internal critical factors to achieve competitive advantage
- Overall assessment of competitive position

Definition of basic strengths and weaknesses

Environmental Scan at the Business Level

(Past performance and future projections)
- Identification of external factors contributing to industry attractiveness
- Overall assessment of industry attractiveness

Identification of opportunities and threats

Formulation of the Business Strategy

A set of multiyear broad action programs

Strategic Programming

Definition and evaluation of specific action programs (covering 6- to 18-months)

Budgeting

Strategic funds programming and operational budgets

programs, allocate resources, make a formal commitment through the agreed-upon budget figures, and define the performance measurements needed to carry out an intelligent strategic management control.

By adhering to this framework, the business strategy becomes the end product of a thoughtful process that includes an environmental scan and an internal scrutiny, and requires a previous articulation of the business mission.

Notes

1. For a historical overview of General Electric's strategic planning system, see the case: General Electric Company, "Background Note on Management Systems: 1981," Case #181-111 (Boston, MA: Harvard Business School, 1981) .

2. For a description of Arthur D. Little's strategic planning approach, see: Arthur D. Little, Inc., A *System for Managing Diversity* (Cambridge,. MA: December 1974); Arthur D. Little, Inc., *Discovering the Fountain of Youth: An Approach to Corporate Growth and Development* (San Francisco,. CA: 1979); Arthur D. Little, Inc., *A Management System for the 1980s* (San Francisco, CA: 1980); and Arnoldo C. Hax and Nicolas S. Majluf, *Strategic Management: An Integrative Perspective* (Englewood Cliffs, NJ: Prentice Hall, 1984).

3. The cornerstone for identifying shared resources opportunities is the value-added chain, which covers all stages of business activities from product development to delivery of the finished product to the final customer. A careful treatment of the value chain and its implications for business strategy is presented in Chapter 6.

4. These four criteria for the definition of an SBU were originally stated by William E. Rothschild, "How to Ensure the Continuous Growth of Strategic Planning," *The Journal of Business Strategy,* 1, no. 1 (Summer 1980), 11–18.

5. A frontal attack on the use of the SBU as a central focus for business strategy has been made by C.K. Prahalad and Gary Hamel in "The Core Competence of the Corporation," *Harvard Business Review* (May-June, 1990), 79–91

6. Michael Porter's five-forces model is explained in depth in his book *Competitive Strategy: Techniques for Analyzing Industries and Competitors* (New York: The Free Press, 1980).

7. Michael Porter's value chain model is discussed in his book, *Competitive Advantage: Creating and Sustaining Superior Performance* (New York: The Free Press, 1985).

4

The Mission of the Business

There are two key strategic decisions a manager has to address at an early stage in a business strategy when defining the mission of the business. These are: defining the business scope—which determines where to compete—and developing the unique competencies associated to the business—which determines how to compete.

The selection of an appropriate business scope implies the selection of the "right" customers and, consequently, the "right" competitors. This means defining the competitive domain in which the business operates. The nurturing and consolidation of the unique competencies involve the development of the key tangible and intangible resources the firm will acquire, as well as the corresponding capabilities that will differentiate the firm from its competitors.[1]

Few decisions are as significant as these. Errors in the definition of the business scope usually have drastic implications for the firm. It might end up missing opportunities by ignoring important emerging business segments, or getting stuck in mature businesses long after their attractiveness has expired. Similarly, the decisions affecting the development of the core competencies of the business are central to achieving superior financial performance. These two decisions—business scope and unique competencies—are embodied in the mission of the business.

Consequently, there are two sets of information that should be contained in the statement of the mission of a business. First, is a clear definition of current and future expected business scope. This is expressed as a broad description of the products, markets, and geographical coverage of the business today and within a reasonable time frame, commonly three-to-five years. The statement of business scope is informative not only for what it includes; it is equally telling for what it leaves out.

The other important piece of information that should be contained in the mission statement of a business is the selection of competencies that uniquely distinguish your business from others in the same industry. They define the way the business pursues a sustainable competitive advantage.

The contrast between the current and future business scope and unique competencies allows us to reflect on the changes that the business is challenged to pursue. These changes will constitute a key input for the strategic action programs that will allow the business to achieve its desired future position.

An important test to judge the quality of the mission of the business is implicit in the degree to which the organization is challenged to achieve truly demanding goals. This has been referred to as the degree of "stretch" intended to move the organization towards a new state of excellence. A disappointing outcome of the statement of the mission of the business will be one in which the managers merely state the current domain and the existing competencies, and record initiatives that are already ongoing as the future business state. In such a mission, no creative stretch is implied. In their celebrated article, "Strategic Intent," G. Hamel and C.K. Prahalad state that rather than trimming ambitions to match available resources, managers should instead leverage resources to reach seemingly unattainable goals.[2] This challenge is at the heart of a proper mission statement.

Often, managers think of the mission statement as a broad declaration of purpose similar to those appearing in annual reports. These statements are typically polished and cosmetic in nature; they are driven primarily by a public relations objective. They tend to be innocuous, and have little, if any, strategic content. This is not what we advocate here.

A Process for Defining the Mission of the Business: An Illustration

THE MISSION AS THE STARTING POINT OF BUSINESS STRATEGY

In our methodology, the mission of the business is the starting point of the formulation of the business strategy. This could appear to be rather controversial, primarily for two reasons. The first one is the result of our previous comment. Managers either tend to trivialize what the content of the mission is, or else they think that they already have a well-established mission statement that does not need to be either revised or challenged. Therefore, when one suggests starting the planning process with a reflection on the mission statement, the first reaction is one of disappointment or rejection, which comes from the misunderstanding of what constitutes the mission of the business. Our definition of the mission is centered on: detecting the changes to be undertaken in business scope and core competencies; identifying the resulting challenges emerging from those changes; and reaching the consensus to be created in the business direction.

The second area of controversy is implicit in the circularity of the strategic planning tasks. One could argue that in order to address the critical decisions of business scope and core competencies, we need first to complete a careful examination of the industry structure and an evaluation of possible options for competitive positions. However, these analyses also require the specification of the business scope, which defines the sectors whose industry structure will be examined, and the unique competencies available to the firm, which allows an examination of competitive positioning. This is the nature of the circularity to which we have alluded.

It is our experience that starting with a thorough review of the mission of the business is the preferred course of action. The methodology that we propose for conducting this analysis leads to a very effective diagnosis that has far-reaching consequences. The questions that are addressed penetrate to the core of the strategic issues of the business. They immediately engage the key executives in a discussion that has enormous relevance. When consensus is reached, and the final effective mission statement is generated, there is a sense of accomplishment that legitimizes the significance of the planning process and provides credibility to its subsequent tasks.

THE ARCHITECTS OF THE MISSION STATEMENT

We believe that the greatest benefit to be derived from an orderly strategic planning process is the dialogue that is facilitated among the key executives responsible for the business's performance. Planning is a key responsibility of the line executives, and is not an activity to be delegated to the staff. Thus, those deliberating on the mission of the business are the managers who will assume the responsibilities for formulating and implementing the business strategy.

We have found it useful, at times, to divide those managers into two groups as equally balanced as possible, assign them the task of defining the mission, and request that they report their conclusions to the full assembly. It should not come as a surprise that groups are often unable to concur with a statement of the current mission, let alone with what future directions should be. Normally, the hottest issue of contention is the identification of what leads to a truly competitive advantage. By examining the sources of disagreement and by debating the essential components of the mission statement, it is possible to engage in a rich communication process, focusing on the heart of what the business should be now, and the major challenges residing in the future.

THE METHODOLOGY FOR DEFINING
THE MISSION OF THE BUSINESS

We present now the different steps of the methodology we suggest for defining the mission of the business using the case of P&G Detergents in Europe. This is an example built from public sources of information with the sole purpose of illustrating the methodology. It is not intended to represent in any way the official statement of P&G strategy in this business.

Step 1. Definition of Time Frame.

In this step we define a time frame for the business strategic plan. This step may seem straightforward, but there are a number of factors to consider. An appropriate time frame for one industry may not be suitable for another. A time frame that is too brief could result in shortsighted planning, and a time frame that is too long could lead to overly speculative planning, especially in a rapidly changing market. Typically, businesses use a three-to-five-year time frame. However, in a volatile industry such as artificial intelligence, a one-or-two year time frame may be appropriate. On the other hand, for an industry that requires long-range investments, such as natural resources, a time frame of ten or more years may be suitable.

For the case of P&G Detergents in Europe, which is a consumer products industry, the time frame deemed appropriate is a planning horizon of five years.

Step 2. Determination of Business Scope and Unique Competencies.

First the firm has to define the existing business scope: the products, markets, and geographic locations that are currently part of the business; and the new business scope: the products, markets, and geographic locations they plan to add to the business. They should also list the capabilities that set the business apart from the competition now—existing unique competencies—and capabilities they hope will set it apart in the future—new unique competencies. As we have indicated before, contrasting the challenges derived from the changes in the existing and new states of the business allows us to detect the *stretch* implicit in the business positioning. After listing existing and new business scopes and unique competencies, we give priorities to each item using the priority assessment charts.

For some firms—usually major business enterprises—creating a list of all the products, markets, and geographic locations could take an enormous amount of time. In such cases—when the scope of the business is very large— the detailed lists could become unmanageable, and would therefore offer little insight. If an SBU fits this description, it might be best to aggregate products, markets, and so forth, at a high enough level to make completing the business scope a reasonable task.

Achieving the proper level of aggregation is important. It is critical how items are categorized; which products, markets, geographic locations, and unique competencies are grouped together and which are listed separately. Going into great detail and listing individual items that could have been handled collectively could lead to information overload. However, too little detail may cause important distinctions to be overlooked.

PRODUCT SCOPE. Products are the goods and services the business provides to customers. The central issue to consider in defining product scope is the categorization of the business products. We may want to group some products into a category so they can be addressed collectively, while listing some more important products separately.

MARKET SCOPE. Markets are usually harder to pinpoint than products. As with product scope definition, the important part of this step is how we segment the market. Market scope should accurately represent the consumers and customers using the products of the business. Important criteria for market segmentation are:

- Type of industry targeted
- Demographics
- Composition of consumers
- Channels of distribution

GEOGRAPHICAL SCOPE. The list of geographic locations should be comprehensive and should be defined at the proper level of aggregation. If the business is undertaking an international expansion, the geographic categories should be chosen to allow an adequate identification of the various countries in which the firm might operate, and their corresponding priorities.

UNIQUE COMPETENCIES. Unique competencies are capabilities that set the business apart from others in the industry. They are abilities that give the business a unique and sustainable advantage over competitors. It is not unusual, when comparing to the definition of business scope, to find that the list of unique competencies is rather short, or even nonexistent. In those circumstances, it is essential to challenge the organization to develop future capabilities that will result in genuine unique competencies.

PRIORITY ASSESSMENT. After listing existing and new products, the items need to be prioritized. Prioritizing the items makes it clear how much effort and how many resources will be allocated in the future. Priorities can have two different meanings, based on whether they are applied to an existing or a new scope item. We present the scale for priority assessment of business scope in Figure 4–1 and the scale of unique competencies in Figure 4–2.

One common concern that we have observed in applying priorities to the various items is the excessive use of the positive side of the scale. Typically, pluses and double pluses far outweigh the counterbalancing minuses and double minuses. A wider and more complete use of the scale is encouraged, reserving the double pluses for items that are truly outstanding and giving double minuses to items that will be deleted within the relevant time frame.

Moreover, priorities signify allocation of resources into the future. For example, an existing product receives a double plus not because it has had the highest priority in the past, but because it will receive the highest priority in the future time frame.

FIGURE 4–1. Priority Assessment Scale for Business Scope

SCOPE	PRIORITY	THE PRODUCT, MARKET, OR GEOGRAPHICAL LOCATION ...
Existing	– –	... is being divested or exited from.
	–	... will be assigned a low level of importance.
	E	... will continue to receive the current level of resources.
	+	... is assigned a high level of importance and additional resources to achieve a better competitive position.
	++	... is assigned the highest level of importance and the resources needed to achieve as outstanding a competitive position as possible.
New	– –	... is very tentatively considered for business activity.
	–	... is tentatively considered for business activity.
	E	... will receive the necessary level of resources.
	+	... will be assigned a high level of importance and the necessary resources to achieve a strong competitive position.
	++	... will be assigned the highest level of importance and the resources needed to achieve as outstanding a competitive position as possible.

FIGURE 4–2. Priority Assessment Scale for Unique Competencies

SCOPE	PRIORITY	THE UNIQUE COMPETENCY ...
Existing	– –	... no longer will provide competitive advantage.
	–	... will only provide a minor competitive advantage.
	E	... will be a source of significant competitive advantage.
	+	... will be a source of very high competitive advantage.
	++	... will be a source of most critical and highly differentiated competitive advantage.
New	– –	... could become a source of competitive advantage, but its significance is highly uncertain.
	–	... could become a source of competitive advantage, but its significance is mildly uncertain.
	E	... will be a source of significant competitive advantage.
	+	... will be a source of very high competitive advantage.
	++	... will be a source of most critical and highly differentiated competitive advantage.

In Figures 4–3 to 4–6, we present business scope and unique competencies for the case of P&G Detergents in Europe, with their corresponding priority assessment.

The categories under the heading "Fabrics" in the existing product scope chart (Figure 4–3) have been expanded into three types of products. These include: Powder (traditional), Powder (concentrated), and Liquid, because they have different priorities for resource allocation. A similar situation happens with the new "Fabric" products, which are further segmented into three new items to be considered. "Refillable Packaging" category receives the highest priority because of the importance given to the manufacture and use of environmentally safe products and packages.

The existing and new market scope (Figure 4–4) shows the different categories used to segment customers, consumers and users. Existing scope deals

FIGURE 4–3. Product Scope for the Case of P&G Detergents in Europe

EXISTING PRODUCT SCOPE

	--	-	E	+	++
▼ Fabrics					
Powder (traditional)	●				
Powder (concentrated)					●
Liquid			●		
Fabric Conditioners					●
Hand Dishwashing Detergents			●		
Machine Dishwashing Detergents				●	
Household Cleaners					●
Bleaches	●				

NEW PRODUCT SCOPE

	--	-	E	+	++
▼ Fabrics					
Refillable package—environmentally safe products and packaging					●
Detergent and Softener combined in same product		●			
Detergent and Bleach in same product (both for colors and whites)		●			
Fabric Conditioners with less environmental impact				●	
Convenience-packaged household cleaners	●				

NOTE: This is not an official document. It is an illustration drawn from public sources.

FIGURE 4–4. Market Scope for the Case of P&G Detergents in Europe

EXISTING MARKET SCOPE

	--	-	E	+	++
Supermarket (mostly food and household goods)					●
Hypermarket (full line of products, including clothing, etc.)					●
Drugstores		●			
Other retail outlets		●			
Men				●	
Women		●			
Low-income families	●				
Medium-income families				●	
High-income families					●

NEW MARKET SCOPE

	--	-	E	+	++
Environmentally concerned					●
Aging population				●	
One-person family units					●

NOTE: This is not an official document. It is an illustration drawn from public sources.

with distribution channels, and the sex and income of consumers; new market scope emphasizes a finer segmentation dealing with behavior: "Environmentally concerned," age ("Aging population"), and social structure of the family ("One-person family units").

The geographical scope (Figure 4–5) shows the different degree of attention given to certain countries in the European Community when compared with other countries in Europe and in the rest of the world. It also shows the high priority granted to countries such as Spain, Portugal, and Italy. It is not that these markets are more important or larger than markets in the United Kingdom or Germany, but that there is a substantial increase in the attention that those countries *should* receive, when compared with their current situation.

The unique competencies (Figure 4–6) are structured around the stages in the value chain. For example, the existing situation of the Technology stage shows the importance of "R&D in packaging and process development," an ability that has to be applied in future developments to get "biodegradable products and packages."

FIGURE 4–5. Geographical Scope for the Case of P&G Detergents in Europe

EXISTING GEOGRAPHICAL SCOPE	--	-	E	+	++
▼ European Community					
United Kingdom and Ireland				●	
Germany				●	
France				●	
Belgium, the Netherlands and Luxembourg			●		
Denmark			●		
Spain and Portugal					●
Italy					●
Greece			●		
Austria			●		
Scandinavian countries			●		
Turkey			●		
Switzerland			●		
Poland and the Czech Republic					●

NEW GEOGRAPHICAL SCOPE	--	-	E	+	++
C.I.S. (Commonwealth of Independent States)		●			
Other Eastern Europe	●				

NOTE: This is not an official document. It is an illustration drawn from public sources.

Step 3. Determination of Product-Market Segments.

A useful way to perform a further analysis in the product- and market-scope dimensions of the business mission statement is exemplified in Figure 4–7. The resultant matrix emphasizes the different alternatives for growth within a product-market scope:

- Market penetration—extend existing products into existing markets. To seek growth opportunities within that context, the firm has to resort to expansion in sales volume, geographical extensions, or market-share improvements.
- Market development—seek new markets for the existing product line.
- Product development—introduce new products into existing markets.
- Diversification—develop new products in new markets.

FIGURE 4–6. Unique Competencies for the Case of P&G Detergents in Europe

EXISTING UNIQUE COMPETENCIES	--	-	E	+	++
▼ Managerial Infrastructure					
Global product management (matrix management)			●		
Employee ownership program			●		
Brand management			●		
▼ Technology					
Highest R&D resources in the industry			●		
R&D sharing across product lines			●		
R&D in packaging and process development					●
▼ Marketing					
Local expertise					●
Strong brand recognition			●		
▼ Retail and Distribution					
Automated distribution, POS information			●		
Strong distribution network			●		
▼ Manufacturing					
Highly automated			●		
Rapid development to market time			●		

NEW UNIQUE COMPETENCIES	--	-	E	+	++
▼ Managerial Infrastructure					
Transnational management					●
▼ Technology					
R&D in biodegradable products					●
R&D in biodegradable packaging					●
▼ Marketing					
Image of environmentally safe company and products					●
▼ Retail and Distribution					
Develop network in Eastern Europe		●			

NOTE: This is not an official document. It is an illustration drawn from public sources.

59

An accepted practice is that the role of the business manager is limited to identifying and fully exploiting the potential extensions of current business into adjacent product and market opportunities. It is not the business manager's responsibility to pursue diversification strategies; rather, this task resides entirely at the corporate level.

Similarly to Product vs. Market Segmentation, we could build a Product vs. Geography Segmentation matrix if that were deemed interesting in order to shed new light on the definition of the business mission.

Figure 4–8 presents the Product vs. Market Segmentation Matrix for the case of P&G Detergents in Europe.

Step 4. Challenges from Changes in the Mission.

In this step we begin to summarize the results of our analysis by listing the new business challenges that arise from the changes we expect in the business. Each critical change—from business scope and unique competencies— is addressed in the form of a challenge. Challenges should be specific and explain what will be done to bring about the desired change.

Later in the strategic planning process we define broad and specific action programs in response to these challenges. If a change is not presented as a challenge, it is likely to be overlooked when action programs are formulated.

Figure 4–9 summarizes the challenges arising from the changes in the mission statement for the case of P&G Detergents in Europe. This includes challenges resulting from changes in product, market, and geographical scope, and

FIGURE 4–7. Definition of Product-Market Segments and Alternative for Growth Strategies

	EXISTING MARKET SCOPE	NEW MARKET SCOPE
EXISTING PRODUCT SCOPE	Market Penetration	Market Development
NEW PRODUCT SCOPE	Product Development	Diversification

FIGURE 4–8. Product vs. Market Segmentation—P&G Detergent Business in Europe

	EXISTING MARKET SCOPE	Supermarket (mostly …)	Hypermarket (full line…)	Drugstores	Other retail outlets	Men	Women	Low-income families	Medium-income families	High-income families	NEW MARKET SCOPE	Environmentally concerned	Aging population	One-person family units
EXISTING PRODUCT SCOPE		++	++	E	E	+	E	−	+	++		++	+	++
▼ Fabrics														
Powder (traditional)	−	○	○	◐	◐	○	○	○	○	○		○	○	○
Powder (concentrated)	++	●	●	●	◐	◐	◐	◐	◐	●		●	◐	●
Liquid	E	◐	◐	◐	◐	◐	◐	◐	◐	◐		◐	◐	◐
Fabric Conditioners	++	●	●	◐	◐	◐	●	○	○	◐		◐	◐	●
Hand Dishwashing Detergent	E	◐	◐	○	◐	◐	●	◐	●	●		○	○	◐
Machine Dishwashing Detergent	+	◐	◐	◐	◐	◐	◐	◐	○	◐		○	◐	◐
Household Cleaners	++	●	●	○	◐	◐	●	●	○	◐		◐	◐	●
Bleaches	−	○	○	○	◐	○	◐	◐	○	◐		○	◐	○
NEW PRODUCT SCOPE														
▼ Fabrics														
Refillable package-en...	++	●	●	●	●	●	●	○	○	●		●	○	○
Detergent and Soft...	E	◐	◐	◐	◐	◐	◐	○	○	◐		◐	○	○
Detergent and Bleach in ...	E	◐	◐	◐	◐	◐	◐	○	○	◐		◐	○	○
Fabric Conditioners ...	+	◐	◐	◐	◐	◐	◐	○	○	◐		◐	○	○
Convenience-packaged ...	−	◐	◐	○	○	◐	○	○	○	○		○	○	○

Key:
- ● high attractiveness
- ◐ medium attractiveness
- ○ low attractiveness

NOTE: This is not an official document. It is an illustration drawn from public sources.

challenges from changes in unique competencies. For example, from the highest priority items in the existing and new product scope, we define as challenges the goal of increasing penetration of concentrated powder products and conditioner lines, as well as focusing on the development of household cleaners with no environmental impact, combining detergent conditioner and detergent bleach.

Step 5. Mission Statement.

The Mission of the Business is a qualitative statement of the overall business position that summarizes the key points with regard to products, markets, geographic locations, and unique competencies. This statement should be brief but substantive. A mission statement abstracts the important points to guide the development of a business. Figure 4–10 on page 64 presents the Mission Statement for the case of P&G Detergents in Europe, which summarizes all the analysis conducted so far.

FIGURE 4–9. Challenges from Changes in the Business Mission—P&G Detergents in Europe

CHALLENGES FROM CHANGES IN PRODUCT SCOPE

To increase the penetration of our concentrated powder products, as they appeal to the customers (smaller packaging and less environmental impact) and the channel (less shelf space and more margin).

To increase the penetration of our conditioner lines (high margin products).

To diminish our push of the traditional powder detergents, keeping them active in the less affluent Western countries and new Eastern European markets.

To introduce refill packs to meet the important environmental and convenience concerns.

Focus great efforts in the household cleaners product lines; they have the largest potential growth in the existing Western European markets.

To develop combined products detergent-conditioner and detergent-bleach. They should be tested in the convenience-oriented markets.

To develop fabric conditioner with no environmental impact, in addition to avoiding plastic containers.

CHALLENGES FROM CHANGES IN MARKET SCOPE

Focus explicitly on developing the strongest possible relationship with the largest distribution channels, hypermarkets, and supermarkets. We should build a partnership leveraging our know-how of IT and POS data analysis gained by the U.S. SBUs.

Target men as users of detergents.

Target with specific products the higher-income families, with environmentally innocuous and extremely convenient products.

Target the environmentally concerned with specific marketing efforts.

Target one-person family units with single-use packaging and other convenience-related products.

CHALLENGES FROM CHANGES IN GEOGRAPHICAL SCOPE

Develop a strong position in Spain, Portugal, and Italy, using the changes that are taking place in the distribution channels.

Enter with all strength the most affluent Eastern European countries, using the basic product line and introducing as fast as the market will accept them, the higher market products.

Develop alliances for distribution of the basic products in the former Soviet Union and other Eastern European countries.

CHALLENGES FROM CHANGES IN UNIQUE COMPETENCIES

Transition from multinational organization to a transnational one.

Develop with other detergent SBUs a research program for environmentally safe and biodegradable products and packages.

Develop local marketing expertise.

Develop an image of being the world-wide leader in environmentally safe detergents and packages.

Develop alliances for distribution in countries without P&G presence.

NOTE: This is not an official document. It is an illustration drawn from public sources.

FIGURE 4–10. Mission Statement—P&G Detergent Business in Europe

P&G European Detergents Division is devoted to providing products of superior quality and value to consumers based on the traditional principles of integrity and doing the right thing. P&G European Detergents Divison is to be recognized as the leader in providing consumers everywhere in Europe with cleaning, conditioning, dishwashing, and household cleaning products. Its purpose is achieved through an organization and working environment able to attract the most qualified individuals.

P&G European Detergents Division is committed to preserving the environment, in its production processes and its products and packaging.

▼ **PRODUCT SCOPE:**

NOW: To manufacture and distribute a complete range of fabric cleaners and conditioners, dishwashing products, household cleaners, and bleaches.

FUTURE: Maintain market leadership in the same segments but focus the development and sale of environmentally friendly products and packaging, convenient applicability of products.

▼ **MARKET SCOPE:**

NOW: Provide products to all individual consumers and institutions through an integrated European-wide network ranging from R&D to manufacturing and distribution. Maintain close ties with distribution networks of other P&G SBUs.

FUTURE: Respond effectively to the ever increasing health and environmental concerns and changes in demographics (aging Western Europe and fast growth in developing Eastern European countries). Market P&G world brands that share global technology but respond to local needs and particularities.

▼ **GEOGRAPHIC SCOPE:**

NOW: All 12 European Community and the other 8 Western European countries.

FUTURE: Expand progressively through distribution alliances into the Eastern European countries.

▼ **UNIQUE COMPETENCIES:**

NOW: R&D leadership has been the foundation of worldwide P&G success. Horizontal integration and multinational management have allowed the firm to compete effectively in Western Europe.

FUTURE: World leadership in environmentally related R&D in the detergent and packaging industries is the global future of P&G. P&G European Detergents is committed to becoming the leader in the protection of the environment. The division will develop a transnational culture to allow for a sharper focus on the differences of various territories and market segments without losing the economies of European-wide market leadership.

NOTE: This is not an official document. It is an illustration drawn from public sources.

Notes

1. Some of the key references that discuss the concept of core competence and the resource-based view of the firm are: C.K. Prahalad and Gary Hamel, "The Core Competence of the Corporation," *Harvard Business Review*, (May–June 1990), 71–91; Margaret A. Peteraf, "The Cornerstones of Competitive Advantage: A Resource-Based View" *Strategic Management Journal*, 14, no. 3 (March 1993), 179–192; Jay Barney, "Firm Resources and Sustained Competitive Advantage," *Journal of Management*, 17, no. 1 (1991), 99–120; Birger Wernelfelt, "A Resource-Based View of the Firm," *Strategic Management Journal*, 5 (1984), 171–180; Pankaj Ghemawat, *Commitment: The Dynamics of Strategy*, (New York: The Free Press, 1991).

2. Gary Hamel and C.K. Prahalad, "Strategic Intent," *Harvard Business Review*, (May–June, 1989), 63–76.

5

Environmental Scan at the Business Level

One of the trademarks of the modern planning approach is its external orientation. We have to address ourselves to the careful appreciation of environmental trends leading to an understanding of the attractiveness of the industry in which the business resides. We should be alert to all developments in our industry, especially to the behavior of competitors. Only a deep knowledge of the structural characteristics of the industry in which we operate along with a sound awareness of competitors' actions, can generate the high-quality strategic thinking required for the healthy long-term development of a firm.

Definition of Industry

An industry can be defined as a group of firms offering products or services that are close substitutes for one another. Thus, the boundaries of the industry are determined from a customer's point of view. The relevant question is: which are the products that an individual trying to satisfy a certain need is willing to consider in his or her buying decision? The answer is: all products that, in the eyes of the individual, perform approximately the same function. Speaking more technically, we could answer that close substitutes are products with high cross elasticity of demand. This can be understood more easily if we think of two products, and only one of them suffers a price increase; close substitutability implies a transfer of the demand from the more highly priced product to the less expensive one.

Definition of Industry
and Competitive Analysis

Industry and competitive analysis is an orderly process that attempts to capture the structural factors that define the long-term profitability prospects of an industry, and to identify and characterize the behavior of the most significant competitors.

Four basic methodologies used to perform this analysis are the subject of our attention in this chapter:

- Porter's framework for the structural analysis of industry: the five-forces model
- Environmental scan at the business level based on external factors analysis
- Strategic groups analysis
- Financial statement analysis framework

Structural Analysis of Industries:
The Five-Forces Model

In order to select the desired competitive position of a business, it is necessary to begin with the assessment of the industry to which it belongs. To accomplish this task, we must understand the fundamental factors that determine its long-term profitability prospects because this indicator embodies an overall measure of industry attractiveness.

By far the most influential and widely used framework for evaluating industry attractiveness is the five-forces model proposed by Michael E. Porter.[1] Essentially, he postulates that there are five forces that typically shape the industry structure: intensity of rivalry among competitors, threat of new entrants, threat of substitutes, bargaining power of buyers, and bargaining power of suppliers. These five forces delimit prices, costs, and investment requirements, which are the basic factors that explain long-term profitability prospects, and henceforth, industry attractiveness. Figure 5–1 illustrates that the generic structure of an industry is represented by the main players (competitors, buyers, suppliers, substitutes, and new entrants), their interrelationship (the five forces), and the factors behind those forces that help to account for industry attractiveness.

INTENSITY OF RIVALRY AMONG
THE INDUSTRY COMPETITORS

The rivalry among competitors is at the center of the forces contributing to industry attractiveness. Out of the many determinants of rivalry presented in

FIGURE 5–1. Elements of Industry Structure: Porter's Five-Forces

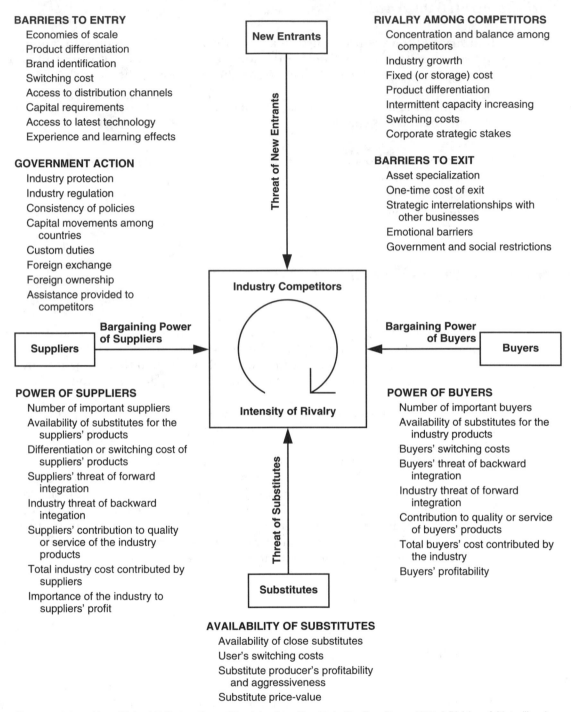

BARRIERS TO ENTRY
Economies of scale
Product differentiation
Brand identification
Switching cost
Access to distribution channels
Capital requirements
Access to latest technology
Experience and learning effects

GOVERNMENT ACTION
Industry protection
Industry regulation
Consistency of policies
Capital movements among
 countries
Custom duties
Foreign exchange
Foreign ownership
Assistance provided to
 competitors

New Entrants

Threat of New Entrants

RIVALRY AMONG COMPETITORS
Concentration and balance among
 competitors
Industry growrth
Fixed (or storage) cost
Product differentiation
Intermittent capacity increasing
Switching costs
Corporate strategic stakes

BARRIERS TO EXIT
Asset specialization
One-time cost of exit
Strategic interrelationships with
 other businesses
Emotional barriers
Government and social restrictions

**Bargaining Power
of Suppliers**

Suppliers

Industry Competitors

Intensity of Rivalry

**Bargaining Power
of Buyers**

Buyers

POWER OF SUPPLIERS
Number of important suppliers
Availability of substitutes for the
 suppliers' products
Differentiation or switching cost of
 suppliers' products
Suppliers' threat of forward
 integration
Industry threat of backward
 integation
Suppliers' contribution to quality
 or service of the industry
 products
Total industry cost contributed by
 suppliers
Importance of the industry to
 suppliers' profit

Threat of Substitutes

Substitutes

POWER OF BUYERS
Number of important buyers
Availability of substitutes for the
 industry products
Buyers' switching costs
Buyers' threat of backward
 integration
Industry threat of forward
 integration
Contribution to quality or service
 of buyers' products
Total buyers' cost contributed by
 the industry
Buyers' profitability

AVAILABILITY OF SUBSTITUTES
Availability of close substitutes
User's switching costs
Substitute producer's profitability
 and aggressiveness
Substitute price-value

SOURCE: Adapted from Michael E. Porter, *Competitive Advantage*, New York: The Free Press, 1985. A Division of Macmillan, Inc.
Reprinted by permission.

the figure, four of them stand out: industry growth, the share of fixed cost to the total value added of the business, the depth of product differentiation, and the concentration and balance among competitors. If an industry exhibits high growth, low relative fixed cost, a wide variety of differentiating capabilities, and a high degree of concentration, then it is most likely that healthy profit opportunities will become available to most participants in the industry. The opposite is also true. Think, for instance, about the domestic airline carriers industry after deregulation, where the four factors just mentioned established conditions that created a largely unattractive base for most of its participants.

It is to be expected that these four factors become dominant determinants of competitive rivalry. First, if the industry is growing aggressively, there are opportunities for everyone involved, and the resultant bonanza produces a source of unlimited prosperity.

Second, fixed costs seem to have an almost psychological impact on the way businesses are managed. When a firm is confronted with high fixed costs, the break-even point rises to a significant fraction of full capacity. If that level of operation is not achieved, the most common reaction is to offer the customer very favorable conditions to boost demand, disregarding the consequences that this action might have on the overall industry performance. Think, for example, of an airline running a regular schedule between Boston and San Francisco, with a Boeing 747 aircraft. After 100 scheduled flights are completed half-full, the burden of absorbing overhead costs may become a major obsession. This may prompt the airline managers to undertake options such as price cutting, the offering of all kinds of frills, and other competitive moves intended to capture passengers, despite the detriment to the overall industry performance.

Third, product differentiation is a most critical factor in the determination of competitive rivalry. Nothing could be more devastating to industry profitability than the "commodity syndrome." A commodity is a product or service that cannot be differentiated. That means that no one can legitimately claim that what it is offering to its customers is superior to an equivalent offering from other competitors. If that is truly the case, a customer decision depends entirely on price; and that means war. When the product features are such that its characteristics fit those of a commodity—such as primary metals—the major strategic challenge is to escape this competitive trap. This means that every effort should be undertaken to differentiate the product, drawing on properties other than its intrinsic attributes. Creative thinking can always identify opportunities for competitive advantage in technical service, financial conditions, delivery lead time, image, marketing skills, customer responsiveness, and whatever other critical attributes are seen as unique in the eyes of the final customer.

And finally, we have the issue of concentration and balance. It is far more desirable to participate in an industry with just four major competitors capturing 85 percent of the market, with a homogeneous competitors philosophy (even if we are not the leading firm), than in an industry with hundreds of players, equally balanced, and with very different competitive perspectives (as is the case of too many diverging international players).

The rationale for this preference is clear. In the first option, we are not likely to expect great surprises. The rules of the game are explicitly or implicitly spelled out. We would be living in a gentle oligopoly, where not a single competitor would have an incentive to undertake a move that, although beneficial to its own position in the short term, is likely to produce adverse consequences for everybody in the long run. This form of constrained behavior is absent when a larger number of quite diverse players converge in the competitive arena.

These are just four of what we regard as the central determinants of the intensity of rivalry among competitors. Other factors included are:

Intermittent Overcapacity.

In industries where capacities are added in large increments such as aluminum, and office space in big cities, the overall supply of the industry tends to go through cycles, alternating periods of large idle capacity, and of insufficient supply that sends prices through the roof. When the incentives of high prices trigger a simultaneous reaction in many competitors, they generate another spurt of larger added capacity, giving rise again to a new cycle of deterioration of the whole industry profitability.

Brand Identity.

This constitutes an important source of differentiation and, therefore, firms try to establish solidly their brands in the market. Brand recognition by consumers is eagerly sought by most companies, and they spend dearly for it. But there are some firms that introduce generic products to the market, attacking the position of fairly differentiated competitors and eroding their profitability base. Numerous examples can be found in over-the-counter pharmaceutical products as well as supermarket products, where generic items are sold at significantly discounted prices compared to products with well-recognized brand names.

Switching Costs.

The easier it is for customers to switch products in a given industry, the higher is the intensity of rivalry. Therefore, it is not surprising that firms might adopt strategies to either make switching difficult, as normally pursued by heavy-equipment manufacturers, or to provide incentives for customers not to switch, which is the intent of the frequent-flyer programs sponsored by most airlines.

Exit Barriers and Corporate Stakes.

A very high exit barrier is a formidable contributor to the deterioration of industry attractiveness in mature and declining markets. When the industry is in the last stages of its life cycle, it is normal to expect a shrinkage in the number of competitors, since opportunities become insufficient to sustain the full roster of participants that were attracted under better structural conditions. However, if exit is very hard or nearly impossible, which is the case when asset specialization and one-time cost of exit are particularly high, an orderly decline is unrealizable. A serious profitability erosion ensues for all competitors.

Not only tangible factors contribute to ease of exit. Sometimes, even more important are the so-called emotional barriers, as well as strategic interrelationships with other businesses, and government and social restrictions, all of which would either prevent or seriously delay the exit decision. Finally, there are firms that deliberately seek to perpetuate themselves in an industry beyond its financial soundness, with the purpose of becoming a "competitive harasser." This tends to happen when firms are *multipoint competitors;* that is, they face each other in a variety of industries with broadly different relative strengths. As an example, consider three well-known financial firms whose individual strengths are rooted in completely different foundations: Merrill Lynch (originally regarded as a brokerage firm); American Express (formerly in the travel-recreation-leisure industry); and Citicorp (a leading U.S. bank with global reach). They are actually or potentially facing each other in a wide variety of industries, such as retail banking, investment and asset management, international banking, travel-financial, communication, and insurance. In the case of multipoint competitors, a firm that faces a serious attack at the core of its central business might counterattack in an area that is of little significance for itself but is critical to that competitor. The competitive-harasser business could therefore be used to provide a signal to another competitor about the destructive nature of excessive aggressiveness.

THREAT OF NEW ENTRANTS

On many occasions, the most critical strategic issue for a given firm does not reside in understanding the existing set of competitors and achieving an advantage over them, but in directing the attention to possible and sometimes inevitable new entrants. This was precisely the case many years ago for AES, a Canadian firm that was then the world leader in stand-alone word processors, and whose distribution branch in the United States was Lanier. It was clearly recognized at that point that the industry was about to attract some of the most formidable firms in the United States, such as Wang, Digital Equipment Corp., and IBM.

A more recent example is represented by PictureTel, a company that in 1994 commanded about 70 percent market share of the video-conference business worldwide. At that time, however, computer manufacturers and communication companies started to search aggressively for opportunities to integrate video capabilities in their product lines. Moreover, the large conference facilities that were the initial conduits for video conferencing, demanding equipment selling for six-figure prices, were being substituted by small personal computers with video-conference equipment selling in the low four-figure range. The comfortable position for PictureTel was being challenged by giants such as AT&T, Intel, and IBM. Under those conditions, the survivability of the challenged firm in its initial position in the industry is highly questionable, because of the inability of a small firm realistically to increase entry barriers due to the size and power of the new entrants. A more credible strategic alternative is to attempt to develop a feasible niche, which is unlikely, or to establish alliances with one of the more powerful new competitors. The questions in this last option are: What can the small firm offer in terms of sustainable advantage? and, How stable and long lasting could the potential alliance be?

This leads us to one of the most important concepts of strategy: the concept of entry barriers and its relationship with the profitability of the industry. Entry barriers are the result of a wide variety of new factors. These include economies of scale, product differentiation, and intensity of capital requirements. Ease of access to distribution channels, critical raw materials, and to the latest technology, as well as the relevance of learning effects and the degree of government protectionism are other crucial factors. Entry barriers also result from some factors that were already present as determinants of rivalry: brand identity and switching costs.

High entry barriers are fundamental to explain a sustained level of strong profitability. A strategy conducive to raising entry barriers to an industry is expected to generate abundant long-term payoffs. Porter proposed a very simple scheme, presented in Figure 5–2, to reflect on the combined impact of exit and entry barriers on the profitability of an industry. High profitability comes with high entry barriers and stability is brought by low exit barriers.

Consequently, the ideal situation is precisely one with high entry barriers and low exit barriers. Unfortunately, these conditions are seldom met simultaneously because the factors that contribute to raising entry barriers at the same time increase exit barriers.

It is clear, then, that when a firm is already in an industry, a high entry barrier is much preferred. In that way the business is protected from a strong

FIGURE 5–2.   The Impact of Entry and Exit
Barriers Over Industry
Profitability

EXIT BARRIERS

		Low	High
ENTRY BARRIERS	High	High and stable profits	High, but possibly unstable, profits
	Low	Low and stable profits	Low and unstable profits

competition easily coming in and wiping out its benefits. But there is a less evident situation. Suppose a firm is not yet *in* an industry, but it is considering entering. Is it better to have high or low entry barriers? When we confront our students with this quandary, there is always one or more who would answer that low entry barriers are to be preferred. The reply we make to the students is, more or less, along the following lines:

"Well, a minute ago I asked you for your preferences for entry barriers when you were in an industry; you said high, and everyone agreed on that answer. Now, you are telling me that when you are outside the industry you would like it low, but as soon as you enter, you would realize that you would rather be in a high entry barrier industry. How do you reconcile this discrepancy?" In time, the true answer emerges: "What you always want is high entry barriers. And when you are weighing the option of entering an industry, you still prefer very high entry barriers for everybody . . . but you." That is the trick. What is needed is to have unique capabilities, not transferable to competitors, that can make entry easy for the firm and unacceptably difficult for everybody else. A typical example of this kind of situation is IBM's entry into the personal computer industry.

THREAT OF SUBSTITUTES

It is not only the firms participating in the industry and the potential newcomers that are central forces in determining industry attractiveness; we have to add firms offering substitutes, which can either replace the industry products and services or present an alternative to fulfill that demand. Substitutes could affect in different ways the attractiveness of an industry. Their mere presence establishes a ceiling for industry profitability, whenever there is a price threshold after which a massive transfer of demand takes place. A famous example that illustrates this point is the conversion from steel to aluminum cans in the American beer and soft-drinks industry. The steel producers kept raising their prices, without giving enough attention to the fact that aluminum prices were not escalating as rapidly. Eventually, a point was reached where the one-time conversion cost was made attractive for the beer and soft-drink manufacturers.

The impact that the threat of substitution has on industry profitability depends on a number of factors, such as availability of close substitutes, user's switching cost, aggressiveness of substitutes' producers, and price-value trade-offs between the original products and its substitutes.

BARGAINING POWER OF SUPPLIERS AND BUYERS

In the original model of industry structure prepared by Porter, he treats the power of buyers and suppliers as mirror images of one another. This becomes patently clear from examining the factors that contribute to the inherent power in these two cases.

Power of Suppliers	*Power of Buyers*
• Number of important suppliers	• Number of important buyers
• Availability of substitutes for suppliers' products	• Availability of substitutes for the industry products
• Differentiation or switching costs of suppliers' products	• Buyers' switching costs
• Suppliers threat of forward integration	• Buyers' threat of backward integration
• Industry threat of backward integration	• Industry threat of forward integration
• Suppliers' contribution to quality or service of the industry products	• Industry contribution to quality or service of buyers' products
• Total industry cost contributed by suppliers	• Total buyers' costs contributed by the industry
• Importance of the industry to suppliers' profit	• Buyers' profitability

Porter's wording, "bargaining power of suppliers and buyers," suggests that there is a threat imposed on the industry by an excessive use of power on the part of these two agents. Porter can be interpreted as indicating that a proper strategy to be pursued by a business firm will have, as a key component, the attempt to neutralize suppliers' and buyers' bargaining power. In today's world, that message is, at best, controversial. The Japanese firms have given us lesson after lesson on the significance of treating suppliers as central partners, whose relationship has to be nurtured and strengthened, so as to become an extension of the firm itself. Moreover, buyers are the most important constituency of the firm, to be treated not as rivals, but as the depositories of a long-lasting, friendly relationship based on performance and integrity.

A Central Dilemma: When to Compete and When to Cooperate
Porter's model represents industries as a battlefield or power game with conflicting and clashing forces. The mere selection of the wording of the model is quite revealing. It talks about *rivalry* among competitors, *threats* of new entrants, *threats* of substitutes, and bargaining *power* of both suppliers and buyers. All of these account for one major message: The business world is tough and competitive. To survive, you have to be better than the best and be prepared to annihilate your opponents and destroy their power base.

As we all know, this conflicting and antagonistic climate does not necessarily explain the most effective or even the most common ways to compete. In the recent past, those firms that are truly smart at conducting their businesses have learned a very important lesson: You need to know when and how to compete; but also, and even more importantly, you need to know when and how to cooperate.

Today, *strategic alliances* represent one of the buzzwords for business. They are formal coalitions between two or more firms, for short- or long-term ventures, born out of opportunistic or permanent relationships that evolve into a form of partnership among players. Some of these alliances, under the more traditional rules, could correspond to agreements among competitors with conflicting interests, they were prohibited in the United States, until very recently, by antitrust legislation which forced American firms to seek covenants only with overseas companies.

The alliances currently under discussion include joint ventures, licensing agreements, supply agreements, venture capital initiatives, joint partnership acquisitions, and many other forms of cooperation. All approaches share the common objective to eliminate or significantly reduce confrontation among competitors, suppliers, customers, potential new entrants, and substitute producers. Certainly, the completion of these alliances is intended to create better conditions for all partners involved through technology acquisition and shared scale economies; access to new markets, raw materials, and components; response to pressures by local governments; and the establishment of agreements for global standardization of products, to mention just the most common among a limitless field of opportunities.

A remarkable example of global strategic alliances is the contrast between the 1965 world automotive industry (Figure 5–3 on page 76) and the 1985 map of global strategic partnerships in that industry (Figure 5–4 on page 77). In 1965, the industry was well defined on a geographic basis, with three major centers of activity in the United States, Japan, and Europe. Out of all the competing firms, only GM, Ford, and Chrysler had overlapping interests in just two of these regions. Moreover, there were not formal relationships among any of the major players. It is striking to look at the world auto industry twenty years later. It is no longer feasible to either separate the geographical scope of the industry participants or to follow up closely the enormous amount of alliances that have been established across the board. Not only that, but the dynamic of change in the industry is so overwhelming it would take a full-time industry expert to be totally up to date with the extensive amount of interfirm agreements that are taking place almost daily.[2]

Two Illustrations of the Structural Analysis of Industries: Pharmaceuticals and Engineering Polymers

The model just presented has an ability to communicate very rapidly and effectively the principal issues that must be recognized in assessing the attractiveness of an industry. To convey that message, we have selected two brief examples. One deals with the pharmaceutical industry, and the other with the engineering polymers industry.

The pharmaceutical industry in the U.S. has enjoyed the highest profitability level of any industry in the recent past. Its attractiveness was extraordinarily high, but new trends are beginning to erode the basis of this superior performance. The five-force analysis allows us to detect the major characteristics of the industry, and to pinpoint the sources of its profitability. Figure 5–5

FIGURE 5–3. 1965 World Automobile Industry

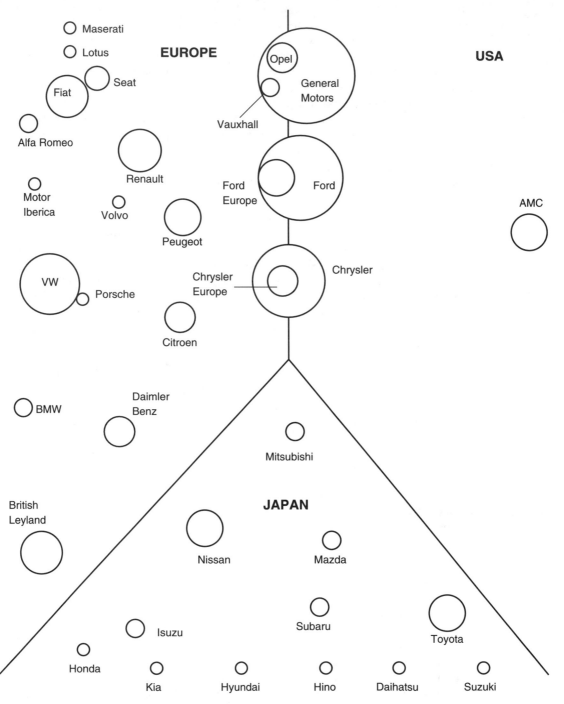

SOURCE: David A. Burgner, "Global Strategy: A Systematic Approach," unpublished masters thesis, Sloan School of Management, MIT, 1986. Reprinted by permission of David A. Burgner.

FIGURE 5–4. Map of Global Strategic Partnerships in the World Automobile Industry

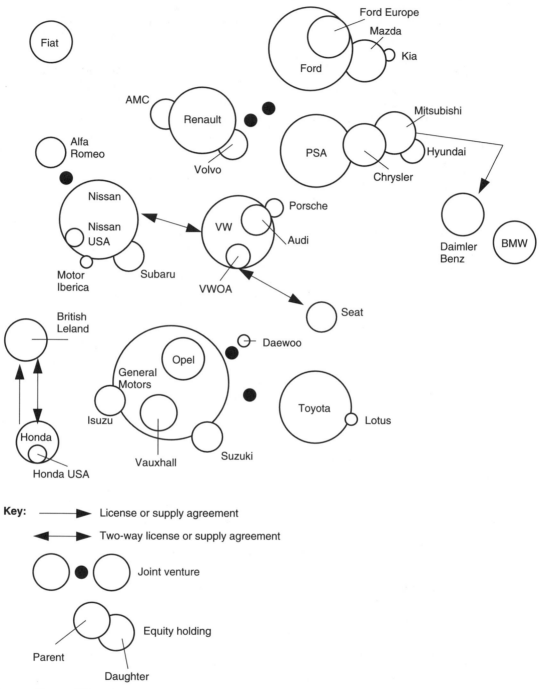

Key:
License or supply agreement
Two-way license or supply agreement
Joint venture
Equity holding
Parent
Daughter

SOURCE: Burgner, "Global Strategy," (1986).

provides a compact description of the primary elements of industry structure through a cross-sectional analysis at the beginning of 1994. Although the industry remains attractive, it is clear that since future trends are cause for concern, particularly an increasing rivalry among the most important manufacturers, the threat imposed by generic and "me-too" drugs, the increasing power of expanded buyers and distributors, and the challenges emerging from biotechnology. In the U.S., the enormous concern about the escalation of health-care costs, which have quadrupled since 1980, is threatening to unleash even more stringent government regulations.

The second example describes the state of the engineering polymers industry in the mid-1980s. These materials are groups of polymers to which engineering equations can be applied, as products are designed and developed.[3] Engineering polymers are capable of sustaining high loads and stresses, and performing under stringent environmental conditions over long periods of time. Members of this family include: nylon, polycarbonates, acetyl, and others. The Du Pont company has played a major role in this industry, having invented many of the products that comprise it. Its major competitor, both in the United States and world markets, is General Electric. A brief summary of Porter's five-forces framework applied to this industry is given in Figure 5–6 on page 80.

In the next chapter we will continue with these two illustrations to examine the competitive position of some of the key companies in these two industries: Merck in pharmaceuticals, and General Electric and Du Pont in engineering polymers.

Further Comments on the Five-Forces Model

BENCHMARKING THE PROFITABILITY OF THE FIRM

There are three points that we would like to make with regard to the impact of industry structure on the profitability of a firm.

First, different industries achieve different levels of average profitability; therefore, the attractiveness of an industry is a factor that is critical to understanding the performance of a firm. In other words, industry *does* matter.

Second, there is a great degree of variability observed in the profitability levels among firms competing in a given industry. Thus, the ability of the firm to deploy resources and develop capabilities to achieve a superior performance, are also very significant. As we have indicated when presenting the business strategy framework in Chapter 3, industry structure and competitive position together affect the performance of a business.

And third, industry behavior seems to change dramatically across time. Industries that enjoyed high levels of profitability in the early 1980s, such as car manufacturers and computer makers, faced either mediocre or poor profitability during the early 1990s. Therefore, timing also matters. This implies that a cross-sectional analysis, which is static in time, has to be complemented by a longitudinal analysis, which explicitly considers the evolution of the industry through time.[4]

FIGURE 5–5. Porter's Five-Forces Model Applied to the Pharmaceutical Industry in the Early 1990s

BARRIERS TO ENTRY (Very Attractive)
- Steep R&D experience curve effects
- Large economies-of-scale barriers in R&D and sales force
- Critical mass in R&D and marketing require global scale
- Significant R&D and marketing costs
- High risk inherent in the drug development process
- Increasing threat of new entrants coming from biotechnology companies

BARGAINING POWER OF SUPPLIERS (Very Attractive)
- Mostly commodities
- Individual scientists may have some personal leverage

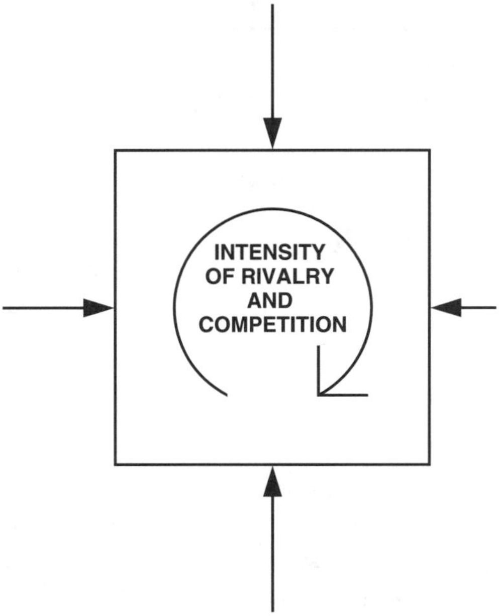

INTENSITY OF RIVALRY AND COMPETITION

BARGAINING POWER OF BUYERS (Mildly Unattractive)
- The traditional purchasing process was highly price insensitive: the consumer (the patient) did not buy, and the buyer (the physician) did not pay
- Large power of buyers, particularly plan sponsors and cost containment organizations, are influencing the decisions to prescribe less expensive drugs
- Mail-order pharmacies are obtaining large discounts on volume drugs.
- Large aggregated buyers (e.g., hospital suppliers, large distributors, government institutions) are progressively replacing the role of individual customers
- Important influence of the government in the regulation of the buying process

THREAT OF SUBSTITUTES (Mildly Unattractive)
- Generic and "Me-too" drugs are weakening branded, proprietary drugs
- More than half of the life of the drug patent is spent in the product development and approval process
- Technological development is making imitation easier
- Consumer aversion to chemical substances erodes the appeal for pharmaceutical drugs

INTENSITY OF RIVALRY (Attractive)
- Global competition concentrated among fifteen large companies
- Most companies focus on certain types of disease therapy
- Competition among incumbents limited by patent protection
- Competition based on price and product differentiation
- Government intervention and growth of "Me-too" drugs increase rivalry
- Strategic alliances establish collaborative agreements among industry players
- Very profitable industry, however with declining margins

SUMMARY ASSESSMENT OF THE INDUSTRY ATTRACTIVENESS (Attractive)

79

FIGURE 5–6. Porter's Five Forces Model Applied to the Engineering Polymers Industry in the Mid-1980s

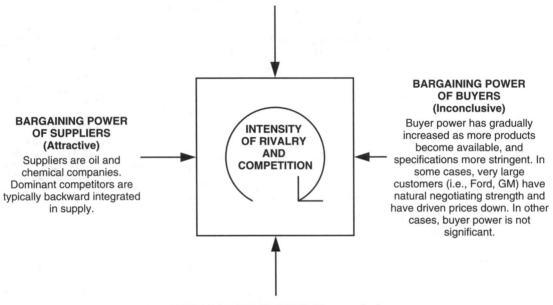

BARRIERS TO ENTRY (Attractive)

Potential entrants face significant barriers to entry, including investment costs (plants are highly capital intensive) and patent protection on many products, as well as extensive product qualification requirements.

BARGAINING POWER OF SUPPLIERS (Attractive)

Suppliers are oil and chemical companies. Dominant competitors are typically backward integrated in supply.

INTENSITY OF RIVALRY AND COMPETITION

BARGAINING POWER OF BUYERS (Inconclusive)

Buyer power has gradually increased as more products become available, and specifications more stringent. In some cases, very large customers (i.e., Ford, GM) have natural negotiating strength and have driven prices down. In other cases, buyer power is not significant.

THREAT OF SUBSTITUTES (Unattractive)

In the early stages of the industry, there were no significant replacements. As it matures, however, substitution is increasingly a factor. Traditional rivals, such as aluminum, have become more competitive in order to preserve their markets. In addition, upscale commmodity polymers threaten the low end as they also improve. Differentiation is becoming more important.

INTENSITY OF RIVALRY (Attractive)

The industry is still very much a gentlemen's oligopoly, as low-cost producers are also price leaders. Both DuPont and GE are lowest-cost producers, but follow quality-differentiated strategies to justify high prices. It is also helpful that these leaders—for the most part—do not compete head-on with their products. Competition then is not to attack each other, but to attempt to capture most of the industry growth so price wars are typically avoided.

CONCLUSION: The industry is still fairly attractive, and can be characterized as being in the growth "shake-out" stage. We already see consolidation as dominant players exercise their market power.

SOURCE: Emmanuel P. Maceda, "Strategic Analysis: Du Pont Company, Engineering Polymers Division," unpublished student paper, Sloan School of Management, MIT, 1988. Reprinted by permission of Emmanuel P. Maceda.

How can we judge the profitability performance of the firm? Among the most widely used competitive benchmarking standards are the average profitability of the industry or industry segments in which the firm is positioned, and the results of leading competitors within the industry.

Once a firm has achieved a level of outstanding profitability within its industry, as in the cases of Merck in the pharmaceutical industry, Nucor in the steel industry, and Wal-Mart in the retailing industry, we might want to raise the level of the yardstick to match the firm's capabilities against world-class performers. This comparison could be carried also function by function, to assure that each critical capability of the firm has achieved world-class excellence in its own right. This last set of standards constitute the most demanding stage in competitive benchmarking.[5]

NOT ALL FORCES ARE EQUALLY IMPORTANT

As happens with any complex evaluation where a host of critical factors is included in the final analysis, not all forces, and for that matter the factors contributing to these forces, have an equal weight. It could very well be that many factors add to an unattractive position, and yet, when judged in its entirety, the industry still presents an attractive picture overall. This simply reinforces the notion that this kind of analysis cannot be carried out in a mechanistic way. It has to be supported by a thorough and sophisticated understanding of the critical factors that contribute the most as determinants of industry attractiveness. These are the central issues that we need to grasp fully and that deserve preferential attention when we decide on the best competitive position of the firm within that industry, and when we consider possible ways, if feasible, to alter industry structure. In fact, the firms that end up achieving extraordinary performance within an industry typically either have set up the standards of the industry in their own favor, such as Motorola in the cellular and paging industry, or have dramatically reshaped industry structure to their own advantage, such as Nucor in the flat-slab industry, and Wal-Mart in rural retailing.

THE DYNAMIC NATURE OF INDUSTRY STRUCTURE

Perhaps the only statement that one could make with certainty about the structure of an industry is that it will change, most likely in unpredictable ways. That by no means invalidates the significance of a carefully done industry analysis, but it serves to reinforce the fact that there is an inherent dynamics in industry structure that we should recognize and attempt to cope with to the best of our abilities. Therefore, despite the criticality and importance of the analysis of the existing structural conditions of an industry and its competitive implications, it has to be followed up with an attempt to recognize the most likely future trends, and the opportunities and threats imbedded in those changes for the business firm. Occasionally, scenario planning is used as a way of configuring meaningful future structural alternatives that could help the organization to prepare itself either to take advantage of optimistic scenarios or to seek protection against pessimistic ones.[6]

Technology and innovation have deeply affected the ways to compete, and have been responsible for creating new industries and significantly changing the structure of existing ones. Perhaps none of the existing technologies can match the potential impact that information technology has in reshaping industry structure and in transforming the nature of businesses and firms. We are living in the information revolution, where computer and communications technologies are affecting every facet of our society. Information technology can offer endless opportunities for a firm to achieve competitive advantage. A company can use information technology to build barriers to entry, to build in switching costs, to completely change the basis of competition, to change the balance of power in supplier relationships, and/or to generate new products.

A Process for Profiling the Industry Attractiveness With the Five-Forces Model: An Illustration

To assist managers with a comprehensive analysis of the industry attractiveness, we provide a disciplined methodology that thoroughly reviews each of the factors of Porter's five-forces model, gives an overall assessment of the attractiveness of the industry, and finally identifies the resulting opportunities and threats posed by the industry. We illustrate this methodology using the case of P&G Detergent Business in Europe. The analysis is carried for the current situation and the one expected to prevail in the future.

STEP 1. PROFILE OF THE INDUSTRY ATTRACTIVENESS

We will be using seven categories to assess the attractiveness of the industry:

- Barriers to Entry
- Barriers to Exit
- Rivalry among Competitors
- Power of Buyers
- Power of Suppliers
- Availability of Substitutes
- Government Actions

The combination of Barriers to Entry and Exit define the Threat of New Entrants, one of Porter's five forces. We have added Government Actions to capture issues of regulation and protectionism that are critical to determine industry attractiveness in a global setting.

The profile will assess the attractiveness of the industry in its current state and provide a projection describing the desired or forecasted attractiveness in the future. The really dominant and successful firms in an industry are those that are able to shape it to its own advantage. Obviously, not all of the industry factors are easily controllable; therefore, we end up with a mix between influence and forecasting in defining the future attractiveness of the industry.

Barriers to Entry.
Clearly, product differentiation, brand identification, access to distribution channels and latest technology, and experience effects are critical determinants of high barriers to entry in this industry (Figure 5–7).

Barriers to Exit.
Surprisingly, the assessment reveals an extraordinary ease of exit in this industry. Neither asset specialization nor emotional barriers seem to be a deterrent to exit (Figure 5–8).

Rivalry among Competitors.
There is a very small number of important competitors of this industry in Europe. Rivalry is not very intense (Figure 5–9).

Power of Buyers.
The major distribution channels are beginning to gain significant strength (Figure 5–10).

Power of Suppliers.
Specialized chemical companies and other critical suppliers could retain significant bargaining power (Figure 5–11).

Availability of Substitutes.
The lack of clear substitutes to detergents make this force attractive (Figure 5–12).

Government Actions.
Government policies tend to be either favorable or not interfering in business activities (Figure 5-13).

Summary of Factor Attractiveness.
Each one of the seven factors analyzed before is given a concluding attractiveness rating. Notice that the five-points scale is retained in this summarization (Figure 5–14).

Overall Assessment of Industry Attractiveness.
After completing the analysis of each factor, one single overall ranking to the industry attractiveness is given. Notice that we switch from a five-point scale to a three-point scale: low, medium, and high attractiveness. This will allow the use of the Industry-Attractiveness/Business-Strength Matrix to assess the strength of the firm's business portfolio, and to suggest guidance for resource allocation and strategic actions (Figure 5–15).

FIGURE 5–7. Attractiveness of Barriers to Entry—P&G Detergent Business in Europe

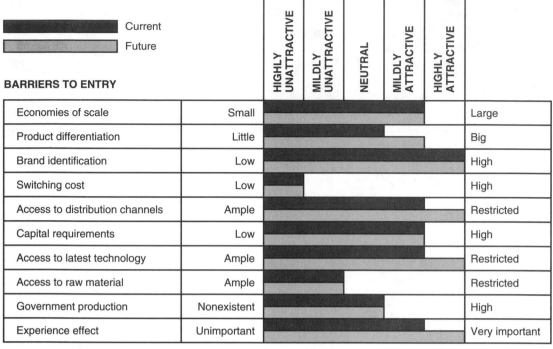

■ Current
▨ Future

BARRIERS TO ENTRY		HIGHLY UNATTRACTIVE	MILDLY UNATTRACTIVE	NEUTRAL	MILDLY ATTRACTIVE	HIGHLY ATTRACTIVE	
Economies of scale	Small						Large
Product differentiation	Little						Big
Brand identification	Low						High
Switching cost	Low						High
Access to distribution channels	Ample						Restricted
Capital requirements	Low						High
Access to latest technology	Ample						Restricted
Access to raw material	Ample						Restricted
Government production	Nonexistent						High
Experience effect	Unimportant						Very important

NOTE: This is not an official document. It is an illustration drawn from public sources.

FIGURE 5–8. Attractiveness of Barriers to Exit—P&G Detergent Business in Europe

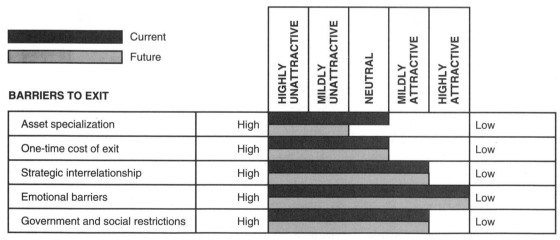

■ Current
▨ Future

BARRIERS TO EXIT		HIGHLY UNATTRACTIVE	MILDLY UNATTRACTIVE	NEUTRAL	MILDLY ATTRACTIVE	HIGHLY ATTRACTIVE	
Asset specialization	High						Low
One-time cost of exit	High						Low
Strategic interrelationship	High						Low
Emotional barriers	High						Low
Government and social restrictions	High						Low

NOTE: This is not an official document. It is an illustration drawn from public sources.

FIGURE 5–9. Attractiveness of Rivalry Among Competitors—P&G Detergent Business in Europe

RIVALRY AMONG COMPETITORS

Legend: ■ Current ░ Future

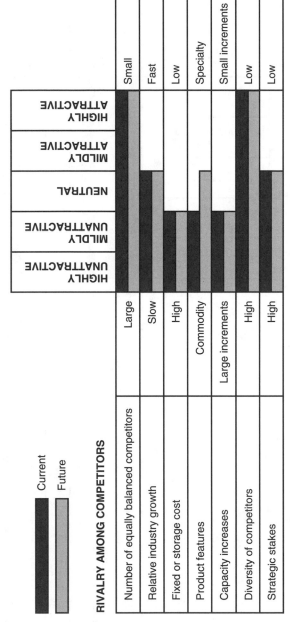

	HIGHLY UNATTRACTIVE	MILDLY UNATTRACTIVE	NEUTRAL	MILDLY ATTRACTIVE	HIGHLY ATTRACTIVE	
Number of equally balanced competitors	Large					Small
Relative industry growth	Slow					Fast
Fixed or storage cost	High					Low
Product features	Commodity					Specialty
Capacity increases	Large increments					Small increments
Diversity of competitors	High					Low
Strategic stakes	High					Low

NOTE: This is not an official document. It is an illustration drawn from public sources.

85

FIGURE 5–10. Attractiveness of Power of Buyers—P&G Detergent Business in Europe

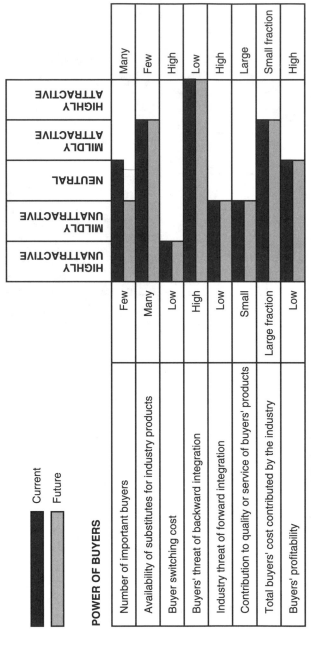

POWER OF BUYERS

		HIGHLY UNATTRACTIVE	MILDLY UNATTRACTIVE	NEUTRAL	MILDLY ATTRACTIVE	HIGHLY ATTRACTIVE	
Number of important buyers	Few						Many
Availability of substitutes for industry products	Many						Few
Buyer switching cost	Low						High
Buyers' threat of backward integration	High						Low
Industry threat of forward integration	Low						High
Contribution to quality or service of buyers' products	Small						Large
Total buyers' cost contributed by the industry	Large fraction						Small fraction
Buyers' profitability	Low						High

Legend: Current / Future

NOTE: This is not an official document. It is an illustration drawn from public sources.

FIGURE 5-11. Attractiveness of Power of Suppliers—P&G Detergent Business in Europe

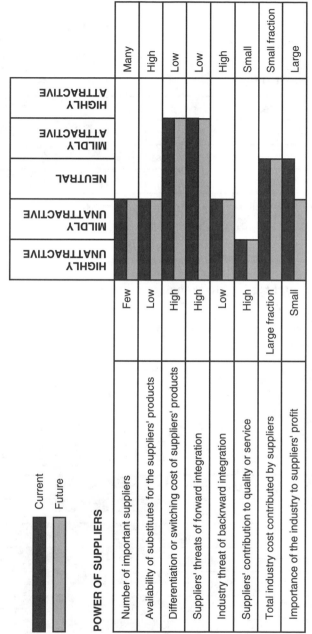

Legend: ■ Current ▨ Future

POWER OF SUPPLIERS

		HIGHLY UNATTRACTIVE	MILDLY UNATTRACTIVE	NEUTRAL	MILDLY ATTRACTIVE	HIGHLY ATTRACTIVE	
Number of important suppliers	Few		■▨				Many
Availability of substitutes for the suppliers' products	Low		■▨				High
Differentiation or switching cost of suppliers' products	High				■▨		Low
Suppliers' threats of forward integration	High				■▨		Low
Industry threat of backward integration	Low		■▨				High
Suppliers' contribution to quality or service	High	■▨					Small
Total industry cost contributed by suppliers	Large fraction			■▨			Small fraction
Importance of the industry to suppliers' profit	Small	■	▨				Large

NOTE: This is not an official document. It is an illustration drawn from public sources.

87

FIGURE 5–12. Attractiveness of Availability of Substitutes—P&G Detergent Business in Europe

■ Current
▨ Future

AVAILABILITY OF SUBSTITUTES

		Highly Unattractive	Mildly Unattractive	Neutral	Mildly Attractive	Highly Attractive	
Availability of close substitutes	Large						Small
User's switching costs	Low						High
Substitute producer's profitability and aggressiveness	High						Low
Substitute price/value	High						Low

NOTE: This is not an official document. It is an illustration drawn from public sources.

Note: Fig 5-13 to be narrowed to 34 picas

FIGURE 5–13. Attractiveness of Government Actions—P&G Detergent Business in Europe

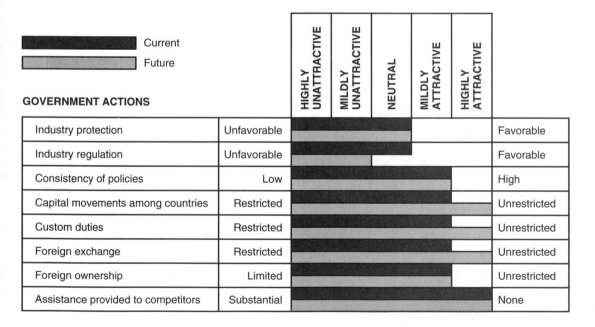

■ Current
▨ Future

GOVERNMENT ACTIONS

		Highly Unattractive	Mildly Unattractive	Neutral	Mildly Attractive	Highly Attractive	
Industry protection	Unfavorable						Favorable
Industry regulation	Unfavorable						Favorable
Consistency of policies	Low						High
Capital movements among countries	Restricted						Unrestricted
Custom duties	Restricted						Unrestricted
Foreign exchange	Restricted						Unrestricted
Foreign ownership	Limited						Unrestricted
Assistance provided to competitors	Substantial						None

88

FIGURE 5–14. Summary of Factor Attractiveness—P&G Detergent Business in Europe

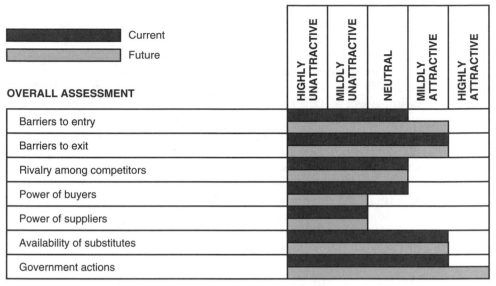

NOTE: This is not an official document. It is an illustration drawn from public sources.

FIGURE 5–15. Overall Assessment of Industry Attractiveness—P&G Detergent Business in Europe

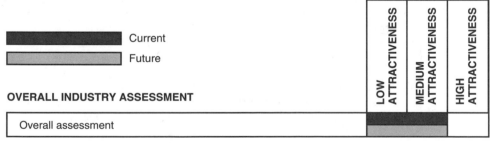

NOTE: This is not an official document. It is an illustration drawn from public sources.

STEP 2. IDENTIFICATION OF OPPORTUNITIES AND THREATS

The final output of the industry analysis is the identification of key opportunities emerging from the favorable factors affecting the industry; and the key threats resulting from the adverse impact to industry attractiveness. These opportunities and threats should be the depositories of all of the critical issues detected during the environmental scanning process.

The business strategy will respond to the opportunities and threats identified in this step, in what is perhaps the gratest challenge in the strategy formulation process. This is so because we are trying to either reshape the industry structure to our own advantage, or respond to events that are not fully under our control. Truly excellent companies have developed the ability to interact effectively with their external environment, either by adapting themselves faster than their competitors, or by capturing opportunities that others have failed to recognize. This ability involves a thorough knowledge and a learning capability to anticipate environmental trends and to place the right bets on the uncertain outcomes associated with them. It all boils down to intelligent risk taking.

The opportunities and threats for the P&G Detergent Business in Europe are exhibited in Figure 5–16.

FIGURE 5–16. Identification of Opportunities and Threats—P&G Detergent Business in Europe

KEY OPPORTUNITIES

- High brand recognition
- Little or no substitute products for detergents
- Low number of main competitors could lead to lower rivalry and oligopolistic opportunities
- The creation of unique market in the European community will permit P&G to use effectively its economy of scale and to compete accordingly
- Good opportunity for growth in the mature basic products in the new Eastern European markets
- The experience acquired in distribution in the U.S. should be used to leverage the access to prominent distribution channels across Europe by the creation of partnerships
- Research and capacity of innovation in packaging and manufacturing process will allow to compete effectively in front of more stringent environmental regulations
- Globalization of tastes and fashions due to the increased use of the communication media

KEY THREATS

- Very low final consumer loyalty and switching costs
- Increase in environmental concerns and regulations
- Increased power of the distribution channel
- Dependence on the oil market
- Appearance of generic and channel-specific brand names will lower margins
- Possible Kao entry

NOTE: This is not an official document. It is an illustration drawn from public sources.

Environmental Scan at the Business Level Based on External Factors Analysis

The environmental scan at the business level is based on the identification of those critical external factors considered to be the central determinants of industry attractiveness in the opinion of key managers of the business. Unlike Porter's model, which is based on a set of fixed factors anchored on industrial organization principles, this model provides the freedom to identify external factors that managers consider particularly relevant to the industry in which the business competes. Managers are required to engage in a totally fresh exercise for deeply probing the identification of those issues that are considered truly significant, and to concentrate their efforts in the assessment of their influence over the industry attractiveness. This inquiry also serves as an effective communication device among top managers, which generates a broad consensus among them, and leads to a collective enrichment of their business understanding. At the same time, it prevents any mechanistic treatment of this all-important strategic question. This approach taps on the broad experiences that the group of managers hold in a given business, and may be more suitable when the firm has had a long-term presence in an industry.

If it were desirable to enrich the conceptual framework used by the managers engaged in the identification and assessment of these critical external factors, one could expose them first to the principles of industrial organization, or to the essence of the five-forces model.

When we use this model, we provide an initial set of factors broken into five major categories: market factors, competitive factors, economic and governmental factors, technological factors, and social factors. The list is included in the illustration provided below. However, we encourage managers to modify the list in order to adjust it to their specific circumstances.

A Process for Profiling the Industry Attractiveness with the External-Factors Model: An Illustration

The process for profiling the industry attractiveness using the external-factors model is quite similar to the one discussed when using the five-forces model. The primary difference is that we start by identifying the critical external factors, which are tailor-made for the industry being analyzed. We illustrate this methodology using, as an example, the life-insurance industry in Taiwan. This study was conducted by Kung-Shih Lee for the Cathay Life Insurance Company.[7]

STEP 1. IDENTIFICATION OF THE CRITICAL EXTERNAL FACTORS FOR INDUSTRY ANALYSIS

The factors identified are described under the five major categories presented in step 2.

STEP 2. PROFILE OF THE INDUSTRY ATTRACTIVENESS

Market Factors.
The analysis indicates that there are favorable trends affecting the life insurance market in Taiwan. The market growth potential is primarily due to increasing income per capita and favorable demographic changes (Figure 5–17).

Competitive Factors.
New entrants, particularly domestic firms familiar with the local culture and markets, are contributing to an increase in competitive intensity. Although this trend is affecting the industry adversely, the final assessment of these factors in the future is neutral attractiveness (Figure 5–18).

Economic and Government Factors.
"The Six-Year National Development Plan" of Taiwan is intended to ensure sustainable economic growth by providing the necessary resources for industrial and infrastructure development. The government has launched major public projects to stimulate the economy, enhance overall productivity, and assure stable economic growth and low inflation. Moreover, the closeness to mainland China opens up an attractive potential for substantial growth opportunities in the entire economy, mainly the service sector. Manpower supply will be tighter due to greater number of competitors (Figure 5–19).

Technological Factors.
The business processes in the various service units of the industry are continuously being improved thanks to the more intensive use of information technologies, but costs are increasing simultaneously. The final impact of technology is to demand higher levels of investment without necessarily allowing for differentiating opportunities among the various players in a sustainable way. At the end, the technology factors are neutral to industry attractiveness (Figure 5-20).

Social Factors.
Greater consumer awareness of the value of life insurance and higher standards of living are contributing to an increased ratio of the number of policies to the total population. Demographic trends that are extending the population age

are also adding attractiveness to the industry. A similar favorable impact will result from increased adaptability of the industry to international markets. The only deteriorating factor is the increasing demand for consumer protection (Figure 5-21).

Summary of Factor Attractiveness.
Each of the five sets of factors previously analyzed are given a summary ranking. Notice that the five-points scale is still used to measure attractiveness (Figure 5–22).

Overall Assessment of Industry Attractiveness.
After completing the analysis of each factor, one single overall ranking to the industry attractiveness is given. Notice that, as in the five-forces model, we switch from a five-point scale to a three-point scale: low, medium, and high attractiveness. This will allow the use of the Industry-Attractiveness/Business-Strength Matrix to assess the strength of the firm's business portfolio, and to suggest guidance for resource allocation and strategic actions (Figure 5–23).

FIGURE 5–17. Attractiveness of Market Factors—Cathay Life Insurance Company in Taiwan

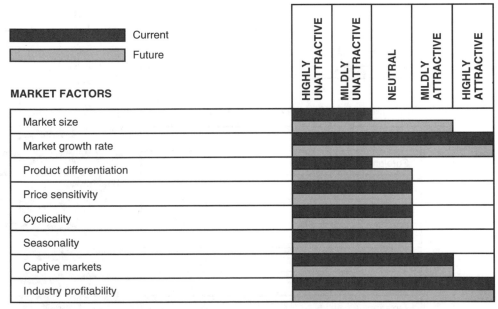

SOURCE: Adapted from Kung-Shih Lee, "A Business Strategy for a Life-Insurance Company," unpublished masters thesis, Sloan School of Management, MIT, (1993).

FIGURE 5–18. Attractiveness of Competitive Factors—Cathay Life Insurance Company in Taiwan

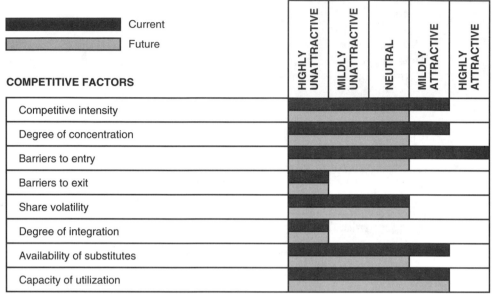

SOURCE: Adapted from Lee (1993).

FIGURE 5–19. Attractiveness of Economic and Governmental Factors—Cathay Life Insurance Company in Taiwan

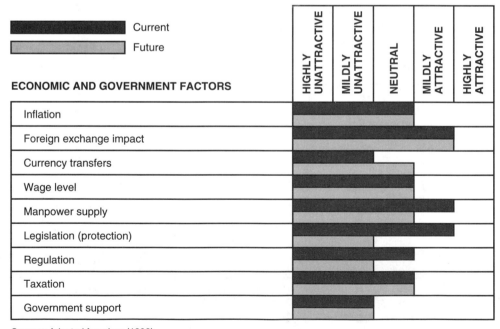

SOURCE: Adapted from Lee (1993).

FIGURE 5–20. Attractiveness of Technological Factors—Cathay Life Insurance Company in Taiwan

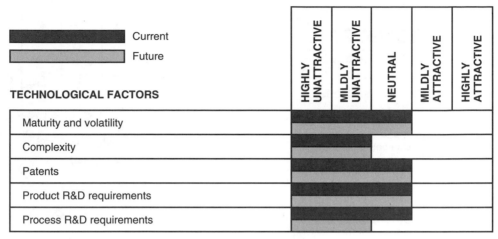

TECHNOLOGICAL FACTORS	HIGHLY UNATTRACTIVE	MILDLY UNATTRACTIVE	NEUTRAL	MILDLY ATTRACTIVE	HIGHLY ATTRACTIVE
Maturity and volatility	▓▓ Current / ░░ Future				
Complexity	▓▓ Current / ░░ Future				
Patents	▓▓ Current / ░░ Future				
Product R&D requirements	▓▓ Current / ░░ Future				
Process R&D requirements	▓▓ Current / ░░ Future				

Legend: ▓▓ Current ░░ Future

SOURCE: Adapted from Lee (1993).

FIGURE 5–21. Attractiveness of Social Factors—Cathay Life Insurance Company in Taiwan

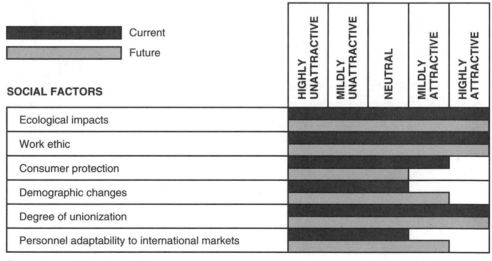

SOCIAL FACTORS	HIGHLY UNATTRACTIVE	MILDLY UNATTRACTIVE	NEUTRAL	MILDLY ATTRACTIVE	HIGHLY ATTRACTIVE
Ecological impacts	▓▓ Current / ░░ Future				
Work ethic	▓▓ Current / ░░ Future				
Consumer protection	▓▓ Current / ░░ Future				
Demographic changes	▓▓ Current / ░░ Future				
Degree of unionization	▓▓ Current / ░░ Future				
Personnel adaptability to international markets	▓▓ Current / ░░ Future				

Legend: ▓▓ Current ░░ Future

SOURCE: Adapted from Lee (1993).

FIGURE 5–22. Summary of Factor Attractiveness—Cathay Life Insurance Company in Taiwan

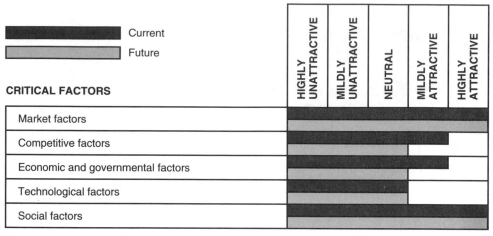

SOURCE: Adapted from Lee (1993).

FIGURE 5–23. Overall Assessment of Industry Attractiveness—Cathay Life Insurance Company of Taiwan

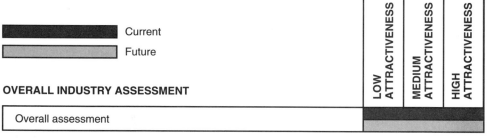

SOURCE: Adapted from Lee (1993).

FIGURE 5–24. Identification of Key Opportunities and Threats—Cathay Life
Insurance Company of Taiwan

KEY OPPORTUNITIES

- The economic growth will be continuously booming through more frequent trade with China and the launching of the National Six-Year Plan, which will stimulate the expansion of the insurance market.
- Very high market growth opportunities.
- Increasing consumer awareness of the benefits of life insurance.
- Social and political changes, and increasing market segmentation are helpful for product development and differentiation.
- The government policy in internationalization is opening up new opportunities for developing the international market.

KEY THREATS

- Deregulation has allowed new entrants and, consequently, more drastic competition.
- Higher costs due to more demanding customers requiring higher levels of professional services and more sophisticated products.
- Higher turnover of human resources due to more intense competition.
- Value of life insurance to customer tends to be challenged by other financial instruments.
- Tendency toward stricter governmental supervision.

SOURCE: Adapted from Lee (1993).

STEP 3. IDENTIFICATION OF OPPORTUNITIES AND THREATS.

The final output of the industry analysis is the identification of key opportunities emerging from the favorable factors affecting the industry; and key threats, resulting from adverse impacts to industry attractiveness (Figure 5–24).

Strategic Groups Analysis

The industry analysis carried forward so far considers all participating firms in a unique pack, implicitly assuming that they share some characteristics, just by the fact of pertaining to the same industry. For a primary level of analysis, this is a good approximation, but it is not enough if we are interested in understanding more deeply the structural qualities of an industry. On a second level of analysis, we need to recognize that firms are not homogeneous. To gain a more profound knowledge of the forms of competition, we must perform a subsequent stage of industry representation aimed, this time, at identifying the *strategic groups.* These groups correspond to aggregations of firms that include in a unique set those competitors that follow a common or similar strategy along well-defined dimensions. We can say then that groups collect firms that are relatively homogeneous in terms of the way they compete .

Porter suggests the following dimensions to identify differences in firm strategies within an industry: specialization, brand identification, a push-versus-pull marketing approach, channel selection, product quality, technological leadership, vertical integration, cost position, service, price policy, financial and operating leverage, relationship with parent company, and relationship to home and host government.[8] We should try to locate in the same group all firms with comparable characteristics and following a similar competitive strategy.

At this more detailed level of analysis, we could still apply the five-forces model to recognize the different degrees of attractiveness within the strategic groups in a process that might be referred to as industry analysis within an industry. Thus, the firm will have higher profits if it is located in a strategic group with the best combination of high *mobility barriers,* insulation from inter-group rivalry and substitute products, and strong bargaining power with adjacent industries. The concept of entry barriers, applicable to the industry as a whole, is replaced by mobility barriers, which capture the difficulty that a strategic group within an industry will encounter when attempting to penetrate into an adjacent strategic group.

The structure within an industry consists of the configuration of strategic groups including mobility barriers, size and composition, strategic distance, and the relative market interdependence.

Essentially, the concept of strategic grouping is a very pragmatic approach aimed at cataloguing firms within an industry in accordance with the way they have chosen to seek competitive advantage. This segmentation is useful when one faces a high diversity of competitive positions in a fairly complex and heterogeneous industry. Typical examples of this situation are global industries with a wide variety of players, some being totally international and some purely local.

A useful tool that can guide the separation of strategic groups in an industry is the so-called *strategic mapping.* This is a two-dimensional display that helps to explain the different strategies of firms. These two dimensions should not be interdependent because otherwise the map would show an inherent correlation .

The two most common dimensions that are used for a strategic mapping purpose are the breadth of the product line and the degree of vertical integration. They allow us to separate firms that have a full coverage of product lines and are fully self-reliant from those firms that are focusing on a very narrow line and concentrating in a short range of the value-added chain. Figure 5–25 illustrates alternative strategic positioning of different competitors on those two dimensions.

To recognize the various strategic groups within an industry, we need to identify the critical explanatory variables that help to discriminate competitive positioning. This is an art more than a science, despite the numerous good-quality statistical efforts in this area. Therefore, we limit ourselves to providing illustrations that might guide the reader into an understanding of this difficult task.

FIGURE 5–25. Strategic Groups Defined in
Generic Terms: An Illustration

DEGREE OF VERTICAL INTEGRATION

	Low	High
Full Line	• Assembler • Very close to suppliers • Most likely differentiated market coverage	• Full line • Vertically integrated • Most likely a low-cost competitor
Narrow Line	• Narrow line • Assembler • High price • High technology • High quality	• Highly focused • Highly automated • Low-cost production

(vertical axis label: **BREADTH OF PRODUCT LINE**)

Our first example has to do with the investment banking industry in the mid-1980s in the United States.[9] In order to separate the various firms competing in that industry, we have chosen the following two dimensions: brand identification and product leadership.

With regard to *brand identification,* the industry can be classified into three tiers, characterized by prestige, type of client served, and special product and service expertise. The first tier includes firms that typically serve the investment banking needs of the largest corporations in the United States. They are among the best capitalized, with firmly established client relationships and extensive distribution systems. The second tier is formed by firms that have strong retail operations with some institutional business, serving smaller companies with smaller debt rating, and are not widely dispersed geographically. The third tier is composed of discount or retail brokers and smaller investment banks that serve the needs of small companies.

Regarding *product leadership,* there are firms known as great innovators, such as First Boston, a pioneer in interest rate swaps, collateralized mortgage obligations (CMO's), public zero-coupon bonds, merger and acquisition strategies, and aggressive entry into international banking. In contrast, there are those who prefer to be followers, the most notable being Goldman Sachs. They are not great innovators but are masters at taking the innovations of others and perfecting them to the point where they have become one of the best at funding new services or products.

Figure 5–26 shows the strategic groups using the U.S. markets as a base, while Figure 5–27 shows the groups using the Eurobonds (international markets) as the base. The size of the circles represents the combined market share of firms in a strategic group within relevant markets.

FIGURE 5–26. Strategic Groups Analysis of U.S. Investment Banks (93 Percent of Market) in the U.S. Underwriting Market in the Mid-1980s

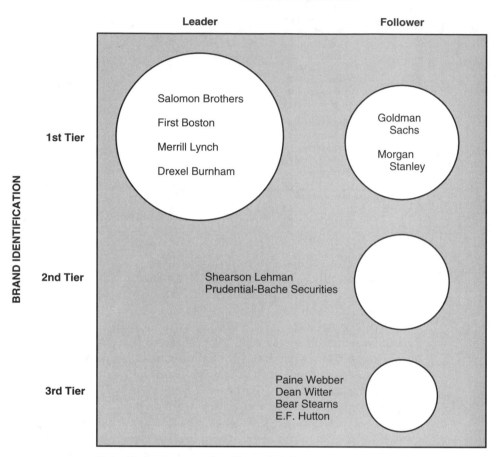

Note: Circle size proportional to market share

SOURCE: Dexter H. Charles, "International Commercial Banks Take On Wall Street: An Analysis and Evaluation," unpublished Masters thesis, Sloan School of Management, MIT, 1986. Reprinted by permission of Dexter H. Charles.

Just as entry barriers protect the industry as a whole, mobility barriers protect the strategic groups. However, these mobility barriers are greater along the vertical dimension (brand identification) than along the horizontal dimension (product leadership). Moving along the horizontal dimension can be achieved to a large extent through raiding the personnel of competitors. In contrast, moving between tiers is very difficult. Factors that determine a firm's tier are its history, culture, contact and public prestige, clients, and so on. In many respects, investment banking is a snobbish industry.

FIGURE 5–27. Strategic Groups Analysis of U.S. Investment Banks (36 Percent of Market) in the Eurobond Underwriting Market in the Mid-1980s

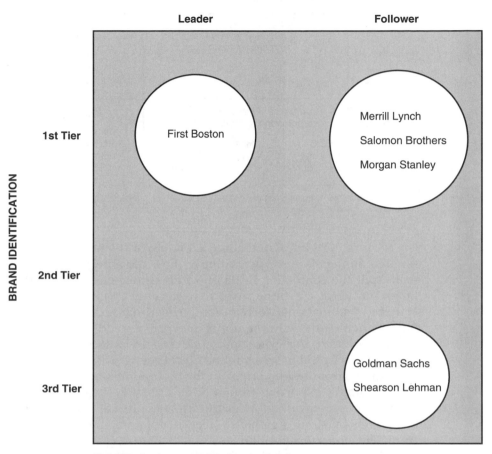

Note: Circle size proportional to market share

SOURCE: Charles (1986).

Our second example is drawn from the worldwide telecommunications equipment industry.[10] We have selected one of the most popular frameworks to characterize strategic groups within a global industry.[11] It uses configuration and coordination of the value-added activities of the firm as the key elements of strategic mapping. The *configuration* dimension addresses the degree of geographical dispersion of the various activities performed by the business firm in a global setting. The *coordination* dimension identifies the degree of centralization that is imposed to properly integrate the activities of the firm.

FIGURE 5–28. Configuration and Coordination of Activities of Telecommunications Equipment Firms in the Mid-1980s

CONFIGURATION

	Mulitple Location	Single Location
Centralized	*High foreign investment with strong control* • GTE • Siemens	*Pure global strategy* • AT&T • Northern Telecom
Decentralized	*Country-centered multinational corporations or domestic firms* • GEC • Hassler (Swiss) • Plesey • STA (Swedish) • ITT Europe • TUN (West German)	*Export-based strategy with decentralized marketing* • LM Ericsson • CIT-Alcatel • Hitachi • Fujitsu • NEC

SOURCE: Lynnet Koh, "Strategic Analysis of the Worldwide Telecommunications Industry," unpublished masters thesis, Sloan School of Management, MIT, 1986. Reprinted by permission of Lynnet Koh.

Figure 5–28 lines up the major players of the worldwide telecommunications equipment industry according to these two criteria. The framework allows us to split the competing firms into four strategic groups. In the bottom left quadrant, there are those firms that are either purely domestic or country-centered multinational corporations, which manage the subsidiaries as totally independent entities. In the upper-left corner, we identify those firms that are heavily centralized, yet whose presence covers a multitude of geographical locations. This is typical of foreign direct investments with a high degree of centralized control from headquarters. In the bottom-right corner, we find those firms that are simply exporting from a home base with a completely decentralized marketing strategy. Finally, in the upper-right corner, we encounter those companies pursuing a global strategy, maintaining a centralized coordination from a headquarters position.

A second framework to identify global strategic groups is based on the breadth of the product line and the global geographical coverage as the two discriminating dimensions.[12] The resultant categorization is presented in Figure 5–29, which segments the firms into five different strategic groups. Firms that offer a broad product range in a global setting can be differentiated by their strategic positioning in an attempt either, to achieve global cost leadership or global differentiation. Those firms retaining a global scope with a narrow range of products are pursuing a niche strategy through global segmentation. Broad product lines at a country level can normally be explained exclusively in terms of protectionistic policies of the local country. And finally, a narrow range at the country level is the residue that belongs to local firms pursuing a limited competitive position responding to national interest or taste.

Figure 5–30 illustrates the five strategic groups just described within the context of the consumer electronic industry in the mid-1980s. It is upsetting to

FIGURE 5–29. Global Strategic Groups: Five Strategic Alternatives for a Global Company

GEOGRAPHICAL SCOPE

	Global	Country
Broad	Global cost Leadership --- Global Differentiation	Protected Markets
Narrow	Global Segmentation	National Responsiveness

BREADTH OF PRODUCT LINE

see the limited role played by American firms RCA and Zenith, which not so long ago were important international players and are now relegated to an insignificant global role. It is also interesting to observe the strategic positioning of the European firms, which are benefiting from a highly protected national environment. However, in the late 1980s this situation did not prevail because changes were fast paced. The Korean and Taiwanese firms are seeking a global positioning from a narrow product line. The key issue with respect to

FIGURE 5–30. An Illustration of Global Strategic Groups: The Consumer Electronic Industry in the Mid-1980s

GEOGRAPHICAL SCOPE

	Global	Country
Broad	Matushita (Japan) Sanyo (Japan) --- Philips (Netherlands) Sony (Japan)	Grunding (West Germany) Thomson-Brand (France) Thorn-E.M.I. (U.K.)
Narrow	Gold Star (Korea) Samsung (Korea) Tatung (Taiwan) Sharp (Japan)	RCA (USA) Zenith (USA)

BREADTH OF PRODUCT LINE

those firms is whether the magnitude of mobility barriers will allow them to move easily into a broad range of products, where they will be facing the most stable Japanese and Dutch competitors.

In conclusion, we would like to reemphasize two points. One, the importance of identifying strategic groups when not all the firms are following the same strategy in a given industry. And two, the need to try many alternative segmentation criteria to generate the insights leading to the appropriate classification of the competing firms into strategic groups.

The Financial Statement Analysis Framework

In this section, we cover a methodological approach to gathering quantitative intelligence at the level of the firm, based on financial statements analysis. One of the most widely distributed sources of information of all firms in any industry are the set of three financial statements—balance sheet, income statement, and statement of changes in the financial position—and the 10K reports, which must be made public periodically by all major corporations. It is only natural, then, to make use of that information for gaining certain understanding of the competitive position of different firms in an industry. The appropriate technique to perform this task has been known for many years; it is called *financial statement analysis* (FSA).

There are two basic procedures to make these figures more easily comparable among different competitors: (1) define common-size financial statements, and (2) perform a financial ratio analysis. Let us review these procedures now.[13]

DEFINITION OF COMMON-SIZE FINANCIAL STATEMENTS

Corporations in an industry are normally of quite different size. Therefore, to say that accounts receivable in firm A are larger than in firm B does not carry too much information. One simple transformation to make financial statements comparable across all firms in an industry is to standardize all of them to a common size, usually 100. In Figure 5–31 we present the common-size balance sheet and income statement for a group of companies in the pharmaceutical industry. We can see, for example, that for Squibb Corp., cash and marketable securities are comparably low, while long-term debt is comparatively high. Also, its income after taxes is the lowest in the industry. This procedure helps us to identify when a player departs from the norms prevailing in the industry and allows us to raise questions with regard to what may be considered as abnormal behavior.

FIGURE 5-31. Common-Size Statements for a Group of Companies in the Pharmaceutical Industry

A. COMMON SIZE BALANCE SHEET (%)

	Abbott Labs	Bristol Myers Co.	Syntex Corp.	Smith-Kline Corp.	Eli Lilly & Co.	Merck Co.	Searle Co.	Squibb Corp.	Group Mean
ASSETS									
Cash & Marketable Securities	5	17	20	21	9	10	20	8	14
Accounts Receivable	16	26	15	21	22	19	19	21	20
Inventories	18	23	19	16	23	22	12	20	19
Other Current Assets	6	6	2	1	3	0	3	5	3
Net Plant and Equipment	31	23	35	31	35	41	26	25	31
Investments & OtherAssets	24	6	9	10	8	8	20	21	13
	100	100	100	100	100	100	100	100	100
LIABILITIES AND EQUITY									
Accounts payable	5	7	8	8	4	13	15	17	8
Other Current Liabilities	31	23	17	17	24	10	18	6	18
Long-Term Debt	9	4	12	10	2	7	8	20	10
Deferred Tax & Other Liabilities	6	3	0	0	5	4	6	4	4
Stockholders' Equity	49	63	63	65	65	66	53	53	60
	100	100	100	100	100	100	100	100	100

B. COMMON-SIZE INCOME STATEMENT (%)

	Abbott Labs	Bristol Myers Co.	Syntex Corp.	Smith-Kline Corp.	Eli Lilly & Co.	Merck Co.	Searle Co.	Squibb Corp.	Group Mean
REVENUES	100	100	100	100	100	100	100	100	100
EXPENSES									
Cost of Goods Sold	55	38	35	31	39	39	33	41	39
Research & Development	5	4	9	8	8	8	9	6	7
Marketing, G&A Expenses	22	42	38	32	30	27	38	36	33
Interest Expense	0	0	0	1	1	1	0	3	1
Other Expense	1	0	0	2	1	1	4	5	2
Tax	6	7	4	8	7	9	6	2	6
Income after Tax	11	9	14	18	14	15	10	7	12
	100	100	100	100	100	100	100	100	100

SOURCE: Adapted from Marianne Kunschak and Luis F. Tena-Ramirez, "Strategic Management for a Pharmaceutical Company: A Case Study," 1983. Reprinted by permission of Marianne Kunschak.

FINANCIAL RATIO ANALYSIS

This is the most extensively used form of financial statement analysis. Ratio analysis is aimed at characterizing the firm in a few basic dimensions considered fundamental to assess the financial health of a company. They are usually categorized in five types:

- Liquidity ratios
- Leverage-capital structure ratios
- Profitability ratios
- Turnover ratios
- Common stock security ratios

Liquidity Ratios

A liquid firm is one that can meet short-term financial obligations without much of a problem when they fall due. This ability is normally measured in terms of three different ratios:

$$Current\ ratio = \frac{Current\ assets}{Current\ liabilities}$$

This is just a ratio between short-term assets and short-term liabilities. *Current assets* are made up of cash, short-term marketable securities, accounts receivable, inventories, and prepaid expenses. *Current liabilities* are made up of accounts payable, dividends, taxes due within one year, and short-term bank loans.

$$Quick\ ratio = \frac{Cash + Short\text{-}term\ marketing\ securities + Accounts\ receivable}{Current\ liabilities}$$

This is a more stringent definition of liquidity, which is commonly called the acid test. Among the short-term assets only the most liquid ones are included, leaving aside inventories and prepaid expenses.

$$Defensive\ interval\ (days) = \frac{Cash + Short\text{-}term\ marketable\ securities + Accounts\ receivable}{Projected\ daily\ operating\ expenditures}$$

This ratio is an estimate of the total number of days of operation that can be financed with the most liquid of short-term assets (also called defensive assets).

Projected daily operating expenditures can be estimated by adding together cost of goods sold; excise taxes; marketing, administrative, and general expenses; interest expenses, and other expenses, and then deducting depreciation and deferred tax and dividing that figure by 365 (days of the year).

The values of these three ratios for a group of companies in the pharmaceutical industry are presented in Figure 5–32. It can be observed that in all three measures, Abbott Labs presents the most critical condition, while Squibb appears well protected for fulfilling its short-term obligations, at least as reflected by the current and quick ratios.

Due to the importance of cash and marketable securities as a source for meeting operative expenditures and other cash demands, three additional financial ratios are sometimes used to define the *cash position* of the firm.

$$\frac{\textit{Cash} + \textit{Short-term marketable securities}}{\textit{Current liability}}$$

$$\frac{\textit{Cash} + \textit{Short-term marketable securities}}{\textit{Sales}}$$

$$\frac{\textit{Cash} + \textit{Short-term marketable securities}}{\textit{Total assets}}$$

Obviously, the greater the value of these ratios, the better the cash position of the firm.

Moreover, increasing emphasis is being given to the capacity of the firm for generating cash. Since most firms do not report directly cash-flow information in their financial statements, additional computations have to be made to figure out "working capital from operations" and "cash flow from operations." These two concepts allow us to compute the following financial ratios, which introduce both working capital and cash flow.

$$\frac{\textit{Working capital from operations}}{\textit{Sales}}$$

$$\frac{\textit{Working capital from operations}}{\textit{Total assets [average]}}$$

$$\frac{\textit{Cash flow from operations}}{\textit{Sales}}$$

$$\frac{\textit{Cash flow from operations}}{\textit{Total assets [average]}}$$

FIGURE 5–32. Liquidity Ratios for a Group of Companies in the Pharmaceutical Industry

	Abbott Labs	Bristol Myers Co.	Syntex Corp.	Smith-Kline Corp.	Eli Lilly & Co.	Merck Co.	Searle Co.	Squibb Corp.	Group Mean
Current ratio	1.22	2.38	2.23	2.28	2.40	2.04	2.40	2.29	2.20
Quick ratio	0.59	1.35	1.35	1.49	1.69	1.09	1.73	1.32	1.33
Defensive intervals (days)	97	135	135	206	220	179	222	126	165

SOURCE: Adapted from Kunschak and Tena-Ramirez (1983). Reprinted by permission of Marianne Kunschak.

FIGURE 5–33. Leverage-Capital Structure Ratios for a Group of Companies in the Pharmaceutical Industry

	Abbott Labs	Bristol Myers Co.	Syntex Corp.	Smith-Kline Corp.	Eli Lilly & Co.	Merck Co.	Searle Co.	Squibb Corp.	Group Mean
Long-term debt / Shareholders' equity	0.18	0.07	0.16	0.11	0.03	0.11	0.33	0.39	0.17
Total debt / Shareholders' equity	0.93	0.59	0.54	0.50	0.46	0.46	0.76	0.84	0.64
Times interest earned	3.2	9.4	4.4	15.8	13.1	11.2	5.3	4.0	8.3

Leverage-Capital Structure Ratios

These ratios measure the use of leverage in the firm (debt versus equity capital) and the ability the firm has to fulfill its long-term commitments with debtholders. These are the most commonly used ratios:

$$Leverage\ of\ long\text{-}term\ debt = \frac{Long\text{-}term\ debt}{Shareholders'\ equity}$$

$$Leverage\ of\ total\ debt = \frac{Current\ liabilities + Long\text{-}term\ debt}{Shareholders'\ equity}$$

These two leverage ratios measure the number of debt dollars (either long-term or total debt) per equity dollar

$$Times\ interest\ earned = \frac{Operating\ income}{Annual\ interest\ payments}$$

where: Operating income − Sales − (Cost of goods sold + Excise tax + Marketing, administrative, and general expenses).

This ratio measures the number of times that interest payments could be covered by operating income (profit before interest and taxes). The larger the ratio, the more certain is the ability of the firm to make its interest payments, and consequently, the lower the risk borne by debtholders.

In Figure 5–33 we present the leverage-capital structure ratios for a group of companies in the pharmaceutical industry. Abbott Labs appears again as the most leveraged company with a 0.93 ratio of total debt to equity; it is closely followed by Squibb which has a 0.84 ratio. Curiously enough, Squibb shows to be very liquid in the short run, but rather illiquid in the long run, with earnings only four times interest payments.

Another debt-service ratio that has been proposed takes into consideration the portion of the annual interest payments covered by cash flow, as follows:

$$\frac{Cash\ flow\ from\ operations}{Annual\ interest\ payments}$$

Profitability Ratios

Profitability ratios measure the ability of the firm to generate profits. There are different measures of profitability, three being the most widely used:

$$Return\ on\ total\ assets =$$

$$\frac{Net\ income\ after\ tax + Interest\ expenses - Tax\ benefits\ of\ interest\ expenses}{Total\ assets}$$

This is a measure of the profitability of the business, independent of the source of financing.

$$Return\ on\ equity = \frac{Net\ income\ after\ taxes\ available\ to\ common\ shareholders}{Common\ shareholders'\ equity}$$

This ratio measures the profitability of the firm to common shareholders, that is, to equity owners. Interest payments are deducted this time from the measure of profit in the numerator.

$$Sales\ margin = \frac{Revenues - Operating\ expenses}{Revenues}$$

This is a measure of the operating profit in relation to revenues from sales.

In Figure 5–34 we present the profitability ratios for a group of companies in the pharmaceutical industry. What is most noticeable in this table is the low sales margin of Squibb Corp. Over total assets, the return is quite comparable with most corporations, except for Smith-Kline Corp., which shows very high profitability in all three indices. But the return on equity is only half the level of other corporations, and the sales margin is still lower. This points again to the capital structure problem, and most likely to an inadequate production-cost structure.

Turnover Ratios

Turnover ratios are also called efficiency ratios because they measure performance in the utilization of assets. The most popular ratios are:

$$Total\ assets\ turnover = \frac{Sales}{Average\ total\ assets}$$

This ratio indicates the number of times that "assets are sold" in a stated period.

$$Average\ collection\ period\ (days) = \frac{Average\ [net]\ accounts\ receivable}{Daily\ sales}$$

This is the average number of days required for the collection of payments on credit sales.

$$Inventory\ turnover = \frac{Cost\ of\ goods\ sold}{Average\ inventory}$$

In this case the ratio refers to the number of times that "inventories are sold."

FIGURE 5–34. Profitability Ratios for a Group of Companies in the Pharmaceutical Industry

	Abbott Labs	Bristol Myers Co.	Syntex Corp.	Smith-Kline Corp.	Eli Lilly & Co.	Merck Co.	Searle Co.	Squibb Corp.	Group Mean
Return on total assets	0.12	0.13	0.14	0.20	0.14	0.15	0.11	0.12	0.14
Return on shareholders' equity	0.21	0.20	0.20	0.30	0.20	0.22	0.17	0.10	0.20
Sales margin (5-year average)	0.44	0.62	0.63	0.66	0.61	0.62	0.67	0.53	0.60

SOURCE: Adapted from Kunschak and Tena-Ramirez (1983). Reprinted by permission of Marianne Kunschak.

FIGURE 5–35. Turnover Ratios for a Group of Companies in the Pharmaceutical Industry

	Abbott Labs	Bristol Myers Co.	Syntex Corp.	Smith-Kline Corp.	Eli Lilly & Co.	Merck Co.	Searle Co.	Squibb Corp.	Group Mean
Total asset turnover	1.06	1.49	0.96	1.15	0.96	1.00	0.86	0.81	1.04
Average collection period (days)	56	57	56	67	83	68	79	101	68
Inventory turnover	5.8	6.3	5.3	6.3	4.1	4.6	7.3	3.9	5.5

SOURCE: Adapted from Kunschak and Tena-Ramirez (1983). Reprinted by permission of Marianne Kunschak.

In Figure 5–35 on page 111 we present the turnover ratios for a group of companies in the pharmaceutical industry. This time Squibb shows the lowest efficiency indicators, with only 0.81 for asset turnover (low sales compared to assets) and 3.9 for inventory turnover (too much inventory for the prevailing level of sales). Also a collection period of over 100 days speaks of credit terms more generous than in other firms in the industry. Is this an intended policy or is it just the result of poor collection practices?

Common Stock Security Ratios

Financial analysts often express some of the information contained in the financial statements on a per-share basis. This is done in order to capture information that is central for the equityholders to be able to judge the firm's performance. The most commonly used of these ratios are:

$$Earnings\ per\ share\ (EPS) = \frac{Net\ income\ available\ for\ common}{Number\ of\ shares\ outstanding}$$

$$Book\ value\ per\ share = \frac{Shareholders'\ equity}{Number\ of\ shares\ outstanding}$$

$$Dividends\ per\ share = \frac{Dividends\ paid\ on\ common}{Number\ of\ shares\ outstanding}$$

$$Dividend\ yield = \frac{Dividends\ per\ share}{Price\ per\ share}$$

$$Market\text{-}to\text{-}book\ value\ (M/B) = \frac{Price\ per\ share}{Book\ value\ per\ share}$$

A highly relevant measurement for assessing the economic performance of a firm in terms of value creation is the market-to-book value ratio, which is discussed extensively in Chapter 15. In Figure 5–36, we provide the trend of M/B values for Squibb Corporation, Smith-Kline (an outstanding performer within its industry), and the drug industry average. The differences observed in these ratios constitute evidence on the actual investment opportunities of the firms as suggested by:

1. Squibb's M/B ratio experiences an important increase in 19X5, when new and quite profitable products were introduced by the company.
2. Smith-Kline's M/B ratio is very high, though it shows a persistent downward trend that could be explained by the prompt expiration of a valuable patent (Tagamet).
3. The average M/B ratio for pharmaceutical companies is relatively high, which indicates a favorable comparison with alternative investment opportunities.

FIGURE 5–36. The M/B Ratio for Squibb Corporation, Smith-Kline Corporation, and the Pharmaceutical Industry

	19x1	19x2	19x3	19x4	19x5
Squibb Corporation	1.88	1.85	1.32	1.38	1.99
Smith-Kline	6.32	5.71	5.34	4.61	3.73
Drug Industry (world-wide)	2.00	1.88	1.76	1.89	2.19

Other Measures of Performance

Besides the five categories of financial ratios we have described it is often useful to include other performance measurements that are particularly critical in a given industry. For instance, for high-technology firms, comparative measures pertaining to R&D expenses could be quite significant. Likewise, for firms with high capital intensity, it could be interesting to observe the ratio of capital investment over sales. In most industries, the firm's growth compared to the industry growth is an important indicator in the changes in relative market share for each of the competitors. Figure 5-37 on page 114 shows additional measures of performance that were considered significant for a group of companies in the pharmaceutical industry. The data associated with sales growth and relative market share positioning (company growth versus industry growth) present Smith-Kline and Syntex Corporation as those gaining competitive positioning more aggressively. All other companies seem more or less to maintain their existing shares. It is clear from the figures that the pharmaceutical industry is exceedingly high in the intensity of R&D expenditures. Abbott Laboratories stands alone as the lowest spender in R&D among the group of companies being considered. This should be a matter of concern for them.

DEFINING THE STANDARD OF COMPARISON: CROSS-SECTIONAL VERSUS TIME-SERIES ANALYSIS

To interpret fully the meaning of a ratio we need standards of comparison. For example, it is a commonly held belief that a corporation with a liquidity ratio of 2 or more and a quick ratio of 1 or more could be considered liquid. But these absolute standards are very hard to justify. For that reason, the preferred two methodologies to define standards for the interpretation of common-size statements and financial ratio analysis use relative indicators. These methodologies follow.

The *cross-sectional analysis* takes all firms in an industry at a given point in time and allows the comparison of their relative standing. The usual reference selected in this case is the mean or the median for the group of industries.

FIGURE 5–37. Other Measures of Performance for a Group of Companies in the Pharmaceutical Industry

Growth Performance Measures Five-Year Average (19x1 Through 19x5)	Abbott Labs	Bristol Myers Co.	Syntex Corp.	Smith-Kline Corp.	Eli Lilly & Co.	Merck Co.	Searle Co.	Squibb Corp.	Group Mean
Average sales growth %*	16	9.4	19	23	13	9	5.3	14	14
19 x 5 sales growth %*	18	14	26	17	12	12	17	18	17
R&D expenses as % of sales	5	9.1	9.1	7.4	8.1	8.2	8	6.1	8
Capital investment/sales	6.5	4.1	8	9.7	7.3	8.7	8.4	6.1	7
Company growth/ industry growth*	1.04	0.99	1.1	1.12	1.03	1.03	.97	.96	1.03

* Real dollars

SOURCE: Adapted from Kunschak and Tena-Ramirez (1983). Reprinted by permission of Marianne Kunschak.

Figures 5–31 through 5–35 and 5–37, which correspond to illustrations of cross-sectional analysis of both common-size statements and financial ratios, include the group mean in the final column.

In the case of *time-series analysis,* the interest is centered on the evolution of an indicator through a period of many years, so the criteria for analysis are not only the behavior of selected indicators for the competitors in the industry, but also the pattern shown by all indicators through time, including the average or median for the group of firms. For example, in Figure 5–38 we present the return on equity and return on total assets for Squibb Corporation and for the industry average between l9X1 and 19X5. In this period, Squibb shows a persistent deterioration of these two indicators, being more pronounced in the return-on-equity ratio. It is interesting to notice that in 19X1, Squibb presented an average profitability as measured by those two indicators, but in all other years it is markedly below the average.

FIGURE 5–38.   Profitability Ratios for Squibb and a Group of Companies in the Pharmaceutical Industry

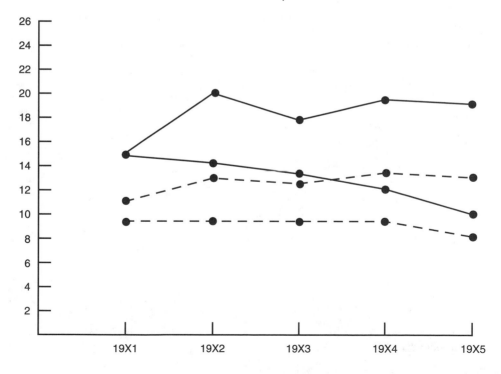

Notes

1. The five-forces model for industry attractiveness is presented in detail in Michael E. Porter, *Competitive Strategy* (New York: The Free Press, 1980). The foundations of the model are rooted in the field of industry organization. For an introduction to the principles of this field, the reader is referred to Richard E. Caves, *American Industry: Structure, Conduct, Performance,* 6th ed. (Englewood Cliffs, NJ: Prentice Hall, 1987); F. M. Scherer, *Industrial Market Structure and Economic Performance,* 2nd ed. (Chicago, IL: Rand McNally, 1980); and Sharon M. Oster, *Modern Competitive Analysis,* 2nd ed. (New York: Oxford University Press, 1994). For a comprehensive application of this model to a wide variety of industries, see Walter Adams, *The Structure of American Industry,* 7th ed. (New York: Macmillan, 1986).

2. Two good general references on the subject of strategic alliances are: Jordan D. Lewis, *Partnerships for Profit: Structuring and Managing Strategic Alliances* (New York: Free Press, 1990); and Peter Lorange and Johan Roos, *Strategic Alliances: Formation, Implementation and Evolution* (Cambridge, MA: Blackwell, 1992). For a discussion on alliances in the computer industry, see Benjamin Gomes-Casseres, "Computers: Alliances and Industry Evolution," in David B. Yoffie (Ed.), *Beyond Free Trade* (Cambridge, MA: Harvard University Press, 1993) 79–128.

3. The presentation of the engineering polymers industry follows Emmanuel P. Maceda, "Strategic Analysis: Du Pont Company, Engineering Polymers Division," unpublished student paper, Sloan School of Management, MIT, 1988.

4. The question of the causes of the firm's profitability is still widely debated in academic circles. Porter's work, from the outset, has assigned a significant importance to industry structure. For a summary of his contribution to the theory of strategic management, see Michael E. Porter, "Toward a Dynamic Theory of Strategy," *Strategic Management Journal* 12, Special Issue (Winter 1991), 95–117. Empirical analysis conducted by Richard Schmalensee, "Do Markets Differ Much?", in the *American Economic Review,* 75 (June 1985) 341–351, seems to corroborate the importance of industry in the performance of the firm. A challenge to the centrality of industry structure in the firm's profitability has been advanced by the so-called resource-based view of the firm, which places the internal resources and capabilities of the firm at the root of its superior performance. For a presentation of those arguments, see Margaret A. Peteraf, "The Cornerstones of Competitive Advantage: A Resource-Based View," *Strategic Management Journal,* 14 (1993) 179–191. For empirical work sustaining the resource-based arguments, see Richard P. Rumelt, "How Much Does Industry Matter?" in the *Strategic Management Journal* 12 (1991) 167–185; and Birger Wernerfelt and Cynthia A. Montgomery, "Tobin's q and the Importance of Focus in Firm Performance," *The American Economic Review,* 76 no. 1 (March 1988) 246–250.

5. There are many sources of information reporting firm and industry performance. Among the most accessible ones are the annual reports on the Fortune 500 and the *Business Week* 1000 firms. A classical reference on benchmarking is Robert C. Camp, *Benchmarking: The Search for Industry Best Practices That Lead to Superior Performance* (Milwaukee, WI: Quality Press, 1989).

6. The following are useful references on scenario planning: P. Wack, "Scenarios: Uncharted Waters Ahead," *Harvard Business Review* (September-October 1985) 73–89; P. Wack, "Scenarios: Shooting the Rapids," *Harvard Business Review* (November-December, 1985) 139–150; Paul J.H. Shoemaker, "When and How to Use Scenario Planning: A Heuristic Approach with Illustrations," *Journal of Forecasting,* 10, (1991) 549–564; Paul J.H. Shoemaker, and Cornelius A.J.M. van der Heijden, "Strategic Planning at the Royal Dutch/Shell," *Journal of Strategic Change,* 2 (1993) 157–171; and Paul J.H. Shoemaker, "Scenario Planning: A Tool for Strategic Thinking," *Sloan Management Review,* 36, no. 2 (Winter 1995), 25–40.

7. Adapted from Kung-Shih Lee, "A Business Strategy for a Life-Insurance Company," unpublished masters thesis, Sloan School of Management, MIT, 1993.

8. For an additional reference of the strategic groups concept, the reader is referred to Michael E. Porter, *Competitive Strategy* (New York: The Free Press, 1980); Kathryn Rudie Harrigan, *Strategic Flexibility* (Lexington, MA: Lexington Books, 1985); and Sharon M. Oster, *Modern Competitive Analysis* , 2nd ed. (New York: Oxford University Press, 1994).

9. The example of the investment banking industry is taken from Dexter H. Charles, "International Commercial Banks Take on Wall Street, An Analysis and Evaluation," unpublished masters thesis, Sloan School of Management, MIT, 1986.

10. This example is drawn from the work of Lynnet Koh, "Strategic Analysis of the Worldwide Telecommunications Industry," unpublished Masters thesis, Sloan School of Management, MIT, 1986.

11. For a further discussion of the configuration-coordination framework, see Michael E. Porter, *Competition in Global Industries* (Boston, MA: Harvard Business School Press, 1986).

12. Porter, *Competition in Global Industries* (1986).

13. For a comprehensive review of financial statement analysis, see George Foster, *Financial Statement Analysis,* 2nd ed. (Englewood Cliffs, NJ: Prentice Hall, 1986).

6

Internal Scrutiny at the Business Level

We have indicated before that there are two key issues regarding the choice of a business competitive strategy. One is the attractiveness of the industry in which the business is placed, assessed primarily by its long-term profitability prospects. The other is the set of factors that determines the competitive position the business will adopt in order to gain a sustainable competitive advantage. It is the second subject that is the central concern of this chapter.

To examine systematically the ways available to a business to achieve a sustainable competitive advantage, it is not possible to look at the firm's activities as a whole. Rather, it is necessary to disaggregate a business unit into strategically relevant stages to take into full account all of the tasks that are conducted to add value. These tasks include: product development and design, production, distribution, marketing, sales, services, and the many forms of support required for the smooth operation of a business. A valuable framework to accomplish this objective is the *value chain,* whose implications to achieve competitive advantages have been thoroughly explored by Porter.[1]

The Value Chain

The focus of analysis of the value chain is the SBU. The underlying principle is that all of the tasks performed by a business organization can be classified into nine different broad categories. Five of them are the so-called *primary activities,* and the other four are labeled *support activities.* A full representation of the value chain is given in Figure 6–1.

The primary activities are those involved in the physical movement of raw materials and finished products, in the production of goods and services, and in the marketing, sales, and subsequent services of the outputs of the business

FIGURE 6–1. The Value Chain

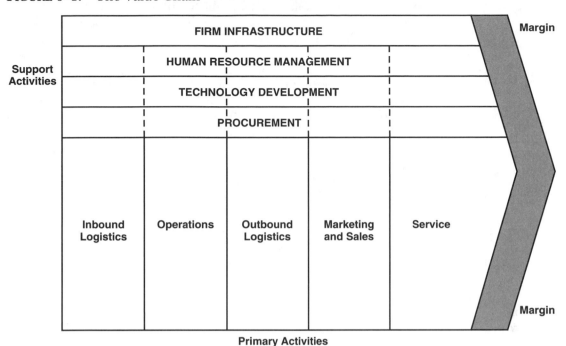

SOURCE: This setup for the value chain was suggested by Michael E. Porter (1985).

firm. To some extent, they can be thought of as the classical managerial functions of the firm, where there is an organizational entity with a manager in charge of a very specific task, and with full balance between authority and responsibility. The support activities, however, are much more pervasive. As their name indicates, their essential role is to provide support not only to the primary activities, but to each other. They are composed of the managerial infrastructure of the firm—which includes all processes and systems to assure proper coordination and accountability—human resource management, technology development, and procurement.

It is easy to see that those support activities are spread out around the whole business organization. The responsibility for financial, human, and technological resources of the business do not reside exclusively with the controller, personnel, and R&D manager, respectively. They are central matters of concern to all of the key managers, regardless of their range of immediate authority. Likewise, procurement is an activity that permeates far beyond the centralized purchasing function.

Perhaps the only point worth stressing is the role that technology is playing in business firms today. Not long ago, technology was regarded as the exclusive province of the R&D managers, not much different from what a manufacturer manager's role is today. Now, particularly with the advent of information technology, this activity is truly pervasive and affects the way to achieve competitive advantage in all of the key managerial tasks of the firm.

Figure 6–2 provides a brief description of both primary and support activities.

Since the value chain is composed of the set of activities performed by the business unit, it provides a very effective way to diagnose the position of the business against its major competitors, and to define the foundation for actions aimed at sustaining a competitive advantage. As opposed to the forces that determine the industry attractiveness to the business, which are largely external and uncontrollable by the firm, the activities of the value chain constitute the foundation of the controllable factors to achieve competitive superiority. Their analysis leads us to identify the critical success factors that are central to compete, and to understand how to develop the unique competencies that provide the basis for sound business leadership.

A final comment has to do with the designation of value. The value generated by a business chain is measured by the total revenues collected by the buyer's payment for the business output. Added value is created whenever the buyer's contribution exceeds the total cost resulting from the completion of all the activities in the chain. The word margin at the end of the chain intends to capture precisely the difference between the total value generated and the aggregated cost of the value activities.

FIGURE 6–2. Definition of Activities in the Value Chain

Primary Activities

Inbound Logistics. Receiving, storing, materials handling, warehousing, inventory control, vehicle scheduling, and returns to suppliers

Operations. Transforming inputs into final product form (e.g., machining, packaging, assembly, equipment maintenance, testing, printing, and facility operations)

Outbound Logistics. Distributing the finished product (e.g., finished goods warehousing, material handling, delivery vehicle operation, order processing, and scheduling)

Marketing and Sales. Induce and facilitate buyers to purchase the product (e.g., advertising, sales force, quoting, channel selection, channel relations, and pricing)

Service. Maintain or enhance value of product after sale (e.g., installation, repair, training, parts supply, and product adjustment)

Support Activities

Procurement. Purchasing of raw materials, supplies, and other consumable items as well as assets

Technology Development. Know-how, procedures, and technological inputs needed in every value chain activity

Human Resource Management. Selection, promotion, and placement; appraisal; rewards; management development; and labor/employee relations

Firm Infrastructure. General management, planning, finance, accounting, legal, government affairs, and quality management

---

Illustration of the Value Chain:
Merck in the Pharmaceutical Industry

The direct illustration of the value chain can be used to summarize in a fairly compact graphical way the competitive positioning of a specific business unit. In Chapter 5, we gave the example of the pharmaceutical industry to summarize the use of Porter's five-forces model. In this section, as a continuation of that illustration, we present Merck's value chain.

Merck & Co., Inc. is the premier firm in its industry. Selected from 1987 to 1993 as the most admired of the Fortune 500 companies in America, Merck is the indisputable global leader in research, manufacturing, and marketing of pharmaceuticals. Although the company is engaged in human and animal health products, as well as specialty chemicals, the human health care business is by far the most important one. This is the business whose value chain is presented in Figure 6–3 on page 122.

Not all of the activities of the value chain are equally important to achieve competitive advantage. Therefore, a central piece of the value chain analysis is to identify the so-called critical success factors, namely, those activities in which the business has to excel to obtain superior performance. What is extraordinary in the pharmaceutical industry is the enormous amount of requirements that are simultaneously demanded for deriving a competitive advantage. The obvious one is superiority in research and development: the drug discovery process is the driving force for performance excellence. However, the process does not limit itself to the development of innovative drugs, but also includes expedient drug approval, and securing proper strategic alliances to extend the base of technological capabilities. In all of these factors, Merck is a genuine leader.

Marketing is an activity as central as R&D for competitive advantage in pharmaceuticals. As we saw in the industry analysis, the power of buyers is shifting and increasing. Major purchasing groups and powerful distributors are concentrating enormous leverage in the purchasing process. Merck has one of the largest and most sophisticated sales forces in the industry, which provides a solid base of strength. Recently, its distribution capabilities have been greatly increased by the acquisition of Medco Containment Services, Inc.

Manufacturing is the third critical activity in pharmaceutical. Not only it is a critical determinant of quality and operational efficiency, but also the conditions of physical facilities are key to obtaining fast drug approval.

To these three activities we have to add the superior quality that Merck has in managerial infrastructure as well as human resources. With this combination of impressive capabilities it is not surprising that Merck emerges as the global leader in its industry.

This summarization, although useful in providing a quick characterization of a business, is of necessity superficial and incomplete. For a comprehensive analysis of competitive advantages, we have to perform a full profiling of competitive positioning. The methodology we recommend for that purpose is covered later in this chapter.

FIGURE 6-3. Merck's Value Chain

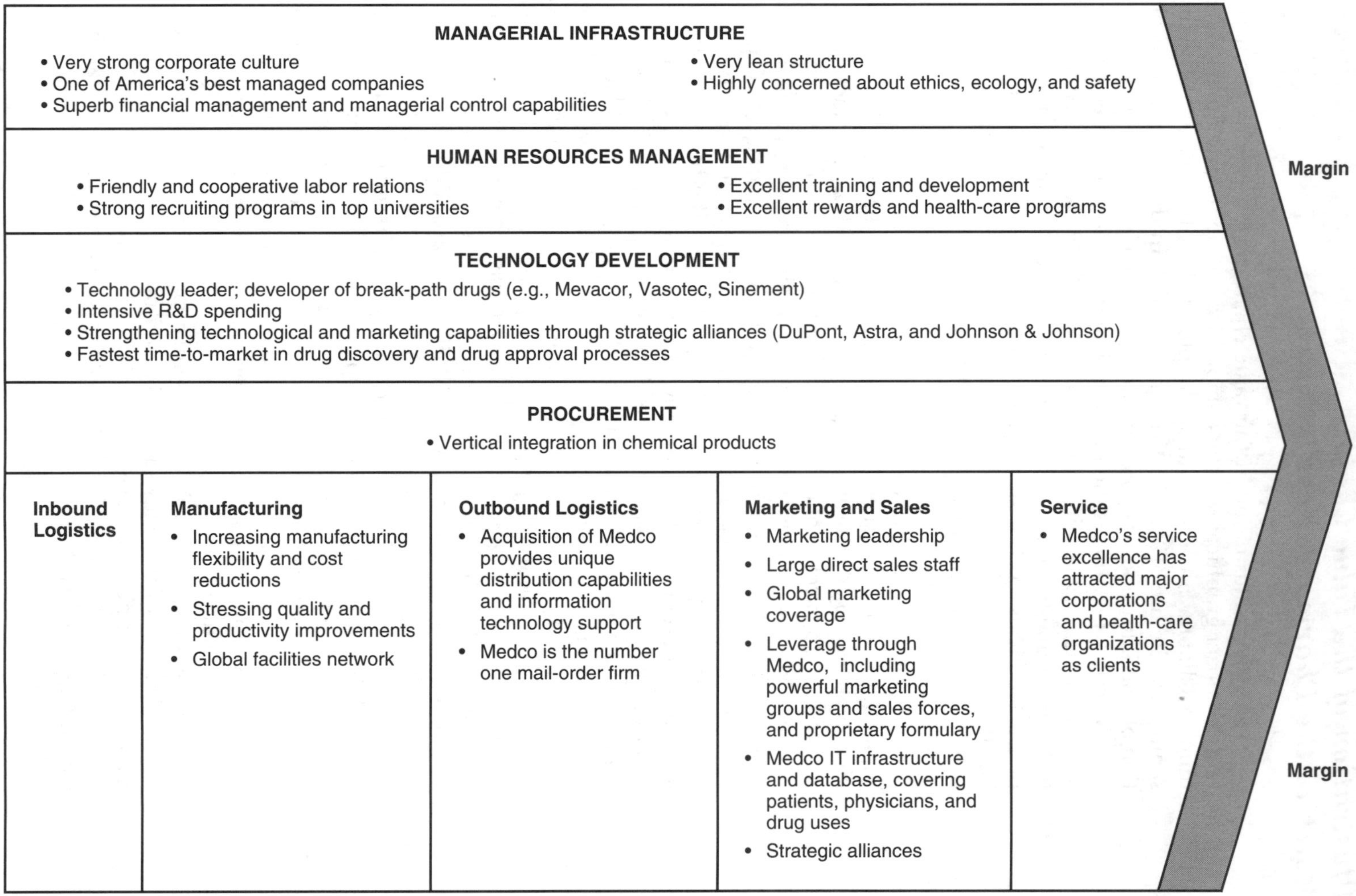

MANAGERIAL INFRASTRUCTURE
- Very strong corporate culture
- One of America's best managed companies
- Superb financial management and managerial control capabilities
- Very lean structure
- Highly concerned about ethics, ecology, and safety

HUMAN RESOURCES MANAGEMENT
- Friendly and cooperative labor relations
- Strong recruiting programs in top universities
- Excellent training and development
- Excellent rewards and health-care programs

TECHNOLOGY DEVELOPMENT
- Technology leader; developer of break-path drugs (e.g., Mevacor, Vasotec, Sinement)
- Intensive R&D spending
- Strengthening technological and marketing capabilities through strategic alliances (DuPont, Astra, and Johnson & Johnson)
- Fastest time-to-market in drug discovery and drug approval processes

PROCUREMENT
- Vertical integration in chemical products

Inbound Logistics	Manufacturing	Outbound Logistics	Marketing and Sales	Service
	• Increasing manufacturing flexibility and cost reductions • Stressing quality and productivity improvements • Global facilities network	• Acquisition of Medco provides unique distribution capabilities and information technology support • Medco is the number one mail-order firm	• Marketing leadership • Large direct sales staff • Global marketing coverage • Leverage through Medco, including powerful marketing groups and sales forces, and proprietary formulary • Medco IT infrastructure and database, covering patients, physicians, and drug uses • Strategic alliances	• Medco's service excellence has attracted major corporations and health-care organizations as clients

Margin

Generic Competitive Strategies

A final concept that Porter introduces in conjunction with the value-chain analysis is that of generic strategies. This concept implies that there are distinct and mutually exclusive ways for a business to achieve competitive advantage. However, these strategies can be applied universally to businesses in a wide variety of industrial settings; thus, the term generic.

Porter states that a business can enjoy a competitive advantage exclusively by one of two basic generic strategies: cost leadership or differentiation. A final understanding of whatever strengths and weaknesses a business could have relative to its competitors can only be explained either by a relative cost advantage or a differentiation capability.

These two generic ways to compete can be combined with the market scope in which the firm attempts to achieve competitive advantage. The resultant alternatives lead to three generic strategies, depending on whether the firm is seeking a competitive position in the overall industry, or whether it will concentrate its activities on a narrow market scope. These generic strategies are: overall cost leadership, differentiation, and or focus. They can be described as follows:

1. Overall cost leadership, by definition, implies that the SBU establishes a position that has a significant cost advantage over all of its competitors in the industry. To achieve such a position, we have to understand first the critical activities in the SBU value chain that are the sources for cost advantage, and then to deploy the necessary capabilities to excel in one or more of them. Cost leadership requires aggressive construction of efficient-scale facilities; vigorous pursuit of cost reductions from experience, tight costs, and overhead control; avoidance of marginal customer accounts, and cost minimization in areas such as R&D, service, sales force, advertising, and so on.[2]

2. Differentiation implies that the business unit has to offer something unique, unmatched by its competitors, and is valued by its buyers beyond offering simply a lower price. Once again it is necessary to understand the potential central sources of differentiation stemming from the activities of the value chain, and the deployment of the necessary skills to enable those potentials to be realized. Differentiation calls for creating something that is perceived *industry-wide* as being unique. Approaches to differentiation can take many forms: design or brand image, technology, features, customer service, dealer network, or other dimensions.[2]

3. Focus consists of concentrating on a particular buyer group, segment of the product line, or geographic market. As with differentiation, focus may take many forms. Although the low-cost and differentiation strategies are aimed at achieving those objectives industry-wide, the entire focus strategy is built around servicing a particular target very well, and each functional policy is developed with this in mind.[2]

Figure 6–4 shows how these strategies relate to the breadth of the strategic scope. As the figure clearly indicates, even when selecting a narrow market

FIGURE 6–4. The Three Generic Strategies

COMPETITIVE ADVANTAGE

		Lower Cost	Differentiation
MARKET SCOPE	Broad	Cost leadership	Differentiation
	Narrow	Cost focus	Differentiation focus

scope the two basic strategies to achieve competitive advantage are cost leadership and differentiation.

What is important to realize is that virtually every activity in the value chain is a potential source for pursuing either cost leadership or differentiation. At the same time, not all of them have the same significance in achieving the desired competitive advantage. Therefore, the process of selecting a competitive position starts with an understanding of the industry structure, the selection of the appropriate generic strategy, and the identification of the crucial activities within the chain that will allow the business to achieve the corresponding sustainable advantage.

Porter is quite adamant in presenting cost leadership and differentiation as the only two ways to compete. He goes further in asserting that seldom, if ever, can a firm achieve these two capabilities simultaneously, because they imply conflicting trade-offs that cannot be overcome. In fact, he argues that if the firm attempts to achieve cost leadership and differentiation at the same time it is likely to be trapped in a mediocre performance, unable to deliver either in a superior way. This is what he labels being *stuck in the middle*. This notion has become a controversial one. Recently, Baden-Fuller and Stopford have joined the many dissenting voices by referring to this as the fallacy of the generic strategy.[3] They claim that the best firms are striving all the time to reconcile the opposites. Consequently, they claim that there are no lasting or enduring generic strategies.

This controversy, to a great extent, is captive of the definitions that Porter has provided to identify the two distinct generic strategies. There is room for only one firm in the cost leadership position and what this firm achieves is a cost reduction with regard to the industry average that allows it to exercise a price discount over the industry price and still make a handsome return. Firms searching for differentiation will spend more than the cost leader, thus incurring an extra cost over the industry average. However, they will demand and obtain a price premium because of nonprice-related value added. This price premium will offset the additional cost, thus also obtaining superior returns. Achieving both cost advantage and obtaining a price premium will require either the use of a different technological base or market imperfections. In either case, the resulting competitive advantage might not be sustainable.

The Engineering Polymers
Example Revisited

In the previous chapter we presented the industry attractiveness analysis for the engineering polymers industry. Now we describe briefly the competitive position of two of its key players.

We have indicated already that GE and DuPont are dominant firms, both domestically and globally. For many years, GE has been experiencing higher growth. As a result of this, GE overtook DuPont in the United States in the mid-1970s, and on a global basis in the mid-1980s. [4]

GE's move into plastics in the early 1960s was a backward integration into materials from their appliance business. A sharp marketing focus and a strategy oriented toward satisfying customer needs was the legacy that came from the business origins. In part, under the leadership of Jack Welch, a Ph.D. chemical engineer and its current CEO, GE achieved dominance in the engineering polymers industry by:

- focusing attention on market needs
- concentratiing on globalization of the markets
- making a commitment to maintain and increase market share
- making a commitment to large investment in production and R&D

Welch's innovative, entrepreneurial, and risk-taking style was vastly different from the stodgy corporate culture that characterized DuPont management. GE's competitive advantage is illustrated in its value chain in Figure 6–5.

On the other hand, DuPont's early formula for success was based on R&D and innovation with an emphasis on the following:

- investment in research
- investment in new products
- obtaining patent protection
- manufacturing products safely and with a high level of quality
- selling everything that could be made at monopoly prices to a waiting market

The stream of inventions became household words, and many of them were plastics and polymers. DuPont created such products as cellophane, nylon, acetal, teflon, dacron, mylar, and many others. The monopolies created, however, attracted the concern of the U.S. government. As a result, the company had several brushes with antitrust situations in the 1950s and 1960s.

With GE's competitive pressures, and with its growth slowing down in the 1970s, DuPont's next step to maintain high returns was to look toward manufacturing. Investment in technology, as well as development of plants exploiting maximum-scale economies and locational advantages in foreign countries, posi-

FIGURE 6–5. GE's Competitive Advantage: Sources of Differentiation

Firm Infrastructure	Top Management Support (Welch Is CEO)						Margin
Human Resources Management	• Superior training			• Use of commission sales incentives			
Technology Development		• Best alloy technology		• Best applications engineering support • Best market research			
Procurement				• Excellent product positioning			
		• High-quality production • Excellent conformance to specifications	• Flexible delivery capability	• Extensive advertising • Strong focus on high growth areas	• High sales force coverage • Strong personal relationships • Extensive credit (GE Credit)	• Easy-to-use products • Extensive training of customers	Margin
	Inbound Logistics	Operations	Outbound Logistics	Marketing	Sales	Service	

• In GE's value chain, the source of differentiation in recent years has primarily been in the marketing/sales area.
• In their future strategy, they expect to emphasize technology development and investment in R&D.
• As they begin to face real competition in their products, they will begin to focus more on generating cost advantage as well.

SOURCE: Maceda (1988).

tioned DuPont as the low-cost manufacturer of its products. Figure 6–6 illustrates the sources of DuPont's competitive advantage through a value-chain analysis.

A close inspection and comparison of the value chains prevailing in the current situation, and shown in Figures 6–5 and 6–6, allow us to draw an interesting conclusion from this case: we observe a convergence of the firms' strategies. DuPont, the technology company, is being forced to enhance its marketing capabilities; and GE, the marketing company, is being driven toward an improvement of its technological skills.

There is a certain danger when the industry players begin to imitate themselves. The essence of a successful strategy is to separate oneself from competitors. When all the firms are pursuing the same strategy, a self-defeating situation emerges. Without a differentiating ability, the opportunities for superior returns are eliminated and the whole industry attractiveness is debilitated.

FIGURE 6–6. DuPont's Competitive Advantage: Sources of Cost Leadership

	Inbound Logistics	Operations	Outbound Logistics	Marketing	Sales	Service	
Firm Infrastructure	History and Tradition of DuPont in Plastics and Materials						**Margin**
Human Resources Management	• Paternalistic culture guarantees security, attracts highest-quality scientists			• Best training, integrating sales and technical service			
Technology Development	• Best polymer R&D • Global scale R&D Technology			• Extensive commitment to process development. Recognized for R&D of customers' manufacturing processes			
Procurement	• Lowest-cost raw materials			• Quality image			
	• Direct supply	• Largest scale economies • Highest product physical properties • High yield, low defects	• Extensive warehouse network • Rapid delivery guaranteed	• Quality image • Horizontal integration of marketing with other DuPont SBUs	• Strong sales force	• Replacement guaranteed • Best customer training • Highest technical service coverage	**Margin**

- In manufacturing, DuPont has developed the lowest cost position through exploitation of the learning curve. There is also extensive horizontal and vertical integration of products across different divisions and departments, since most materials have the same building blocks, and DuPont is basic in almost every area.
- The majority of their advantages have been in research, technology, and manufacturing. The current strategy is to develop strength in the marketing and sales area to compete better with GE.

SOURCE: Maceda (1988).

A Process for Profiling the Competitive Positioning of a Business: An Illustration

We have already discussed the basic concepts behind the task of defining the competitive position for a business. We propose now a systematic and disciplined approach to guiding a manager through all the necessary steps to perform the internal scrutiny at the business level. This process leads to the identification of the major strengths and weaknesses of the firm against its most relevant competitors. We illustrate this methodology using the case of P&G Detergent Business in Europe. This is a continuation of the case we used to illustrate how to profile the industry atttractiveness. These two processess are the inputs for defining the business strategy.

STEP 1: IDENTIFICATION OF THE MOST RELEVANT COMPETITORS

A relevant competitor is one who fulfills one or more of the following conditions: From a market point of view,

- it has a high market share.
- it has experienced a sustained market growth.
- it earns high levels of profitability with regard to the industry average.
- it has demonstrated an aggressive competitive attitude against your entire business or important segments of your business.
- it has a highly vulnerable position against your own competitive actions.

From a functional point of view,

- it has the lowest cost structure.
- it has the strongest technical base.
- it has the strongest marketing.
- it offers the best product quality.
- it shows the highest level of vertical integration.
- it exhibits the highest level of capacity utilization.

Any sound strategy has to be supported by a thorough understanding of the firm's most relevant competitors, since a business strategy aims at achieving a sustainable advantage over them. Unless this is derived from a sound intelligence gathering, we would be playing the business game blindly. Figure 6–7

FIGURE 6–7. The Key Competition of P&G Detergent Business in Europe in the Early 1990s

Relevant Competitors

Competitors	Market Point of View			
	Last year's sales	3 years average growth rate of sales	3 years average profitability (ROE)	Last year's market share
Unilever	1748.0	15.0	High	21.0
Henkel	1203.0	15.0	Average	15.0
Colgate-Palmolive	577.0	10.0	Low	7.0
Kao	0.0	0.0	Very Low	0.0
Other competitors	3037.0	11.0	Average	37.0
P&G	1644.0	16.0	High	20.0
Total for the Market	8209.0	11.2	Average	100.0

provides the list of the key competitors of P&G in the Detergent Business in Europe, with a few comparative indicators. As before, this is just an illustration; therefore the numbers should not be taken as accurate.

Normally, it is important to collect as much quantitative and qualitative information as required to construct a well-rounded overall competitive profile. The financial statement analysis framework, which we discussed in Chapter 5, constitutes a sound first step in this direction.

STEP 2: SELECTING THE CRITICAL SUCCESS FACTORS

The value-chain concept provides a valuable framework for organizing the tasks undertaken at the business level. It serves as a guideline to perform a diagnosis of current strengths and weaknesses, and to identify the capabilities to be mobilized in order to achievie competitive advantage. However, its categories are still too broadly defined. They do not incorporate enough detailed content to facilitate the selection of the critical success factors leading to the identification of key strengths and weaknesses of the SBU.

An approach to conducting the internal scrutiny at the business level is to look at the business in its entirety from a very broad perspective. As with the environmental scan, the top business managers are called upon to provide an initial overall assessment of the business position. The group is asked, as a first step, to identify the central competitive skills that are the foundation for determining the business position in its industry. In subsequent steps, the managers are asked to agree on a diagnosis of the current situation, and to define collectively a desired state of the future competitive positioning of the business.

We recommend classifying the activities of the value chain into seven different categories that are slightly different than those proposed by Porter:

- Managerial Infrastructure
- Finance
- Human Resources Management
- Technology
- Procurement
- Manufacturing
- Marketing and Sales

The first activity of Porter's value chain, the Firm Infrastructure, is divided into two components: Managerial Infrastructure, which includes the administrative processes of the firm, organizational structure, culture, and leadership capabilities; and Finance, a key centralized function that deserves separate attention. The activity referred to as Manufacturing includes Inbound Logistics, Operations, and Outbound Logistics. Manufacturing should be interpreted as the activity linked to the movement, production, and delivery of the products and services generated by the business. Finally, the activity referred to as Marketing and Sales includes these two functions as well as Service. Under these seven categories we provide a comprehensive list of attributes to be analyzed for competitive profiling. These lists should be modified to adjust them to fit the particular circumstances of each individual business unit.

STEP 3. COMPETITIVE PROFILING OF YOUR BUSINESS AGAINST EACH OF ITS MOST RELEVANT COMPETITORS

The internal scrutiny is a much more comprehensive task than the environmental scanning. In the latter, we limit ourselves to analizing a single industry. In the former, we have to compare our business against each of the most relevant competitors. We will undertake this task by showing the competitive profile of P&G against Unilever, its toughest competitor. The profile is done using the seven categories of critical success factors outlined above.

Competitive profiling assesses the strengths of your business now and in the future. When addressing the current state, we try to be as objective as possible in describing our competitive position against each of the key competitors. However, when addressing the future, we should be both realistic—in terms of our capabilities to improve our relative position—and challenging enough to mobilize the energies of the business to realize a superior performance. This is not a forecasting exercise, because we are not dealing with totally uncontrollable events; this is a commitment to action and a challenge to achieve higher levels of excellence.

Competitive Assessment of Managerial Infrastructure.
P&G has enjoyed a competitive advantage due to better planning and control systems, and a more appropriate global organizational structure. Unilever is matching these strengths. P&G is attempting to develop a stronger transnational organization, as well as better global communication and information systems (Figure 6–8).

Competitive Assessment of Finance.
The strengths of P&G and Unilever are fairly equally matched when it comes to financial capabilities. P&G has a slight edge on the management of its pension plans, while Unilever enjoys a minor advantage in its financial organization (Figure 6–9).

Competitive Assessment of Human Resources Management.
P&G's advantages stem from a better reward system than Unilever, particularly in the area of stock options for its top executives. On the other hand, Unilever has better international training and development capabilities (Figure 6–10).

Competitive Assessment of Technology .

P&G has maintained a slight advantage over Unilever as the result of a more effective transfer of product and process technologies across their businesses. Significant emphasis is being placed on improvements in new products development—particularly in biodegradeable and ecologically friendly products and packaging innovations (Figure 6–11).

Competitive Assessment of Procurement.

The capabilities of both firms are exactly even in these activities (Figure 6-12).

Competitive Assessment of Manufacturing.

The competitive position of P&G against Unilever in this area is quite similar. The only sources of advantage are a higher degree of automation and a better responsiveness in the timing of new products (Figure 6–13).

Competitive Assessment of Marketing and Sales.

The comparison of P&G against Unilever shows a strong distribution network, with a high level of automation and point-of-sales intelligence. However, Unilever is an extraordinary competitor with remarkable marketing capabilities, and it is difficult to surpass (Figure 6–14).

Summary of the Competitive Assessment against Each Competitor.

After completing the assessment of each critical success factor, this step summarizes the overall competitive position of P&G against each of its most relevant competitors. The figure shows the profile against Unilever (Figure 6–15).

The Ranking of All Competitors.

After the competitive profile has been completed for each of the most relevant competitors, it is possible to make a summary of their ranking. This is shown in Figure 6–16. Notice that P&G has emerged as the leading competitor, followed by Unilever, Henkel, Colgate-Palmolive, and finally Kao.

Strengths and Weaknesses of Each Competitor.

This step provides a qualitative statement of the strengths and weaknesses of each competitor, as well as the issues to be addressed by P&G to either neutralize their strength or exploit their weaknesses. We have presented only the case of Unilever as an illustration of this step. Similar charts should be prepared for all relevant competitors (Figure 6–17).

FIGURE 6–8. Competitive Assessment of Managerial Infrastructure—P&G vs. Unilever—Detergent Business in Europe

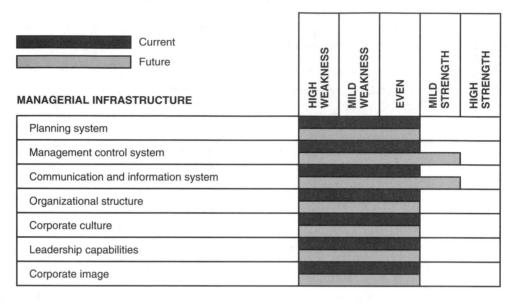

FIGURE 6–9. Competitive Assessment of Finance—P&G vs. Unilever—Detergent Business in Europe

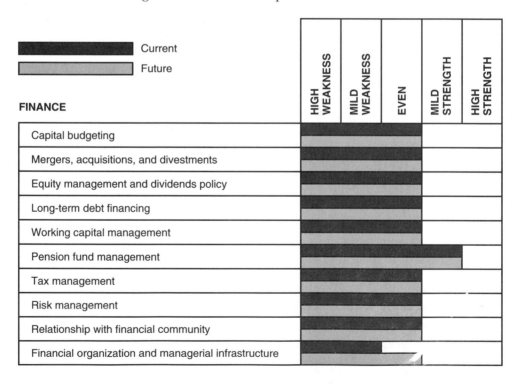

FIGURE 6–10. Competitive Assessment of Human Resource Management—P&G vs. Unilever—Detergent Business in Europe

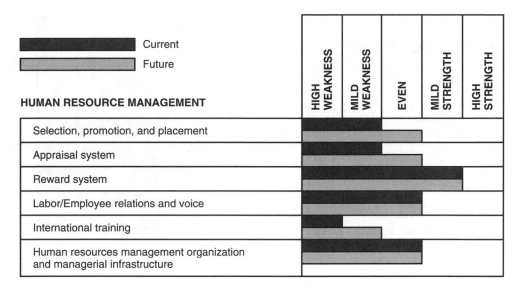

FIGURE 6–11. Competitive Assessment of Technology—P&G vs. Unilever—Detergent Business in Europe

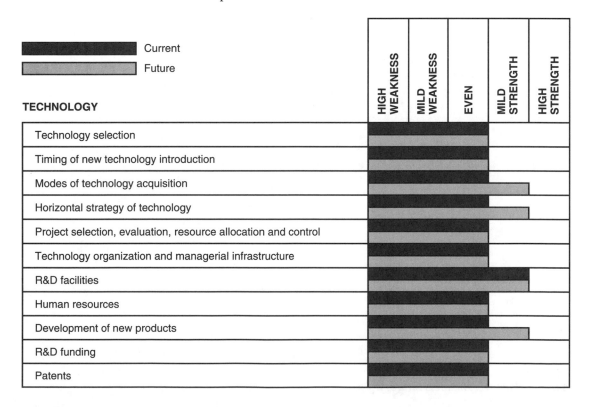

FIGURE 6–12. Competitive Assessment of Procurement—P&G vs. Unilever—Detergent Business in Europe

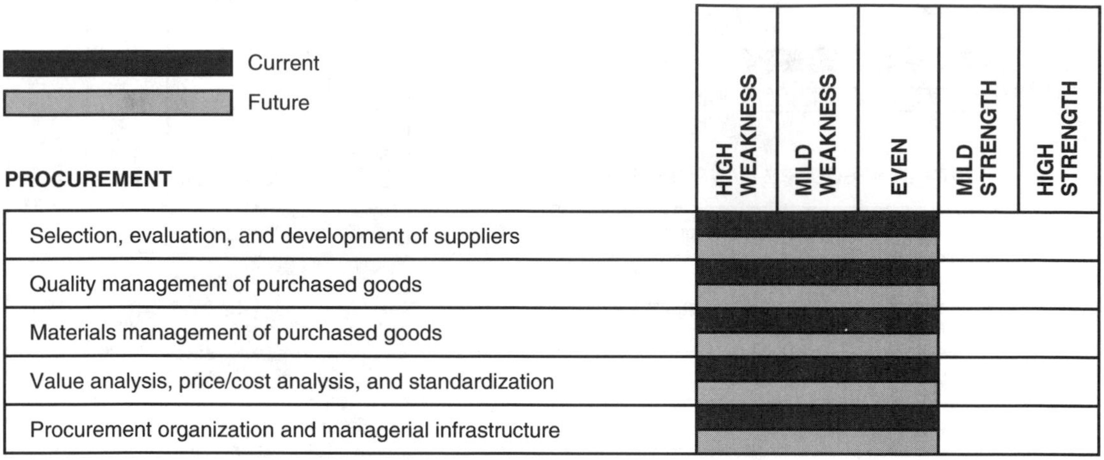

Legend: Current (black bar), Future (gray bar)

PROCUREMENT	HIGH WEAKNESS	MILD WEAKNESS	EVEN	MILD STRENGTH	HIGH STRENGTH
Selection, evaluation, and development of suppliers	██████	██████	██████		
Quality management of purchased goods	██████	██████	██████		
Materials management of purchased goods	██████	██████	██████		
Value analysis, price/cost analysis, and standardization	██████	██████	██████		
Procurement organization and managerial infrastructure	██████	██████	██████		

FIGURE 6–13. Competitive Assessment of Manufacturing—P&G vs. Unilever—Detergent Business in Europe

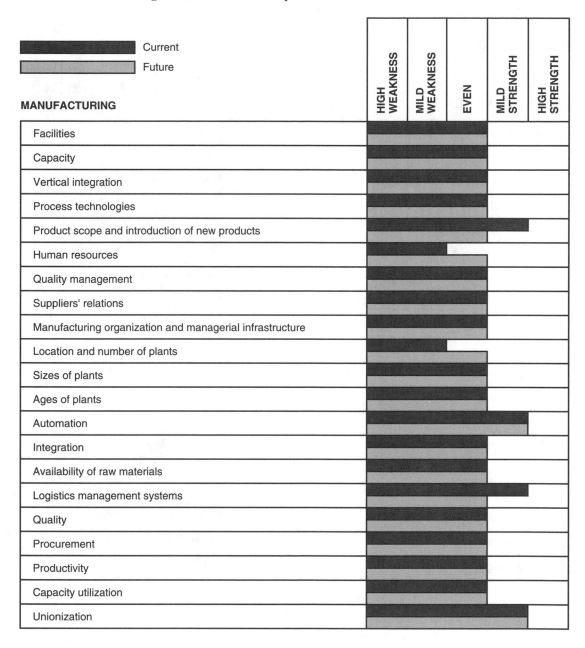

FIGURE 6–14. Competitive Assessment of Marketing and Sales—P&G vs. Unilever—Detergent Business in Europe

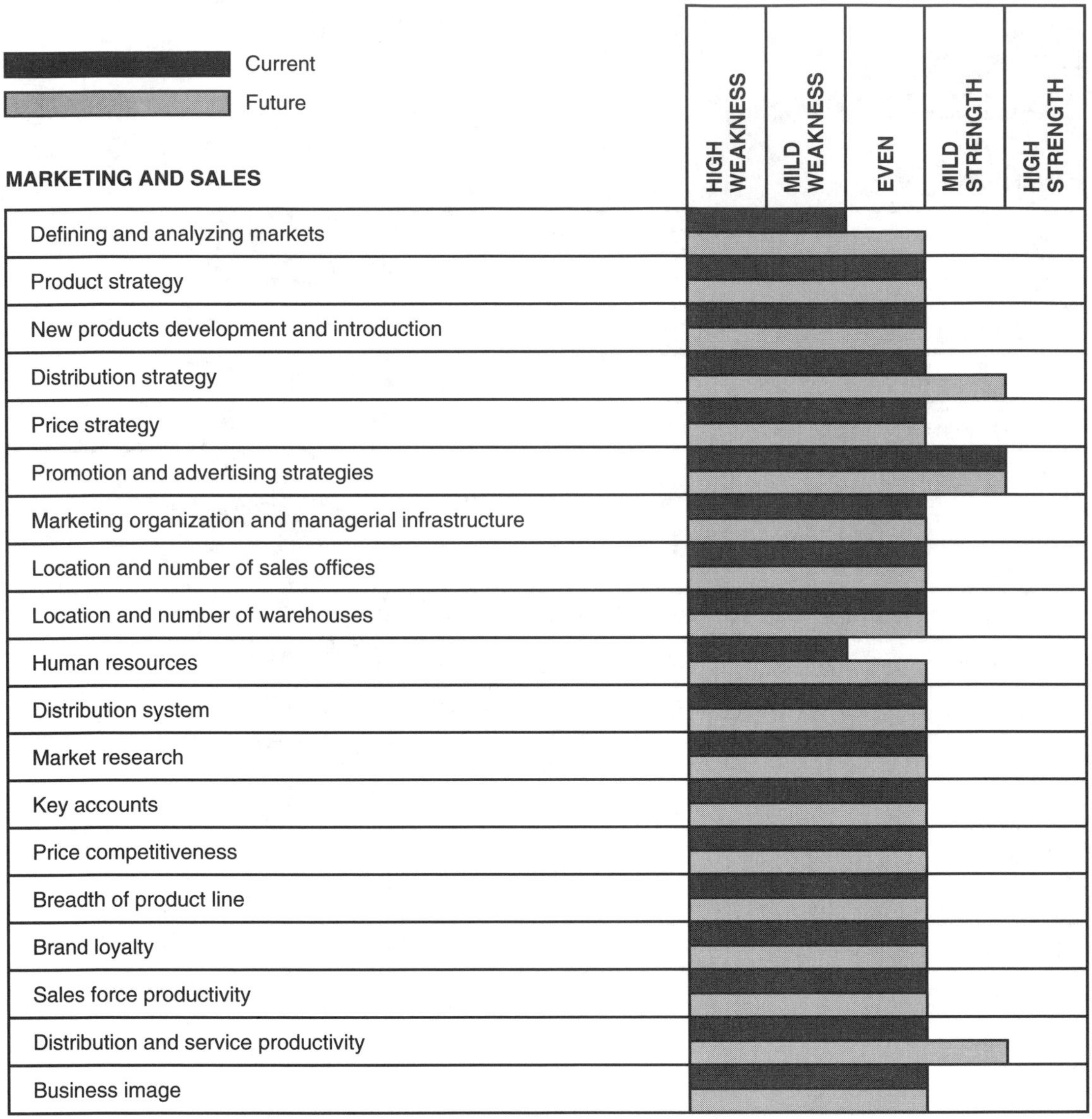

Legend:
- ▮ Current
- ▮ Future

MARKETING AND SALES	HIGH WEAKNESS	MILD WEAKNESS	EVEN	MILD STRENGTH	HIGH STRENGTH
Defining and analyzing markets					
Product strategy					
New products development and introduction					
Distribution strategy					
Price strategy					
Promotion and advertising strategies					
Marketing organization and managerial infrastructure					
Location and number of sales offices					
Location and number of warehouses					
Human resources					
Distribution system					
Market research					
Key accounts					
Price competitiveness					
Breadth of product line					
Brand loyalty					
Sales force productivity					
Distribution and service productivity					
Business image					

FIGURE 6–15. Summary of the Competitive Assessment of P&G vs. Unilever— Detergent Business in Europe

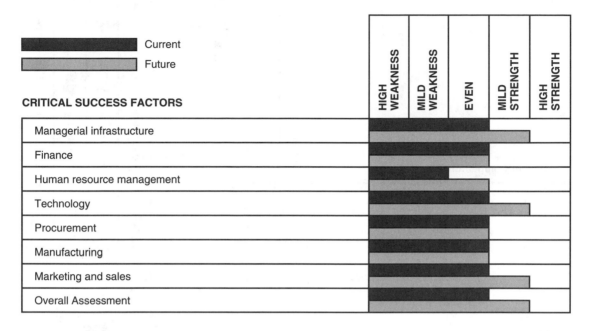

FIGURE 6–16. Ranking of All Competitors—P&G Detergent Business in Europe

Relevant Competitors / Critical Success Factors	Managerial Infrastructure	Finance	Human Resource Management	Technology	Procurement	Manufacturing	Marketing and Sales	Overall Ranking of Each Competitor
Unilever	E	E	–	E	E	E	E	2
	+	E	E	+	E	E	+	
Henkel	E	+	+	+	+	E	E	3
	+	+	+	++	++	+	+	
Colgate-Palmolive	+	+	+	+	+	+	+	4
	+	+	+	++	+	++	+	
Kao	++	+	+	+	++	++	++	5
	++	+	++	+	++	++	++	
P&G								1

Key:
- ++ P&G is much stronger than the competitor
- \+ P&G is stronger than the competitor
- E P&G is even with the competitor
- – P&G is weaker than the competitor
- – – P&G is much weaker than the competitor

FIGURE 6–17. Strengths and Weaknesses—Unilever Detergent Business in Europe

Strengths
- European firm
- Starting to produce in one factory in Eastern Europe
- Already distributing in many Eastern European countries
- High price competitiveness
- Good managerial infrastructure
- Good R&D
- Strong brand loyalties and identities

Weaknesses
- Weak in selected geographies for some specific products
- Seemingly poor R&D-to-marketing link

Issues to Be Addressed
- Unilever has more knowledge of the European market
- Unilever is ahead in the Eastern European markets

STEP 4. IDENTIFICATION OF STRENGTHS AND WEAKNESSES OF YOUR BUSINESS

By completing the competitive profiles of your business against each of the most relevant competitors, ranking them, and examining their inherent strengths and weaknesses, we have developed a strong base from which to catalog our own set of strengths and weaknesses. We accomplish this with the following two tasks.

In Figure 6–18 we present the Overall Competitive Assessment of P&G, which identifies its strengths and weaknesses in each of the critical success factors categories. Notice that we switch from a five-point scale to a three-point scale: low, medium, and high strength. This will allow the use of the Industry-Attractiveness/Business-Strength Matrix to assess the strength of the firm's business portfolio, and to suggest guidance for resource allocation and strategic actions. P&G has a competitive advantage, which results primarily from the quality of its human resources and managerial infrastructure, its superior technology, and its marketing capabilities.

Figure 6–19 on page 140 provides the final list of strengths and weaknesses in the case of P&G.

It is an obvious assertion that an effective business strategy should reinforce the strengths and correct the weaknesses observed at the end of this process. Without denying the importance of this conclusion, we should go further than this.

FIGURE 6–18. Overall Competitive Assessment—P&G Detergent Business in Europe

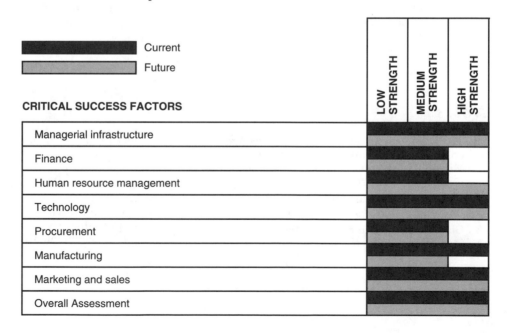

FIGURE 6–19. Strengths and Weaknesses—P&G Detergent Business in Europe

---

Strengths

- High brand recognition
- High-quality products
- Strong environmental awareness
- Rapid product introduction across markets
- High employee commitment
- Outstanding R&D capacity
- Strong links with distribution channels

Weaknesses

- Weak in responding to local consumer needs
- Lack of manufacturing and distribution in Eastern Europe
- Not recognized as the environmental leader

NOTE: This is not an official document. It is an illustration drawn from public sources.

The exhaustive competitive profiling that has been completed should give us a comprehensive understanding of the necessary capabilities the firm has to develop to truly achieve sustainable advantage. The final product of this analysis allows us to detect the existing and desired core competencies that distinguish ourselves from the rest of our competitors. The essence of business strategy is trying to be different; in other words, separating ourselves from competitors rather than imitating them. This will give us a genuine claim for business leadership, and provide the basis for achieving superior performance.

Notes

1. The value chain as a way of achieving competitive advantage is examined in Michael E. Porter, *Competitive Advantage* (New York: The Free Press, 1985).

2. These definitions are adapted from Porter, *Competitive Advantage* (1985).

3. Charles Baden-Fuller and John M. Stopford, *Rejuvenating the Mature Business: The Competitive Challenge* (London: Routledge, 1992) .

4. The presentation of the engineering polymers industry follows Emmanuel P. Maceda, "Strategic Analysis: DuPont Company, Engineering Polymers Division," unpublished student paper. Sloan School of Management, MIT, 1988.

7

The Formulation of the Business Strategy

All of the analyses conducted so far—the mission of the business, the environmental scan to determine industry attractiveness, and the internal scrutiny to identify competitive strengths—should lead to an intelligent formulation of the business strategy. This is captured in Figure 3–1 which describes the fundamental elements in the definition of a business strategy.

A business strategy is a well-coordinated set of action programs aimed at securing a sustainable competitive advantage. These action programs should respond to the desired changes in the business mission, properly address the opportunities and threats revealed by the environmental scanning process, and reinforce the strengths and neutralize the weaknesses uncovered in the internal scrutiny.

The business programs are defined at two different levels of specificity: broad action programs typically covering a multiyear planning horizon, which are normally understood to represent the long-term strategic objectives of the SBU; and specific action programs, covering a six- to eighteen-month period, which represent the tactical support needed for the realization of the strategic objectives.

These programs, broad and specific, often involve functional commitments, transforming a business strategy in the articulation of properly integrated multifunctional activities. Furthermore, the final output of the business strategy is translated into a budget. This is an important document, because it represents an agreement reached by the key managers of the business and becomes the yardstick by which to measure their performance. The budget is the bridge between the strategic planning process—which defines the action programs—and the management control process—which make the managers accountable for the implementation of those programs.

A Process for Formulating Business Strategy: An Illustration

We start this stage with a broad understanding of all of the relevant issues—external as well as internal—that are central to enhancing the business performance. Now we move from reflection into action. Formulating the business strategy implies defining the managerial agenda with a set of concrete, action-driven programs.

Step 1. Positioning the Business in the Industry-Attractiveness / Business-Strength Matrix

A useful tool to summarize a critical output of our previous analysis is the Industry-Attractiveness/Business-Strength Matrix, which is presented in Figure 7–1 for the case of P&G Detergent in Europe. This matrix captures in a graphical display the competitive standing of the business unit in the two critical

FIGURE 7–1. Positioning in Industry Attractiveness – Business Strength Matrix—P&G Detergents in Europe

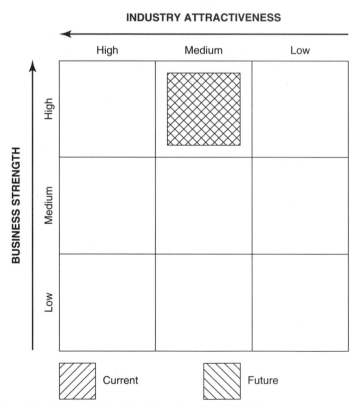

NOTE: This is not an official document. It is an illustration drawn from public sources.
In this example the current and future positions overlay in the same cell.

dimensions: Industry Attractiveness (captured in the Overall Assessment of Industry Attractiveness in Figure 5–15), and Business Strength (captured in the Overall Competitive Assessment in 6–18).

There are some useful implications that emerge from the current and future positions of the business unit in this matrix. One is the direction of change that this business is expected to follow during the planning horizon being considered. In the P&G example, the analysis did not reveal any change in the business's position. That implies that we are neither expecting a change in industry attractiveness nor in the competitive strength of P&G. The lack of mobility should not be interpreted as a lack of challenge, since retaining the leadership position is in itself, a demanding task.

Second, depending on where the business resides, the Industry-Attractiveness Business Strength Matrix suggests what is referred to as a *generic strategy*; namely, a course of action that is congruent with the attractiveness of the industry and the competitive strength of the businesses within that industry. The nine generic strategies associated with the matrix are presented in Figure 7–2. Notice that the P&G position has the following recommendations: identify growth segments, invest strongly, and maintain position elsewhere. Implicit in this statement is the notion that a "medium" industry attractiveness requires

FIGURE 7–2. Generic Strategies Associated with the Industry Attractiveness – Business Strength Matrix

INDUSTRY ATTRACTIVENESS

	High	Medium	Low
High	Grow Seek dominance Maximize investment	Identify growth segments Invest strongly Maintain position elsewhere	Maintain overall position Seek cash flow Invest at maintenance level
Medium	Evaluate potential for leadership via segmentation Identify weaknesses Build strengths	Identify growth segments Specialize Invest selectively	Prune lines Minimize investment Position to divest
Low	Specialize Seek niches Consider acquisitions	Specialize Seek niches Consider exit	Trust leader's statesmanship Sic on competitors' cash generators Time exit and divest

BUSINESS STRENGTH

SOURCE: Reproduced by permission of A. T. Kearney, Inc., Chicago, Illinois.

some selectivity, because not every segment of the industry is equally attractive. The generic strategy—both current and future—should only be regarded as a point of reference for the subsequent definition of action programs.

A final inference from this matrix has to do with managing the portfolio of the different businesses of the firm. The notion is that not every business is equally deserving of the scarce resources of the firm. Therefore, different priorities should be used to recognize the distinct potentials of these businesses. Figure 7–3 suggests a list of different priorities consistent with the various positions of a business unit in the portfolio matrix. In the case of P&G, we selected "build gradually" as the appropriate priority for resource allocation.

FIGURE 7–3. Business Strategic Priorities Emerging from the Portfolio Approach to Strategic Planning

---

Build aggressively: The business is in a strong position in a highly attractive, fast-growing industry, and management wants to build share as rapidly as possible. This role is usually assigned to an SBU early in the life cycle, especially when there is little doubt as to whether this rapid growth will be sustained.

Build gradually: The business is in a strong position in a very attractive, moderate-growth industry, and management wants to build share, or there is rapid growth but doubt as to whether this rapid growth will be sustained.

Build selectively: The business has good position in a highly attractive industry and wants to build share where it feels it has strength, or can develop strength, to do so.

Maintain aggressively: The business is in a strong position in a currently attractive industry, and management is determined to aggressively maintain that position.

Maintain selectively: Either the business is in a strong position in an industry that is getting less attractive, or the business is in a moderate position in a highly attractive industry. Management wishes to exploit the situation by maximizing the profitability benefits of selectively serving where it best can do so, but with minimum additional resource deployments.

Prove viability: The business is in a less-than-satisfactory position in a less attractive industry. If the business can provide resources for use elsewhere, management may decide to retain it, but without additional resource support. The onus is on the business to justify retention.

Divest-Liquidate: Neither the business nor the industry has any redeeming features. Barring major exit barriers, the business should be divested.

Competitive harasser: This is a business with a poor position in either an attractive or highly attractive industry, and where competitors with a good position in the industry also compete with the company in other industries. The role of competitive harasser is to attack sporadically or continuously the competitor's position, not necessarily with the intention of long-run success. The objective is to distract the competition from other areas, deny them from revenue business, or use the business to cross-parry when the competition attacks an important sister business of the strategic aggressor.

SOURCE: Adapted from Ian C. MacMillan, "Seizing Competitive Initiative." Reprinted by permission of *The Journal of Business Strategy*, Spring 1982. Copyright, Warren, Gorham, & Lamont, Inc., Boston, MA. All rights reserved.

Step 2. Definition of Broad Action Programs

A key requirement for an effective formulation of a business strategy is the consistency between the strategic action programs—to be generated at this stage of the process—and the results from the previous analyses—challenges from changes in the mission (Chapter 4); opportunities and threats emerging from the environmental scan (Chapter 5); and the strengths and weaknesses resulting from the internal scrutiny (Chapter 6).

The action programs are stated at two different levels of aggregation. First, we define the full set of broad action programs, which should cover the complete strategic agenda of the business unit. There should not be too many—thus the connotation of broad—and should permit an appropriate coordination of the many tasks that are conducted at the business level. The acid test for their correct formulation is whether they are comprehensive enough—meaning that they respond to all of the key issues uncovered in our strategic analysis—and whether they are challenging enough so as to stretch the organization to a higher level of performance. Each broad action program, in turn, will be supported with a set of specific action programs which carry the detailed tasks to be accomplished. Broad and specific action programs are equivalent to strategies and tactics, a terminology often used in military and business contexts.

There is an easy way to assure, or at least to check, how comprehensive is the full set of broad action programs. This is done by reflecting on the requirements imposed by the three major pieces of our analysis: the challenges emerging from changes in product, market, and geographical scopes, and unique competencies (Figure 7–4 on page 146); the opportunities and threats from the environmental scan (Figure 7–5 on page 147), and the strengths and weaknesses from the internal scrutiny (Figures 7–6 on page 148). The figures remind us of the major conclusions reached at the end of these three stages of the strategic audit, which should be important inputs to the process of generating broad action programs. In the P&G case, we end up with eight broad action programs, which are listed in Figure 7–7 on page 149 and appear as columns in the previous figures. Defining and linking broad action programs should be done concurrently.

The dots in Figures 7–4 to 7–6 simply indicate which broad action program is responding to the various requirements. The test for comprehensiveness becomes straightforward with these aids.

There is some valuable information that should be used in the characterization of each broad action program.

- *Description*: to state the purpose and goal of the broad action program.
- *Responsible manager* : a single individual who will be responsible for overseeing the implementation of the broad action program.
- *Key indicators for management control* : stable factors used to assess the performance of the business.
- *First major milestone description* : the first tangible output of the broad action program.
- *First major milestone date* : the date at which the milestone should be reached.

FIGURE 7–4. Linkages of Broad Action Programs with Changes in the Mission—P&G Detergent Business in Europe

Definition of Broad Action Programs	Expand geographical penetration	Push existing environmentally friendly products	Develop distribution channels in Eastern Europe	Exploit distribution channels	Environmental leadership in product and packaging	Strengthen relations with largest distribution chains	Develop, produce and market convenience products	Develop transnational P&G organization in Europe
Challenges from Changes in Product Scope								
Increase penetration of concentrated powder products	●				●	●		
Increase penetration of conditioner lines (high margin)	●					●		
Keep traditional detergents in less affluent countries		●						
Introduce refill packs to meet environmental concerns					●			
Focus on household cleaners product lines	●							
Develop and test detergent-conditioner and bleach							●	
Develop environmentally friendly fabric conditioners					●			
Challenges from Changes in Market Scope								
Strengthen relationship with largest distribution channels						●		
Target men as a user of detergents	●	●			●			
Target higher-income families with convenient products	●	●			●			
Focus marketing efforts on environmental concerns		●			●			
Target one person family units with single use packaging							●	
Challenges from Changes in Geographical Scope								
Develop a strong position in Spain, Portugal, and Italy	●	●			●	●	●	
Enter strongly most affluent Eastern European countries			●	●				
Distribution of products in formerly communist countries			●					
Challenges from Changes in Unique Competencies								
Move from multinational to transnational organizations								●
R&D for environmentally safe products and packages					●		●	
Develop local marketing expertise		●			●		●	●
Image of leadership in concern for the environment		●			●			
Alliances for distribution in countries without presence			●					

NOTE: This is not an official document. It is an illustration drawn from public sources.

FIGURE 7–5. Linkages of Broad Action Programs with Opportunities and Threats—P&G Detergent Business in Europe

Definition of Broad Action Programs	Expand geographical penetration	Push existing environmentally friendly products	Develop distribution channels in Eastern Europe	Exploit distribution channels	Environmental leadership in product and packaging	Strengthen relations with largest distribution chains	Develop, produce and market convenience products	Develop a transnational P&G organization in Europe
▼ Key Opportunities								
High brand recognition	●	●		●		●	●	
Little or no substitute products for detergents								
Lower rivalry and new opportunities (less competitors)	●	●	●	●	●	●	●	
Economies of scale in common European markets						●		
Growth opportunities in new Eastern European markets			●	●				
Creation of partnerships in distribution						●		
Innovations to meet stringent environmental regulations					●		●	
Globalization of tastes and fashions	●	●			●	●	●	
▼ Key Threats								
Very low final consumer loyalty and switching costs		●			●	●	●	
Increase in environmental concerns and regulations		●			●			
Increased power of the distribution channel						●		
Dependence on the oil market								
Appearance of generic and channel-specific brand names						●		
Possible KAO entry	●	●				●	●	

NOTE: This is not an official document. It is an illustration drawn from public sources.

FIGURE 7–6.   Linkages of Broad Action Programs with Strengths and Weaknesses—P&G Detergent Business in Europe

Definition of Broad Action Programs	Expand geographical penetration	Push existing environmentally friendly products	Develop distribution channels in Eastern Europe	Exploit distribution channels	Environmental leadership in product and packaging	Strengthen relations with largest distribution chains	Develop, produce and market convenience products	Develop a transnational P&G organization in Europe
▼ Strengths								
High brand recognition	●	●					●	
High quality products	●	●	●			●	●	
Strong environmental awareness					●		●	
Rapid product introduction across markets					●		●	
High employee commitment								●
Outstanding R&D capacity					●		●	
Strong links with distribution channels						●		
▼ Weaknesses								
Weak in responding to local consumer needs		●			●	●	●	●
Lack of manufacturing and distribution in Eastern Europe			●	●				
Not recognized as the environmental leader		●			●		●	

NOTE: This is not an official document. It is an illustration drawn from public sources.

FIGURE 7–7. List of Broad Action Programs—P&G Detergent Business in Europe

▼	Expand geographical penetration by increasing market share in selected countries
▼	Push existing environmentally friendly products in all markets
▼	Develop distribution channels in Eastern Europe
▼	Exploit existing distribution channels
▼	Develop environmental leadership in product and packaging
▼	Strengthen relationship with largest distribution chains
▼	Develop, produce, and market convenience products
▼	Develop a transnational organization within the context of P&G Europe

NOTE: This is not an official document. It is an illustration drawn from public sources.

Figure 7-8 gives the definition of the first broad action program of the P&G Detergent Business in Europe: "Expand geographical penetration by increasing market share in selected countries."

Step 3. Definition of Specific Action Programs

Each broad action program is supported by a set of specific action programs that help provide a sense of concreteness to the strategic managerial work. Specific action programs are tangible, short-term tasks that can be precisely identified, monitored, and evaluated.

Figure 7-9 lists all the specific action programs that support the first broad action program of the P&G Detergent Business in Europe: "Expand geographical penetration by increasing market share in selected countries." The five action programs listed in the figure address those countries that, in the geographical scope part of the mission statement, were given the highest priority (see Figure 4–5).

The definition of a specific action program includes the following information:

- *Description* : a narrative of the program activities.
- *Statement of priority* : conveys how critical the action program is to the business. The three priority categories used are in Figure 7–10.
- *Statement of costs* : estimation of the costs associated with implementing the action programs. The figures should be broken down into the three components of strategic funds: investments, increases in working capital, and developmental expenses. This subject is discussed in the next step, when defining the budget for the business unit.

FIGURE 7–8. Definition of Broad Action Programs—P&G Detergent Business in Europe

▼ **Expand geographical penetration by increasing market share in selected countries**
▼ **Description** There are a number of products that have a potential for growth in selected geographic regions. We shall develop specific product-region strategies targeted to increase market share in those countries where our share is comparatively smaller. Special efforts should be devoted to our line of household cleaners.
▼ **Responsible Manager** P&G European Detergents marketing manager, coordinating individual product and country managers.
▼ **Key Indicator(s) for Management Control** Market share in different countries
▼ **First Major Milestone Description** Concrete action plans for each product-region
▼ **First Major Milestone Date** Date for the approval of the plan

NOTE: This is not an official document. It is an illustration drawn from public sources.

- *Statement of benefits*: estimates of the financial and nonfinancial rewards associated with the implementation of the action programs.
- *Scheduled completion:* the deadline of the execution of the action program.
- *Responsible manager*: a single individual who will be responsible for overseeing the implementation of the broad action program.
- *Procedure for controlling completion*: indicating the mechanisms to be used for monitoring, evaluating, and if needed, taking corrective actions with regard to the program implementation.
- *Statement of performance and goals*: targets to be accomplished by the program execution.

FIGURE 7–9. List of Specific Action Programs That Support a Broad Action Program—P&G Detergent Business in Europe

▼ **Expand geographical penetration by increasing market share in selected countries**
▶ Market Penetration in Spain
▶ Market Penetration in Portugal
▶ Market Penetration in Italy
▶ Market Penetration in Poland
▶ Market Penetration in the Czech Republic

NOTE: This is not an official document. It is an illustration drawn from public sources.

FIGURE 7–10. Priorities for Specific Action Programs

STATEMENT OF PRIORITY	DEFINITION
Absolutely first priority	Postponement will hurt the competitive position significantly. (Lack of implementation will seriously damage the SBU's competitive position.)
Highly desirable	Postponement will affect the competitive position adversely. (Implementation will significantly help the SBU's competitive position.)
Desirable	If funds were available, the competitive position could be enhanced. (This program would be helpful, but can be postponed or cancelled if resources are not available.)

NOTE: This is not an official document. It is an illustration drawn from public sources.

Figure 7–11 provides a definition of the specific action program: "Market penetration in Spain," associated with the P&G case.

Step 4. Budgeting and Strategic Funds Programming

Budgets represent projections of revenues and costs normally covering one or more years. The *master budget* of a firm includes all those activities whose monitoring is judged to be important for a healthy development of the firm's businesses: among them are sales, manufacturing, administrative activities, investment, and cash management. Figure 7–12 provides a schematic view of the primary elements in a master budget.

The result of the business planning process leads toward the development of an *intelligent budget,* which is not a mere extrapolation of the past into the future, but an instrument that contains both strategic and operational commitments. Strategic commitments pursue the development of new opportunities, which very often introduce significant changes in the existing business conditions. Operational commitments, on the other hand, are aimed at the effective maintenance of the existing business base.

A way to break this dichotomy within the budget is to make use of strategic funds and operational funds to distinguish the role that those financial resources will have. *Strategic funds* are expense items required for the implementation of strategic action programs whose benefits are expected to be accrued in the long term, beyond the current budget period.[1] *Operational funds* are those expense items required to maintain the business in its present position.

There are three major components of strategic funds:

1. *Investment* in tangible assets, such as new production capacity, new machinery and tools, new vehicles for distribution, new office space, new warehouse space, and new acquisitions.

FIGURE 7–11. Definition of Specific Action Programs—P&G Detergent Business in Europe

▼ **Market Penetration in Spain**
▼ **Description**
Improve competitive position in Spain. Primary targets are the major metropolitan areas in Madrid, Barcelona, Bilbao, Valencia, and Seville. Emphasize distribution through hypermarkets and superstores like Corte Ingles. Build up promotion and marketing efforts.
▼ **Statement of Priority**
Absolutely first priority
▼ **Statement of Costs**
See attached budgeting projections
▼ **Statement of Benefits**
See attached budgeting projections
▼ **Scheduled Completion**
One year from the beginning of the plan
▼ **Responsibililty**
Spain country manager
▼ **Procedure for Controlling Completion**
Monthly reports by metropolitan area, major accounts, and product lines comparing actual vs. budget figures.
▼ **Statement of Performance and Goals**
Market share, profit margins, and return on investment for each metropolitan area, major account, and product lines.

NOTE: This is not an official document. It is an illustration drawn from public sources.

2. *Increases (or decreases) in working capital* generated from strategic commitments, such as the impact of increases in inventories and receivables resulting from an increase in sales; the need to accumulate larger inventories to provide better services; increasing receivables resulting from a change in the policy of loans to customers, and so on.

3. *Developmental expenses* that are over and above the needs of existing business, such as advertising to introduce a new product or to reposition an existing one; R&D expenses of new products; major cost reduction programs for existing products; introductory discounts, sales promotions, and free samples to stimulate first purchases; development of management systems such as planning, control, and compensation; certain engineering studies, and so on.

It is important to recognize these three forms of strategic funds. Although all of them contribute to the same purpose, namely, the improvement of future capabilities of the firm, financial accounting rules treat these three items quite

FIGURE 7–12. A Schematic Representation of a Master Budget

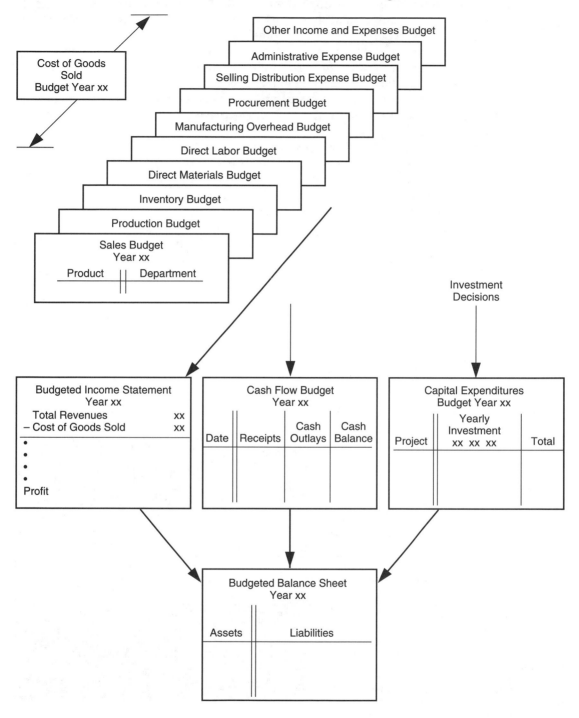

differently. Investment is shown as an increase in net assets in the balance sheet and as annual expenses through depreciation in the profit and loss statement. Increases in working capital also enlarge the net assets of the firm, but they have no annual cost repercussion. Developmental expenses are charged as expenses in the current year income statement and have no impact on the balance sheet. Since there are no immediate profitability results derived from these strategic funds, it is important to make a manager accountable for the proper and timely allocation of those expenditures using performance measurements related to the inherent characteristics of the action programs they are attempting to support.

If the business has developed a sound strategy, it will be easy to see how the key performance variables begin to improve with the years. What is more difficult is to measure the short-term contribution of a multitude of programs requiring strategic expenses. Often, it is necessary to resort to the project-management type of control mechanisms, centered in cost and time efficiency, as the only way to measure the quality of the implementation of strategic funds.

The strategic funds are defined when we allocate the costs associated with each specific action program. Figure 7–13 shows the stream of strategic funds that are required in the P&G case for the action program "Market penetration in Spain." The investment stream primarily consists of new warehousing facili-

FIGURE 7–13. Strategic Funds for a Specific Action Program—P&G Detergent Business in Europe

	1992	1993	1994	1995	1996	1997
▼ **Expand geographical penetration**						
▼ **Market Penetration in Spain**						
• Investments	1.3	0.0	0.0	1.6	0.0	0.0
• Changes in Working Capital	5.1	2.6	1.3	1.8	2.5	3.3
• Development Expenses	3.5	2.5	1.5	1.7	1.9	2.1
Total Strategic Funds	9.9	5.1	2.8	5.1	4.4	5.4
▶ **Market Penetration in Portugal**						
▶ **Market Penetration in Italy**						
▶ **Market Penetration in Poland**						
▶ **Market Penetration in Czech Republic**						

NOTE: This is not an official document. It is an illustration drawn from public sources.

ties and new assets for the distribution system. Increases in working capital are primarily due to larger inventories and receivables. Developmental expenses result from additional promotions and advertising efforts.

Finally, Figure 7–14 give us an illustration of a budget that contains the differentiation between operational and strategic funding. The numbers attached to the figure are totally artificial; they merely represent an example. What is important, however, is to emphasize some of the key conceptual differences that this type of budget has compared with a conventional one.

The budget presents both a history and a future projection. This is helpful for understanding the evolution of the financial results and the extent of drastic departures from expected to past performance. The budget starts with figures measuring the Total Market of the industry where the business resides. This will allow us to see immediately the market share position of the business and the evolution of the industry life-cycle. The relationship between the Total Market and the Company Sales determine the Market Share of the business.

From the Company Sales we subtract the Operating Cost of Goods Sold and the Operating SG&A (Sales, General, and Administrative Expenses). The key word here is "operating;" namely, we are not allocating any overhead or expenses that have strategic purposes. This allows us to obtain an Operating Margin of the business. From that we subtract Strategic Expenses, Capital Investments, and Increases in Working Capital—the three components of the Strategic Funds of the business. By separating the operating from the strategic expenses, we can track the financial performance of the business in these two different modes. One derives from the existing activities of the business; the other comes from its future potential.

The bottom line measures what is usually defined as the "free cash" generated by the business. This is cash coming from operations after the deduction of interest, taxes, and all the strategic funds committed, and the addition of depreciation.

The flow of free cash is what has to be discounted to obtain the net present value of the business, which measures the wealth created for shareholders.

(Figure 7-14 follows on page 156)

FIGURE 7-14. Strategic Funds Programming and Operational Budgets—An Illustration

	History					Current Year		Projections			
	1988	1989	1990	1991	1992	Actual	Budget	1994	1995	1996	1997
Total Market	4032.0	4994.0	5822.0	6722.0	7820.0	0.0	9266.0	11120.0	13123.0	16012.0	19312.0
Market Share (%)	52.0	51.0	52.0	49.0	49.0	0.0	49.0	50.0	50.0	51.0	52.0
Company Sales	2083.0	2568.0	3002.0	3316.0	3799.0	0.0	4502.0	5522.0	6577.0	8123.0	9966.0
– Operating Cost of Goods Sold	1789.0	2138.0	2499.0	2771.0	3165.0	0.0	3760.0	4612.0	5492.0	6789.0	8336.0
Gross Operating Margin	294.0	430.0	503.0	545.0	634.0	0.0	742.0	910.0	1085.0	1334.0	1630.0
– Operating SG&A	62.0	103.0	110.0	121.0	138.0	0.0	162.0	199.0	241.0	295.0	366.0
Operating Margin	232.0	327.0	393.0	424.0	496.0	0.0	580.0	711.0	844.0	1039.0	1264.0
– Strategic Expenses	130.0	165.0	204.0	213.0	251.0	0.0	321.0	396.0	497.0	626.0	789.0
SBU Margin	102.0	162.0	189.0	211.0	245.0	0.0	259.0	315.0	347.0	413.0	475.0
– Taxes	5.0	18.0	23.0	27.0	32.0	0.0	35.0	43.0	56.0	70.0	93.0
SBU Net Income	97.0	144.0	166.0	184.0	213.0	0.0	224.0	272.0	291.0	343.0	382.0
+ Depreciation	18.0	21.0	26.0	32.0	38.0	0.0	46.0	56.0	67.0	82.0	100.0
– Capital Investments	32.0	57.0	87.0	128.0	115.0	0.0	150.0	195.0	169.0	202.0	183.0
– Increases in Working Capital	0.0	0.0	0.0	0.0	0.0	0.0	0.0	0.0	0.0	0.0	0.0
Contribution/Request of Funds to the Corporation	83.0	108.0	105.0	88.0	136.0	0.0	120.0	133.0	189.0	223.0	299.0

Notes

1. The concept of strategic funds was first advanced by Richard F. Vancil in "Better Management of Corporate Development." Harvard Business Review, 50, no. 5 (September–October 1972), 53–62; and Paul J. Stonich, "How to Use Strategic Funds Programming," *The Journal of Business Strategy*, no. 2 (Fall 1980), 35–50.

CHAPTER 8

Strategic and Economic Evaluation of the Merits of a Strategy

In the previous chapters we have provided guidelines for the formulation of a business strategy. The final task that still has to be completed is the assessment of the contribution that this strategy makes to the value of the firm. There are four major questions that lead to a proper evaluation of the merits of a strategy:

1. How unique is the competitive advantage created by the strategy?
2. How sustainable is that advantage, once it has been created?
3. How much economic value does the strategy add?
4. Is the strategy flexible enough to adjust to alternative courses of action?

To guide us in this strategic evaluation analysis, we propose the positioning-sustainability-valuation-flexibility framework.[1] Positioning addresses the issue of the uniqueness of the competitive advantage; sustainability deals with the capacity to maintain that advantage through time; valuation attempts to capture the economic value of the strategy under different scenarios; and flexibility refers to the ability of the firm to change its course of action if confronted with unexpected events.

We illustrate the application of this framework by examining one of the most surprising and intriguing strategic decisions that took place in the U.S. industry in 1993: the acquisition of Medco Containment Services by Merck & Company—a premier pharmaceutical firm. When the announcement of this acquisition was made, its implications went far beyond a vertical integration decision. Merck, a company that had been voted by the CEO's of Fortune 500 companies for seven years in a row the most admired corporation in America, and which had a track record of serving society by developing highly differentiated products with a high content of R&D, paid a hefty price for a distributor of generic and brand-name drugs. This decision puzzled the business community, both for the apparent lack of strategic fit, as well as the enormity of the price tag.

We turn now to the positioning-sustainability-valuation-flexibility framework to probe the rationale behind that critical decision. This is an illustration of a methodology that we feel can be helpful in addressing decisions like this one. We are not judging the merits of the actual decision of Merck in its acquisition of Medco.

The framework can be used to analyze the complete strategy of a business, or to assess the goodness of a critical strategic decision, such as the Merck-Medco acquisition.

The Positioning-Sustainability-Valuation-Flexibility Framework

1. POSITIONING: THE ASSESSMENT OF THE UNIQUENESS OF THE COMPETITIVE ADVANTAGE

The critical requirement for a strategy is to generate a unique competitive advantage. This means that the firm understands the structure and trends of the industries in which it competes, and deploys the necessary resources and capabilities that will allow it to differentiate itself from its competitors. The resulting unique competitive advantage should allow the firm to achieve a superior financial performance.[2]

2. SUSTAINABILITY: THE ASSESSMENT OF THE DURABILITY OF THE COMPETITIVE ADVANTAGE

The key issue is whether the unique competitive advantage that emerges from the firm's positioning in its industry is sustainable through time, and the duration of such advantage. There are three major requirements for sustainability.

Commitment, explains both the persistence in the business performance, as well as the difference in performance enjoyed by distinct firms competing in the same industry. Commitment defines strategies as a continuous pattern of decision making, which are punctuated by discontinuities due to commitment changes.

Commitment is the result of investments in the development of unique resources and capabilities inside the firm, which are scarce, durable, specialized, and untradeable; consequently, they are hard to imitate or substitute by other players in the industry. These resources could be both tangible—such as financial and physical assets—and intangible—such as reputation, brand power, product innovation, and superior customer orientation. Resources of this kind require investments in the so called "sticky factors," which are enduring in nature, and are thus maintained over a rather long period of time. From an economic point of view, they are largely sunk costs. Resources are converted into capabilities when the firm develops the necessary organizational routines to use them effectively.

Scarcity implies that the resources and capabilities that are the sources of competitive advantage must continue to be scarce. The threats of imitation and substitution are the two most critical elements that might impair the scarcity value of factors. Lack of imitation assures that competitors will not be able to reproduce easily the strategic advantage acquired by the firm. Lack of substitution implies that the resources that are the foundation of such advantage cannot be replaced by plausible alternatives.

Appropriability means that the organization should retain a significant portion of the value generated by its unique competitive advantage. There are two principal threats against the appropriation by its owners of the wealth generated by a firm.

First, what is referred to as the threat of holdup, comes from nonowners controlling complementary and specialized factors. Perhaps the most remarkable example in recent history is Intel's and Microsoft's claim of 65 percent of the wealth created in the personal computers industry. While computer manufacturers have engaged in an intensive rivalry that has generated lackluster performance for themselves, Intel (the provider of the computer chip) and Microsoft (the developer of the operating system and of critical software for the industry) enjoy extraordinary profitability levels. The threat of holdup does not necessarily reduce the overall economic wealth available to the industry participants; it simply assigns that wealth in a way that works against the firm's owners. The size of the pie remains the same; it is the size of the wedges that goes to the industry actors that gets redefined.

The second threat is the so-called threat of slack, which comes from internal members of the organization, most likely its own employees. In the U.S., the most common threat of slack originates from rivalry between owners and unionized employees. This rivalry results in a reduction of the potential wealth that the business could otherwise have created, due to inefficiencies and unwarranted benefits. Now the size of the pie is reduced. In the long run, this will have unfavorable implications for all the players. The U.S. domestic airline industry is perhaps the clearest example that comes to mind. In the early 1990s, Robert Crandall, the CEO of American Airlines, insistently voiced his frustration regarding the inability of his company to generate any kind of returns for its shareholders. He pointed to the lack of competitive cost structure derived from excessive demands from its pilots and flight attendants. United Airlines, which experienced a similarly frustrating performance, finally agreed to a leveraged buyout from its employees in a desperate attempt to line up the interests of owners and employees. Both airlines lost close to $1 billion each during 1993.

3. VALUATION: THE ASSESSMENT OF THE VALUE CREATED BY THE PROPOSED STRATEGY

Having understood the sources of competitive advantage and the degree of its sustainability through time, we need to perform a financial evaluation of the strategy to assess the value that it creates for the firm owners. From a methodological point of view, this is a fairly conventional step in the evaluation of the merits of a strategy. It simply consists of projecting the cash flows through a reasonable time horizon and discounting them using a rate that takes inflation and risk into account, in order to obtain the corresponding net present value. Although this is a very straightforward exercise, there are some important issues to bear in mind:

• The projection of cash flows are invariably supported by critical assumptions regarding key uncertain parameters that eventually will determine the size of the investment to be made, the magnitude of the revenues, and the associated expenses. The economic evaluation is heavily dependent upon the assumptions built into the financial analysis. Seldom, if ever, does the concluding financial evaluation determine the final selection of the preferred strategy. It is essential to address the impact that unforeseen events will have on the economic value that is being created. The financial analysis will give us a sense of the robustness of a strategy, as well as the dependency of the final outcomes on critical uncertain events.

• At the risk of being trivial, we want to include a word of caution regarding the use of nominal and real figures in the economic evaluation of strategic decisions. One of the most common mistakes is to mix nominal and real figures in the projections of financial figures. Nominal projections imply using data that have imbedded inflationary trends, while real projections do not assume any inflationary trend, but work with normalized currency of a fixed date, say 1996. The central warning is consistency. Either we use nominal cash flow projections and nominal discount rates, which allow for inflationary and risk discounting; or else we use real financial projections and real cost of capital, which do not include inflationary corrections. Failing to achieve this consistency can produce significant distortions in the financial evaluation. As a matter of fact, in past years, nominal discount rates have ranged between 15 percent and 20 percent, while real discount rates have been often below 10 percent.

• A third point that needs to be addressed is the assumption regarding the terminal value of the economic activity being analyzed; that is, the value at the end of the selected planning horizon. There are various ways of accounting for that terminal value. The most common ones are to assume a book value representing the equity of the investment at that point, or to allow for a perpetuity—a stable cash flow to be realized after the planning horizon—under various assumptions of growth rates.

Financial evaluation appears to convey an objective, quantitative measure of the worth of a strategy. However, it is our experience that it is important to combine a deep understanding of the sources of competitive advantage—which is usually highly subjective and heavily dependent on qualitative judgments—with a serious attempt to measure the economic value created by a strategy. This evaluation is closely linked to the final step of our analysis, which deals with the flexibility implicit in the strategic commitments being made.

The positioning and sustainability analysis are aimed at understanding the sources for sustainable competitive advantage. The valuation stage assigns an economic value to the strategy being evaluated. This stage is not geared only to the generation of a quantitative assessment of the worth of the strategy; but, most importantly, it is aimed at the identification of the critical factors determining the final outcomes of the firm's strategy. A sensitivity analysis is a helpful tool to pinpoint the critical controllable factors that we have to monitor, as well as the uncontrollable external factors that are the most influential on the value of the strategy. By recognizing the critical determinants of the value of the strategy, we can lay out the flexible responses required under different plausible scenarios.

4. FLEXIBILITY: THE ASSESSMENT OF THE ADAPTABILITY OF THE PROPOSED STRATEGY

Besides the achievement of a unique competitive advantage—which emanates from an effective positioning and the sustainability of this advantage—an enduring strategy has to be flexible. Flexibility is required because of the inherent uncertainty the firm faces due to an unexpected external environment, as well as unforeseeable actions by the firm's competitors. Technically, flexibility is the added expected value generated by the ability of the firm to revise its strategy by adopting alternative courses of action as the outcomes of uncertain events unfold. The value added by flexibility stems from the degree of preparedness in which the firm must commit the necessary resources and deploy the required capabilities to pursue different courses of action as events unfold. Flexibility is not the optimization of the value of the firm with regard to just one single set of assumptions, but rather the selection of a strategy that can be adjusted under a wide range of critical outcomes.

Strategic Evaluation
of the Merck-Medco Acquisition

In July 1993, Merck & Co., one of the world's largest pharmaceutical manufacturers, agreed to purchase Medco Containment Services, one of the largest Pharmacy-Benefits Management (PBM) firms and the largest mail-order drug company[3]. The $6.6 billion acquisition shocked the pharmaceutical industry. Why did Merck purchase Medco and why did it pay almost 47 times Medco's 1993 net income for the company? What competitive advantages were created via this purchase? Are these advantages sustainable? Was value created for Merck's shareholders? We evaluate these issues following the positioning-sustainability-valuation-flexibility framework.

POSITIONING OF MERCK-MEDCO

To understand the implications of the Merck-Medco merger from a positioning point of view, we need to address two primary questions. The first is how the industry will be restructured after the merger, and whether such restructuring will generate additional opportunities for the combined firm. To answer this question we examine both the Pharmaceutical Industry and the Pharmacy-Benefits Management Industry, as well as exploring their consolidation. The second issue to be examined, besides the additional benefits stemming from the industry restructuring, is to understand the potential gains in developing unique competitive advantages within the combined industry. This question leads to the analysis of the value chain of the merged organization, to detect those activities that will allow further differentiation of the firm positioning.

The Drug Manufacturers and the PBM Industry Attractiveness

In Chapter 5 we used Porter's five-forces model to characterize the pharmaceutical industry in 1993. This analysis is reproduced in Figure 8–1.

Although the pharmaceutical industry enjoyed superior profitability performance, the current trends are somewhat concerning. They involve the emergence of generic and "me-too" drugs, and the increased power of the managed care and cost containment organizations, which exert considerable influence on prescribing physicians. This has resulted in enormous pressures to drive prices down thereby making the overall industry less attractive. These trends are compounded by the seemingly out of control health-care costs, which are motivating new government legislation leading toward further price erosion.

Figure 8–2 attempts to represent the changes that have taken place in the past decade regarding the influences over prescribing physicians. In 1993, we noticed the emergence of plan sponsors—particularly Health Maintenance Organizations (HMOs), Preferred Provider Organizations (PPOs), and cost containment organizations such as Medco—which are influencing decisions to prescribe less expensive drugs and thus reduce costs to their clients. The practice they follow is to produce formularies recommending the drugs that participating doctors should prescribe, backed up with sales forces that follow up these recommendations with the doctors. Buyers have also increased their power due to the increased importance of mail-order pharmacies. These organizations have million of patients under their control, and can command significant discounts on drugs from pharmaceutical manufacturers. Moreover, large retail pharmacy chains, which can command large discounts on volume drugs, have proliferated. The pharmaceutical industry remains attractive largely

FIGURE 8–1. Porter's Five-Forces Model Applied to the Pharmaceutical Industry in the Early 1990s

BARRIERS TO ENTRY (Very Attractive)
- Steep R&D experience curve effects
- Large economies-of-scale barriers in R&D and sales force
- Critical mass in R&D and marketing require global scale
- Significant R&D and marketing costs
- High risk inherent in the drug development process
- Increasing threat of new entrants coming from biotechnology companies

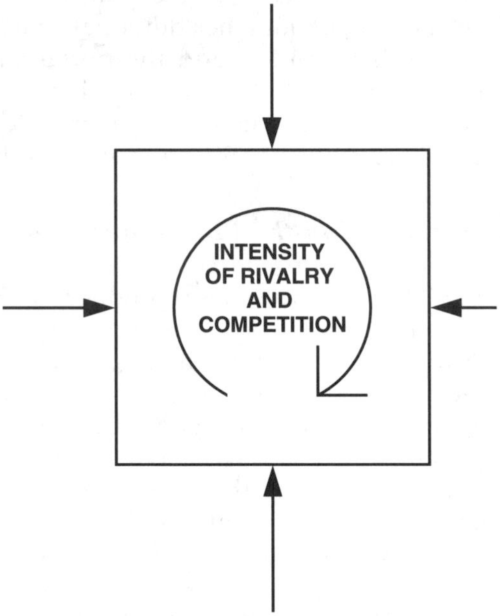

BARGAINING POWER OF BUYERS (Mildly Unattractive)
- The traditional purchasing process was highly price insensitive: the consumer (the patient) did not buy, and the buyer (the physician) did not pay
- Large power of buyers, particularly plan sponsors and cost containment organizations, are influencing the decisions to prescribe less expensive drugs
- Mail-order pharmacies are obtaining large discounts on volume drugs.
- Large aggregated buyers (e.g., hospital suppliers, large distributors, government institutions) are progressively replacing the role of individual customers
- Important influence of the government in the regulation of the buying process

BARGAINING POWER OF SUPPLIERS (Very Attractive)
- Mostly commodities
- Individual scientists may have some personal leverage

INTENSITY OF RIVALRY AND COMPETITION

THREAT OF SUBSTITUTES (Mildly Unattractive)
- Generic and "Me-too" drugs are weakening branded, proprietary drugs
- More than half of the life of the drug patent is spent in the product development and approval process
- Technological development is making imitation easier
- Consumer aversion to chemical substances erodes the appeal for pharmaceutical drugs

INTENSITY OF RIVALRY (Attractive)
- Global competition concentrated among fifteen large companies
- Most companies focus on certain types of disease therapy
- Competition among incumbents limited by patent protection
- Competition based on price and product differentiation
- Government intervention and growth of "Me-too" drugs increase rivalry
- Strategic alliances establish collaborative agreements among industry players
- Very profitable industry, however with declining margins

SUMMARY ASSESSMENT OF THE INDUSTRY ATTRACTIVENESS (Attractive)

FIGURE 8–2. Change of Prescribing Influence in Pharmaceutical Value Chain

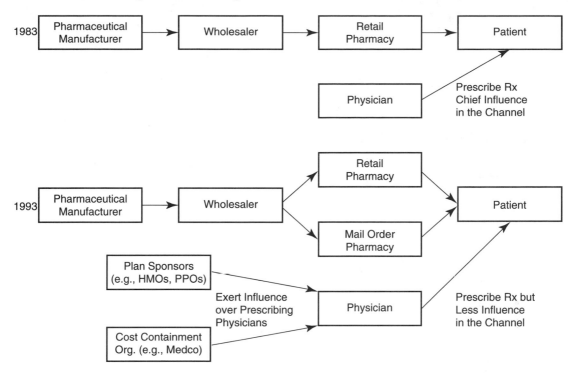

because of patent protection, but it has become much more competitive, with profit being squeezed from the drug manufacturers by other players in the industry.

To understand the industry structure implications of the acquisition of Medco by Merck, we should turn our attention to the PBM industry. What exactly is a PBM? According to Bill Tindall, Director of the Academy of Managed-Care Pharmacies, a PBM "should have a formulary[4], a program promoting generic substitution, an academic detailing program in which decisions are called to prescribe more cost-effective drugs, and a drug utilization review program."[5] Some PBMs also have sophisticated information systems that can file data on patients, physicians' prescriptions, drug usage, and much more.

PBMs are exercising an increasing influence over the pharmaceutical manufacturers to ensure that their drugs are listed on the PBM's formularies. Figure 8.3 shows the dramatic increase in price discounting to different types of pharmacies from 1987 to 1992.

PBMs encompass both categories B and C on Figure 8-3. Combining these categories, PBMs had about a 16 percent share of the prescription market in 1987. This share increased to a colossal 50 percent in just five years. The other key information emerging from this figure is the level of discounting received

FIGURE 8–3. Increase in Price Discounting and Managed Pharmacy Care

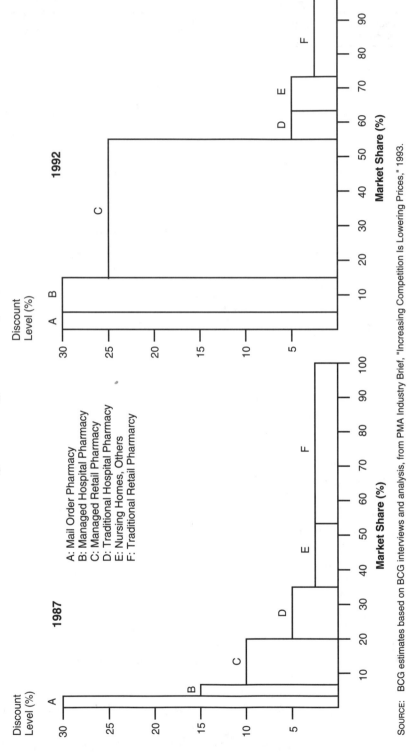

A: Mail Order Pharmacy
B: Managed Hospital Pharmacy
C: Managed Retail Pharmacy
D: Traditional Hospital Pharmacy
E: Nursing Homes, Others
F: Traditional Retail Pharmacy

SOURCE: BCG estimates based on BCG interviews and analysis, from PMA Industry Brief, "Increasing Competition Is Lowering Prices," 1993.

by the different players in the market. The higher discounts are given to PBMs and to mail-order pharmacies, which many PBMs own and operate. PBMs have increased the discount level received from pharmaceutical manufacturers from 10–15 percent in 1987 to 25–30 percent in 1992. The increased market share, and thus the prescribing influence of PBMs in the industry, has driven these substantial discounts from drug manufacturers.

The brief commentary on the factors and PBM cost containment in organizations makes apparent the great benefits to be derived from an industry structure point of view on the Merck-Medco merger. Rather than establishing a costly rivalry between drug producers and distributors, the merger of these two giants in their respective industries facilitates a consolidation of power that makes the combined industry much more attractive.

The Merck-Medco Competitive Positioning

Having considered the changing dynamics in the pharmaceutical and PBM industries, we now turn our attention to the competitive positioning of Merck and Medco within their respective industries, and the resulting competitive positioning of the integrated merged company.

Figure 8–4 shows worldwide market shares for the fifteen leading pharmaceutical companies in 1993, the year Merck acquired Medco. The data presented in the figure represent gross estimates, since many pharmaceutical

FIGURE 8–4. 1993 Estimated Market Share of Top Fifteen Pharmaceutical Firms

COMPANY	MARKET SHARE (%)
Merck	5.2%
Glaxo	5.2%
Bristol-Myers Squibb	4.2%
Hoechst	3.9%
Ciba-Geigy	3.3%
Sandoz	3.2%
SmithKline Beecham	3.1%
Bayer	3.0%
Roche	2.9%
Eli Lilly	2.9%
American Home Products	2.9%
Rhone-Poulenc Rorer	2.7%
Johnson & Johnson	2.7%
Pfizer	2.7%
Abbott Laboratories	2.5%
Other	49.6%
Top 4 Firms	18.5%
Top 8 Firms	31.1%
Estimated Total Market	$200 billion

SOURCE: Market share based on estimates from literature including *Manufacturing Chemist*, (December 1992), p.8.

manufacturers sell products other than drugs, which makes rather difficult an accurate estimation of sales for drugs only. The figure shows an extremely fragmented pharmaceutical market with a low degree of concentration. Merck, along with Glaxo, is the largest pharmaceutical firm in the world, yet it has only slightly over 5 percent of global market share. The top four players account for a mere 18.5 percent share and the top eight players have slightly more than a 30 percent share.

Though competitive advantages have not allowed any one pharmaceutical firm to capture a significant share of the market, Merck does have some strengths compared to the competition that have propelled the firm to be the leader in the industry. They are:

- *Management.* Merck is perceived by physicians and patients to be highly credible and ethical. This reputation is matched by few others in the industry. Merck has arguably the best management in the business. They combine tremendous technical ability with business prowess. Roy Vagelos, the CEO of Merck in 1993 and now retired, has been the embodiment of this superb management team, having revised a once struggling research department and having provided strategic vision for the future. This management team has come to lead the pharmaceutical industry in terms of implementing many new strategies and tactics. For example, Merck was the first company in the industry to implement the idea of selling a generic version of one of its drugs prior to it coming off patent in order to capture a share in the generic market as well as the branded market. Though this cannibalizes sales, a good manager knows that it is better to cannibalize your own sales than let someone else cannibalize them for you.

- *Manufacturing.* Merck has given a very high priority to modernizing its manufacturing facilities, increasing manufacturing flexibility, and improving productivity and costs. The cost of materials and production has been around 23 percent.

- *Research & Development.* Merck is known to have the shortest average product development lead-times in the industry. Over the past decade, Merck has averaged over one major product introduction per year, better than all of its competitors. Historically, the firm has had a strong pipeline. Currently, it has two billion-dollar drugs: Mevacor, a treatment for high cholesterol and Vasotec, for the treatment of hypertension and congested heart failure. R&D expenditures have exceeded 11 percent of sales during the last ten years.

- *Marketing and Sales.* Merck has one of the largest and most efficient marketing groups and sales forces in the industry. Merck has trained them well to contact effectively and promote Merck's products to millions of physicians and managed care groups each year. Marketing and administrative expenses have accounted for about 30 percent of sales.

Merck possesses the above strengths, which has enabled the firm to be the leader in the industry. However, could Merck capture more market share relying on these competitive advantages alone? Are these advantages even sustainable? In 1993 Merck felt the answer to both questions to be "no." They believed they needed to position themselves in the PBM market and subsequently purchased Medco.

Figure 8–5 provides some key information of the top eight PBM organizations. As is obvious from the figure, the PBM industry is much more concentrated

FIGURE 8–5. Comparison of Leading Eight PBMs

PBM	Total Patients Covered	Market Share (%)	Mail-Order?	Network of Pharmacies
PCS Health Systems	45 million	23.6%	recently entered	54,000
Medco	38 million	19.9%	largest in the nation	48,000
Diversified Pharmaceutical Services	14 million	7.3%	no	39,000
Caremark	13 million	6.8%	yes	52,000
Diagnostek	13 million	6.8%	n.a.	n.a.
Value Health	11 million	5.8%	n.a.	n.a.
Express Scripts	5 million	2.6%	n.a.	n.a.
Systemed	4 million	2.1%	n.a.	n.a.
Other	48 million	25.1%		
Total	191 million	100.0%		
Top 4 Firms	110 million	57.6%		
Top 8 Firms	143 million	74.9%		

SOURCE: *The New York Times*, May 5, 1994, p. C1, from Sanford C. Bernstein's estimates plus additional literature review and analysis.

than are pharmaceutical manufacturers. Although there are over 150 PBM organizations in the U.S., the top four firms control 15.6 percent of the market and the top eight command three quarters of the total market, with a total coverage of nearly 150 million patients. Their influence on prescribing doctors is enormous, often encouraging the least expensive drugs and generic versions.

Medco is well positioned in both the prescription-influenced channel and the distribution channel. Its competitive strengths are:

- *Management.* Medco's reputation is similar to Merck's, in that it is a highly credible organization in the eyes of physicians and patients.
- *Information Technology.* Another key strategic advantage of Medco (some argue that it is their most vital advantage), is the strength of its information systems and databases. The firm has built a solid IT infrastructure and tracks detailed data concerning patients, physicians, drug use, dosage, prescription success, etc. A few of the other major PBMs have strong information systems, such as PCS and Diversified, but few are as good as Medco.
- *Leading Mail-Order Company.* This is a significant competitive advantage. The other PBMs do not have the same size mail-order, and thus less prescriptions flow through other firms. Being the number one mail-order firm gives Medco growing influence in the distribution channel. Thus, Medco is gaining market power with

the pharmaceutical producers by telling the doctors what to buy and then selling the drugs to the patients, themselves.

- *Strong Marketing and Sales.* Medco's detailed marketing group and sales force promote the drugs on their formulary by calling physicians and requesting changes in prescriptions if they prescribe off-formulary drugs. This sales force is very talented and known to succeed often in changing the minds of doctors. Due to their talent, pharmaceutical manufacturers give substantial discounts to Medco just to be on the formulary. Being off the formulary can mean a great loss of market share.

- *Excellent Service.* The product/service that Medco offers is well established and popular with large corporations and organizations, who are the clients of PBMs. PBM clients include corporations, such as IBM and GM, and health care organizations, such as Blue Cross/Blue Shield and HMOs. These organizations pay Medco monthly fees per employee to manage their prescriptions to ensure lower overall drug costs. This excellence has propelled Medco to be number two in the industry, in terms of number of patient lives covered, behind PCS.

Strategic Reasoning behind the Acquisition

Merck has bought Medco to gain a dual-prescribing and distribution influence in the value chain. This will allow Merck to capture the largest rents. If profits begin to be siphoned out of the pharmaceuticals to the PBMs or mail-order firms, Merck will now be in a position to collect these rents.

Though gaining influence in the channel is obviously a driver for Merck, it is useful to look more deeply at the synergy between Merck and Medco to recognize the underlying strategic intent of the acquisition. Merck is attempting to develop a new model for a pharmaceutical company; one where it can combine its ever strong R&D capabilities with a large and thorough information database to improve the quality of health care, help contain costs, and increase Merck's share of the pharmaceutical industry. Prior to the acquisition, Merck already excelled in the drug discovery process that has permitted the development of blockbuster drugs that propelled Merck to the top of the pharmaceutical industry. However, Merck did not have access to the information database.

Recently retired CEO of Merck, Roy Vagelos, stated that "the company that does the best job of understanding how information flows in the managed care environment will ultimately prevail."[6] Medco controls 38 million patient lives and has computer systems that monitor patient prescriptions and usage, doctors' patterns of prescribing, the pricing of drugs, and other market information. To demonstrate how Merck can use this database to its advantage, consider the following example. Medco tracks the use of medications by its patients. Reports have shown that many patients stop taking their medications even though this can be very harmful to their health. When they stop taking the medication, patients often become very ill, requiring extensive hospital stays, surgery, etc. Through Medco's information system, the firm can alert the patient's physician when he or she stops using the medication (they don't purchase refills), and the doctor can urge the patient to keep taking the drugs. The doctor is happy because he or she benefits from a doctor's visit fee and helps the patient with preventative medicine; Merck/Medco is happy because they increase sales; the plan sponsors are happy because, though they pay the medication fees, they pay less in the long run due to better prolonged patient heath; and the patient is happy because he or she remains healthier and benefits in the long run.

Merck can increase its share of the pharmaceutical industry in more mundane ways through Medco, as well. The simplest example is that Medco makes about 3 million calls per year to physicians for various reasons, including to ask them to switch to less expensive prescriptions. When medically appropriate, these salespeople can push Merck products whether they are branded or one of Merck's generic products. Merck recently acquired a generics firm to produce an array of products from brands to generics to offer through Medco and through alliances with other PBMs. This allows Merck to increase its market share of new and existing products in the pharmaceutical industry. Currently, Merck products represent 11 percent of Medco sales. With this marketing push, Merck hopes to increase this percentage and use increased profits to fund more R&D. This is a positive circular loop. The more market share Merck gets, the greater the revenue, the greater the funds available for R&D, the better likelihood a blockbuster drug will be discovered, and the more share and revenue Merck will get.

The Merck/Medco deal combines two of the most reputable firms in their respective industries. Merck offers superb products with a strong R&D bent, while Medco offers excellent service with a powerful information system. The combined marketing group and sales force also offers a competitive advantage over the competition because between the two teams they reach most of the physicians across the country. The only dilemma comes in how to manage these two organizations. This can be a very difficult task, especially incorporating two very different cultures into one. Medco is a cost-cutting, discount environment that plays in a very competitive industry, while Merck historically has been playing in a highly profitable, country club setting. The competitive advantage that could make this acquisition work is the superb management team at Merck that is committed to success.

From the analysis we have conducted so far, it is quite clear that Merck and Medco are leading companies in their respective industries. Moreover, the strengths of these companies are not overlapping but complementary in nature. Merck excels in the upstream activities of the value chain, while Medco strengths are abundant in the downstream activities. The merge results in an extraordinary combined force, as is depicted in Figure 8–6 which shows a summary of the Merck-Medco competitive capabilities.

THE SUSTAINABILITY OF THE MERCK-MEDCO STRATEGY

The competitive positioning analysis we just concluded indicates that the Merck-Medco merger has resulted in an even stronger unique competitive advantage than either one of the individual firms enjoyed prior to the acquisi-

FIGURE 8–6. Merck-Medco Competitive Positioning

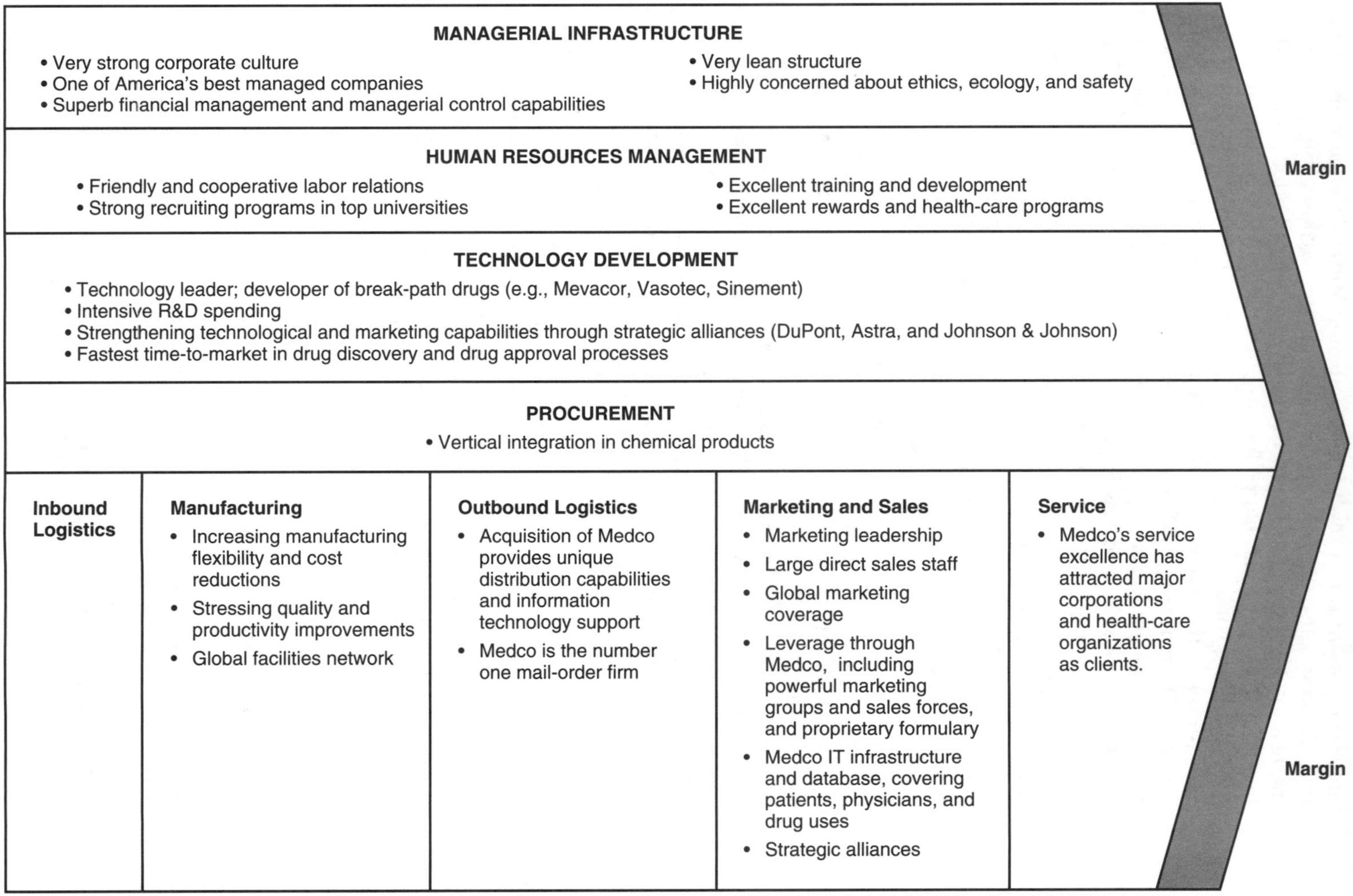

MANAGERIAL INFRASTRUCTURE
- Very strong corporate culture
- One of America's best managed companies
- Superb financial management and managerial control capabilities
- Very lean structure
- Highly concerned about ethics, ecology, and safety

HUMAN RESOURCES MANAGEMENT
- Friendly and cooperative labor relations
- Strong recruiting programs in top universities
- Excellent training and development
- Excellent rewards and health-care programs

TECHNOLOGY DEVELOPMENT
- Technology leader; developer of break-path drugs (e.g., Mevacor, Vasotec, Sinement)
- Intensive R&D spending
- Strengthening technological and marketing capabilities through strategic alliances (DuPont, Astra, and Johnson & Johnson)
- Fastest time-to-market in drug discovery and drug approval processes

PROCUREMENT
- Vertical integration in chemical products

Inbound Logistics	Manufacturing	Outbound Logistics	Marketing and Sales	Service
	- Increasing manufacturing flexibility and cost reductions - Stressing quality and productivity improvements - Global facilities network	- Acquisition of Medco provides unique distribution capabilities and information technology support - Medco is the number one mail-order firm	- Marketing leadership - Large direct sales staff - Global marketing coverage - Leverage through Medco, including powerful marketing groups and sales forces, and proprietary formulary - Medco IT infrastructure and database, covering patients, physicians, and drug uses - Strategic alliances	- Medco's service excellence has attracted major corporations and health-care organizations as clients.

Margin

Margin

tion. We explore now whether the competitive advantage realized can indeed be sustainable. As we indicated in the introduction to this chapter, sustainability is explained through three fundamental concepts: commitment, scarcity, and appropriability.

Commitment

The root of commitment is the investment in scarce, durable, specialized, and untradeable factors. This investment represents decisions that are, to a great extent, irrevocable and hard to revert. The $6.6 billion spent by Merck is about 50 percent of the after-merger equity. Unquestionably, Merck's acquisition of Medco stands as a strong example of a major commitment. It goes far beyond the $ 6.6 billion investment. It is an attempt to restructure the industry and create new sources of competitive advantage. By buying Medco, Merck bought information on, and control of, 38 million patients' prescription usage. Merck spent 47 times Medco's net income and has incurred considerable debt to finance the deal. Merck has already shown commitment to the new firm by spending considerable funds to further improve the information systems, improve and retain the marketing and sales staff, and incorporate the two cultures. Through a financial commitment in people and systems, Merck hopes to bring out the synergy of the two entities and develop capabilities that lead to a sustainable competitive advantage.

Scarcity

For a strategy to be sustainable, it has to rely on the development of resources and capabilities that cannot be easily imitated or substituted. The threat of imitation is quite real. In fact, immediately after Merck announced Medco's acquisition, Eli Lilly purchased PCS Health Systems for $4 billion, and Smith-Kline Beecham purchased Diversified Pharmaceutical Services for $2.3 billion. PCS is the number one firm in the PBM industry, and Diversified Pharmaceutical Services is number three. Medco's acquisition is perhaps more expensive, in spite of being the second largest PBM, because it controls the largest mail-order house. The fourth largest PBM is Caremark, which will probably remain independent because it just formed very strong alliances with three pharmaceutical manufacturers: Pfizer, Rhone-Poulenc, and Bristol-Myers Squibb. This seems to indicate that the best acquisition targets have been already preempted, thus decreasing opportunities for further imitation.

The threat of substitution can be addressed by asking whether pharmaceutical firms can create their own PBMs or purchase small PBMs and build them up. It is unlikely that this can be done in a way that can seriously challenge the Merck-Medco competitive positioning, without incurring a major investment and requiring significant amount of time for its implementation. Time is the critical issue in the substitution argument. Merck could have developed distribution capabilities on its own, but by acquiring Medco, it added instantaneously those capabilities, which are difficult to imitate or substitute.

Appropriability

The relevant question regarding the appropriability issue for the Merck-Medco strategy is whether the merged company will retain the greatest share of the wealth created in the new industry environment. The basic threats against appropriability are holdup and slack.

First considering holdup, there is another rising influence in the prescribing channel that has been previously mentioned but not fully explained. Cost-containment organizations, like Medco, are not the only rising influence in the channel. Reviewing Figure 8–2, we see that plan sponsors, such as HMOs and PPOs, are also gaining influence over physicians. Currently, plan sponsors sometimes outsource their prescription management to PBMs, because this is their specialty; plan sponsors concentrate on providing health care, while PBMs concentrate on providing low-cost prescriptions. The threat of holdup will become real if the plan sponsors become the chief influence in the prescribing channel and they gain market share over PBMs. In this case, HMOs and PPOs may either contract with the PBMs to handle their formulary developments and prescription services, demanding significant rents from them, or they can just circumvent the PBMs altogether and provide pharmacy-benefits services themselves. Although this threat is real, the likelihood of presenting a significant challenge to the sustainability of the Merck-Medco strategy seems relatively low, at least in the short run.

Slack is also a possibility with this strategy. There could be considerable friction between the two merged organizations because of the inherent different cultures previously discussed. However, it is likely that the strong management of Merck will overcome the slack between the two groups and turn this aspect of the acquisition into a competitive advantage.

In summary, the commitment, scarcity and appropriability arguments tend to indicate that Merck-Medco competitive advantage is likely to be sustainable for a significant period of time.

THE VALUE CREATED BY THE MERCK-MEDCO ACQUISITION

From the positioning and sustainability analysis conducted so far, it is clear that there are benefits to be derived from the acquisition of Medco. These benefits stem from the potential sales increase for Merck (as a result of the industry restructuring), as well as the cost reduction (due to added capabilities and synergy), particularly in distribution. Similarly, there are likely to be favorable impacts on Medco coming from the exploitation of synergy between the two companies and resulting in the improvement of the sales margin.

To quantify the economic consequences of these benefits, we need to perform a financial analysis. An in-depth study of a decision as critical as the one we are examining requires a great deal of sophistication. It is usually based on a model relating financial performance with innumerable factors that can be managed and controlled by the organization. If done properly, the analysis not only gives a sense of the economic value created by a major investment, such as the one being analyzed, but also enlightens the strategic action programs a firm should follow to assure its financial performance. Moreover, investments of this magnitude can be greatly influenced by the financing conditions the firm chooses to use to pay for the investment, conditions that often have significant tax implications. For reasons of limited scope and lack of access to the relevant financial managerial data, we are not able to deliver such a sophisticated financial model. On the contrary, our analysis is exceedingly simple, based on the most modest assumptions that could characterize the broadest implications of the acquisition. Our hope is that this simple exercise can provide some approximation to assess the value created by the Merck-Medco deal.

For the valuation of this decision, we have to make some assumptions in order to project the cash flows within a reasonable time frame, and to assign a terminal value at the end of the planning horizon. The selection of the time frame for the analysis, and the amount for the terminal value, are closely related to the size of the competitive advantage created by the acquisition and its sustainability through time. The final question is whether the value created by the merger will offset the acquisition cost of $6.6 billion.

The valuation approach we present is composed of three distinct analyses. The first is aimed at determining the value of Merck without the merger; the second, the value of Merck with the merger; and the third, the value of Medco after the merger. We also include a sensitivity analysis of the figures obtained by these valuation processes.

1. The Value of Merck without the Merger.

Figure 8–7 displays the calculation we have made to assess the present value of Merck without the acquisition. We have used a planning horizon of five years because it is within this time frame that the benefits from the acquisition should be consolidated. The three years prior to 1994 are used to provide the foundations to extrapolate the performance from Merck. The critical assumptions are:

- A constant sales growth of 10%, which follows past trends
- A cost of goods sold of 63% of sales, also consistent with past performance
- Capital expenditures are evaluated at 50% of net income
- The discount rate used is 13.5 %
- The terminal value is obtained assuming that the cash flow of 1998 grows at 7% in perpetuity.

Under these assumptions, the total present value of Merck, without the merger, is $26.87 billion. Keep in mind that we are trying to assess the value added by the merger. Therefore, the meaningful evaluations will be the incremental value added as opposed to the absolute net present value of each of these economic entities.

FIGURE 8–7. The Value of Merck without the Merger ($ figures in billions)

	Past 1991	1992	1993	91+92+93			Future 1994	1995	1996	1997	1998	Terminal Value
Sales	8.60	9.66	10.50	28.76		Sales	11.55	12.71	13.98	15.37	16.91	
		12.	9.			Sales growth (%)	10.	10.	10.	10.	10.	
	1.93	2.10	2.50	6.53		Materials and Production						
	2.57	2.96	2.91	8.44		Marketing and Administrative						
	0.99	1.11	1.17	3.27		Research and Development						
	5.49	6.17	6.58	18.24		Cost of goods sold	7.28	8.00	8.80	9.69	10.65	
	64.	64.	63.	63.		% of sales	63.	63.	63.	63.	63.	
			0.78	0.78		Restructuring charge						
	3.11	3.49	3.14	9.74		Income before taxes	4.27	4.70	5.17	5.69	6.26	
	1.04	1.12	0.94	3.10		Taxes on income	1.37	1.50	1.65	1.82	2.00	
	33.	32.	30.	32.		% of income	32.	32.	32.	32.	32.	
		0.46				Effect of accounting changes						
	2.07	1.91	2.20	6.18		Net income	2.91	3.20	3.52	3.87	4.25	
	24.1	19.8	21.0	21.5		% of sales	25.2	25.2	25.2	25.2	25.2	
	1.04	1.07	1.01	3.12		Capital Expenditures	1.45	1.60	1.76	1.93	2.13	
	50.	56.	46.	50.		as % of net income	50.	50.	50.	50.	50.	
	0.25	0.30	0.39			Depreciation and amortization	0.30	0.33	0.36	0.40	0.44	
		8.				Increase in W.C. (8% sales gr.)	0.084	0.092	0.102	0.112	0.123	
						Cash Flow	1.669	1.836	2.019	2.221	2.444	37.593
						Discount Factor	1.135	1.288	1.462	1.660	1.884	
						Discounted cash flow	1.470	1.425	1.381	1.339	1.297	
					6.91	Present value of cash flow						
					19.96	P.V. of Terminal Value						
					26.87	Total P.V.						

NOTE: This is not an official document. It is an illustration drawn from public sources.

2. The Value of Merck with the Merger.

Figure 8–8 provides the computation to assess the evaluation of Merck taking into account the benefits that are derived from the acquisition of Medco. The figures do not consolidate Medco's financial results. This is done independently in the next step. The basic assumptions are:

- Sales grow at a constant rate of 11% per year. Notice that this represents a 1% increment from the previous case, where Merck was standing alone. This one percent is attributed to a newly expanded market that can be reached through the acquisition of Medco.
- The cost of goods sold declines from 63% in the previous case to 62%, due to realized synergy with Medco, particularly in sales and distribution.
- There is an additional cost represented by the amortization of goodwill. The total goodwill in Merck's 1993 annual report is $6.6 billions, an amount that is amortized over a period of 30 years.
- Capital expenditures continue to be 50% of net income.
- The discount rate is also maintained at the level of 13.5%.
- The terminal value, as before, assumes a perpetuity of the 1998 cash flow growing at 7% per year.

The resulting total present value of Merck, with the merger, is $30.17 billions.

3. The Value of Medco after the Merger

Figure 8–9 gives us the basic figures of the valuation of Medco after the merger. The following are the critical assumptions:

- Sales growth is at 37.5% in 1994, 30% in 1995, 22.5% in 1996, and 15% in 1997 and 1998.
- Net income, as a percentage of sales, is constant at 6%. This represents a slight increase over past performance as a result of the merger.
- The discount rate is maintained at 13.5%.
- The terminal value is derived from the 1998 cash flow assumed to grow as a perpetuity at 7% per year.

The resulting total value of Medco after the merger is $2.86 billions.

Adding the value of Merck after the merger ($30.17 billions) to the value of Medco after the merger ($2.86 billions) give us the total value of the combined Merck-Medco company, equal to $33.03 billions.[7] Therefore, the value created by the merger is as follows:

Total value of Merck-Medco	$33.03 billions
-Total value of Merck without the merger	-$26.87
Total value added by the merger	$ 6.16

FIGURE 8-8. The Value of Merck with the Merger (without consolidating Medco) ($ figures in billions)

	Past				Future					Terminal Value
	1991	1992	1993	91+92+93	1994	1995	1996	1997	1998	
Sales	8.60	9.66	10.50	28.76	11.66	12.94	14.36	15.94	17.69	42.266
Sales growth (%)		12.	9.		11.	11.	11.	11.	11.	
Materials and Production	1.93	2.10	2.50	6.53						
Marketing and Administrative	2.57	2.96	2.91	8.44						
Research and Development	0.99	1.11	1.17	3.27						
Cost of goods sold	5.49	6.17	6.58	18.24	7.23	8.02	8.90	9.88	10.97	
% of sales	64.	64.	63.	63.	62.	62.	62.	62.	62.	
Restructuring charge		0.78	0.78							
Amortization of goodwill					0.22	0.22	0.22	0.22	0.22	
Income before taxes	3.11	3.49	3.14	9.74	4.21	4.69	5.24	5.84	6.50	
Taxes on income	1.04	1.12	0.94	3.10	1.35	1.50	1.68	1.87	2.08	
% of income	33.	32.	30.	32.	32.	32.	32.	32.	32.	
Effect of accounting changes		0.46								
Net income	2.07	1.91	2.20	6.18	2.86	3.19	3.56	3.97	4.42	
% of sales	24.1	19.8	21.0	21.5	24.5	24.7	24.8	24.9	25.0	
Capital Expenditures	1.04	1.07	1.01	3.12	1.43	1.60	1.78	1.98	2.21	
as % of net income	50.	56.	46.	50.	50.	50.	50.	50.	50.	
Depreciation and amortization	0.25	0.30	0.39		0.52	0.55	0.59	0.63	0.68	
Increase in W.C. (8% sales gr.)		8.			0.09	0.10	0.11	0.13	0.14	
Cash Flow					1.860	2.048	2.257	2.490	2.747	
Discount Factor					1.135	1.288	1.462	1.660	1.884	
Discounted cash flow					1.638	1.590	1.544	1.500	1.459	
Present value of cash flow	7.73									
P.V. of Terminal Value	22.44									
P.V. Total	30.17									

NOTE: This is not an official document. It is an illustration drawn from public sources.

FIGURE 8-9. The Value of Medco after the Merger ($ figures in billions)

	Past					Future					
	1991	1992	1993	91+92+93		1994	1995	1996	1997	1998	Terminal Value
Sales	1.39	1.89	2.62	5.90		3.60	4.68	5.74	6.60	7.59	4.189
Sales growth (%)		36.	39.			37.5	30.	22.5	15.	15.	
Net income	0.061	0.106	0.141	0.308		0.216	0.281	0.344	0.396	0.455	
% of sales	4.4	5.6	5.4	5.2		6.0	6.0	6.0	6.0	6.0	
Capital Expenditures	0.040	0.034	0.069	0.143		0.108	0.140	0.172	0.198	0.228	
as % of net income	66.	32.	49.	46.		50.	50.	50.	50.	50.	
Depreciation	0.016	0.024	0.032			0.040	0.052	0.064	0.073	0.084	
		4.									
Increase in W.C.(4% sales gr.)						0.039	0.043	0.042	0.034	0.040	
Cash Flow						0.109	0.149	0.194	0.237	0.272	
Discount Factor						1.135	1.288	1.462	1.660	1.884	
Discounted cash flow						0.096	0.116	0.132	0.143	0.145	
Present value of cash flow					0.63						
P.V. of Terminal Value					2.22						
Total P.V.					2.86						

NOTE: This is not an official document. It is an illustration drawn from public sources.

179

This is the critical figure that has to be compared with the $6.6 billion dollars paid by Merck for the acquisition. The figures seem to be close enough, particularly given the roughness of our calculation, to permit us to conclude that the price was about the break-even point. It does not seem either to add or destroy significant value to Merck. Undoubtedly, it has enhanced the competitive capabilities of Merck and stopped the likely erosion that might have taken place without the acquisition. But clearly, the acquisition price was not a bargain, particularly if one realizes that the balance sheet of Medco is quite soft. If the merger were not to succeed, Medco's resale value would be quite low compared to the price paid by Merck.

4. Sensitivity Analysis.

Any financial analysis of this magnitude leaves us with some degree of frustration due to our inability to forecast the future with any degree of high confidence. This makes it important to test the analysis by constructing different scenarios that will give us a sense of how sensitive the financial results are to changes in the most critical variables.

Figure 8–10 shows the changes in market value of Merck after the merger when we change the three most critical parameters of our initial assumptions: sales growth (which ranges from 10% in the pessimistic scenario to 12% in the optimistic one); cost of goods sold (63% in the pessimistic scenario and 61% in the optimistic one); and terminal value (which grows at 5% in the pessimistic scenario and 9% in the optimistic one). All these changes are related to the base case that has a total present value of $30.17 billions.

It emerges from this figure that the most critical assumption is the one related to the growth after the planning horizon captured by the terminal value

FIGURE 8–10. Sensitivity Analysis for Merck After the Merger (Not Including Medco)

CRITICAL PARAMETERS	SCENARIOS		
	Pessimistic	Base Case	Optimistic
Sales growth Change in P.V.	10 % – 0.96	11 % 0	12 % 0.99
Cost of goods sold Change in P.V.	63 % – 0.66	62 % 0	61 % 0.66
Terminal value of growth Change in P.V.	5 % – 5.28	7 % 0	9 % 9.97

Notes:
Changes in present value with regard to the base case are measured in $ billions.
The total present value in base case is $ 30.17 b.

NOTE: This is not an official document. It is an illustration drawn from public sources.

FIGURE 8–11. Sensitivity Analysis for Medco

CRITICAL PARAMETERS	SCENARIOS		
	Pessimistic	Base Case	Optimistic
Sales growth Change in P.V.	– 5 % – 0.36	* 0	+ 5 % 0.39
Net income ($ sales) Change in P.V.	5 % – 0.41	6 % 0	7 % 0.40
Terminal value of growth Change in P.V.	5 % – 0.53	7 % 0	9 % 0.98

Notes:
Changes in present value with regard to the base case are measured in $ billions.
The total present value in base case is $ 2.86 b.
* Sales growth is assumed to be 37.5% for 1994, 30% for 1995, 22.5% for 1996, and 15% for 1997 and 1998.

NOTE: This is not an official document. It is an illustration drawn from public sources.

assumption. This is closely linked to the sustainability of the competitive advantage created by the merger, and the duration of the period where this advantage is translated into superior financial performance.

Similarly, Figure 8–11 reports the sensitivity analysis for the market value of Medco after the merger.

Finally, Figure 8–12 gives the sensitivity analysis for the total value added by the Merck-Medco merger. This time we compare the various outcomes to the $6.16 billion, which represents the value added in the base case by the merger. Also remember that $6.6 billions is the price paid by Merck for Medco. The outcome of the optimistic scenario would clearly justify that price. The opposite is true under the pessimistic outcome. The message that is coming from this computation is quite clear. The merits of the acquisition rely quite heavily on

FIGURE 8–12. Sensitivity Analysis for the Total Value Added by the Merck-Medco Merger (figures in $ billions)

CRITICAL PARAMETERS	SCENARIOS		
	Pessimistic	Base Case	Optimistic
Sales growth	4.84	6.16	7.54
Cost of goods sold	5.09	6.16	7.22
Terminal value of growth	5.04	6.16	8.24

NOTE: This is not an official document. It is an illustration drawn from public sources.

the capacity of both companies in the combined organization to increase the rate of growth of their sales, to reduce the cost of goods sold and improve their sales margin, and to extend as much as possible the duration of these benefits. If these conditions do not materialize, it might be that Merck paid in excess of market value for the acquisition of Medco.

THE FLEXIBILITY OF THE MERCK-MEDCO STRATEGY

There are both positive and negative implications for the flexibility that Merck enjoys after the merger.

On the positive side, Merck emerges as a stronger company with added capabilities that will allow the firm to respond more effectively to consumer demands and to the competitive conditions of the industry. Moreover, having access to the valuable databases of Medco, which include patients, physicians, competitors, and customer-oriented organizations, will enhance Merck's competitive strengths, allowing for quicker and more intelligent responses to industry pressures.

On the negative side, the association of a leading drug manufacturer with a PBM may cloud the objectivity that should guide the PBM to satisfy customer needs without favoring any specific manufacturer. This apparent lack of objectivity might not only impair Medco's position in the market, but could also affect adversely the desire of other PBMs to push strongly Merck's products. Merck has become both a competitor and a client of other PBMs.

The other negative implications have to do with loss in financial flexibility. The extraordinarily high price of Medco's acquisition has resulted in a $2.4 billion dollar increase in debt, creating additional interest costs of about $130 million annually. Moreover, the price paid has generated a noncash cost due to the amortization of goodwill estimated at $220 million per year. The weakening of Merck's balance sheet due to this additional debt could also curtail the ability of Merck to pursue alternative major investment opportunities.

CONCLUSIONS

The positioning-sustainability-valuation-flexibility framework is a powerful paradigm to review the merits of a strategy.

Was the acquisition of Medco by Merck a sound decision? The positioning and sustainability arguments give an affirmative answer. From a positioning point of view, the combined company would have restructured the industry to its own advantage, and realized sustainable competitive capabilities. From a flexibility point of view, the answer is less categorical, since there are risks inherent in this major decision that will introduce some limitations in Merck's competitive moves, particularly in the short run.

Was $6.6 billion the right price to pay for Medco? Our valuation analysis seems to indicate that the value created by the merger can only exceed its cost if the combined company can benefit from the potential synergies, and extend as much as possible the opportunities created by the merger. This would mean a sales growth increase and added efficiency—lower costs and higher sales margin.

Roy Vagelos, the CEO of Merck at the time of the acquisition, might have had these considerations in mind when he wrote in August 29, 1993, in a Report to Shareholders: "To complement our efforts on managed care, we expect to create with Medco a bold new approach called Coordinated Pharmaceutical Care. The merger will allow us to link payers, patients, doctors, pharmacists, other health-care providers, and pharmaceutical companies for the best patient care at the best prices regardless of which company makes the drugs. We expect to generate additional earnings through incremental increases in our product volumes, and by reducing our costs through greater efficiencies in marketing, packaging labels and promotions."

Notes

1. This framework relies heavily on the work Pankaj Ghemawat presented in his book, *Commitment: The Dynamic of Strategy* (New York: The Free Press, 1991). He provides an original breakthrough to the framework that we are adapting in this chapter. He integrates the concepts of commitment, sustainability, and flexibility to offer a novel way at framing strategic issues. We are borrowing heavily from his concepts and ideas in this chapter.

2. The issue of competitive advantage for a business strategy has been thoroughly discussed in Chapters 3 through 7.

3. This section draws from Daniel DiSano, "Strategic Implications of the Merck-Medco Acquisition," unpublished student paper, Sloan School of Management, MIT, December 1994.

4. A formulary is a list of drugs put together by a PBM and delivered to all physicians on the cost containment plan. Physicians are encouraged to prescribe to patients drugs that are on the formulary.

5. Quoted from Greg Muirhead, "The ABC's of PBMs: Pharmacy Benefit Managers Control Pharmacy Industry," *Drug Topics*, 138, no.17 (September 5, 1994), 76.

6. Nancy A. Nichols, "Medicine, Management, and Mergers," *Harvard Business Review*, (November–December 1994), 110.

7. The $33.03 billion was compared against the total market value of Merck in 1993. The average number of shares in that year was 1,156 million, and the average common stock market price was about $33 per share. This gives a total market value of $38 billion. Although there is a discrepancy, as is to be expected, the numbers are comparable. No effort has been made to improve the estimated values, because the important part of the valuation exercise is the comparison of the market values with and without the merger.

CHAPTER 9

Corporate Strategy: The Core Concepts

THE THREE PERSPECTIVES OF STRATEGY

We distinguish three perspectives in a formal strategic planning process: corporate, business, and functional. These perspectives are different both in terms of the nature of the decisions they address, as well as the organizational units and managers involved in formulating and implementing the corresponding action programs generated by the strategy formation process.

At the corporate level we deal with the tasks that cannot be delegated downward in the organization, because they need the broadest possible scope—involving the whole firm—to be properly addressed. At the business level we face those decisions that are critical for establishing a sustainable competitive advantage, leading toward superior economic returns in the industry where the business competes. At the functional level, we attempt to develop and nurture the core competencies of the firm—the capabilities that are the sources of the competitive advantages.

Strategic Tasks at the Corporate Level

This chapter deals exclusively with corporate strategic tasks. There are three different imperatives—leadership, economic, and managerial—that are useful for characterizing these tasks, depending on whether we are concerned with shaping the vision of the firm, extracting the highest profitability levels, or assuring proper coordination and managerial capabilities.

THE LEADERSHIP IMPERATIVE

This imperative is commonly associated with the person of the CEO, who is expected to define a vision for the firm and communicate it in a way that generates contagious enthusiasm.

The CEO's vision provides a sense of purpose to the organization, poses a significant yet attainable challenge, and draws the basic direction to the pursuit of that challenge. Successful organizations invariably seem to have competent leaders who are able to define and transmit a creative vision, which generates a spirit of success. In other words, success breeds success.

Much has been written and said about leadership including the controversy on "nature or nurture"—whether leaders are born or made—and on the existence of common characteristics to describe successful leaders.[1] We will not review this literature here, since we will be concentrating on the economic and managerial imperatives of the corporate strategic tasks. Nonetheless, the set of corporate tasks that will be the subject of this part—dealing with the economic and managerial imperatives—are the critical instruments to imprint the vision of the firm. The leadership capabilities are expressed and made tangible through thc tasks that are discussed herein.[2]

THE ECONOMIC IMPERATIVE

This imperative is concerned with creating value at the corporate level. The acid test is whether the businesses of the firm are benefiting from being together, or if they would be better off as separate and autonomous units. From this point of view, the essence of corporate strategy is to assure that the value of the whole firm is bigger that the sum of the contributions of its businesses as independent units.

The economic imperative involves three central issues: the definition of the businesses of the firm; the identification and exploitation of interrelationships across those businesses, and the coordination of the business activities that allow sharing assets and skills.[3]

There are eight corporate tasks that we associate with the economic imperative of corporate strategy. The first one is the environmental scan at the corporate level, which allows us to start the reflection of the corporate and competitive position through a thorough understanding of the external forces that it is facing. One of the principal objectives of strategy is to seek a proper alignment between the firm and its environment. Therefore, it seems logical to start the corporate strategic planning process with a rigorous examination of the external environment.

The seven additional tasks imply critical strategic decisions seeking the attainment of corporate strategic advantages. They are the mission of the firm, business segmentation, horizontal strategy, vertical integration, corporate philosophy, strategic posture of the firm, and portfolio management.

We provide now a preview of each of these tasks, which we cover extensively in the remaining chapters of Part III.

1. Environmental Scan at the Corporate Level: Understanding the External Forces Impacting the Firm.

The environmental scan provides an assessment of the distinct business opportunities offered by the geographical regions in which the firm operates. It also examines the general trends of the various industrial sectors related to the portfolio of businesses of the corporation. Finally, it describes the favorable and unfavorable impacts to the firm from technological trends; supply of human resources; and political, social, and legal factors. The output of the environmental scan is the identification of key opportunities and threats resulting from the impact of external factors.

2. The Mission of the Firm: Choosing the Competitive Domains and the Way to Compete.

Conceptually, the mission of the firm is identical to the mission of the business. It defines the business scope—products, markets, and geographical locations—as well as the unique competencies that determine the capabilities of the firm. However, there are two important differences that contrast the mission of a firm with that of a business.

One is the level of aggregation used to express these mission statements. At the level of the firm the statements are very broad, because we need to encompass all the critical activities and capabilities of the corporation. At the level of the business, we are much more specific in providing a sharper focus to define the business scope and the way we select to compete.

The second difference has to do with the criticality of the decisions implicit in both statements. The mission of the firm defines the overall portfolio of businesses. It selects the businesses in which the firm will enter or exit, as well as the discretionary allocation of tangible and intangible resources assigned to them. The selection of a business scope at the level of the firm is often very hard to reverse without incurring significant or prohibitive costs. The development of unique competencies shape the *corporate advantage,* namely, the capabilities that will be transferred across the portfolio of businesses.

The mission of the firm involves two of the most essential decisions of corporate strategy: selecting the businesses of the firm, and integrating the business strategies to create additional economic value. Mistakes in these two categories of decisions could be painful, because the stakes that are assigned to the resulting bets are very high indeed.

3. Business Segmentation: Selecting Planning and Organizational Focuses.

The mission of the firm defines its business scope, namely the products and services it generates, the markets it serves, and the geographical locations in which it operates. The business segmentation defines the perspectives or dimensions that will be used to group these activities in a way that will be managed most effectively. It adds planning and organizational focuses, which are central for both the strategic analysis and the implementation of the business strategies. This concept is of great importance in the conduct of a formal strategic planning process, since the resulting businesses are the most relevant units of analysis in that process.

4. Horizontal Strategy: Pursuing Synergistic Linkages Across Business Units.

One could argue that horizontal strategies are the primary sources for corporate advantage of a diversified firm. It is through the detection and realization of the existing synergy across the various businesses that significant additional economic value can be created. The value chain is the basic framework that is used to detect opportunities for sharing resources and activities across businesses. The resulting degree of linkages among businesses determines their relative autonomy and independence. The mission of the firm defines the business scope; business segmentation organizes the businesses into planning and managerial units; horizontal strategies determine their degree of interdependence. Consequently, these tasks are highly linked. Moreover, the mission of the firm also defines the current and future corporate core competencies, which are the basis that supports the relationship among the various businesses, and the role to be played by horizontal strategy.

5. Vertical Integration: Defining the Boundaries of the Firm.

Vertical integration determines the breadth of the value chain, as well as the intensity of each of the activities performed internally by the firm. It specifies the firm's boundaries, and establishes the relationship of the firm with its primary outside constituencies: suppliers, distributors, and customers.

The major benefits of vertical integration are realized through: cost reductions from economies of scale and scope; creation of defensive market power against suppliers and clients; and creation of offensive market power in order to profit from new business opportunities. The main deterrents of vertical integration are: diseconomies of scale from increases in overhead and capital investments; loss of flexibility; and administrative penalties stemming from more complex managerial activities.[4]

6. Corporate Philosophy: Defining the Relationship Between the Firm and Its Stakeholders.

The corporate philosophy provides a unifying theme and a statement of basic principles for the organization. First, it addresses the relationship between the firm and its employees, customers, suppliers, communities, and shareholders. Second, it specifies broad objectives for the firm's growth and profitability. Third, it defines the basic corporate policies; and finally, it comments on issues of ethics, beliefs, and rules of personal and corporate conduct.

The corporate philosophy is the task that is most closely related to the leadership imperative, insofar as bringing a capability for articulating key elements of the CEO's vision.

7. Strategic Posture of the Firm: Identifying the Srategic Thrusts, and Corporate Performance Objectives.

The strategic posture of the firm is a set of pragmatic requirements developed at the corporate level to guide the formulation of corporate, business, and functional strategies. The strategic thrusts define the strategic agenda of the firm. They identify all of the key strategic issues, and signal the organizational units responsible for responding to them. The corporate performance objectives define the key indicators used to evaluate the managerial results, and assign numerical targets as an expression of the strategic intent of the firm. The strategic posture captures the outputs of all of the previous tasks and uses them as challenges to be recognized and dealt with in terms of action-driven issues.

8. Portfolio Management: Assigning Priorities for Resource Allocation and Identifying Opportunities for Diversification and Divestment.

Portfolio management and resource allocation have always been recognized as responsibilities that reside squarely at the corporate level. We have already commented that the development of core competencies shared by the various businesses of the firm constitutes a critical source of corporate advantage. Those competencies are borne from resources that the firm should be able to nurture and deploy effectively, including: physical assets, such as plant and equipment; intangible assets, such as highly recognized brands; and capabilities, such as skills associated with product design and development.

The heart of an effective resource allocation process is the capacity to create economic value. Sometimes, this value emerges from internal activities of the firm; in other cases it is acquired from external sources through mergers, acquisitions, joint ventures, and other forms of alliances. On occasion value can even be created by divesting businesses that are not earning their cost of capital; i.e., they are destroying, instead of adding value to, the firm. Portfolio management deals with all of these critical issues.

In the last decade, most developed economies have been facing periods of stagnation that have forced firms to implement drastic restructuring policies. Restructuring leads to the realignment of physical assets—including divestment—human resources, and organizational boundaries of the various businesses with the intent of reshaping their structure and performance. Restructuring decisions are also part of portfolio management.[5]

THE MANAGERIAL IMPERATIVE

This imperative is the major determinant for a successful implementation of corporate strategy. It involves two additional important corporate tasks: the design of the firm's managerial infrastructure, and the management of its key personnel.

9. Managerial Infrastructure: Designing and Adjusting the Organizational Structure, Managerial Processes, and Systems in Consonance With the Culture of the Firm to Facilitate the Implementation of Strategy.

Organizational structure and administrative systems constitute the managerial infrastructure of the firm. An effective managerial infrastructure is critical for the successful implementation of the strategies of the firm. Its ultimate objective is the development of corporate values, managerial capabilities, organizational responsibilities, and managerial processes to create a self-sustaining set of rules that allow the decentralization of the activities of the firm.

Today, the term organizational architecture is commonly used to designate the design efforts that produce an alignment between the environment, the organizational resources, the culture of the firm, and its strategy.[6]

10. Human Resources Management of Key Personnel: Selection, Development, Appraisal, Reward, and Promotion.

Regardless of how large a corporation is, it will always be managed by a few key individuals. Percy Barnevik, the CEO of Asea Brown-Boveri, a successful global company, stated that one of ABB's biggest priorities (and potential bottlenecks) is to create global managers. However, he immediately added that a global company does not need thousands of them. At ABB, five hundred out of a total of fifteen thousand managers are enough to make ABB work well.[7]

Tom MacAvoy, the former president of Corning-Glass Works used to talk, in a rather colorful way, about the need for "one hundred centurions" to run an organization. These are huge corporations, with operations in over one hundred countries. When it comes to identifying the key personnel they need, the numbers are surprisingly small; yet, the process of identifying, developing, promoting, rewarding, and retaining them is one of the toughest challenges that an organization faces.[8]

The Fundamental Elements in the Definition of Corporate Strategy

We can organize the corporate strategic tasks in a strategic planning framework that closely parallels the one used for the definition of business strategy in Figure 3–1. The framework, which we label "The Fundamental Elements of the Definition of Corporate Strategy: The Ten Tasks," is presented in Figure 9–1.

The first element of the framework is to identify the entity that is going to be part of the corporate strategic analysis. As opposed to the business strategy case, where the unit of analysis is the SBU, corporate strategy can be applied at

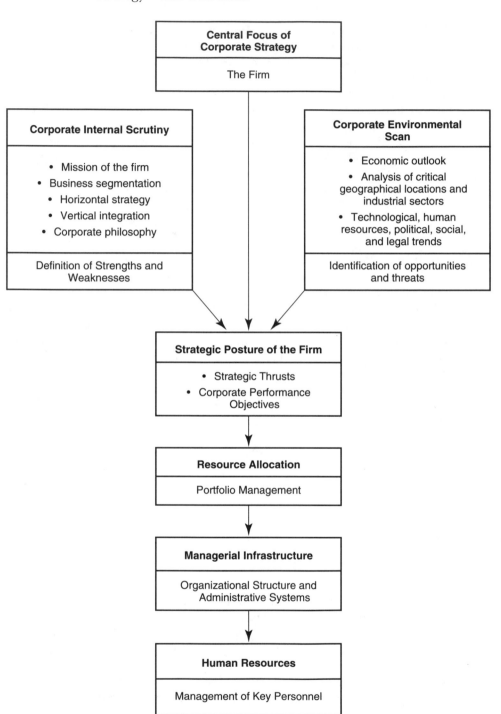

FIGURE 9–1. The Fundamental Elements of the Definition of Corporate Strategy—The Ten Tasks

Central Focus of Corporate Strategy

The Firm

Corporate Internal Scrutiny

- Mission of the firm
- Business segmentation
- Horizontal strategy
- Vertical integration
- Corporate philosophy

Definition of Strengths and Weaknesses

Corporate Environmental Scan

- Economic outlook
- Analysis of critical geographical locations and industrial sectors
- Technological, human resources, political, social, and legal trends

Identification of opportunities and threats

Strategic Posture of the Firm

- Strategic Thrusts
- Corporate Performance Objectives

Resource Allocation

Portfolio Management

Managerial Infrastructure

Organizational Structure and Administrative Systems

Human Resources

Management of Key Personnel

190

different levels in a large, diversified organization. The amplest possible scope is the firm as a whole, which is the most relevant entity of the corporate strategic analysis. However, it may be that we choose a smaller entity, which still encompasses a number of different business units. This could be a sector, a group, a division, or any aggregation of business units requiring an integrative strategic analysis.

Next, there are two important set of issues that, as before, we have labeled environmental scan and internal scrutiny. This time, however, these are performed at the corporate level as opposed to the business level.

We should recognize, from the outset, the dynamic nature of this framework. There is an underlying time frame that has to be spelled out at the beginning of the planning process. Throughout the corporate strategic analysis, we are contrasting existing conditions with future ones. In the case of the environmental scan, the future conditions normally require a forecast of uncontrollable external factors, except when the firm has an ability to influence external events to its own advantage. The internal scrutiny deals primarily with exercising decisions controllable by the firm, and with the allocation of the firm's resources aiming at a more desirable future position.

The corporate environmental scan should be conducted first in the planning process, because it serves to frame the impacts of the external environment, and to provide an understanding of the important trends associated with the industries and geographical locations relevant to the firm. The corporate environmental scan also has the important role of transferring a common set of assumptions to the various businesses and functional units of the firm, to serve as inputs of their own strategic planning efforts. It gives a sense of uniformity to the strategic planning thinking across all the key organizational units of the firm. As before, this task culminates with the recognition of opportunities—the favorable impacts of the external environment that we would like to seize—and threats—the unfavorable impacts that we would like to neutralize.

The corporate internal scrutiny captures the key actions and decisions the corporation has to address to gain a competitive position that is in line with the challenges generated by the external environment and conducive to the development of a sustainable corporate advantage. As we have indicated before, this advantage is transferable to the various business units of the firm, and enhances its resources and capabilities. The tasks that are part of the internal scrutiny in our framework are:

- Mission of the firm
- Business segmentation
- Horizontal strategy
- Vertical integration
- Corporate philosophy

In all of these decisions we contrast the current state with a desirable future one, and we proceed to define the challenges those changes generate for the formulation of corporate strategy. The internal scrutiny concludes with an overall statement of corporate strengths—which the firm wishes to maintain and reinforce—as well as a statement of corporate weaknesses—which the firm wishes to correct or eliminate.

The corporate environmental scan and internal scrutiny provide the basic inputs that will define the strategic posture of the firm. This task serves as a synthesis of the analysis conducted so far, and captures the strategic agenda of the firm. The strategic thrusts are a powerful expression of all the issues that, from the perspective of the firm, need to be addressed to consolidate an integrative strategy.

The corporate performance objectives define the key indicators that will be used to detect the operational and strategic effectiveness of the firm. The strategic posture is the essence of the formulation of the corporate strategy, and as such, it is a task that should receive the utmost attention. When properly conducted, the firm is able to frame the activities, responsibilities, and performance measurements that are critical for its superior strategic position.

The subsequent task—resource allocation and portfolio management—permits backup for the strategic actions implicit in the strategic posture of the firm, with the necessary resources needed for their deployment. We are now entering into the realm of strategy implementation.

These implementation efforts are going to be strongly reinforced by the remaining two corporate tasks: managerial infrastructure and human resources management of key personnel.

Notes

1. Two useful references on leadership are: Edgar E. Schein, *Organizational Culture and Leadership*, 2nd ed. (San Francisco, CA: Jossey-Bass, 1992); and John P. Kotter, *The Leadership Factor* (New York: Free Press, 1988).

2. An important related topic to leadership is the issue of power. From this perspective, management is perceived as a political process addressing the creation, exercise, retention, and transfer of power. Power plays the central role in the implementation of strategy by influencing people's behavior, making them do things that they otherwise would not do, and changing the course of events. For an excellent treatment of the subject, see Jeffrey Pfeffer, *Managing with Power: Politics and Influence in Organizations* (Boston, MA: Harvard Business School Press, 1992).

3. Michael E. Porter, "From Competitive Advantage to Corporate Strategy," *Harvard Business Review*, 65, no. 3 (May–June 1987), 43–59 suggests a typology with four corporate strategies: portfolio management, assets restructuring, transfer of skills, and shared activities. The first two can be accomplished with unrelated businesses; the last two are based on interrelationships among businesses.

Portfolio management is commonly perceived as one of the most passive corporate strategies, where the contribution of the firm simply consists of allocating resources—primarily financial ones—across businesses, according to priorities that reflect their various degrees of attractiveness. Restructuring involves the realignment of assets, including divestment, human resources, and organizational boundaries of the various businesses, with the intent of reshaping their structure and performance. It is a strategy that is commonly pursued after major acquisitions or when the corporation faces moments of significant crisis or takeover threats. The last two strategies—transfer of skills and shared activities—are the basis for the *horizontal strategies* and *vertical integration* of the corporation. They imply identifying and exploiting interrelationships among distinct but related businesses.

4. Some sources for the topic of vertical integration are: John Stuckey and David White, "When and When Not to Vertically Integrate," *Sloan Management Review* (Spring 1993) 71–83; Kathryn Rudie Harrigan, *Strategic Flexibility: A Management Guide for Changing Times* (Lexington, MA: Lexington Books, 1985); Gordon Walker, "Strategic Sourcing, Vertical Integration and Transaction Costs," *Interfaces,* 19 (May–June 1988), 62–73; and David J. Teece, "Profiting from Technological Innovations: Implications for Integration, Collaboration, Licensing, and Public Policy," in David J. Teece, ed., *The Competitive Challenge: Strategies for Industrial Innovations and Renewal* (Cambridge, MA: Ballinger Publishing Co., 1987).

5. For an excellent presentation on the nature, process, and management of restructuring, see Gordon Donaldson, *Corporate Restructuring, Managing the Change Process from Within* (Boston, MA: Harvard Business School Press, 1994).

6. For a discussion of "organizational architecture'" see David A. Nadler, Marc S. Gerstein, Robert B. Shaw, and Associates, *Organizational Architecture: Designs for Changing Organizations* (San Francisco, CA: Jossey-Bass, 1992).

7. William Taylor, "The Logic of Global Business: An Interview with ABB's Percy Barnevik," *Harvard Business Review* , 69, no. 2 (March–April 1991), 91–105.

8. For a forceful treatment of the role of human resources in seeking competitive advantage, see Jeffrey Pfeffer, *Competitive Advantage through People* (Boston, MA: Harvard Business School Press, 1994).

10

Environmental Scan at the Corporate Level

Environmental scan is the first task to be conducted in the definition of the corporate strategy, because it formalizes the process of understanding the external forces that are impacting the firm. There are three different elements that guide the environmental scan: economic overview, primary industrial sectors, and basic external factors.

The *economic overview* attempts to capture the existing conditions and trends that characterize the economic activities in all the major geographical locations relevant to the firm. It involves segmenting the geographical areas into regions, countries, or other relevant units that are going to be treated as homogeneous in terms of their economic behavior; selecting the factors that will provide the economic assessment (such as GNP growth, inflation rate, unemployment, disposable personal income, prime rate, etc.); and establishing numerical values to those factors, measuring the historical performance as well as the future projection.

The *primary industrial sectors* analysis attempts to diagnose the past and future conditions of the industries related to the portfolio of businesses of the corporation. It requires the firm to define those businesses, suggest indicators to monitor their evolution (such as total market, market growth rate, total company sales, market share, etc.), and quantify the past performance and future projections for each of those indicators.

The *basic external factors* analysis consists of describing the favorable and unfavorable impacts to the firm from technological trends, supply of human resources, political factors, social factors, and legal factors. These external factors are, by and large, uncontrollable by the firm, but are critical for defining the attractiveness of the environment in which it operates. We need to define those factors, understand their past as well as future behavior, and extract from them the opportunities and threats presented to the firm.

What we have just described seems to make a great deal of sense in terms of capturing the environment in which the firm operates. What we are saying is that we need to understand economic trends, industrial trends, and other important critical external factors that are going to affect the firm's performance. What truly complicates this analysis is the enormous complexity that is added when a firm operates in a global setting. All of these dimensions are completely different in the regions and countries in which the firm operates. Therefore, although it is hard to argue against the need to collect specific environmental information in all the dimensions we have identified, the task of gathering that intelligence, country by country, could be truly overwhelming.

A Process for Performing the Environmental Scan at the Corporate Level

When a firm operates in a global environment with a presence in many different countries, the environmental scanning process can be enormously demanding, due to the massive amount of statistics that need to be collected in each individual geographical location. The execution of this task can be simplified through proper delegation of information gathering at the local level. However, we feel it is essential for the firm to have a central point for processing the resulting information to achieve an overall view of the corporate environment.

To illustrate the process of performing the environmental scan at the corporate level, we use as an illustration the case of the materials sector of NKK Corporation. NKK is one of the biggest Japanese companies, with net sales of Y1.3 trillion, and net income of Y 36 billion. The materials sector, including steel and advanced materials businesses, is the core of the company, representing 74 percent of its total sales (1991 FY). NKK is the fifth largest producer of steel in the world.[1]

Step 1. Definition of Time Frame.
In this step we define a time frame for the corporate strategic plan. The time frame is described by using past, current, and future specifications. Typically, firms use a three-to-five-year future time horizon, although this could be greatly affected by the characteristics of the industries relevant to the firm. The past time frame is used to gather statistics pertaining to historical behavior; its length is often dictated by the availability of the necessary data. Contrasting past and future projections is useful for detecting the evolution of the factors being examined as well as the soundness of future projections.

In the case of NKK, we are using 1989–1991 as the past time frame; 1992 as the present; and 1993–1995 as the future. It was judged that the dynamics of the industry was so fast that a longer time frame might not be meaningful.

Step 2. Geographic Segmentation.
The environmental scan varies within the different geographical regions in which the firm operates. The economic, political, and social factors affecting

one country are different from those affecting another. The geographical segmentation should lead to the identification of units that behave similarly with regard to these external factors.

Figure 10–1 shows the geographical segmentation for NKK materials sectors. Notice that we separate existing and new geographical scopes. There is also a very different level of detail in the segmentation of each geographical area. Japan, which is the dominant market for NKK, is broken into eight different geographical areas; while Latin America and Africa, markets of small importance for NKK, are lumped into one single category each.

Step 3. Identification and Analysis of Economic Factors.

This step involves the task of identifying the critical economic factors to be used in describing the economic conditions of each geographical unit, and quantifying the historical and future performance of each factor to facilitate an economic analysis of each area.

FIGURE 10–1.   Geographical Segmentation— NKK Materials Sector

Existing Geographical Scope
• Domestic
Kanto (including Tokyo)
Kansai (including Osaka)
Hokkaido
Tohoku
Chubu (including Nagoya)
Chugoku
Shikoku
Kyushu
• China
• Far East
• ASEAN
• Other Asia (including Oceania)
• Middle East
• U.S.A.
• Latin America
• Western Europe
• Former Soviet Union
• Africa
New Geographical Scope
• Eastern Europe

SOURCE: Masayuki Tada, "Corporate Strategy for a Japanese Steel Manufacturing Company," unpublished masters thesis, Sloan School of Management, MIT, 1993. This is not an official document of NKK Corporation.

Figure 10–2 both identifies and describes the economic factors for Japan in the NKK case. The figure summarizes the statistics for the domestic market, although pertinent information is also gathered in more detail for the eight Japanese regions shown in Figure 10–1.

The figure shows some of the deteriorating conditions of the Japanese economy. The expectation is for a gradual recovery due in part to active investment by the Japanese government. However, even after the recovery, the Japanese economy would not be able to exhibit the strength of the late 1980s.

The projections provided here, as well as in the remaining steps of the environmental scan, are based on a most likely scenario. At the end of this process, we offer optimistic and pessimistic scenarios as alternatives. These represent the full range of the realization of expected events, which allow us to have a sense of the intensity of the uncertainty affecting the firm, as well as providing the basis for appropriate contingency planning.

The economic analysis performed at this step is a fairly broad overview. As we have seen in the business strategy part, a more detailed analysis is conducted at the level of the business unit.

Step 4. Identification and Analysis of Primary Industrial Sectors.

Together with the economic factors, the performance of the industrial sectors in which the firm competes are key in defining the growth and profitability

FIGURE 10–2. Identification and Analysis of Economic Factors—NKK Materials Sector

	Past			Current	Future		
	1989	1990	1991	1992	1993	1994	1995
Japan							
Real GNP Growth (%)	4.7	5.5	3.4	2.1	3.5	3.7	3.8
Inflation Rate (CPI)	2.9	3.1	2.8	2.1	2.3	2.5	2.5
Unemployment Rate (%)	2.2	2.1	2.2	2.3	2.3	2.1	2.1
Prime Rate (%)	5.9	7.9	7.5	5.3	5.3	5.5	6
Growth in Private Housing Starts	0.5	4.9	-10.1	0.1	1.3	1.5	1.5
Growth in Private Investment in Plant & Equipment	16.6	12.1	3.1	2.7	5.1	6.5	6.5
Growth in Public Investment in Infrastructure	-2.2	4.4	5.4	5.8	6	6	6
Crude Oil Price ($/Barrel)	17.8	22.9	20.7	19.1	20	22.1	24.2
Yen Rate (¥/$)	143	141	133	120	118	116	114
Population Growth (Millions)	0.4	0.4	0.3	0.3	0.25	0.25	0.2

SOURCE: "Japan Economic Almanac '92," Tokyo, Nihon Keizai Shimbun, Inc. "Monthly Kaigai Keizai Data," Economic Planning Agency, Tokyo, Japan. Tada (1993). This is not an official document of NKK Corporation.

opportunities. A very diversified corporation covers a wide array of different, or even unrelated, industries. On the contrary, a very focused firm, although it might be participating in a broad portfolio of businesses, tends to concentrate its activities in a few highly related industries. There is a great strategic significance attached to this issue, because there seems to be ample evidence that related diversification leads to higher profitability levels than unrelated diversification. The conglomerate firm, the extreme version of unrelated diversification, seldom, if ever, is able to sustain superior economic performance.[2]

This step identifies the most important industrial sectors of the firm and describes quantitatively its past and future performance. Figure 10-3 illustrates the step for the NKK case. The steel industry is preponderant in the materials sector of NKK. Therefore, the figure concentrates exclusively on identifying factors that lead to explaining variations in steel consumption. Reflecting the recession of the Japanese economy, the production of automobiles, housing, construction, electronic, and not electronic machinery have decreased significantly since its 1990 levels. In the future, although it is expected that all of these industries will experience a recovery, strong growth is coming only from shipbuilding and public spending in infrastructure.

Step 5. Analysis of Basic External Factors and Definition of Alternative Planning Scenarios.

To the economic overview and the primary industrial sectors analysis we have already conducted, we should add a reflection on a host of more subtle but often crucial issues embodied in the category of basic external factors. The first of these factors is represented by technological trends, a critical environmental

FIGURE 10–3. Identification and Analysis of Primary Industrial Factors—NKK Materials Sector

	Past			Current	Future		
	1989	1990	1991	1992	1993	1994	1995
Automobile Production (000)	12,954	13,592	13,146	12,580	12,260	12,740	13,210
Housing Starts (000)	1,673	1,665	1,343	1,382	1,400	1,420	1,440
Construction (000 sq. meters)*	11,986	12,656	11,958	11,898	12,000	12,200	12,400
Public Works Starts (¥ bil.)	12,187	13,390	15,174	16,000	17,000	17,500	17,500
Electronic Machinery Index ('85=100)	143	154	157	148	148	149	150
Machinery Index ('85=100)	123	130	124	111	112	115	118
Shipbuilding Starts (000 G/T)	5,705	6,886	6,942	8,120	7,580	7,990	8,400

* Nonhousing construction

SOURCE: "Tekko Jyukyu No Ugoki, vol. 167," Kozai Club, Tokyo, Japan. NKK In-House Report. Author's Estimation. Tada (1993). This is not an official document of NKK Corporation.

force in every significant industry today. Human resources, the next of the basic factors in our list, is equally important. The quality, availability, and depth of human resources—particularly with regard to key professional and technical skills—often constrain or stimulate the opportunities of the firm. To complete the analysis of the environmental scan, we add political, social, and legal factors. They include issues that are central to most business firms, such as regulatory matters, questions of unionization, minority concerns, environmental policies, public opinion pressures, community activities, and the like.

In this step, after defining the factors, we proceed to examine the impact they would have on the businesses of the firm. Often, it is useful to describe their past trends and project them toward the future. The objective of this exercise is not to produce accurate forecasts of these factors' behavior. We all know that this is an impossible task. Rather, we want to have a deep reflection on what are possible outcomes that might come from the environment, understand how they will affect the firm, and be ready to exercise flexibility in the way we respond to unanticipated events. For these reasons, we find useful to describe three different scenarios associated with each factor: a most likely, a pessimistic, and an optimistic scenario.

Figure 10–4 describes those scenarios for the case of NKK Materials Sector. Notice that we have added a narrative for economic and primary industrial sector factors. Although these were treated specially in the previous steps, in order to describe their performance quantitatively, they now reemerge as we provide a more qualitative description of their impact on the firm.

Step 6. Identification of Key Opportunities and Threats.

The final output of the environmental scan is the identification of key opportunities emerging from favorable factors affecting the firm; and key threats resulting from adverse impacts from those factors. These opportunities and threats should capture all of the critical issues detected from the environmental scanning process.

A big challenge is how these issues are going to affect the various managers and organizational entities of the firm. Later, in the Strategic Posture phase of our analysis, we identify which organizational units will be responsible for coming out with action programs aimed at seizing opportunities and neutralizing threats.

Figure 10–5 lists the opportunities and threats impacting the NKK materials sector. We have included also Figure 10-6, which provides a similar list for the case of P&G. We carry on the P&G example throughout this part, as an illustration of the various tasks of corporate strategy. In the business strategy part, we presented the case of Detergents in Europe, a unit of P&G; in this part, we address the corporation as a whole.

(Figures 10-4 through 10-6 follow on pages 200-202)

FIGURE 10–4. Definition of Alternative Planning Scenarios—NKK Materials Sector

BASIC FACTORS	PESSIMISTIC	MOST LIKELY	OPTIMISTIC
Economic Overview	• Increasing government debt & its reluctance to invest in infrastructure • Failure to decrease trade surplus • Increasing debt of U.S. government and decrease of credibility of U.S. treasury bonds • Stagnant GNP growth in Japan & U.S. < 3.0%; China & ASEAN < 6% • High and rapid appreciation of yen (¥100/$) • Crude oil price goes up to $25/Barrel	• Government invests in infrastructure • Structural change of Japanese economy is started • Trade surplus and trade conflicts are maintained under control • Steady and strong GNP growth • Steady growth in Japan and U.S. around 3.5%; China and ASEAN 8% • Yen appreciation (¥120/$) • Crude oil price at $20/Barrel	• Success in structural changes of the Japanese economy strengthening the domestic market • Decreasing trade conflicts in foreign countries, especially the U.S. • Steady and strong GNP growth in Japan and U.S. > 4.0%; China and ASEAN > 10% • Stable Yen rate (¥120-130/$) • Crude oil price keeps less than $20/Barrel
Primary Industrial Sectors Overview	• Automobile production level remains at less than 13,000,000 until '95 • Housing starts and nonhousing construction keep decreasing through '95	• Automobile production level reaches 13,000,000 in '95 • Housing starts and construction stop decreasing in '94	• Recovery of automobile production level to 13,000,000 in '94 and continuous growth afterward • Increase of housing starts to 15,000,000 units in '94
Technological Trends	• Quantity of steel used in a car decreases by 250kg/car by '95 • Failure of development of steel-making process that can respond to needs from environmental concerns (especially recycling)	• Maintenance in use of steel • Continue efforts to develop environmentally clean smelting process	• Successful development of value-added and light-weight steel sheets which can compete with aluminum sheets effectively • Successful development of DIOS (Direct Iron Ore Smelting) process technology
Supply of Human Resources	• Decrease of loyalty toward the company among employees due to massive restructuring between '93 and '95 • Increase of difficulty in hiring excellent young people as steel manufacturers, especially engineers and shop floor workers	• Loyalty toward the company is acceptable • Attraction of young people still a concern	• Manufacturing recovers popularity as an employer among young people
Political Factors	• Japanese government introduces world's strictest environmental regulations • Japanese government introduces "Land Price Tax"	• Environmental regulations and tax do not change significantly	• Japanese government gives up the introduction of "Land Price Tax"
Social Factors	• Concern for environmental issues is increased to the same level as in Germany	• Increased concern for environmental issues	• Concern for environmental issues remains at present level
Legal Factors	• Houses introduce product liability law as tough as U.S. law	• New product liability law does not mean major cost increase	• Houses (National Diet) give up introduction of product liability law

SOURCE: Adapted from Tada (1993). This is not an official document of NKK Corporation.

FIGURE 10–5. Identification of Opportunities and Threats—NKK Materials Sector

KEY OPPORTUNITIES	
Economic Overview	• Stable growth of public investment in infrastructure • Stable improvement of U.S. economy • High growth of Chinese economy • Continuous growth of ASEAN
Primary Industrial Sectors	• Increase of public works starts • Increase of shipbuilding starts
Technological Trends	• Increasing needs for value-added steel • Development of Direct Iron Ore Smelting (DIOS) process technology • Increasing needs for lightweight material (especially in auto industry) • Development of materials with high corrosion and heat resistance • Increasing number of ships that need double hulls • Development of FMS (Flexible Manufacturing Systems) • Development of new iron-making process using scrap
Supply of Human Resources	• Less need for shop floor workers due to introduction of further automation
Political Factors	• Strong support for further Investment in maintenance of infrastructure • Transferring the country's Capitol outside Tokyo • Adoption of some antidumping action against low-price foreign producers by Japanese government
Social Factors	• Increasing concern for environmental issues
KEY THREATS	
Economic Overview	• Slowdown of the growth of the Japanese economy • High appreciation of Yen
Primary Industrial Sectors	• Dull growth of Japanese auto industry • Depressed production of machinery
Technological Trends	• Increasing needs for lightweight material (especially in auto industry) • Diversified needs for material and small-lot production • Improvements of process technology of minimills • Downsizing of information systems
Supply of Human Resources	• Increase of average age of employees • Unpopularity of manufacturing jobs among young people • Trend of reducing working hours in Japan
Political Factors	• More strict environmental regulation • Enforced Fair Trade Commission in Japan • Increasing trade conflicts between Japan and U.S. • Abuse of antidumping by the U.S. competitors • Introduction of Land Price Tax by the Japanese Government
Social Factors	• Increasing concern for environmental issues • Change of Japanese lifestyles (less work, more leisure)
Legal Factors	• Introduction of product liability related law

SOURCE: Adapted from Tada (1993). This is not an official document of NKK Corporation.

FIGURE 10–6. Identification of Opportunities and Threats—The Case of P&G

KEY OPPORTUNITIES	
Economic Overview	• The creation of unique markets in the European Community, North America and the South Cone of Latin America should allow us to use our size to compete effectively on quality, brand recognition, and pricing. • Rapid population growth in the Third World, and economic rebound in developing countries.
Primary Industrial Sectors	• In cosmetics and personal care, high brand recognition and leadership in R&D should be used to increase market share.
Technological Trends	• Our leadership in R&D should be focused on environmental issues, to be recognized— if possible with proprietary technologies—as the "environmental company." • Opportunity to become leaders in small and recyclable packaging before its use is mandatory.
Supply of Human Resources	• Availability of skilled inexpensive labor in Latin American and Eastern European areas.
Political Factors	• The creation of a politically unified Europe will bring stability to the area; the same will probably happen in the South Cone of Latin America.
Social Factors	• Similarity of needs, tastes, and fashions around the world leads to globalization of markets favorable to P&G products.
KEY THREATS	
Economic Overview	• Margins for consumer goods in the U.S. markets are likely to keep on declining.
Primary Industrial Sectors	• Very hard competition in growing markets, especially Latin America, where Unilever is very well positioned. • Europe and North America are mature in all markets except men's cosmetics.
Technological Trends	• Increasing investment by pharmaceutical competitors are affecting the prescription drug and over-the-counter businesses.
Supply of Human Resources	• Intensive competition for talented individuals, particularly global managers with multicultural and multilanguage skills. • Unionization in the European Community may be problematic.
Political Factors	• Uncertainty, conflicts, and chaos in former communist countries. • Potential for increasing friction among block trading partners.
Social Factors	• Reduction in size of the diaper market due to a decrease in births. • Increased concern over the environment could become a threat if we cannot become leaders in environmentally sound products and processes.

NOTE: This is not an official document. It is an illustration drawn from public sources.

Notes

1. The case of NKK has been adapted from: Masayuki Tada, "Corporate Strategy for a Japanese Steel Manufacturing Company," unpublished masters thesis, Sloan School of Management, MIT, 1993.

2. Michael E. Porter, "From Competitive Advantage to Corporate Strategy," Harvard Business Review, 65, no. 3 (May–June 1987), 43–59.

CHAPTER 11

The Mission of the Firm

The mission of the firm addresses the essence of what the firm is all about. It has two major components: the definition of the business scope, and the unique competencies that the firm has developed and will continue to promote into the future.

The business scope makes explicit, the areas in which the firm competes. It defines the overall portfolio of businesses, indicating the businesses in which the firm will enter or exit, as well as the discretionary allocation of tangible and intangible resources assigned to them. Pragmatically, it means identifying the products and services generated, the markets served, and the geographical reach covered. In addition, it includes the task of assigning priorities for resource allocation. The three dimensions—product scope, market scope, and geographical scope—are critical in defining the competitive domain of the firm. We have found it useful to address the business scope definition of a mission statement by first describing what is the current state of affairs; namely, what products, markets, and geographical locations define the domain in which the firm is operating. Then we reflect on a future state; that is to say, what products, markets, and geographical locations we should be serving. The contrast between the existing and the desired state generate the challenges and bring forth the definition of priorities for resource allocation that requires a response from strategic programs. This should lead to a redirection of the firm. After all, management of change is the essence of strategy.

The second dimension of the mission of the firm has to do with how to compete. It involves the definition of the unique competencies that the firm possesses now and those that it will be establishing in the future to acquire differentiating capabilities from its competitors. These unique competencies are born from resources and capabilities developed by the firm, and are the foundation of sustainable competitive advantages.

Establishing the mission of the firm is a major corporate task in our planning process. It constitutes the initial effort that provides top managers with an opportunity to reflect seriously on the current status of the overall firm activities, and to reach consensus with regard to the desired changes they would like to carry into the future. The declaration made explicit in the mission statement contains an inherent definition of priorities for the strategic agenda of the firm and identifies the major opportunities for growth and the capabilities that have to be enhanced to achieve a superior competitive advantage. As such, it provides basic guiding principles and a set of expectations that are going to condition the rest of the strategic activities at all managerial levels of the firm.

The proper amount of detail to be used in addressing each component of the mission depends on the complexity of the firm and, primarily, on its degree of diversification. In highly diversified multinational firms, the statements of product and market scope should be carried out at the level of an industry; the geographical scope might be described by listing the countries in which the firm operates or serves. Much finer details could be both feasible and useful in a less complex organization.

We have given a great deal of attention to these issues in Chapter 4 of this book, when we commented on the mission of the business. The process that we went through in that chapter, with all its laborious details, is directly applicable to the mission of the firm. Conceptually we are facing identical issues: defining the business scope—that is where to compete—and the unique competencies—how are we going to establish a competitive advantage. The differences between the mission of the business and the mission of the firm are scope and aggregation.

When defining the mission of the business, we are focusing on fairly well constrained product-market segments. However, when defining the mission of the firm, there is a much broader scope that encompasses all the business activities that are relevant to the corporation. By necessity, therefore, we should aggregate the activities of the firm in a way that captures its essence, without distracting us with unnecessary details. Those critical details will be addressed at the business and functional levels.

We will not revisit in this chapter all the steps that we recommend to define the mission of the business, and translate them to the mission of the firm. There is such an obvious parallel that we do not need to repeat the detailed tasks here. Again, the only difference is one of aggregation. We are dealing with broad issues at the firm level, while we are being much more specific at the business level.

Alternatives for Growth and Diversification: A Guide to Assessing the Future Scope of the Firm

Growth is the dominant force that drives future changes in the mission statement. The patterns of growth in the American industry have been well documented by the prominent business historian, Alfred D. Chandler, Jr.[1] The major generic alternatives for growth are depicted in Figure 11–1. After the introduction of a successful product the first logical strategy to follow is that of

FIGURE 11–1. Alternatives for Growth and Diversification: A Guide to Assessing the Future Scope of the Firm

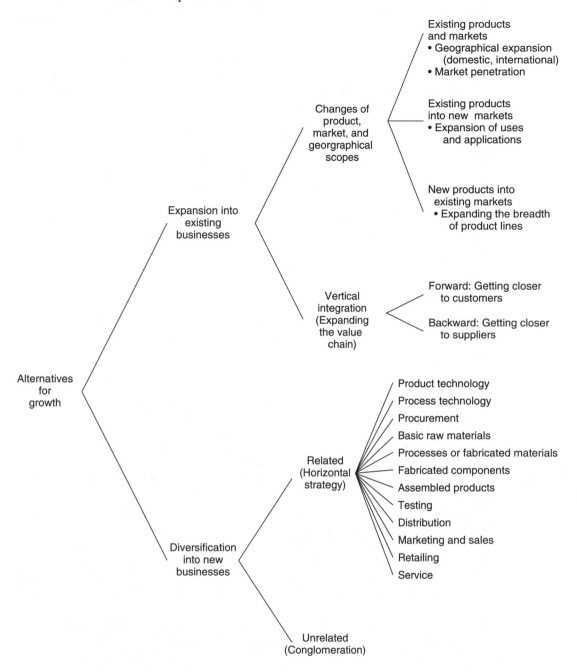

expanding the existing business within its current product-market structure. This can be accomplished by further penetration leading to increased sales volumes and geographical expansion, including, perhaps, international coverage. Moreover extensions of the existing market and product breadths are basic strategies for growth in existing businesses.

The second major strategy available to firms is vertical integration, which is an attempt at increasing value added within a given business base. There are two forms of vertical integration: forward, which leads the firm closer to its customers; and backward, which moves it closer to its suppliers.

A logical next step is to seek entry into new businesses via diversification. The nature of the diversification may be either related or unrelated, the latter type conducive to what is referred to as conglomeration. Related diversification is supported by expertise residing in one or more stages in the value chain. Thus the firm could attempt to enter into new businesses where the key for success can be traced back to one or more of the following stages of value added in which the firm currently excels: product and process technology, procurement, basic raw materials, processed or fabricated materials, fabricated components, assembled products, testing, distribution, marketing and sales, retailing, and services.

All of these alternatives for growth can be achieved either through internal development or acquisition. The pursuit of internal development has the advantage of establishing a strong base with deep cultural consistency. The obvious advantage of acquisition is its speedy and expedient accessibility to skill and competency not available internally to the firm. Acquisition prevails in the execution of unrelated diversification.

The selection of the strategies for growth as well as the intensity to carry out each one of them requires the exercise of a high level of judgment. There are clear dangers in not pursuing a strategy of extending the product line, for example, when competitors are including various features to differentiate their products. However, there are also serious problems in going too far in product-line extension, when product differences only contribute to increased inventory and lower productivity without adding significant value to the business.

Even more difficult is designing a proper strategy of vertical integration. If one is too aggressive in implementing a forward integration strategy, one could antagonize its own customers and pay dearly for it. Likewise, a backward integration strategy might result in severe negative responses on the part of one's own suppliers. Yet if key competitors seek a strategy of value-added maximization, it will be hard to compete if vertical integration is not properly undertaken. And then, there is always the risk that your own customers integrate backward or the suppliers integrate forward. This subject is treated more thoroughly in Chapter 14.

We have found that a discipline enforced by carefully analyzing each one of these strategies for growth contributes to the quality of the overall assessment of the opportunities available to a firm. This framework could generate alternatives to be subjected to a careful economic analysis, ultimately leading toward a preferred strategic direction for a firm.

Defining the Mission of the Firm: The Cases of NKK and P&G

Arriving at a proper statement of the mission of the firm is one of the most insightful corporate strategic tasks. It is the process leading to its formulation that contributes to making this task so important. Most significantly, we need to involve all the key managers in the process of the mission formulation to gain two things: the deep knowledge that resides in the backgrounds and experiences of those managers, and the consensus that will emerge after the commonly agreed mission statement is reached.

As we have already commented in Chapter 4, when presenting the detailed tasks that need to be completed to arrive at the definition of a mission statement, the process of defining that mission contains a number of different steps. We repeat these steps briefly here through the example of the Materials Sector of NKK.

The first step is the formulation of the business scope and unique competencies. In Figures 11–2 through 11–5 we identify existing and new products, markets, geographic locations, and unique competencies respectively. As shown in these figures, we need to reflect also on our current as well as desired scope and capabilities, and assign priorities to them to identify their relative importance. For example, the products receiving the highest priorities are "hot-rolled and cold rolled sheets," and "surface treated sheets" among existing products and "stainless steel sheets" the only new product added. Similarly, the automobile industry is the most important market; and China and the ASEAN countries are the most relevant among international geographical locations. Finally, unique competencies present a most formidable challenge, because many of them demand prime attention; most notably, the importance of achieving a substantial cost leadership, and effectively integrating factories, which are ongoing efforts. At the same time they are: looking for an alliance with Toa steel in low-end products; using National Steel as base to develop the business in the Americas; and having Thai Coated Steel as a base for further inroads into the ASEAN countries.

Next, we prepare some qualitative statements that document the challenges resulting from changes in business scope and unique competencies. These challenges contrast the existing conditions with the desired ones, and reflect upon the actions needed to fill in the gaps. Figure 11–6 presents the challenges emerging from the analysis done in the NKK case. There are challenges stemming from changes in the product scope, such as No. 3, "expand the share of stainless steel, especially sheets." In term of the market scope, No. 1 focuses on the adoption of light-weight materials for auto makers. In the are of geographical scope, we have No. 5, which calls for an increase in the resources assigned to the Chinese market. In the category of unique competencies, No. 1 refers to the need for further cost rationalization and No. 5 deals with the joint strategy with Toa Steel to promote low-end products.

FIGURE 11–2. Existing and New Product Scope and Priority Assessment Charts—The Case of NKK

Existing Product Scope	– –	–	E	+	++
• Carbon and low-alloy steel			●		
Pipes and tubes			●		
Plates			●		
Hot rolled and cole rolled sheets					●
Surface treated sheets					●
Bars and shapes		●			
• Stainless and specialty steel					
Pipes and tubes				●	
Plates				●	
Specialty steel sheets				●	
Bars and shapes				●	
• Polymer products			●		
• Titanium		●			
• Aluminum			●		
• Ferroalloys		●			
• Specialty metals		●			
• Chemicals				●	
• Ceramics			●		
• Precision metal products			●		
New Product Scope	– –	–	E	+	++
• Stainless steel sheets					●

SOURCE: Tada (1993). This is not an official document of NKK Corporation.

208

FIGURE 11–3. Existing and New Market Scope and Priority Assessment Charts—The Case of NKK

Existing Market Scope	− −	−	E	+	++
• Constructors				●	
• Automobile industry					●
• Electronic machinery industry			●		
• Machinery industry			●		
• Shipbuilding industry			●		
• Aerospace industry				●	
• Steel industry		●			
• Distributors			●		
• Exports		●			

New Market Scope	− −	−	E	+	++
• Design House			●		

SOURCE: Tada (1993). This is not an official document of NKK Corporation.

FIGURE 11–4. Existing and New Geographical Scope and Priority Assessment Charts—The Case of NKK

Existing Geographical Scope	– –	–	E	+	++
• Domestic					●
Kanto (including Tokyo)					●
Kansai (including Osaka)					●
Hokkaido			●		
Tohoku			●		
Chubu (including Nagoya)				●	
Chugoku				●	
Shikoku			●		
Kyushu			●		
• China					●
• Far East			●		
• ASEAN					●
• Other Asia (including Oceania)			●		
• Middle East			●		
• North America			●		
• Latin America			●		
• Western Europe			●		
• Former Soviet Union		●			
• Africa			●		
New Geographical Scope	**– –**	**–**	**E**	**+**	**++**
• Eastern Europe		●			

SOURCE: Tada (1993). This is not an official document of NKK Corporation.

210

FIGURE 11–5. Existing and New Unique Competencies and Priority Assessment Charts—The Case of NKK

Existing Unique Competencies	– –	–	E	+	++
• High brand recognition				●	
• Traditionally close relationship with suppliers				●	
• Close relationship with customers				●	
• Cost leadership					●
• Effective and integrated factories					●
• Excellent human resources				●	
• Intensive research and development			●		
• Using synergy with Engineering Division					●
New Unique Competencies	– –	–	E	+	++
• Alliances with Toa Steel in low-end products					●
• Use of National Steel as a base in American continents					●
• Use of Thai Coated Steel as a base in ASEAN					●

SOURCE: Tada (1993). This is not an official document of NKK Corporation.

FIGURE 11–6. Challenges Emerging from Changes in the Mission of the Firm—The Case of NKK

CHALLENGES EMERGING FROM CHANGES IN PRODUCT SCOPE

1. Develop further position in hot and cold rolled sheets by improving quality.
2. Improve the cost competitiveness of surface treated sheets.
3. Expand the share of stainless steel, especially sheets.
4. Transfer the production of low-end products to Toa Steel (bars and shapes, as well as low-end sheets).
5. Continue to search for business chances in aluminum business.
6. Shrink the business of ferroalloys.
7. Move toward more value-added areas and develop a significant position in chemical areas.
8. Restructure the titanium business and reduce its product lines.

CHALLENGES EMERGING FROM CHANGES IN MARKET SCOPE

1. Pay attention to the movement of adoption of lightweight materials by automakers and keep responding promptly to their requests.
2. Work jointly with Toa Steel and develop further our position in construction material markets.
3. Improve the presence in the aerospace material market by continuing to offer advanced materials.
4. Strengthen our reputation among design houses and architects.
5. Decrease dependence on exports.

CHALLENGES EMERGING FROM CHANGES IN GEOGRAPHICAL SCOPE

1. Keep the significant presence in Kanto (the biggest domestic market).
2. Increase market share in Kansai by strengthening Osaka Sales Office.
3. Strengthen the tie up activity with the Fukuyama Works to increase market share in Chugoku.
4. Establish close relationship with JVs between Japanese and local companies in ASEAN countries.
5. Keep allocating significant resources for the Chinese market.
6. Investigate business opportunities in Eastern Europe.
7. Shrink businesses in former Soviet Union.

CHALLENGES EMERGING FROM CHANGES IN UNIQUE COMPETENCIES

1. Retain cost leadership by further rationalization, especially indirect costs.
2. Continue to put emphasis on quality of products and services, and keep close relationship with big customers.
3. Seek to implement more integrated production system.
4. Put more energy into realizing a synergy with Engineering Division.
5. Develop a joint strategy with Toa Steel and work with it in low-end products.
6. Use National Steel as a marketing base on both American continents.
7. Keep brand recognition among both customers and students who will be our future employees by wise use of PR.
8. Keep close relationship with financial communities by improving ROE.

SOURCE: Tada (1993). This is not an official document of NKK Corporation.

After all of these steps, we conclude with a definition of the mission of the firm, as shown in Figure 11–7 for the case of NKK.

In a similar way we have gone through an analysis of the mission for the case of P&G. But in this case, we limit ourselves to producing in Figure 11–8 the final statement of the mission for this company. The statement adheres to the format that we recommend, which is a direct result of the methodology applied. First, it provides a broad statement of intent, which resembles what one finds in annual reports. But then, most importantly, this is expanded into a more detailed description of the existing and new product, market, and geographical scope, as well as unique competencies, giving us a sense of the existing and future state of the competitive domain of P&G, and of the way in which P&G expects to sustain its competitive advantage. These last comments are intended to summarize the major findings of the mission statement process, and carry with them a commitment toward action.

(Figures 11-7 and 11-8 follow on pages 214-15.)

Note

1. Alfred D. Chandler, Jr., in *Strategy and Structure* (Cambridge, MA: The MIT Press, 1962).

FIGURE 11–7. Mission Statement—The Case of NKK

Based on the results of the priority assessment and the challenges emerging from changes in business scopes, we developed the mission statement of NKK's Materials Sector:

MISSION STATEMENT

NKK's mission in material areas is to become an excellent total material manufacturing company by offering a wide array of materials. NKK is committed to steel production, the core business, and the base material for all products, by increasing its cost competitiveness in the long run and strengthening our joint strategy with NKK group companies in both Japan and overseas. In addition, NKK continues to develop other materials businesses, especially advanced materials by intensified R&D, aggressive marketing, as well as supporting subsidiaries that are spun off from NKK and that deal with materials other than steel.

PRODUCT SCOPE

- Now: Emphasis on carbon and low-alloy steel, especially sheets, and the broad development of advanced material businesses.
- Future: Emphasize high-end, value added steel such as stainless steel more than now, as well as carbon and low-alloy sheets. Restructure titanium and specialty metal businesses. Shrink ferroalloy business.

MARKET SCOPE

- Now: Most important industries are automobile and construction industries.
- Future: Keep the emphasis on the above industries. Penetrate more into the aerospace industry, which uses a lot of advanced materials.

GEOGRAPHICAL SCOPE

- Now: Emphasis is put on domestic market, especially Kanto market. However, fair amount of effort is spent on exporting.
- Future: Put more energy into increasing market share in Kansai area. Reduce dependence on export while making much of ASEAN and China.

UNIQUE COMPETENCIES

- Now: Cost leadership by effective and integrated production facilities in addition to traditional close relationship with customer has been the foundation of NKK's competitiveness.
- Future: NKK should maintain cost leadership by further rationalization and integration of the production system. Further use of synergy with the Engineering Division, and an alliance with Toa Steel and National Steel make NKK more competitive.

SOURCE: Tada (1993). This is not an official document of NKK Corporation.

214

FIGURE 11–8. Mission Statement—The Case of P&G

- P&G is devoted to providing products of superior quality and value to the world's consumers based on the traditional principles of integrity and doing the right thing. P&G is to be recognized as the world leader in providing consumer everywhere with cleaning, personal care, medicinal, and food products. Its purpose is achieved through an organization and working environment able to attract the most qualified individuals.
- P&G is committed to preserving the environment in its production processes, and its product and packaging.
- P&G provides its shareholder with long-term growth and profitability by establishing and maintaining leadership position in all markets.

PRODUCT SCOPE
- Now: Manufacture and distribute laundry and cleaning, food and beverage, personal care, pharmaceutical, and pulp and chemical products of superior quality to best fill the needs of the world customers.
- Future: Maintain market leadership in the same segments, but focus on the development and sale of convenient products, and environmentally friendly products and packaging.

MARKET SCOPE
- Now: Provide products to all individual consumers and institutions through an integrated, global network that includes R&D, manufacturing, marketing, sales, distribution, and services.
- Future: Respond effectively to the ever increasing health concerns, demographics changes, aging in U.S., and fast growth in developing countries. Market world brands that share global technology but respond to local needs.

GEOGRAPHICAL SCOPE
- Now: Worldwide with different product scopes in different world regions.
- Future: Expand distribution of basic products (laundry and personal care) to East European countries with the highest per capita income. Establish a strong position in South America to compete effectively in the newly liberalized markets.

UNIQUE COMPETENCIES
- Now: R&D leadership has been the foundation of P&G success. Horizontal integration and multinational management have allowed the firm to compete effectively.
- Future: P&G is committed to becoming the leader in the protection of our environment, through environmentally related R&D in the detergent and packaging industries. The firm will develop a transnational culture to allow for a sharper focus on the differences of local market segments, but without losing the economies of global leadership.

NOTE: This is not an official document. It is an illustration drawn from public sources.

CHAPTER 12

Business Segmentation

The cornerstone of the strategic planning process is the segmentation of the firm's activities into business units. Within our recommended process, business segmentation is one of the most critical corporate strategic tasks. It comes after the performance of the environmental scan, which allows to frame all the external forces that will be impacting the firm, and after the statement of mission of the firm, which defines the business scope (where the firm will compete), and the unique competencies (how the firm will compete). The third task in our framework implies the segmentation of the businesses of the firm, which requires grouping the firm activities into coherent categories that will allow a most effective management of the firm's resources. This is a subject that we introduced in Chapter 3 of this book. We defined the strategic business unit (SBU) as an operating unit or a planning focus that sells a distinct set of products or services to a uniform set of customers, facing a well-defined set of competitors. Also, we identified the basic criteria for SBU definition and we commented about the nature of interactions that normally exist across business units.

Business segmentation is important for all the strategic tasks of the firm. Corporate strategy deals primarily with the shrewd management of the portfolio of businesses, which includes the proper allocation of resources among them, the sharing of these resources across them, and the use of the organizational resources and capabilities for the development of new businesses. The recognition of this portfolio of businesses allows the firm to focus proper attention on the development of each business to its maximum potential, which is the essence of business strategy. Finally, functional strategies are intended to develop and cultivate the capabilities of the firm that will support the corresponding business strategy.

We are revisiting this subject now, because business segmentation is an important task to be undertaken by the top managers of the firm. We commented in Chapter 1, when analyzing one perspective of strategy as the definition of the competitive domain of the firm, that segmentation is a very difficult task that has no clear guidelines to assure a proper outcome. It goes far beyond selecting the focuses for managerial attention, although most of the analysis, formulation, and implementation of strategic activities have the SBU as the central concern. When defining the business units, top managers are creating the domains in which the strategy of the firm will become explicit. This is a most powerful way of conveying the sense of direction and priorities that will lead the overall managerial decision-making process, because it is not just a verbal declaration of intent, but an actual manifestation of the perspectives selected by the firm to compete in the markets in which it participates.

It is important to have a thorough understanding of the key dimensions that could be legitimate candidates for business segmentation. The first and most obvious is the set of products of the firm. In fact, most organizations have a natural tendency to define SBUs according to product lines, simply because they are the tangible outputs of managerial activities. Without denying the importance of products as a key to segmentation, they do not carry a sense of exclusiveness or might not even be the most relevant. In some specific circumstances, markets, functions, and geographical areas could be equally valid dimensions of business segmentation, because of the significance that they bring to strategic positioning.

Another important aspect of business segmentation is that it does not have to be based on one single predominant criterion. Most likely, we will have an array of product, market, functional ,and geographical dimensions to take into consideration. The essence of segmentation is the identification of all matters demanding focused strategic attention. Consequently, we may well end up with a selection of critical areas that are not mutually exclusive, but have partially overlapping focuses of attention. That is to say, the resultant business segments may imply a fair amount of double counting. For example, the segmentation process might finish with the identification of an array of comprehensive world-wide products as a definition of critical businesses. It might also include Japan and financial services as two additional SBUs—where some or all of the previously identified products converge—simply because of the critical importance of that country and that market, respectively. Even a function such as technology or a core capability such as the entire logistics process could become the basis for SBU segmentation, because of their potential for becoming the foundation for the development of new businesses.

Consequently, business segmentation is a complex and multidimensional representation of the organizational purpose. It is a dynamic representation that evolves and is reflected in those matters selected as focuses of organizational attention, which thus give rise to the creation of units or the identification of special areas of concern during the process of strategy formation.

Business segmentation requires continuous redefinition and adjustments to align the business definition with the permanent transformation in today's rapidly changing environment. It also requires the formal recognition of the expansion of the businesses into global markets, and the way in which technology is affecting how businesses compete in those markets.

The business entities that result from the segmentation process should not be treated independently and run autonomously. In fact, the greatest corporate strategic challenge is to resolve the many paradoxes that exist in running the business units and, particularly, the dimensions of centralization versus decentralization, and globalization versus localization. We want to share resources and capabilities across the businesses, which calls for centralized management actions to take place; but, at the same time, we want to foster entrepreneurship autonomy and independence to make the business more flexible and more agile. Similarly, we want to have a global reach exploiting global brand names and global product positioning, while being responsive to the local idiosyncrasies. The next two tasks that are part of the corporate strategic planning framework address the issues of horizontal and vertical integration. This means that immediately after having defined the businesses, we will ask the degree of interrelationship they should have, as well as how much value added will be provided to these businesses within the corporation.

The Core Competence and the Challenge to the SBU concept

C.K. Prahalad and Gary Hamel, in their article, "The Core Competence of the Corporation,"[1] state a very strong challenge to the concept of the SBU. This article has generated enormous impact and exerts significant influence on American management thinking on issues of strategy. In fact, this article currently has the largest number of reprints in the history of *The Harvard Business Review*. Since its message challenges the concept of the SBU as the central piece of strategic management, it is only appropriate that we subject some of the implications of Prahalad and Hamel's work to the framework that we advocate for the proper conduct of the strategic planning process. We comment first on what we regard to be central ideas presented in the work of Prahalad and Hamel, and then on their contribution to strategic management thinking.

They establish three main ideas in their paper. First, they state that the roots of competitive advantage "derive from an ability to build, at lower cost and more speedily than competitors, the core competencies that spawn unanticipated products. The real sources of advantage are to be found in management's ability to consolidate corporate-wide technologies and production skills into competencies that empower individual businesses to adapt quickly to changing opportunities." Second, they postulate that "the tangible link between identified core competencies and end products is what they call the core products—the physical embodiment of one or more core competencies." And third, they state that "senior management should spend a significant amount of its time developing a corporate-wide strategic architecture that establishes objectives for competence building. Strategic architecture is a road map of the future that identifies which core competencies to build and their constituent technologies."

The basic messages in these viewpoints are: that the central source for strategic advantage resides at the corporate level, where core competencies are developed; that core competencies are not directly applied to end products (instead, core products are the recipients of the core competencies of the firm, and they provide platforms from which to respond to the dynamics of the environment); and finally, that developing the strategic architecture is what guides competence building.

The concept of core competence has obvious merits: it calls for an elevation of the strategic issues of the firm to the corporate level; it forces a reflection for top managers to understand the fundamental foundations of competitive engagement; it focuses the technological and production skills of the firm to concentrate on a long-lasting, farreaching set of outputs (core products instead of end products); and, finally, it identifies as a priority agenda for top managers the development of the strategic architecture and capabilities of the firm.[2] The message has been impacting because it attempts to address many of the deficiencies that took place in American management during the 1970s and the 1980s.

It is hard to disagree with the overall content of this message, except for several concerns that we have. First, we wish that there were a sharper and clearer definition of the concept of core competency. What really are the core competencies of the firm? How could the firm acquire them? How could it make them unique? How could it make them sustainable? How could the firm appropriate them preventing imitation or substitution? How are they transferred to core products? What is the essence of the core product definition? How are those core competencies and core products passed onto end products? What are the relevant features of strategic architecture? This host of questions simply points to one concern: how could we, in a useful and pragmatic way, translate these very broad concepts into meaningful practical diagnostic and prognostic managerial capabilities.

The second major concern we have with regard to the implications of the core competence message is the dismissal of the SBU as a focus of analysis; in fact, Prahalad and Hamel refer to it as the "tyranny" of the SBU. Core competencies, from their perspective, become an alternative to the SBU as a central focus for strategic analysis. They invoke the need for new principles and new terms of competitive engagement. In their opinion, the need for these principles is most obvious in companies organized according to the logic of the SBU.

They summarize the two alternative courses for structuring the corporation in the first three columns of Figure 12–1, which presents the differences between the SBU and the core competence form of management according to some key dimensions. The contrast that emerges is quite sharp and very demeaning to the SBU. It could very well be that Prahalad and Hamel are properly describing an SBU management practice that is still observed in many organizations today. Obviously, this is not what we are advocating as the SBU-driven form of management. The concept of SBU that emerges from their description, which is based upon autonomy and independence, is a rather antiquated and anachronistic model that was in vogue throughout the1970s.

In the last column of Figure 12–1 we offer our own commentaries, in which we attempt to build a bridge between these two paradigms. What are the issues?

FIGURE 12–1. Two Concepts of the Corporation: SBU or Core Competence

	SBU	CORE COMPETENCE	OUR COMMENTARY
Basis for competition	Competitiveness of today's products	Interfirm competition to build competencies	The SBU is the depository of the core competencies of the firm.
Corporate structure	Portfolio of businesses related in product-market terms	Portfolio of competencies, core products, and businesses	Horizontal strategies—developing and sharing core competencies across distinct but related SBUs is a corporate task even more central than portfolio management.
Status of the business unit	Autonomy is sacrosanct; the SBU "owns" all resources	SBU is a potential reservoir of core competencies	The SBU should not be an autonomous entity. Corporate and functional strategies integrate the business units within the corporate umbrella.
Resource allocation	Discrete businesses are the unit of analysis; capital is allocated business by business	Businesses and competencies are the unit of analysis; top managment allocates capital and talent	Resource development and resource allocation should be done from a corporate and business perspective.
Value added of top management	Optimizing corporate returns through capital allocation trade-offs among businesses	Enunciating strategic architecture and building competencies to secure the future	Strategic management addresses the proper integration of strategy, structure, processes, performance, and culture.

SOURCE: The first three columns of this figure are reprinted by permission of *Harvard Business Review*. An exhibit from "The Core Competence of the Corporation" by C. K. Prahalad and Gary Hamel, May–June 1990. Copyright ©1990 by the President and Fellows of Harvard College; all rights reserved. The last column provides our own commentary.

With regard to the basis for competition, we believe that the SBU should be the recipient of the core competencies that are developed at the corporate level. How else are these capabilities going to be transferred in a productive and meaningful way? It does not seem to be fair to characterize SBU management as dealing exclusively with today's products. In fact, the bridging concept intends to resolve this paradox: core competencies provide the long-term capabilities of the firm, while the SBU uses those capabilities to enhance the current competitiveness of the firm.

With regard to the corporate structure, we need to balance both the portfolio of competencies and the portfolio of businesses. In our opinion, horizontal strategy plays the key role in sharing core competencies across distinct, yet related, businesses.

With regard to the status of the business unit, it seems an anachronism to conceive of an SBU as possessing a "sacrosanct autonomy." Corporate and functional strategies serve to integrate the business unit so as to develop the overused but still relevant formula for corporate success: *the whole has to be greater than the sum of the parts.*

With regard to resource allocation, although businesses are relevant units of analysis, it does not mean that resources are to be allocated discretely business by business. We need a broader view, which is provided by the corporate strategy umbrella.

Finally, when it comes to the value added of top management, we wholeheartedly subscribe, as proponents of any sensible management philosophy would, to the idea that there is a higher level task of strategic concern. Prahalad and Hamel call it strategic architecture. We prefer to use the term *strategic management,* which addresses the proper integration of strategy, structure, processes, performance, and culture.

The core competence approach begs for enhancing the centrality of corporate strategy. In fact, in this article, Prahalad and Hamel ask how many senior executives discuss the crucial distinction between competitive strategy at the level of a business and competitive strategy at the level of an entire company; they imply that the answer is too few. We feel that both levels of strategy are central, and we advocate for a much clearer definition of what competitive strategy at the level of the entire company should be. Our answer is contained in the ten corporate strategic tasks that we are discussing in this part of the text.[3]

Matching Organizational Structure and Business Segmentation

Business segmentation is strongly influenced by the principles commonly used for designing the organizational structure of a firm. The central questions in organizational design are: how to identify the key *responsibilities,* representing the major tasks of the organization; and how to allocate the proper levels of *authorities,* to facilitate the use of the necessary resources to execute the assigned tasks. The process that leads toward the final organizational structure of the firm is only possible through the wise exercise of a large number of tradeoffs and compromises. Because of the inherent limitation of the span of control, one has to identify just a very few critical dimensions as the basis for the primary segmentation of organizational tasks. This is what one normally observes in the first echelon of the organization chart of a firm. But the process of segmentation does not end there. It continues to flow through finer and finer segmentation, until we have a subordinate hierarchy incorporating all of the critical dimensions that address the overall allocation of responsibilities and authorities.

Likewise, the business segmentation process is applied at different hierarchical levels in the organization. There is a span of control issue when identifying businesses from the corporate perspective. The resultant number of SBUs should not be so large as to impair the ability of top managers to understand the broad characteristics of each business and to contribute effectively to their proper management. By necessity, therefore, the corporate segmentation in a large firm is rather broad and aggregated.

Normally, the resultant SBUs are thus composed of a plurality of products and markets, which have to be properly identified by a secondary segmentation taking place at the business level. This segmentation provides the necessary intelligence for the SBU manager to establish meaningful priorities for the development of each individual segment. This may mean possible abandonment of some of them in order to concentrate all of the business competencies in a more narrowly focused market.

Although the two processes of business segmentation and organizational structure design do not have the same final objective, they are strongly linked. One could argue that a complete match between business segmentation and organizational structure is highly desirable. This match would greatly facilitate the formulation and implementation of strategy, the congruency between operational and strategic commitments, and the resultant accountability in both modes. Whenever organizational and business segmentation do not result in a perfect alignment, a significant ambiguity regarding the strategic and operational responsibilities is generated. In this case, considerable efforts would have to be made to match strategy and structure.

When we face a situation where there is a complete mismatch between the tasks that determine the organizational design and the business focuses that lead to a proper business segmentation, we need to put in place an infrastructure of horizontal coordinating mechanisms. The most common among them are: assigning a manager as liaison, formation of task forces and committees, appointing either temporary or permanent coordinating managers, or recognizing formally the dual responsibilities and authorities by means of a matrix organization.

Making Explicit the Business Segmentation

Regardless of the final dimensions selected to resolve the way the business segmentation process is conducted, it is important that top managers reach a final consensus on the resultant business units, the rationale for segmentation, and the identification of the individuals responsible for the formulation and implementation of the corresponding business strategy.

Normally, it is rather hard to achieve a rapid consensus on business segmentation among top managers of the firm. This tends to underscore the inherent complexity associated with this task, as well as the centrality of carrying it through to a successful completion. Figure 12-2 identifies the fifteen business

FIGURE 12–2. Business Segmentation—The Case of P&G

	BUSINESS UNIT	RATIONALE FOR SEGMENTATION
1	Cellulose	Unique competitors, technology, and customers
2	Tissue and Paper Towel Products	Unique competitors and technology
3	Disposable Diapers	Largest unit Unique competitors and technology
4	Coffee	Different suppliers and customers Most profitable food segment
5	Cake Mixes	Unique competitors and technology
6	Shortening Oils	Unique competitors and technology
7	Potato Chips/Peanut Butter	Unique competitors and technology
8	Drinks	Different R&D and competitors Separated to facilitate possible divestment
9	Cosmetics	Well-defined set of customers, competitors, and technologies
10	Oral Care	Different customers and competitors
11	Soaps-Shampoos	Different customers and competitors
12	Detergents	Core product with large external market Well-defined customers and competitors
13	Chemicals	Different customers, channels, and competitors
14	OTC Drugs	Different R&D and competitors
15	Prescription Drugs	Different R&D, competitors, customers, and channels Separated to facilitate possible divestment

NOTE: This is not an official document. It is an illustration drawn from public sources.

units that we recognize for P&G. Notice that all of them have product connotations. This is not an exception to the rule, since the product dimension seems to prevail in business segmentation. Moreover, we have attempted to provide a brief rationale for the reasons to adopt each business unit. These reasons, by and large, result from differences in competitors, technology, customers, and channels of distribution. Occasionally, a business unit can be singled out for possible divestment, as is the case of "Drinks" in our example.

Similarly, Figure 12–3 shows the business segmentation and assignment of business responsibilities for NKK. In this case, we can observe, for example, that steel products are disaggregated into three SBUs: high-end, low-end, and stainless steel. Other metals are aggregated into one SBU: titanium, aluminum, and specialty metals. Also, there is an SBU that offers more value added to the customer: precision metal products. In this figure, we have also identified the manager in charge of each business.

FIGURE 12–3. Business Segmentation and Assignment of Managerial Responsibility—The Case of NKK

BUSINESS UNIT	RESPONSIBLE MANAGER	RATIONALE FOR SEGMENTATION
High-end carbon and low-alloy steel	Executive Director, Steel Div.	Different customers and independent strategic actions
Low-end carbon and low-alloy steel	President, Toa Steel	Different customers and independent strategic actions
Stainless steel and specialty steel	General Manager, Specialty Steel Product Dept.	Independent strategic actions
Polymer products	General Manager, Polymer Products Dept.	Different competitors and independent strategic actions
Titanium, aluminum, and specialty metals	General Manager, Titanium and Advanced Metals Dept.	Independent strategic actions
Ferroalloys	General Manager, Toyama Works	Different competitors and customers, independent strategic actions
Chemicals	President, ADCHEMCO	Different competitors and customers, independent strategic actions
Precision metal products	President, NKK Seimitsu Corp.	Different competitors and customers, independent strategic actions

SOURCE: Tada (1993). This is not an official document of NKK Corporation.

Notes

1. C. K. Prahalad, and Gary Hamel, "The Core Competence of the Corporation," *Harvard Business Review*, (May–June, 1990), 79–91; and Gary Hamel and C.K. Prahalad, *Competing for the Future* (Boston, MA: Harvard Business School Press, 1994).

2. The strategic architecture concept is related to what we call the strategic management paradigm. It was discussed as the last of our five frameworks for the study of strategy that we covered in Chapter 2.

3. The reader may refer back to Chapter 1 to review the various dimensions of strategy, with particular emphasis on the impact of core competencies and the resources based view of the firm. Figure 1–3 offers the mission of the business as a bridge that would allow the core competencies to be transferred to the end products, markets, and geographical locations of the business.

CHAPTER 13

Horizontal Strategy

Having segmented the businesses of the firm, the critical question to be resolved is the extent to which potential synergism across businesses could be identified and properly exploited in order to add value beyond the simple sum of independent business contributions. This activity is the distinctive form in which a diversified firm enhances its competitive advantage, and it is the heart of the development and implementation of horizontal strategy. Since its managerial scope embraces the totality, or at least a partial group, of businesses of the firm, it is defined in our context as a corporate task. Depending on the specific organizational structure of the firm, it could reside exclusively at the level of top corporate officers or be shared with other high-ranking managers of the firm at the group or sector echelons.

For many organizations, the appropriate pursuit of horizontal strategy becomes one of the most critical ways to establish a superior competitive position. This is particularly so when the firm's strategy stems from a unique competency residing, normally, in one stage of the value chain that has permitted the company to enter successfully into a wide variety of business enterprises, all of which share that particular resource. Countless examples from actual companies can be cited to stress this point. Among them are: the original strategy of Procter & Gamble, exploiting its clout in distribution, particularly through supermarket chains; Texas Instruments using electronic technology to support a large array of industrial consumer products; and Corning-Glass Works, with a similar, wide-range coverage of products, all of them sharing specialty glass technology. Even a company as widely diversified as General Electric can legitimately claim that all of its businesses stem from what Jack Welch refers to as the three circles of excellence: the traditional "core" businesses, the high-technology businesses, and the service businesses.

Most top managers today are keenly aware of the importance of carefully developed horizontal strategies. If a firm does possess opportunities for exploiting synergism across businesses and is incapable of doing so, it is literally throwing away what could become a source of significant competitive strength. Moreover, horizontal strategies do not tend to emerge spontaneously. This is because the organizational structure of the firm tends to promote a vertical flow of information but seldom generates on its own the lateral communications that are needed for grasping horizontal opportunities. In fact, we could say that the natural response of a vertical organization is to impede and oppose the support of horizontal interrelationships. This is due to a wide variety of factors, such as asymmetric benefits, protection of turf, conflicts over priorities, biased incentive systems, cultural and managerial differences, and excessive decentralization forces.

What we conclude from these comments is: first, that the pursuit of horizontal strategy is a central task for corporate management; and second, that it will not materialize unless there exists a determined will to make it happen. In this chapter we reflect on the guiding principles that facilitate the formulation of horizontal strategies, as well as the organizational mechanisms that can be used to assure their implementation.[1]

Interrelationship Among Business Units

Horizontal strategy is a set of coherent, long-term objectives and action programs aimed at identifying and exploiting interrelationships across distinct but related business units. Therefore, a crucial first step in the definition of horizontal strategy is to identify the sources of possible interrelationships. Michael Porter proposes three types:

- Tangible interrelationships, arising from opportunities to share activities in the value chain.
- Intangible interrelationships, involving the transference of management know-how among separate value chains.
- Competitor interrelationships, stemming from the existence of rivals that actually or potentially compete with the firm in more than one business unit.

Tangible interrelationships are the easiest to detect and capitalize. The sources of competitive advantage that they support are founded on the actual sharing of concrete assets or managerial capabilities in one or more activities of the value chain. It is not surprising, therefore, that tangible interrelationships constitute the most likely sources for horizontal strategy development.

Going back to the concept of generic strategies, a tangible interrelationship can either be used to obtain cost leadership, often by means of economies of scale and scope, or to improve the differentiating capabilities of businesses. However, sharing activities of the chain brings additional costs, such as the cost of coordination, and the cost of compromising. Another cost is the added inflexibility created when businesses have to share activities that have become outdated and are hard to renew. This inflexibility might present an obstacle to react quickly to moves by competitors that do not have this burden. For example, in the U.S. commercial airlines market, Southwest Airlines has a more favorable cost structure than American Airlines, which cannot match Southwest's structure, among other things, because of the inflexibility of its labor contracts. This has made Southwest one of the few profitable airlines in the early 1990s.

In order to simplify the analysis of tangible interrelationships, Porter combines the value-chain activities into five categories: managerial infrastructure, including central administrative functions, financial management, and human resources management; technology; procurement; manufacturing; and marketing. Figures 13–1 through 13–5 summarize some sources of tangible interrelationships according to these five categories. In addition, they list possible forms of sharing, comment on the potential competitive advantage to be gained, and provide an indication of the costs to be borne.

Intangible interrelationships lead to competitive advantage through sharing managerial skills among different value chains. They involve interactions across independent SBUs that are placed in different industries but retain generic similarities such as:

- same generic strategy
- same type of buyers
- similar configurations of the value chain (e.g.,. value chains in different countries)
- similar important value activities (e.g., relationships with government)

FIGURE 13–1.   Infrastructure Interrelationships

SOURCE OF INTERRELATIONSHIP	POSSIBLE FORM OF SHARING	POTENTIAL COMPETITIVE ADVANTAGE	COMPROMISE COST
Common firm infrastructure needs	Shared accounting Shared legal department Shared government relations Shared hiring and training	Smaller support staff Lower costs Critical mass to attract top-level managers	Need for coordination is higher People may have differing interests Conflicts may occur more often Needs of different types of people
Common capital	Shared raising of capital Shared cash utilization	Lower cost of financing	Increased complexity leads to higher overhead

SOURCE: Alain C. Boutboul, "A Framework for Analyzing Acquisition and Divestitures Decisions," unpublished masters thesis, Sloan School of Management, MIT, 1986. Reprinted by permission of Alain C. Boutboul.

FIGURE 13–2. Technology Interrelationships

SOURCE OF INTERRELATIONSHIP	POSSIBLE FORM OF SHARING	POTENTIAL COMPETITIVE ADVANTAGE	COMPROMISE COST
Common product technology	Joint technology development	Lower product or process costs Larger critical mass in R&D	Technologies are the same, but the tradeoffs in applying the technology are different among business units
Common process technology		Enhanced differentiation	
Common technology in other value activities			
One product incorporated into another	Joint interface design	Lower interface design cost Higher differentiation	A nonstandard interface reduces the available market
Interface among products			

SOURCE: Boutboul, (1986).

Intangible interrelationships can also be an important source in seeking cost advantage or in gaining differentiation capabilities. However, they are much more difficult to apprehend and exploit. Because of the wide array of similarities existing across value chains of different business units, it is impossible to provide a full cataloguing of all types of interrelationships. Instead, careful attention to the nature of the value chains of the firm's business units constitutes an effective source of analysis from which intangible interrelationship opportunities might emerge.

Competitor interrelationships exist when a firm competes with diversified rivals in more than one business unit. Multipoint competitors necessarily link industries together because actions toward them in one business may have implications in another.

The presence of multipoint competitors expands the scope of competitive analysis. In this case, rather than searching for opportunities to share resources and skills to enhance one's own competitive position, the focus is on retaliatory actions that a firm could undertake in response to the overall competitive standing of a rival firm. The clearest example of this kind of issue arises in global competition. When Michelin successfully penetrated the American market with radial tires, Goodyear was confronted with a very difficult strategic

FIGURE 13–3. Procurement Interrelationships

SOURCE OF INTERRELATIONSHIP	POSSIBLE FORM OF SHARING	POTENTIAL COMPETITIVE ADVANTAGE	COMPROMISE COST
Common purchased inputs	Joint procurement	Lower cost of input	Input needs are different in terms of quality or specifications, leading to higher cost than necessary in business units requiring less quality
		Improved input quality	Technical assistance delivery needs vary
		Improved service from vendors in terms of responsiveness, holding of inventory, conditions of sale	Centralization can reduce the information flow from factory to purchasing, and make purchasing less responsive

SOURCE: Boutboul, (1986).

FIGURE 13–4. Manufacturing Interrelationships

SOURCE OF INTERRELATIONSHIP	POSSIBLE FORM OF SHARING	POTENTIAL COMPETITIVE ADVANTAGE	COMPROMISE COST
Common location of raw materials	Shared inbound logistics	Lower costs	Plants are located in different areas
Identical or similar fabrication process	Shared component fabrication	Lower costs	Needs for component design and quality differ
Identical or similar assembly process	Shared assembly facilities	Better capacity utilization; lower costs	Less flexibility Different needs
Identical or similar testing/quality control procedures	Shared testing/quality control	Lower testing costs	Testing procedures and quality standards differ
Common factory support needs	Shared indirect activities	Lower cost Improved quality	Different needs More difficult to manage a larger work force

SOURCE: Boutboul, (1986).

FIGURE 13-5. Marketing Interrelationships

SOURCE OF INTERRELATIONSHIP	POSSIBLE FORM OF SHARING	POTENTIAL COMPETITIVE ADVANTAGE	COMPROMISE COST
Common buyer	Shared brand name	Lower advertising cost Reinforcing product images	Product images are inconsistent Buyer is reluctant to purchase too much from one firm Diluted reputation if one product is inferior
	Shared advertising	Lower advertising cost Greater leverage in purchasing advertising space	Appropriate media or messages are different Advertising effectiveness reduced by multiple products
	Shared promotion	Lower promotion costs	Appropriate forms and timing of promotion differ
	Cross selling of products to each other's buyers	Lower cost of finding new buyers Lower cost of selling	Product images are inconsistent or conflicting Buyer is reluctant to purchase too much from one firm
Common channel	Shared channels	Higher bargaining power Lower infrastructure cost	Too much dependency on channel Channel unwilling to allow a single firm to account for a major portion of its sales
Common geographic market	Shared sales force	Lower selling cost Better sales force utilization	Different buyer purchasing behavior Different type of salesperson is more effective
	Shared service network	Lower servicing costs More responsive servicing Better capacity utilization	Different equipment necessary to make repairs Different needs of buyers
	Shared order processing	Lower order processing costs Better capacity utilization	Differences in the form and composition of typical orders Differences in ordering cycles

SOURCE: Boutboul, (1986).

230

response. Fighting Michelin aggressively in the U.S. markets had very asymmetric consequences for both players, with Michelin having little to lose, and Goodyear being threatened at the primary source of its profitability. Goodyear's answer to this puzzle was to retaliate aggressively in the French market. This strategic action, besides the ultimate financial implications that it might generate, has the purpose of providing a signal to a competitor that sets up the rules of the game. What we have described is a turf battle: Michelin was charging into Goodyear's "profit sanctuary." A smart response was for Goodyear to do likewise and charge against Michelin's profit sanctuary.

Multipoint competitors are important because they might force us to consider different forms of retaliation in jointly contested industries, as well as providing opportunities to exploit our overall corporate position.

Identification of Sources of Interrelationships: Some Illustrations

The first step in the development of a horizontal strategy is to identify the tangible and intangible interrelationships that could potentially be shared across SBUs. Tangible interrelationships are analyzed by examining potential sharing across businesses by each activity of the value chain. The simplest way of identifying opportunities for horizontal integration is illustrated in Figures 13–6 and 13–7, which show the most important sources of tangible and intangible interrelationships across the primary business units of AMAX, Inc. This is a widely diversified metals and energy company based in Greenwich, Connecticut, which operates on a world-scale basis, which was recently acquired by Cyprus Minerals. In Figure 13–6 we observe a strong need for corporate involvement in the areas of mining, technology, R&D, and human resources management to assure that these sources of commonalty among businesses are properly exploited. This is also valid, to a lesser extent, in the areas of marketing and sales, and exploration.

Figure 13–7 stresses the importance of establishing coordinating mechanisms to exploit intangible interrelationships in the metal industry, where competition from companies controlled by foreign governments is widespread. Opportunities for transferring know-how across geographical areas, both domestically and internationally, are of the highest priority among all businesses, except coal and fertilizer. There also seem to be opportunities for sharing skills through commonality of major clients—such as Bethlehem Steel—and industries—such as the steel industry. Finally, all of the business units share a declining consumption rate relative to GNP, which places them in the same generic industry environment, calling for a common managerial approach.

The most comprehensive and laborious way to identify sources of tangible interrelationships is to examine each value-added activity independently, one at a time. We select one activity—say, manufacturing—and proceed to make pairwise comparisons among business units to detect the extent to which this activity is shared between every pair of businesses. Figure 13–8 illustrates this process in the case of P&G. There are four activities represented in this figure:

FIGURE 13–6. AMAX, Inc.: Tangible Interrelationships

VALUE-CHAIN ACTIVITIES	Molyb	Nick	Tung	Copp	Ld/Zn	Silv	Specialty Metal	Iron	Alum	Magn	Oil & Gas	Fert	Coal
Product R&D	X	X		X	X		X			X			
Process R&D	X	X	X	X	X	X	X	X	X	X		X	X
Purchasing of Raw materials													
Transportation of Raw Materials													
Exploration	X		X	X				X			X		X
Mining Technology and Mining Operation Know-How	X		X	X	X	X		X					X
Marketing	X	X	X	X	X								
Sales	X	X	X	X	X								
Distribution													
Human Resources	X	X	X	X	X	X	X	X	X	X	X	X	X

Note: X indicates sharing

Key: Molyb   Molybdenum   Copp   Copper   Alum   Aluminum
       Nick   Nickel   Ld/Zn   Lead/Zinc   Magn   Magnesium
       Tung   Tungsten   Silv   Silver   Fert   Fertilizer

SOURCE: Gray (1984).

FIGURE 13–7. AMAX, Inc.: Intangible Interrelationships

VALUE-CHAIN ACTIVITIES	Molyb	Nick	Tung	Copp	Ld/Zn	Silv	Specialty Metal	Iron	Alum	Magn	Oil & Gas	Fert	Coal
Major Clients	X	X	X				X		X	X			
Domestic Areas (U.S.)	X	X	X	X	X	X	X	X	X	X			
Major Geographic International Areas	X	X	X	X	X	X	X	X	X	X	X		
Industries	X	X	X	X	X		X	X	X	X			
Foreign Government Controlled Production	X	X		X	X	X			X		X	X	
Declining Consumption Rate Relative to GNP	X	X	X	X	X	X	X	X	X	X	X	X	X

Note: X indicates sharing

Key: Molyb Molybdenum   Copp   Copper   Alum   Aluminum
     Nick   Nickel   Ld/Zn Lead/Zinc Magn Magnesium
     Tung   Tungsten   Silv   Silver   Fert   Fertilizer

Source: Gray (1984).

233

FIGURE 13–8. Tangible Horizontal Interrelationships Among Business Units—The Case of P&G

Key: • denotes sharing of wholesale distribution activities across business units. A,B,C,D identify clusters of sharing of manufacturing activities across business units. For instance, cellulose, tissue paper, and disposable diapers all have a common manufacturing activity designated by A. Cake, shortening, potato chips, and peanuts also have common manufacturing activities designated by B, but these are different than A.

WHOLESALE DISTRIBUTION

	Cellulose	Tissue	Diapers	Coffee	Cake	Shortening	Potato Chips/Peanuts	Drinks	Cosmetics	Oral	Soap	Detergents	Chemicals	OTC
Tissue & Papers														
Disposable Diapers		•												
Coffees		•	•											
Cake Mixes		•	•	•										
Shortening		•	•	•	•									
Chips/Peanuts		•	•	•	•	•								
Drinks		•	•	•	•	•	•							
Cosmetics		•	•	•	•	•	•	•						
Oral Care		•	•	•	•	•	•	•	•					
Soap-Shampoos		•	•	•	•	•	•	•	•	•				
Detergent		•	•	•	•	•	•	•	•	•	•			
Chemicals		•	•	•	•	•	•	•	•	•	•	•		
OTC Drugs		•	•	•	•	•	•	•	•	•	•	•	•	
Prescription Drugs														•

MANUFACTURING

	Cellulose	Tissue	Diapers	Coffee	Cake	Shortening	Potato Chips/Peanuts	Drinks	Cosmetics	Oral	Soap	Detergents	Chemicals	OTC
Tissue & Papers	A													
Disposable Diapers	A	A												
Coffees														
Cake Mixes														
Shortening					B									
Chips/Peanuts					B	B								
Drinks														
Cosmetics														
Oral Care									C					
Soap-Shampoos									C	C				
Detergent									C	C	C			
Chemicals									C	C	C	C		
OTC Drugs									C	C	C	C	C	
Prescription Drugs														D

	Cellulose	Tissue	Diapers	Coffee	Cake	Shortening	Potato Chips/Peanuts	Drinks	Cosmetics	Oral	Soap	Detergents	Chemicals	OTC
Tissue & Papers	A	A												
Disposable Diapers	A	A												
Coffees														
Cake Mixes														
Shortening														
Chips/Peanuts														
Drinks														
Cosmetics									B					
Oral Care									B	B				
Soap-Shampoos									B	B	B			
Detergent									B	B	B	B		
Chemicals									B	B	B	B	B	
OTC Drugs									B	B	B	B	B	
Prescription Drugs														D

RESEARCH AND DEVELOPMENT

	Cellulose	Tissue	Diapers	Coffee	Cake	Shortening	Potato Chips/Peanuts	Drinks	Cosmetics	Oral	Soap	Detergents	Chemicals	OTC
Tissue & Papers	A	A												
Disposable Diapers	A	A												
Coffees														
Cake Mixes														
Shortening					B									
Chips/Peanuts						B								
Drinks														
Cosmetics									C					
Oral Care									C	C				
Soap-Shampoos									C	C	C			
Detergent									C	C	C	C		
Chemicals									C	C	C	C	C	
OTC Drugs									C	C	C	C	C	
Prescription Drugs														D

NOTE: This is not an official document. It is an illustration drawn from public sources.

wholesale distribution, manufacturing, raw-materials procurement, and R&D; each one of them having a very different pattern of sharing. P&G has always been recognized by its enormous clout in distribution, and its ability to use it as one of its most formidable sources of competitive advantage. This fact becomes patently clear in the first picture of the figure. Virtually all the businesses share the same distribution channels. The only exceptions are cellulose—which is a backward integrated business that does not relate with anyone in terms of distribution—and prescription drugs, which only shares distribution channels with the OTC drugs business. Manufacturing, Raw Materials, and R&D behave quite differently. They share activities with clusters of businesses. For instance, cellulose, tissue paper, and disposable diapers constitute one manufacturing cell, while cake-mixes, potato chips, peanut butter, and shortening oils represent another. Figure 13-8 clearly demonstrates the visual impact portrayed by this process of detecting interrelationships. One can easily detect the degree of relatedness of the business portfolio by each critical activity of the value chain.

Configuration of Activities of the Value Chain: The Case of the Telecommunications Equipment Industry WorldWide

A key decision to be made in the development of a horizontal strategy is to decide on the physical configuration of the value chain. Depending on the potential that exists for achieving economies of scale and scope, it could be advantageous to centralize one activity in a single location, or to disperse it across multiple areas in the world. This choice often leads to profound differences in the managerial systems required to integrate the resulting administrative tasks. The issues of *configuration* of the value chain, and *coordination* of the value activities represent key design questions of a horizontal strategy.

We use the worldwide telecommunications equipment industry in 1986 as an illustration of the important issues of configuration and coordination in the deployment of a horizontal strategy.[2] In 1986, worldwide sales in this industry were close to $30 billion, and growing fast. The industry is very heavily concentrated, with five firms supplying more than half of total demand. The leading competitors are the following:

FIRM	1985 WORLD WIDE MARKETSHARE (%)	COUNTRY OF ORIGIN
AT&T Technologies, Inc.	20	U.S.
ITT	12	U.S.
L.M. Ericsson	7	Sweden
Siemens	6	W.Germany
GTE	6	U.S.
NEC	4	Japan
OKI	4	Japan
Hitachi	4	Japan
Fujitsu	4	Japan

Market sales of telecommunications equipment falls into four major categories: cable, main-exchange switchgear, transmission equipment, and station equipment. All of these products complement each other and are required in a balanced mix for the development of a telecommunications equipment network. The issues that affect the configuration and coordination for the overall industry are summarized in Figure 13–9. It is apparent that the central activities providing the foundation for horizontal strategy are research and development; components manufacturing; assembly, testing, and quality control; and marketing, distribution, and sales. Figure 13–10 presents the main advantages and disadvantages for a centralized configuration and a high coordination in each one of the respective value activities. The resulting analysis allows us to conclude that R&D and components manufacture would have the highest potential for sharing resources across all businesses. This imposes a great deal of pressure to centralize these activities in one, or a very few, world locations, and to exercise a high degree of coordination to reap the resulting benefits. At the other extreme, assembly, marketing, distribution, and services present little potential for economies of scale and scope, and, therefore, there is little pressure to concentrate and integrate those activities. Somewhere in between resides the testing and quality control activity, where some regionalization and coordination appears to be advantageous.

The reader might want to go back to Chapter 5, where we use the same example to illustrate the concept of strategic groups. Figure 5–28 divides the

FIGURE 13–9.   Factors Affecting Configuration and Coordination in the Worldwide Telecommunications Equipment Industry

Factors Favoring Centralized Configuration	• The existence of unexploited economies of scale beyond the size of national markets • Rising R&D, production, logistics, and distribution economies • Lowering of trade barriers • Falling of transportation costs • Homogenizing of marketing systems, business practices, and infrastructure • Falling communication and coordination costs and increasing speed and scope of communication technology • Homogenizing of product needs among countries • Flexible manufacturing allows production of multiple varieties in a given facility
Factors Favoring High Coordination	• Computerization of manufacturing process and other coordination among activities • Greater mobility of buyers internationally • More multinational and global buyers

SOURCE: Koh (1986).

FIGURE 13–10. Factors Affecting Configuration and Coordination in the Main Activities of the Value Chain of the Worldwide Telecommunications Equipment Industry

ACTIVITIES OF THE VALUE CHAIN	CENTRALIZATION CONFIGURATION		HIGH COORDINATION	
	ADVANTAGES	DISADVANTAGES	ADVANTAGES	DISADVANTAGES
R&D	• Go down the learning curve faster • Gain economies of scale and scope • Gain protection against leakage of technology to outsiders	• Failure to respond to heterogeneous local product needs • Failure to respond to government requirements in some countries	• Bargaining advantages with governments • Share know-how and learning • Better serve multinational buyers	• Government restrictions on flow of information • Coordination costs • Organizational difficulty in achieving transfer of technology among subsidiaries
Components manufacturing	• Gain scale economies • Go down the learning curve faster	• Transport and storage costs • No hedge against the risks of single site • Unable to encourage nationalistic purchasing	• Share know-how and learning • Bargaining advantages with governments	• Coordination costs • Government restrictions on the movement of components
Assembly	• Better quality control	• Higher costs • Failure to respond to heterogeneous local product needs • Failure to respond to local government requirements • Failure to encourage nationalistic purchasing	• Share know-how and learning • Flexibility in responding to competitors • Respond to changes in comparative advantage among countries	• Coordination costs • Government restriction on flows of goods and information
Testing and quality control	• Some economies • Some learning curve effects	• Failure to differentiate product in final production stages to address local market segments • Failure to encourage nationalistic purchasing • Failure to respond to government requirements	• Share know-how and learning • Solidify brand reputation of the product throughout the world	• Coordination costs
Marketing, distribution, and sales	• Standard marketing policies worldwide • Solidify brand reputation worldwide	• Failure to respond to heterogeneous local product needs • Failure to encourage nationalistic purchasing • Failure to respond to government requirements	• Solidify brand reputation worldwide • Better serve multinational buyers • Gain flexibility in responding to competitors	• Coordination costs • Organizational difficulty in achieving cooperation among subsidiaries • May not respond well to heterogeneous local conditions

players in the telecommunication equipment industry—using the configuration and coordination dimensions—into four distinct competitive groups.

Organization and Managerial Infrastructure for Horizontal Strategy

We said in the introduction of this chapter that the vertical nature of flows prevailing in the conventional organizational structure is an impediment to the proper execution of horizontal strategy. Therefore, to assure successful implementation, we need to create horizontal mechanisms that cut across the existing organizational units of the firm. There is a wide variety of ways to adapt the organizational structure, the administrative processes and systems, and even the culture of the firm to be more responsive to the demands of horizontal strategy.

There are two important critical dimensions for deciding the proper design of an organizational structure: segmentation and coordination. From a segmentation point of view, we can define formal units within the organization whose primary roles are that of assuring horizontal responsiveness among businesses. This is commonly done by grouping distinct yet related businesses within clusters, and assigning the management of those businesses to a group or sector manager, whose primary role is the integration of key activities common to the subordinated businesses.

Whenever segmentation alone is not enough, we have to resort to lateral coordinating mechanisms, the most popular among them being the creation of liaison roles, task forces, committees, integrating managers, and matrix relationships, which allow preservation of a dual focus of managerial attention: one pertaining to business development, and the other concerned with identifying and exploiting lateral synergism.

Another device that has proven to be enormously effective in reinforcing horizontal strategic commitment is the intelligent use of key managerial processes and systems available to the firm: planning, control, communication and information, and reward systems.

The planning process, when properly instituted, can become a powerful integrative instrument, which facilitates the recognition of the critical tasks confronted by the firm, and the achievement of a healthy consensus on how to go about the execution of those tasks. Within the numerous encounters, retreats, and analytical sessions that are intrinsic to a well-run planning process, there are many opportunities to address sharing resources and concerns, and to develop the proper commitment to carry on the demanding obligations imposed by a horizontal strategy.

The management control system is the key for monitoring, evaluating, and reformulating the action programs that emerge from the planning process. When horizontal strategies are an important part of the overall strategic blueprint of the firm, the control system should properly identify the way to follow up the shared responsibilities, and to assure that their execution reaches a healthy congruency. A key consideration in this respect is the development of performance measures and procedures that stimulate the intended behavior on the part of all managers involved. Transfer price systems, make-or-buy policies, revenue and cost allocation procedures, and capital budgeting systems for joint projects are just a handful of examples of mechanisms that could make or break the kind of climate needed for cooperative behavior among independent managers.

Communication and information systems are also key elements to support the horizontal structure. Not only do they constitute the backbone for facilitating the flow of information across all of the organizational entities, but they can become the central vehicles to instill the desired sense of direction, and to resolve conflicts whenever they emerge. Managing the interface of a variety of independent businesses, functions, and geographical areas—including, possibly, a wide number of countries with completely different cultural backgrounds—requires enormous communication and informational skills, and extraordinary wisdom to reconcile legitimately different points of view. The communication process becomes the foundation for the negotiations that have to take place in order to develop constructive relationships among a wide variety of heterogeneous players. Facilitating that process is an indispensable factor in the successful execution of a horizontal strategy. This also calls for the dissemination or acceptance of clear procedures for conflict resolution, including direct access to top managers entrusted with the authority for sanctioning eventual appeals.

The rewards and human resources management system are the final, but perhaps the most important, of all of the managerial processes available to firms to facilitate horizontal integration. Rewards are key for motivating people, and motivation shapes behavior. Therefore, it is imperative to recognize the complexities of rewarding individuals not only for actions that belong to their own private domain, but also for those that reside outside their scope of authority, but bring in positive results for the overall organization. Moreover, human resource practices pertaining to selection, promotion, placement, appraisal, management development, and employee relations can truly facilitate the intended collaboration across business units. Among the most commonly used practices in that regard, we can mention: personnel rotation, organizationwide selection and training of personnel, promotion practices that encourage broad experiences, and personnel development programs with ample scope.

SOME FINAL COMMENTS

We have not exhausted the issue of horizontal strategy. There is still much to be said with regard to the role that lateral interrelationships play in diversification strategies, as well as in supporting vertical integration decisions. In the next chapter we address the important question of vertical integration, which refers to the extent of the activities that a firm chooses to perform internally. That decision depends upon the degree to which value activities can be shared by the business units of the firm. We are leaving for the next chapter a description of an integrative methodology that allows us to consider the interaction of horizontal and vertical issues.

Notes

1. Often in this chapter we rely for our presentation on Michael E. Porter's able treatment of this subject. Michael E. Porter, *Competitive Advantage: Creating and Sustaining Superior Performance* (New York: The Free Press, 1985).

2. The description of the telecommunications equipment case study was begun in Chapter 5. It is based on Lynnet Koh, "Strategic Analysis of the Worldwide Telecommunications Equipment Industry," unpublished masters thesis, Sloan School of Management, MIT (1986).

14

Vertical Integration

Vertical integration involves a set of decisions that, by the nature of their scope, reside at the corporate level of the organization.[1] These decisions are threefold:

1. Defining the boundaries a firm should establish over its generic activities on the value chain (the question of make versus buy, or integrate versus contract).
2. Establishing the relationship of the firm with its constituencies outside its boundaries, primarily its suppliers, distributors, and customers.
3. Identifying the circumstances under which those boundaries and relationships should be changed to enhance and protect the firm's competitive advantage .

This set of decisions is of critical importance in defining what the firm is and is not, what critical assets and capabilities should reside irrevocably within the firm, and what type of contracts the firm should establish to deal with its external constituencies.

We have conceptualized the firm as a chain of activities that relates to the administration, production, distribution, and marketing of the goods and services that constitute its primary outputs. The degree of ownership the firm chooses to exercise over these activities will eventually determine the breadth and extent of its vertical integration. To decide this question, the firm has to weigh carefully the economic, administrative, and strategic benefits against the costs resulting from vertical integration. As indicated earlier, this is a question that goes far beyond the simple economic analysis of make-or-buy decisions. It also involves issues of flexibility, balance, organizational market incentives and capabilities for managing the resulting enterprise.

Characterization of Vertical Integration

Before entering into more substantive discussions on the advantages and disadvantages of vertical integration and the ways to achieve it, we provide a few definitions to characterize and measure the vertical integration of the firm through four dimensions: direction, degree of integration and forms of ownership, breadth, and extent.

1. *The direction of vertical integration* recognizes two different ways of adding value to the inputs and outputs of the firm, respectively: *backward,* which means getting closer to suppliers by incorporating into the firm a given input to the current core; and *forward,* which involves a greater proximity to customers by putting a given output of the core under the firm's umbrella. These two forms of vertical integration are sometimes referred to as upstream and downstream extensions, respectively.

2. *The degree of integration and forms of ownership* are defined for each one of the important inputs and outputs of the firm. The categories used to describe vertical integration according to this dimension are the following:

Full integration

A firm that is fully integrated backward on a given input satisfies all the needs for that particular input from internal sources. Likewise, when a firm is fully integrated forward for a given output, it is self-sufficient in providing internally the demand for that product or service. Fully integrated companies have complete ownership of their assets.

Quasi-integration

Quasi-integrated firms do not have full ownership of all of their assets in the value chain related to a given input or output. Rather, they resort to several mechanisms to assure steady relationships with their external constituencies, which reside somewhere between long-term contracts and full ownership. Prevalent forms of quasi-integration are joint ventures or alliances, minority equity investments, loans, loan guarantees, licensing agreements, franchises, R&D partnerships, and exclusivity contracts.

Tapered integration

Tapered integration represents a partial integration, backward or forward, that makes the firm dependent on external sources for the supply of a portion of a given input, or for the delivery of a portion of a given output. For the fraction of the input or output that the firm handles internally, it can resort to either a full integration or a quasi-integration mode of ownership.

Nonintegration

A firm that decides not to integrate on a given input or output depends completely on external providers for its necessary support. The commitments that facilitate the reliance on those external parties are usually drafted in terms of contracts that represent joint responsibilities but no internal integration.

Common forms of contracts are competitive bids, long-term contracting, and rent of assets.

The degree of backward integration can be measured by the percentage of requirements of a particular input that the firm secures from internal sources. Similarly, the degree of forward integration for a given output can be measured by the percentage of it that is transferred directly to an organizational unit adjacent to the core of the firm.

3. *The breadth of integration* measures how broadly or narrowly the firm depends on its own internal sources for all of its important inputs and outputs. Breadth can be measured as the fraction of value provided by the internal inputs or outputs of the firm with regard to the total value of its internal and external transactions, for a given organizational unit.

4. *The extent of integration* refers to the length of the value chain housed by the firm, whether it is limited to just a few stages or if it covers the whole array. One way of measuring the extent of integration is through the fraction of the final value of a product or service that is added by the firm.

Benefits and Costs of Vertical Integration

As with any other crucial decision that has significant strategic importance, vertical integration is affected by a complex trade-off. All of the benefits that support a movement toward increased vertical integration have to be balanced against potential costs. The final decisions as to the direction, degree, breadth, and extent of vertical integration have to be undertaken based not only on numerical computations of the financial consequences of those decisions, but with a broader understanding of the strategic implications of the competitive standing of the firm.

To save the reader from a lengthy commentary on detailed factors that support and discourage vertical integration, we simply present Figures 14–1 and 14–2 with a listing of benefits and costs related to vertical integration decisions.

The major benefits of vertical integration can be classified into four categories: (1) *cost* to internalize economies of scale and scope, and avoid transaction costs from imperfect markets; (2) *defensive market power,* which provides autonomy of supply or demand, as well as protection of valuable assets and services; (3) *offensive market power,* which allows access to new business opportunities, new forms of technology, and differentiation strategies; and (4) *administrative and managerial advantages* arising from a more simplified managerial infrastructure when basic tasks are brought inside as opposed to left outside the firm.

Those benefits have cost counterparts that represent barriers to vertical integration. The deterrent factors can also be grouped under four major labels: (1) *cost* represented by increased overhead and capital investment requirements, and the inability to reach operational break-even; (2) *flexibility loss*

FIGURE 14–1. Benefits from Vertical Integration

COST REDUCTIONS

- Internalize economies of scale resulting in a cost lower than that of outside suppliers and distributors.
- Avoid high transaction costs from many sources; e.g., expensive physical transfer of goods and rendering of services, writing and monitoring contracts with external providers, excessive coordination, and heavy administrative burden.
- Eliminate cost penalties from unpredictable changes in volume, product design, or technology that the firm requires to be introduced in contracts with providers.
- Generate economies from combined operations, sharing of activities, and maintenance of a stable throughput in a long stretch of the value chain.

DEFENSIVE MARKET POWER

- Provides autonomy in supply or demand that shields the firm from foreclosure, inequitable exchange relationships, and opportunistic behavior and overpricing on the part of upstream or downstream providers of goods and services.
- Provides for the firm protection of valuable assets and know-how from unwanted imitation or diffusion.
- Allows the retention of exclusive rights to the use of specialized assets.
- Protects the firm from poor service provided by external suppliers that may have special incentives to favor competitors.
- Guards against important attributes being degraded, distorted, ignored, or impaired by sloppy distribution, marketing, or service operations.
- Raises entry or mobility barriers.

OFFENSIVE MARKET POWER

- Increases opportunities for entering new businesses, upstream or downstream.
- Makes new forms of technology available for existing business base.
- Promotes strategy of differentiation through the control of the interface with final customers.
- Improves market intelligence.
- Facilitates a more aggressive strategy to gain market share.

ADMINISTRATIVE AND MANAGERIAL ADVANTAGES

- Impose throughout the firm a market discipline through direct dealing with providers, up and downstream.
- Increase the interchange of information with external sources.
- Ameliorate the need for a heavy organizational structure and large bodies of personnel.

---

resulting from the difficulties in responding quickly to changes in the external environment because of being locked into a more rigid position than competitors when vertical integration is higher; (3) *balance penalties* resulting from underutilized capacities or unfulfilled demands originated from drastic changes in demand patterns; and (4) *administrative penalties* derived from the burden of managing a more complex and heterogeneous set of activities.

FIGURE 14–2. Costs of Vertical Integration

COST INCREASE
- Increased operating leverage implies a greater fraction of fixed costs and a corresponding greater business risk.
- Higher capital investment requirements.
- Possibility of increased overhead costs.

FLEXIBILITY LOSS
- Flexibility to diversify is reduced.
- Ability to tap different distributors and suppliers is curtailed.
- Harder to compete when the environment takes a negative turn.
- Higher exit barriers and larger volatility in earnings.
- Greater difficulties in getting rid of obsolete processes.

BALANCE REQUIREMENTS
- Vertical integration forces the firm to maintain a balance among the various stages of the value chain. Otherwise external shocks might produce cost penalties on several counts: excess capacities and unfulfilled demand simultaneously.

ADMINISTRATIVE AND MANAGERIAL PENALTIES
- Vertical integration forces the use of internal incentives (as opposed to market incentives), which are more arbitrary in character and might produce strong distortion if not properly applied.
- Vertical integration could affect adversely the flow of information to the firm from either customers or suppliers.
- Vertical integration may impose an additional burden on the organizational structure, managerial processes, and systems in order to deal effectively with increased heterogeneity and complexity.

Conceptual Frameworks for Vertical Integration

There are two frameworks that are particularly helpful in guiding managers to a better understanding of vertical integration decisions. The first one, proposed by Gordon Walker, uses two basic dimensions as the key to analyzing these kinds of issues: the qualifications of the buyer relative to the best outside suppliers, and the degree of strategic risk associated with sourcing from an outside supplier. Qualifications of the inside and outside sources are determined by their capabilities to meet specific performance criteria such as price, delivery, quality, and technological leadership. Strategic risk has three components: (1) *appropriation risk* represented by the ability of the firm to appropriate the rent generated by its assets; (2) *diffusion risk* corresponding to the possibility of unwanted imitation and the difficulties of protecting the know-how of the firm when external vendors are used; and (3) *degradation risk* refering to the deterioration of product characteristics and service to clients when distribution and sales are not the responsibility of the firm. Figure 14–3 represents the alternatives for vertical integration decisions associated with different combinations of strategic risk and buyer qualification.

The second framework for vertical integration, proposed by David Teece, exploits even further the concepts of rent appropriation just described. It postulates that the ability of the firm to appropriate the rent depends on two main factors: (1) *regimes of appropriability* or the ability to maintain exclusive know-how or effective legal protection of key value activities of the firm; and (2) the *access to complementary assets*, which are those required for manufacturing and commercializing a product in addition to the assets owned by the firm. Complementary assets can be classified into three different groups: (1) *generic*, when assets are widely available and can serve the needs of many firms; (2) *specialized*, when the firm is fully dependent for its smooth operation on the use of a scarce asset, but this asset can easily be modified to serve other needs; and (3) *co-specialized*, when it is a specialized asset that cannot be modified to serve other needs.

The implications for vertical integration and contracting options, which are derived from these concepts, are clearly spelled out in the flow chart given in Figure 14–4. This indicates that the firm has to integrate vertically whenever a number of conditions are fulfilled simultaneously: complementary assets are specialized, the appropriability regime is weak (it does not offer enough protection from copying and imitation), specialized assets are critical, the cash position allows for an investment, and the firm finds itself in a favorable position with regard to competitors. Otherwise, the firm would have to negotiate part of its share of profits away to contract for the required access to specialized complementary assets.

FIGURE 14–3.   Strategic Risk vs. Buyer Qualification Matrix for Vertical Integration Decisions

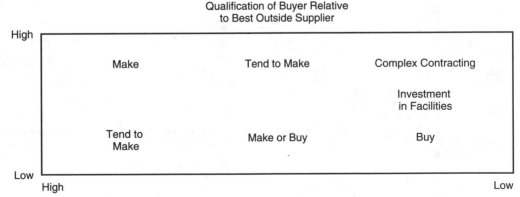

SOURCE: Gordon Walker, "Strategic Sourcing, Vertical Integration and Transaction Costs," *Interfaces*, 19, no. 3, May-June 1988: 62-73. The Institute of Management Sciences, 290 Westminster St., Providence, RI 02903 USA. Reprinted by permission.

FIGURE 14–4. Selecting Between Vertical Integration and Contracting Options

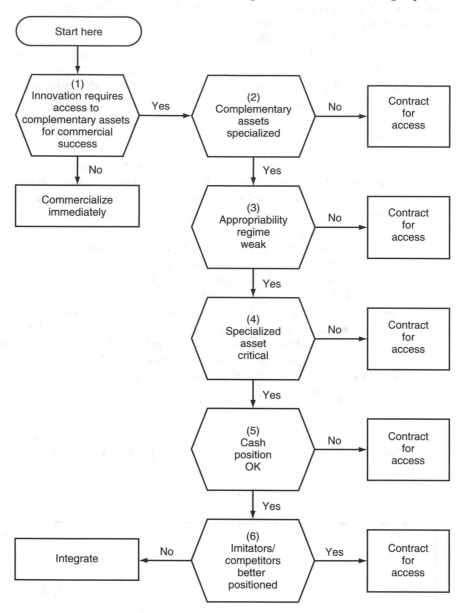

SOURCE: From *The Competitive Challenge* edited by David J. Teece, copyright 1987 by The Center for Research in Management, School of Business Administration, University of Calfiornia, Berkeley. Used by permission of Harper-Business, a divison of HarperCollins publishers.

The main lessons to be learned with regard to vertical integration are that:

- Critical complementary assets must be owned (mainly when they are specialized for the needs of the firm), unless there is a cash constraint. In this last case, the firm should try to form a partnership with at least aminority position.
- When critical complementary assets are not owned, the firm should secure early access to them, mainly when its product is not protected by a tight regime of appropriability (it is an easy matter to copy it), and when the capacity of complementary assets is in short supply and may become a bottleneck.

WHEN NOT TO VERTICALLY INTEGRATE

John Stuckey and David White[2], who have studied vertical integration extensively, provide this final advice regarding vertical integration decisions: "Do not vertically integrate, unless absolutely necessary." They claim that this strategy is too expensive, risky, and difficult to reverse for two reasons. First, although objectives such as reducing cyclicity, assuring market access, increasing value added, or getting closer to the customer are sound reasons to vertically integrate, very often they are not realized, for their cost largely outweighs the benefits to be derived. And second, quasi-integration strategies can be far superior to full vertical integration in both benefits and costs. Long-term contracts, joint ventures, strategic alliances, technology licenses, and franchising often involve lower capital costs and greater flexibility on vertical integration.

Stuckey and White conclude by pointing out the general trend toward vertical disintegration during the late 1980s and early 1990s. The intensive globalization of the businesses has contributed greatly to this trend, by increasing the number of buyers and sellers, augmenting the number of component buyers in various countries, expanding the need for customer flexibility and corporate focus, and favoring the practice of establishing long-term supplier relationships.

A Methodology for Linking
Horizontal Strategy and Vertical Integration

Horizontal strategy and vertical integration are very closely linked. A business unit that is considering extending its value chain independently of other businesses might conclude that it is both infeasible and uneconomical due to its own reduced scope. However, when the issue of adding another value activity is examined from the overall point of view of the firm, it might be perfectly affordable and desirable to add that activity because it would be shared by a large number of business units. That is the central linking between vertical integration decisions, which extend the activities of the value chain, and horizontal strategies, which share activities across businesses within the value chain.

A simple way of identifying potential opportunities for horizontal and vertical integration is presented in Figure 14–5, for the case of P&G. This figure represents a much more compact way of addressing the interrelationships among activities than the pair-wise comparisons shown in Figure 13-8. Moreover, it allows us to make explicit the linkage between horizontal and vertical integration decisions. The illustration shows the high degree of horizontal integration of P&G activities (primarily in manufacturing and R&D); as well as the various degrees of vertical integration existing in its business units. The contrast

FIGURE 14–5. Horizontal and Vertical Integration—The Case of P&G

STAGES OF VALUE CHAIN	CEL	TP	DD	COF	CM	SO	PCP	DR	COS	OC	SSD	DE	CH	OTC	PD	Current H	Current M	Current L	Desired H	Desired M	Desired L
Wholesale distribution		X	X	X	X	X	X	X	X	X	X	X	X	X&Y	Y	√			√		
Manufacturing	A	A	A		B	B	B		C	C	C	C	C	C&D	D		√		√		
Raw materials	E	E	E						F	F	F	F	F	F&G	G		√				√
R&D	H	H	H		I	I	I		J	J	J	J	J	J&K	K	√			√		
Vertical Integration — Current H		√	√						√	√	√	√	√								
Vertical Integration — Current M	√				√	√	√							√	√						
Vertical Integration — Current L				√				√													
Vertical Integration — Desired H		√	√		√	√	√		√	√	√	√	√								
Vertical Integration — Desired M	√													√	√						
Vertical Integration — Desired L				√				√													

Key:
Letters identify clusters of sharing value chain activities across the various businesses of P&G. At the margins we indicate the current and future levels of horizontal and vertical integration.

SBU:
CEL	Cellulose	COS	Cosmetics
TP	Tissue & Paper	OC	Oral Care
DD	Disposable Diapers	SSD	Soap, Shampoo and Deodorants
COF	Coffee	DE	Detergents
CM	Cake Mixes	CH	Chemicals
SO	Shortening Oils	OTC	OTC Drugs
PCP	Potato Chips and Peanuts	PD	Prescription Drugs
DR	Drinks		

NOTE: This is not an official document. It is an illustration drawn from public sources.

between current and future states generates requirements for strategic action programs.

Although this is a highly simplified representation of the horizontal and vertical interrelationships, the figure can be useful in guiding integration decisions. First, we have to reflect on the current state of the firm's activities, and attempt to identify for each stage in the value chain the existing breadth or coverage of each activity across the business units. This effort leads to an assessment of the overall degree of vertical integration by business unit, and the current degree of exploitation of horizontal strategy across business entities. The next task is to reflect on the desired changes. We could proceed by analyzing the desired degree of vertical integration by business unit, and then capture how these expectations can be supported by the sharing of value-chain activities across business units through meaningful horizontal strategies.

Figure 14–6 provides an illustration of the horizontal and vertical interrelationships across the business units of the Materials Sector of NKK. As we examine the implications of this chart, the following challenges emerge.

1. Develop new products by using and combining existing product technology.
2. Open new distribution channels other than trading firms.
3. Explore the possibility of expanding the sharing of outbound logistics among SBUs.
4. Integrate the Chemical business with the other SBUs.
5. In the Stainless Steel business, add value through integration into cold rolled and color sheets.

The chart is clearly an oversimplified way of addressing horizontal and vertical integration, yet we believe it contains the heart of the issues to be resolved in the proper reconfiguration of this critical decision.

(Figure 14-6 follows on page 252)

FIGURE 14–6. Horizontal and Vertical Integration—The Case of NKK

STAGES OF VALUE CHAIN	Business Units								Overall Degree of Horizontal Integration					
									Current			Desired		
	H	L	S	P	T	F	C	PM	H	M	L	H	M	L
Product R&D	#	#	#		#					√		√		
Process R&D	*	*	*		*	*			√			√		
Raw materials	∞	∞		∞	∞				√			√		
Inbound logistics	§	§	§		§				√			√		
Testing	Δ	Δ	Δ	Δ	Δ	Δ		Δ	√			√		
Distribution	X	X	X		X	X		X	√				√	
Outbound logistics	Y	Y	Y								√		√	
Service	Z	Z	Z		Z					√			√	

Overall Degree of Vertical Integration			H	L	S	P	T	F	C	PM
Overall Degree of Vertical Integration	Current	H	√	√						
		M			√	√	√	√	√	√
		L								
	Desired	H	√	√	√			√		
		M				√	√	√		√
		L								

Key:
			SBU:		
H	High		H	High-end steel
M	Medium		L	Low-end steel
L	Low		S	Stainless and specialty steel
#	Common (material) product technology		P	Polymer products
*	Common (material) process technology		T	Titanium and Aluminum
∞	Common purchased inputs		F	Ferroalloys
§	Common transportation methods		C	Chemicals
Δ	Similar testing procedures		PM	Precision metal products
X	Common channels			
Y	Common transportation methods			
Z	Common required technology for service			

Notes

1. The primary sources for the topic of vertical integration that we have used throughout this chapter are: Kathryn Rudie Harrigan, *Strategic Flexibility: A Management Guide for Changing Times* (Lexington, MA: Lexington Books, 1985); Robert H. Hayes and Steven C. Wheelwright, *Restoring Our Competitive Edge: Competing through Manufacturing* (New York: John Wiley & Sons, 1983); Michael E. Porter, *Competitive Strategy: Techniques for Analyzing Industries and Competitors* (New York: The Free Press, 1980); Gordon Walker, "Strategic Sourcing, Vertical Integration and Transaction Costs." *Interfaces,* 19, (May–June 1988), 62–73; and David J. Teece, "Profiting from Technological Innovations: Implications for Integration, Collaboration, Licensing, and Public Policy," in David J. Teece, ed., *The Competitive Challenge: Strategies for Industrial Innovations and Renewal,* (Cambridge, MA: Ballinger Publishing Co., 1987).

2. John Stuckey and David White, "When and When Not to Vertically Integrate," *Sloan Management Review,* 34, no. 3 (Spring 1993), 71–83.

15

Corporate Philosophy

Corporate philosophy is a rather permanent statement, articulated primarily by the CEO, addressing the following issues:

1. The relationship between the firm and its primary stakeholders—employees, customers, shareholders, suppliers, and the communities in which the firm operates.
2. A statement of broad objectives of the firm's expected performance, expressed primarily in terms of growth and profitability.
3. A definition of basic corporate policies with regard to issues such as management style, organizational policies, human resources management, financial policies, marketing, and technology.
4. A statement of corporate values pertaining to ethics, beliefs, and rules of personal and corporate behavior.

The corporate philosophy has to provide a unifying theme and a vital challenge to all organizational units, communicate a sense of achievable ideals, serve as a source of inspiration for confronting daily activities, and become a contagious, motivating, and guiding force congruent with the corporate ethic and values. The corporate philosophy is a statement of basic principles that sets apart those firms that have been able to articulate it in a positive manner from those that lag behind in this respect.

An individual working for a firm has to become an active collaborator in the pursuit of the corporate purposes; he or she must share the vision of the firm and feel comfortable with the way it is translated or expressed in traditions and values. The behavior of individuals is conditioned by this framework and they must intimately sense that, by following these guidelines, they are fulfilling their most personal needs for achievement. The corporate philosophy is a personal drive for their own lives.

It is interesting to observe that those firms that have taken the time to truly reflect on the essence of their purpose and communicate it in writing through a public statement of corporate philosophy tend to produce documents that look very much alike. A cynical interpretation of this convergence of principles might be that they are empty of any significance—the so-called motherhood-and-apple-pie values—which do not convey any meaning for individual behavior. Normally, the reality is quite the opposite. In actuality, these firms adhere to a code of conduct that goes far beyond a narrow expectation of profitability, and project the firm as a public entity with full acceptance of a wide range of societal responsibilities.

A good example of a forceful declaration of corporate philosophy that conveys the communicational power of this type of statement is provided in Figure 15–1 for Analog Devices.

Methodology for a Diagnosis of Corporate Philosophy

Having referred to corporate philosophy as a statement that contains the fundamental and permanent values of the organization, one wonders why we are defining it as a corporate strategic task, implying that it needs, at least, a certain periodic review. When addressing this task, we take a completely different approach than attempting to charter its content with a sense of permanence. Instead, we define the task as a critical and insightful diagnostic on how the corporation is performing in accordance with all the various perspectives that we stated in the definition that we gave in the introduction to this chapter. Rather than the CEO alone, we want to embark the key top executives on a candid evaluation of what is happening in the company in each of the dimensions of the corporate philosophy. It might be useful for the reader to look at Figures 15–2 and 15–3 as previous background of the issues that we are about to address.

1. Relationships with stakeholders.
We ask the managers to be as objective as possible in responding to the following questions: What does it feel like to be an employee, a customer, a shareholder, and a supplier? How do the communities in which the firm operates perceive the firm's impact on them? Whenever possible, the managers should try to survey the stakeholders, so that their views, and not the managers' views, are recorded. This results in a statement of the existing state of relationships with stakeholders. Then we turn to the desired state, and ask the managers how they want these relationships to be.

FIGURE 15–1. The Statement of Corporate Philosophy of Analog Devices, Inc.

CORPORATE PURPOSE AND SCOPE OF BUSINESS

Our purpose is to search continuously for opportunities where we can make unique or valuable contributions to the development and application of analog and digital signal processing technology. In so doing, we strive to offer our customers products that improve the performance, quality and reliability of their products, and thereby increase the productivity of human and capital resources, and contribute generally to upgrading the quality of life and the advancement of society.

Our primary product focus is on monolithic integrated circuits manufactured on semiconductor processes developed by and proprietary to Analog Devices. We also manufacture hybrid circuits and assembled products, including components and board-level subsystems and systems.

Our customers consist primarily of original equipment manufacturers (OEMs) who incorporate Analog's products into a wide variety of instruments and systems. The Company's served markets include laboratory and industrial automation, defense/avionics, telecommunications, transportation, computer peripherals, and selected high-end consumer products. We pursue business in these markets on a world-wide basis.

OUR EMPLOYEES

Our employees' personal motivation and interests are primarily related to ascending needs for security, safety, purpose, recognition, identity, and the realization of one's full potential. Our corporate goals are thus best achieved in an environment that encourages and assists employees in the achievement of their personal goals while helping Analog Devices achieve its goals. We therefore seek to offer our employees a challenging and stable work environment where they can earn above average compensation for above average performance and contribution to the Company. It is our policy to offer unrestricted opportunity for personal advancement irrespective of race, creed, color, sex, national origin, age, or disability.

Our objective is to build mutual respect, confidence and trust in our personal relationships based upon commitments to integrity, honesty, openness, and competence. Our policy is to share Analog Devices' success with the people who make it possible.

OUR CUSTOMERS

Satisfying our customers' needs is fundamental to our survival and our prosperity. These needs can best be understood in terms of the support we lend our customers in helping them meet their objectives with the minimum use of their resources. Thus, our goals must be to provide superior, easy to use, reliable products that conform to specifications and offer innovative solutions to our customers' problems. We must back up these products with excellent product literature and strong customer service that includes highly effective applications assistance, quick response to inquiries, and dependable delivery. We must work hard at understanding our customers' businesses so that we may anticipate *their* needs and enhance *their* effectiveness. We wish to be major suppliers to our key customers and to establish long lasting business relationships based on quality, performance and integrity.

OUR STOCKHOLDERS

Our responsibility to our stockholders is to satisfy their desire for a secure and liquid investment that provides an attractive rate of return. Our objective is to consistently earn a return on invested capital that is well above average for all manufacturing companies and comparable to the most successful companies in our industry. By achieving consistent growth with a high return on capital we can offer our stockholders an attractive opportunity for capital appreciation.

OUR SUPPLIERS

Our suppliers are partners in our efforts to develop market share by fulfilling our customers' needs. This requires that we be open and frank about our plans and requirements as they would affect our suppliers. It also requires that we seek to understand the constraints placed upon our suppliers by their technology, cost structure, and financial resources. We place strong emphasis on associating with suppliers who are financially stable, competent, and honest and who are consistent in meeting their delivery and quality commitments to us.

OUR COMMUNITY

Our goal is to be an asset to every community in which we operate by offering stable employment and by lending effort and support to worthy causes. We encourage our employees to take an active interest in their communities and contribute their efforts toward making their communities better places to live and work. We make a special effort to aid and support those universities and colleges that are an important source of scarce resources.

GROWTH

Growth is an important means by which we satisfy the interests of our employees, our stockholders, and our customers. High caliber people look for opportunities for personal development and advancement which can best be achieved in a growth environment. Our stockholders are looking for an above average return, which is much more likely to be achieved by a growth company.

To achieve growth we continuously search out and focus on application for our products and technology that have above average long-term potential. We also continuously broaden the range of our products and technology, mostly through internal development.

PROFIT

Profit generated by our business is the primary source of the funds required to finance our growth. Without growth and profits we cannot achieve our corporate objectives. Our financial goals are to generate profit after tax and return on capital comparable to the best-performing companies in our industry and - without taking unreasonable risks - self-fund our growth.

MARKET LEADERSHIP

Our goal is to obtain the largest share of each market segment we serve. We believe the key to achieving market share is to enter growth markets early with superior, innovative products, and to provide a high level of quality and customer service. Our markets are world-wide in scope, and our objective is to achieve comparable penetration in every major geographical market.

QUALITY

Customer satisfaction, and thus our success, is critically dependent on dependable delivery of high quality products and services. A high quality product or service is one that is delivered when promised and performs as specified under all intended operating conditions throughout its intended life.

The achievement of high quality begins with product planning, but it must also be an integral part of product design and the design and implementation of manufacturing processes. High quality depends upon the commitment of all employees to the on-time production of defect free products and services.

High quality is not a static condition. It is susceptible to continuous improvement through systematic identification and elimination of causes of errors and variances, through development of improved designs and processes and through education and training. Continuous improvement of quality leads not only to greater customer satisfaction but also to higher productivity and lower costs.

The concept of quality improvement is applicable to every area of the Company, including marketing, customer service, finance, and human resources, as well as manufacturing and engineering. Every employee should be committed to quality improvement and should be determined to "do it right the first time and do it better the next time."

SUMMARY

Achieving our goals for growth, profits, market share, and quality creates the environment and economic means to satisfy the interests and needs for our employees, stockholders, customers, and others associated with the firm. Our success depends on people who understand the interdependence and congruence of their personal goals with those of the Company, and who are thus motivated to contribute toward the achievement of these goals.

SOURCE: Analog Devices, Inc., "Corporate Objectives." Reprinted by permission of Analog Devices, Inc., Norwood, MA.

We are dealing with issues that are at the heart of what the corporation is and should be. Marked differences between these two states can indicate serious strategic deficiencies that need to be corrected. Often, passionate discussions emerge, and subjects that are seldom openly vented begin to receive proper attention and consideration. A subject that, on the surface, could appear as vague and irrelevant becomes central and insightful.

2. Broad Corporate Objectives.
These issues do not have the emotional intensity that we captured in the previous dimension of corporate philosophy. We are dealing, first, with the characterization of the growth and profitability that the firm has enjoyed in the past; and then, the recording of the expectations that managers have with regard to desirable targets.

3. Corporate Policies.
This time the issues are centered on the perceptions that managers have regarding the way that the firm addresses its internal affairs. The questions are: How can we characterize the management style of the firm? The existing organizational policies? The practices of human resources? The management of finance? And the marketing, manufacturing, and technological capabilities of the firm?

Again, contrasting the existing conditions with the desired ones is the key part of this assignment. A significant gap is indicative of serious weaknesses that will generate significant strategic action programs to be corrected.

4. Corporate Values.
Now we come to one of the most elusive issues of corporate philosophy: the current ethical beliefs and rules of personal behavior, and the possible transformations we would like to see in them.

Figure 15–2 illustrates the output of the process of reexamining the corporate philosophy of the firm, by using the case of P&G. Perhaps the content of that figure does not capture the richness of this task, because, as we have said before, the P&G case is used in this book only as an illustration, in which no P&G managers have been involved.

Figure 15–3 gives an illustration of the corporate philosophy analysis for the Materials Sector of NKK. From this analysis, the following challenges emerge:

1. Pursue integrated management through the realization of synergy
2. Strengthen cooperation among the companies in the group
3. Accelerate the restructuring of total assets
4. Globalize the R&D function establishing facilities overseas and closer relationships with foreign universities
5. Put more energy into fundamental research

FIGURE 15–2. Corporate Philosophy—The Case of P&G

	Existing	Desired
RELATIONSHIPS WITH STAKEHOLDERS		
Employees	Competition among individuals, brands, and teams. Commitment to recruiting and retaining talented people irrespective of creed, race, sex, or national origin.	Extend coordination and cooperation across different organizational units. Make corporate profit a goal of all individuals. Continue and expand the employee ownership program.
Customers	U.S. customer dominant in defining product characteristics.	Our customers are the people of the world. Detect geographical differences and account for the ever increasing power of the distribution channels. Our customers will choose P&G products for their outstanding value.
Shareholders	High returns and stock appreciation.	Continue providing high returns and stock appreciation.
Suppliers	Regarded as important partners. Solid relationships in the U.S.; uneven in the rest of the world.	Recognize them as essential partners in our global value chain.
Communities	Environmental concerns.	Attain indisputable environmental leadership.
BROAD CORPORATE OBJECTIVES		
Growth	Continuous market share increases in the past years.	Growth should not be limited to market share. It includes product development and the entrance in geographical areas in which P&G has no presence.
Profitability	Above average returns.	Maintain above-average returns.
CORPORATE POLICIES		
Management Style	Mainly centralized. U.S. focused.	Become truly global and decentralized in those aspects needing local focus. Create a transnational culture.
Organizational Policies	Focus on the ability to transfer technology and retain individuals.	Adopt the philosophy of the learning organization.
Human Resources Management	Good professionals with individual focus.	Increase mobility and team spirit. Emphasize international training.
Finance	Local funding and management of currency exchanges.	Centralize access to worldwide markets.
Marketing	Localized.	Disseminate knowledge. Local focus.
Manufacturing	Good with some aging plants.	Improve cost structure; emphasis on process advantages.
Technology	Innovative in all products and markets.	Become "the environmental company," both in products and packages as well as production processes.
CORPORATE VALUES		
Ethics	Good reputation	Environmental focus.
Beliefs	Honest dealings are rewarded.	Honest dealings will always be rewarded.
Rules of Personal Behavior	The power resides in the individual.	Add long-term perspective all in areas.

NOTE: This is not an official document. It is an illustration drawn from public sources.

FIGURE 15–3. Corporate Philosophy—The Case of NKK

	Existing	Desired
RELATIONSHIPS WITH STAKEHOLDERS		
Employees	Employees are a really important resource. NKK keeps lifetime employment system and basically adheres to the seniority system. Management has a good relationship with the unions.	Keep treating employees as an important asset. Keep good relationship with the unions. Change the organization and systems so that the full scope of employees' abilities is employed.
Customers	NKK is really responsive to customers. NKK keeps traditional close relationship with many big customers.	Retain close relationship with big customers. Try to grasp customers' intangible needs and create new market for them.
Shareholders	NKK pays out certain dividend per year (10% of face value per stock).	Increase dividend payout.
Suppliers	NKK keeps long term relationship with suppliers.	Support their cost cutting and quality improvement activities and share the benefits.
Communities	NKK acknowledges communities as NKK's stakeholders and contributes to their activity.	Contribute more actively to the improvement of lives in communities, just not being asked but by taking initiatives.
BROAD CORPORATE OBJECTIVES		
Growth	Growth through diversification strategy and expansion of engineering businesses.	Growth through the expansion of existing new businesses.
Profitability	Increase in profitability through rationalization of the steel and engineering businesses.	Improvement through further value-adding to core businesses and contribution of new businesses.
CORPORATE POLICIES		
Management Style	Decentralization. Active pursuit of diversification strategy. Worldwide business development.	Further decentralization and utilization of synergy among divisions and group companies.
Organizational Policies	Divisional structure.	Divisional structure with systems which realize synergy among divisions and group companies.
Human Resources Management	Continuous hiring of college graduates. Combination of in-house training and on-the-job training. Common HRM systems for almost all divisions.	Exchange of human resources among group companies. Establish HRM system which is suitable for each business.
Finance	Reduction of debt through equity finance and reduction of inventory level.	Strict control over investment in new businesses (adoption of ROA as investment criteria). Optimization of funds utilization among group companies. Accelerate the restructuring of total assets.
Technology	Putting emphasis on R&D of new products for NKK. Construction of information infrastructure. Development of sophisticated but broad technology that supports integrated management.	Strengthening of fundamental research. Establishment of a global R&D network.
CORPORATE VALUES		
Beliefs	NKK contributes to the establishment of a rich environment for human beings through the formation of industrial and life infrastructures.	
Rules of Personal Behavior	NKK supplies the best quality goods from materials through service by realizing customers' needs and wants. NKK continues to be a competitive company through its global viewpoint, keeping the future and continuous improvement in mind.	

SOURCE: Tada (1993). This is not an official document of NKK Corporation.

Finding major differences between the existing and desired states calls for serious reflection and important action programs, which are sometimes difficult to implement because they point at transformations in deeply rooted cultural behavior. Whenever this process leads to the identification of significant changes in the current corporate philosophy, we usually face a task of unquestionable difficulty, since these changes most likely force adaptations of deeply ingrained attitudes and cultural values.

Summary of the Corporate Internal Scrutiny: The Strengths and Weaknesses of the Firm

The completion of the corporate philosophy signifies the end of the corporate internal scrutiny. As we indicated in Figure 9-1, we now need to summarize the overall strengths and weaknesses of the firm. There is an intrinsic bonding of the five tasks that are part of this internal scrutiny. The mission of the firm and the business segmentation serve to define the areas of strategy formulation and implementation; horizontal and vertical integration provide the necessary linkages to these resulting business entities; and corporate philosophy is the glue that adds the set of values that will direct the management of those businesses. The businesses are not regarded as independent and autonomous activities, but are integrated into the coherent whole which is the corporation. The corporation is particularly shaped by the five tasks that we refer to as the corporate internal scrutiny.

Figure 15–4 summarizes the corporate strategic strengths for the case of P&G. Likewise, Figure 15–5 conveys similar information for the case of NKK Materials Sector.

This final step of the corporate internal scrutiny provides an opportunity for the top managers of the organization to make a broad reflection about the nature of the existing and required competencies, and about the efforts that will be required to preserve the competitive advantage into the future.

(Figures 15-4 and 15-5 follow on pages 262 and 263)

FIGURE 15–4. Summary of the Corporate Internal Scrutiny: Strengths and Weaknesses of the Firm—The Case of P&G

CURRENT CORPORATE STRENGTHS

1. Information technology linking customers to production.
2. Application of R&D for innovation to extend product life cycle.
3. Advanced R&D capabilities to generate new products. Regional R&D centers focused on regional differences.
4. Human resource management.
5. Marketing and advertisement.
6. Brand management.
7. International management experience.
8. Proactive environmental policies.
9. Vertical integration from paper and packaging to a broad distribution network ending at the store shelf.
10. Employee stock ownership plan.

REQUIRED CORPORATE STRENGTHS (CURRENT CORPORATE WEAKNESSES)

1. Increase knowledge of the food and beverage businesses.
2. Attain cost leadership in as many product lines as possible.
3. Develop transnational infrastructure and corporate culture.
4. Expand in newly opening markets.
5. Improve responsiveness to local markets.
6. Become the environmental leader.

NOTE: This is not an official document. It is an illustration drawn from public sources.

FIGURE 15–5. Summary of the Corporate Internal Scrutiny: Strengths and Weaknesses of the Firm—The Case of NKK

CURRENT CORPORATE STRENGTHS OF NKK'S MATERIAL SECTOR

1. High brand recognition.
2. Traditional close relationship with big customers.
3. Effective and integrated steel factories.
4. Excellent human resources.
5. Most advanced process technology in upstream area of steel manufacturing.
6. Having manufacturing bases in Thailand (TCS) and USA (National Steel).
7. Intensive R&D.
8. Having a powerful mini-mill (Toa Steel) in the NKK Group.

REQUIRED CORPORATE STRENGTHS (CURRENT CORPORATE WEAKNESSES) OF NKK'S MATERIAL SECTOR

1. Improve financial strength.
2. Use synergy with other divisions, including Engineering Division, more aggressively.
3. Strengthen the cooperation among NKK Group companies.
4. Aim to become the highest quality carbon and stainless steel sheet manufacturer in the world.
5. Improve the efficiency of R&D.
6. Find a strong ally in the aluminum business.
7. Expand market share in Kansai area.
8. Develop a more aggressive and creative culture.
9. Increase the cost competitiveness of nonsteel products.

SOURCE: Tada (1993). This is not an official document of NKK Corporation.

CHAPTER 16

Strategic Posture of the Firm

The strategic posture of the firm is a set of pragmatic requirements developed at the corporate level to guide the formulation of corporate, business, and functional strategies. It is expressed primarily through the formulation of corporate strategic thrusts and corporate performance objectives. As shown in Figure 9–1, the principal inputs to define the strategic posture of the firm come from the corporate environmental scan and the corporate internal scrutiny. These have been the subjects of discussion in Chapters 9 through 15.

Corporate Strategic Thrusts: The Agenda, the Assignment of Responsibilities, and the Measures of Control

The corporate strategic thrusts constitute a powerful mechanism for translating the broad sense of directions the organization wants to follow into a practical set of instructions to all key managers involved in the strategic process. We define strategic thrusts as the primary issues the firm has to address during the next three to five years to establish a healthy competitive position in the key markets in which it participates. There are three dimensions involved in defining the strategic thrusts of the firm:

1. The Agenda.

The strategic thrusts constitute the strategic agenda of the firm shaped by its top managers. They must be the depositories of all the previous analyses that we have conducted so far. This is a test of comprehensiveness. To assure that this test is passed, we have to reflect back on the tasks that we have conducted so far, to make sure that the strategic thrusts respond to all the challenges coming from:

- the statement of opportunities and threats resulting from the environmental scan
- the collective set of issues that emerge from the corporate internal scrutiny. This involves the challenges emerging from the changes in the mission, business segmentation, horizontal and vertical integration, corporate philosophy, and the final summary identifying the strengths and weaknesses of the firm.

Having satisfied the test for comprehensiveness, we have to consider the test for stretch. When we look at the strategic agenda of the firm condensed in the strategic thrusts, we must ask ourselves the following questions: Do we feel that its realization will effectively move the firm to its most desirable competitive stage? Are we just repeating the old formulas? Are we feeling too comfortable about the challenges that are implicit in the thrusts? Are we truly responsive to the dynamic changes that are emerging from industrial restructuring and competitors' moves? And, most of all, for a wide variety of firms, do we truly understand the challenges of globalization and the role that technology is playing in defining our way to compete? And as a bottom line, are we internalizing all of these challenges in a way that deals with the human resources of the firm as the most important source of competitive advantage?

2. The Assignment of Responsibilities.
If we address properly all the questions that we have just stated, we will end up with a powerful set of strategic initiatives. The second major issue that needs to be resolved is answering the question of responsibility and accountability. We can not disassociate formulation from implementation, nor responsibility from accountability. This calls for identifying all the key organizational units of the firm, or better yet, the specific individuals who are responsible for those organizational units. This approach can provide a mapping between the responsibilities that originate in each individual strategic thrust. It can also delineate the accountability that will rest on those in charge of defining the action programs that respond to each thrust and will enable them to monitor the consequent implementation of these programs.

In the previous step we checked the quality of the strategic agenda in terms of the comprehensiveness and stretch of the strategic thrusts; now we are concerned about defining, as clearly as we can, the assignments of responsibility and accountability that every major player in the organization will assume in order to manage the firm strategically.

3. The Measures of Control.
The strategic thrusts should reveal the strategic agenda of the firm and be translated into a set of tasks unequivocally assigned to each of the organizational units and the responsible managers of the firm. The third issue to be resolved has to do with developing the necessary metrics to monitor the progress being made by the firm to live up to the challenges of the strategic thrusts. We have to define the basis for the information and control systems required to monitor the progress of the strategic agenda. It is at this point that we make explicit the linkage between planning and control. If the strategic thrusts truly represent

the strategic agenda of the firm, they should become the foundation for the development of the executive information systems of the firm.

The formulation of strategic thrusts frames all the critical issues and raises the central questions the firm should address for a meaningful strategic development. They establish a coherent and relatively stable framework for conducting the remaining part of the strategic planning process.

Corporate Strategic Thrusts: Some Illustrations

Figure 16–1 illustrates in a very succinct way the statement of strategic thrusts for P&G and the assignment of responsibilities to the organizational levels in charge of responding to those thrusts. The statement also includes relevant measures of performance intended to monitor the operational and strategic results associated with each thrust. Notice that there is a priority assigned to those planning challenges, depending on the intensity of the necessary participation required by each of the relevant organizational units. The first column of the chart identifies corporate responsibilities; the next fifteen business columns correspond to the business units described in Figure 12–2; the activities of the value chain are represented in the six functional columns: finance, procurement, production, marketing, technology, and managerial infrastructure (which includes human resources management).

The chart containing strategic thrusts can be read in three different ways, which correspond to the three dimensions that we have identified in the previous section. First, we could analyze the quality of the agenda emerging from the overall set of strategic issues, placing particular attention on whether they capture the totality of the strategic initiatives facing the corporation—its comprehensiveness—and the extent to which they represent a forceful and impacting challenge—its stretch.

Second, we can read each thrust horizontally to make sure that we have properly identified the organizational units and the managers who should be involved in formulating the action programs addressing each thrust, as well as supporting their implementation. When a strategic thrust cuts across several functions and business units of the firm, it is an indication that a business process might be identified by that thrust. Business process reengineering has become one of the most widely used and best business practices. The literature on the subject is very vague on how to define business processes. We believe that the strategic thrusts chart, such as the one in Figure 16-1, provides a proper insight into this matter.[1]

Third, we can read this chart vertically to detect the role assigned to each individual organizational unit. This allows us to spot potential bottlenecks and the criticality of the involvement of each unit. To some extent, this also gives us another check of completeness, because it allows us to examine the involvement of each organizational unit as well as the functional support needed to back up each strategic thrust.

FIGURE 16–1. Statement of Strategic Thrusts—The Case of P&G

STRATEGIC THRUST	COR	1	2	3	4	5	6	7	8	9	10	11	12	13	14	15	Fin	Proc	Prod	Mkt	Tec	MI	PERFORMANCE MEASUREMENTS
1. Concentrate on the profitability of food and beverages. Divest if necessary.	1				1	1	1	1	1								1	2	2	2	2	2	Sales, profit, and margin
2. Emphasize environmentally friendly product, particularly compact and liquid detergents.	2												1				2	2	2	2	1		Sales and product mix
3. Develop OTC product lines.	2														1	1	2	2	2	1	1		Size of product line, and overall market share
4. Increase R&D in process manufacturing.	2	2	2	2	2	2	2	2		2	2	2	2	2	2	2		2	1	1	1		Production costs and environmental impact
5. Develop biodegradable diapers.		1	2	1														2	2		2		Time to market
6. Constantly monitor changes in tastes and health concerns.			1	1	1	1	1	1		1	1	1	1	1	1	1				1	1		Number of consumer surveys and product improvements
7. Develop geographical strategies for different regions, with emphasis on Latin America, W. Europe, and Asia.	1		2	2	2	2	2	2		2	2	2	2	2	2	2	2	2	2	1	2	1	Regional market shares
8. Develop specialty stores as a channel for prestige care products.										1	1	1								1			Market share
9. Improve relationships with suppliers.	2	1	1	1	1	1	1	1		1	1	1	1	1	1	1		1	2			2	Increase % of supplier sales to P&G
10. Encourage communication between market research and product R&D.	2	2	2	2	2	2	2	2		2	2	2	2	2	2	2		2	2	1	1	2	Customer-driven product innovations
11. Develop a full line of men's cosmetics.										1	1	1					2		2	1	1		Product line market share
12. Develop combined products, both in the food and detergent segments.					1	1	1	1		1	1	1	1						2	1	1		Number of products, sales, market share
13. Develop distribution channels through wholesale clubs and discount drugstores.				1	1	1	1	1		1	1	1								1			Market share
14. Develop entry strategies for China and countries without P&G presence in Eastern Europe, Latin America, and Africa, through distribution alliances.	1		2	2						2	2	2	2		2		2			1		1	Market share per product introduced and country
15. Develop a transnational organization.	1	2	2	2	2	2	2	2	2	2	2	2	2	2	2	2	2	2	2	2	2	1	Completion of a first proposal

NOTE: This is not an official document. It is an illustration drawn from public sources.

CODE: 1—Key role in formulation and implementation; 2—Important support role.

CODE: COR - Corporate

CODE FOR BUSINESS NUMBERS:

1. Cellulose 2. Tissue and Towel Paper Products 3. Disposable Diapers 4. Coffee 5. Cake Mixes 6. Shortening Oils 7. Potato Chips/Peanut Butter 8. Drinks 9. Cosmetics 10. Oral Care 11. Soap-Shampoos 12. Detergents 13. Chemicals 14. OTC Drugs 15. Prescription Drugs

Finally, the last column, which defines the performance measurements selected to monitor the progress of each strategic thrust, gives us a sense of the critical indicators that are relevant to the top managers of the firm.

Another example is provided in Figure 16–2 for the Materials Sector of NKK. A first observation is the broadness of the nineteen strategic thrusts responding to all the issues raised in the previous step of the analysis—a test for comprehensivness. Also, there are ambitious thrusts, like the development of new materials to replace steel—a test for stretch. Reading the figure horizontally, we can see, for example, that strengthening the sales offices in Osaka and Singapore—thrust no. 2—and looking for synergy with other companies of the NKK group—thrust no. 3—attract attention of all the businesses; while developing the chemical business—thrust No 13—is centered exclusively in that SBU. Looking at the columns, we see that all businesses and functions are presented with demanding challenges, but the three steel businesses have an especially heavy agenda. Finally, the performance measurements include indicators of profitability, market share, growth, and other.

Corporate Performance Objectives

Corporate objectives are quantitative indicators of the overall performance of the firm. Typically, companies choose to express corporate objectives via a selective number of indices, which are predominantly of a financial nature. Although there is no universal set of such indices, we can classify them into two major categories.[2] The first includes quantitative financial measures that relate to size, growth, profitability, capital markets, and a host of other financial variables. The second is oriented at measuring the overall efficiency of the managerial capabilities of the firm.

The first category—quantitative measures of financial performance—is of the greatest importance, because quantitative measures address objectives that are central to the short-term well being of the firm, as well as its long-term survival and development. Also, the financial standing of the firm and its position in the capital markets constitute parameters of undeniable managerial significance. American managers have often been criticized for paying excessive attention to the response of capital markets and being obsessed by short-term (even quarterly) financial performance. Without denying the importance of financial performance, managers should aim at having a balance between short- and long-term consequences, acting in a way that does not distort one of these dimensions in favor of the other. Figure 16–3 suggests performance variables to measure this category of financial indicators. We attempt to contrast current and past performance, and to set up objective targets for the short and the long term.

Various considerations serve as a base to arrive at a numerical expression of those targets: first, the historical performance achieved by the corporation; second, the projected trends expected from the existing and new business lines;

FIGURE 16–2. Statement of Strategic Thrusts—The Case of NKK

STRATEGIC THRUST	HES	LES	SUS	PP	TI&AL	FA	CHE	CER	CP	R&D	HRM	IS	C	FIN	Others	PERFORMANCE MEASUREMENTS
1. Establish a joint strategy with Toa Steel.	1	1							1				2	2		Total market share: ROA of NKK and Toa.
2. Strengthen sales offices in Osaka (to deal with the Kansai area) and Singapore (to address the ASEAN countries).	1	1	1	1	1	1	1	1	1		2				1	Milestones of the plan; regional market share.
3. Look for synergies with other companies of the NKK group, in logistics, procurement, finance, and information systems.	1	1	1	1	1	1	1	1	1		2	1	1	1	1	% of cost reduction.
4. Study the restructuring of current assets of each company in the NKK group.	1											1	2	2	1	% inventory reduction.
5. Establish a marketing strategy, based on National Steel, to deal with AFTA.	1	1	2						2						1	Growth of regional market share.
6. Establish a marketing strategy for steel products in ASEAN countries, based on Thai Coated Steel (TCS) and the strengthened Singapore Office.	1	1	2						2						1	Growth of regional market share.
7. Keep cost leadership for steel products through further rationalization and integration of plants.	1	1	1	1											1	Our cost vs. the cost of the most relevant competition.
8. Improve process and product technology for steel sheets.	1	1	1							1						Benchmarking with Nippon Steel.
9. Empower marketing and sales departments for automakers and constructors.	1	1	2												1	Market share and customer satisfaction.
10. Seek a strong ally in the aluminum business.	1								1	2						Identify, at least one candidate for the alliance.
11. Evaluate and divest the less profitable ferroalloy products.	2	2														ROA.
12. Restructure the titanium business.			2		1				2	2						ROA and market share of each product.
13. Develop the chemical business by forward integration.	2						1		2	1			2	2		ROA and market share.
14. Develop and grow new materials that can replace steel in the future and for which we have the technology (both process and product).	1	1	1		1					2						Number of new products and their market share.
15. Introduce more work stations instead of mainframes.	2	2	2	2	2	2	2	2	2	2	2	1	2	2	2	% of cost reduction.
16. Exchange employees among group companies and divisions to realize synergy.	2	2	2	2	2	2	2	2	2	2	1	2	2	2	1	Milestones in the plan.
17. Establish HRM systems that transfer researchers to marketing sections temporarily so as to grasp intangible market needs directly.	2	2	2	2	2	2	2	2		1	1					Milestones in the plan.
18. Seek proper sites for R&D center in USA and Europe.									1	1	2				1	Identification of proper sites.
19. Form a task force with a researcher of the R&D Division to look for synergies among the companies of the NKK group.	2	2	2	2	2	2	2	2	1	1	2				2	Number of products developed by task force.

Columns grouped: **BUSINESSES** (HES, LES, SUS, PP, TI&AL, FA, CHE, CER); **FUNCTIONS** (CP, R&D, HRM, IS, C, FIN, Others).

SOURCE: Adapted from Tada (1993). This is not an official document of NKK Corporation.

CODE: 1 – Key role in formulation and implementation; 2 – Important support role. CODE FOR SBUs: HES—High-end steel, LES—Low-end steel, SUS—Stainless and specialty steel, P—Polymer products, TI&AL—Titanium, aluminum and specialty metals, FA—Ferroalloys, CHE—Chemicals, CER—Ceramics, PM—Precision metals, CODE FOR FUNCTIONAL UNITS: CP—Corporate Planning Dept., R&D—R&D Division, HRM—Personnel Dept. & Labor Relations Dept., IS—Information Systems Dept., C—Comptroller's Dept., FIN—Finance Dept.

FIGURE 16–3. Corporate Performance Objectives: Size, Growth, Profitability, Capital Markets, and Other Financial Measures

PERFORMANCE INDICATORS		Past Years			Current Year	Objective Markets	
		19x1	19x2	19x3	19x4	Short Term	Long Term
Size	Sales Assets Profits Market value Number of employees						
Growth	Sales Assets Profits Market value Number of employees						
Profitability	Profit margin Return on assets (ROA) Return on equity (ROE) Spread (ROE-k_E)						
Capital Markets	Dividend yield (Dividend/Price) Total return to investors Price/Earning ratio (P/E) Market-to-book value ratio (M/B) Payout (Dividend/Earning) Price per share (P) Book value per share (B)						
Liquidity	Current ratio Quick ratio Defense interval Cash position Working capital from operations Cash flow from operations						
Leverage	Debt-to-equity ratio Short-term vs. long-term debt Times interest earned Cash flow vs. interest payments						
Turnover	Total assets turnover Average collection period Inventory turnover						
Other Financial	Bond rating Beta Cost of equity capital (k_E) Cost of debt Weighted average cost of capital						

third, the financial position of the firm's competitors; and fourth, the performance measurements of the so-called "best in class," which identify superior firms, whether we are competing against them or not. It is important to recognize the financial performance of the key competitors not only from the perspective of comparative analysis, but also because firms in the same industry attract the same group of investors in the capital markets.

These corporate performance objectives should not be applied indiscriminately to every business of the firm, but should be adjusted to recognize the different contribution they make to the short- and long-run performance of the firm.

Figure 16–4 lists the financial performance indicators for the case of P&G, registers its historical values, and set up objective targets. Figure 16–5 displays similar information for the case of the Materials Sector of NKK.

FIGURE 16–4. Corporate Financial Performance Objectives—The Case of P&G

Performance Indicators	Past Years			Current	Objectives
	1989	1990	1991	1992	1993–1997
Sales 　　　　Total 　　　Growth (%)	21,398	24,081 12.5	27,026 12.2	29,306 8.4	To $42 billion by 1997. Increases mainly overseas. Monitor by product, specifically OTC and cosmetics.
Profits 　　　　Total 　Profit Growth (%) 　　Profit/Sales	1206 5.64%	1602 32.8 6.65%	1773 10.7 6.56%	1879 6.0 6.41%	Maintain profits above 6% of sales. Monitor by product line. Concentrate in food and decide on divestment.
Assets 　　　　Total 　　　Growth	16,351	18,487 13.1	20,464 10.7	21,696 6.0	Continue investing at current levels.
Capital Structure 　Long-Term D/E 　Long-Term D/TC	59.5 43.7	47.7 40.4	53.1 53.1		Maintain current ratios.
Profitability 　　　　ROE 　　　　ROA	23.1 7.4	24.6 8.7	30.9 8.7		Maintain around 25%. Maintain around 9%.
Earnings/Share	3.47	4.27	4.62		Maintain around 4.5%.
Division/Earnings	41	41	42		Above 40%.
Market/Book	3.37	4.63	4.56		Maintain above 4.0.

NOTE: This is not an official document. It is an illustration drawn from public sources.

FIGURE 16–5. Corporate Financial Performance Objectives—The Case of NKK

Performance Indicators	Past Years			Current	Objectives		
	1989	1990	1991	1992	1993	1994	1995

Size
   Sales ¥(Billion)*
Operation Income
   (¥Billion)*
Number
   of Employees
	1208.2
	
	195.4
	
	15,711
		1219.2
		
		135.5
		
		15,279
			118.8
			
			108
			
			15,331
				1190
				
				72
				
				15,000
					1190
					
					72
					
					14,000
						1230
						
						102
						
						13,000
							1260
							
							123
							
							12,300

Profitability
   ROA (%)**
   ROE (%)**
	1.4
	8.3
		1.04
		5.1
			1.59
			7.5
				0
				0
					0.5
					2.5
						1
						5
							2
							10

Liquidity
   Current Ratio
      (%)**
	98.7	85.5	83.6	85	90	100	110

Leverage
   Equity Ratio
      (%)**
	20.3	20.5	21.2	20.5	21	21.5	23

Efficiency
   Total Assets
   Turnover **
	0.43	0.47	0.46	0.45	0.5	0.6	0.75

Other Bond Rating**	AA-	AA--	AA-	AA-	AA-	AA-	A

*These figures are total of NKK's Steel Division, New Business Center, and Toa Steel.
**These figures are those of NKK as a firm (i.e., they are total of all divisions of NKK and do not include Toa's figure).

SOURCE: Tada (1993). This is not an official document of NKK Corporation.

The second major category of corporate performance objectives, which is oriented at measuring managerial capabilities, focuses particularly on human resources, technology, procurement, manufacturing, and marketing. Incorporating these functional measures at the corporate level is relevant whenever we deal with centralized functions. Otherwise, the functional measures should become part of either divisional or business performance indicators, depending on where the function resides within the organization. Figure 16–6 lists functional indicators in a format quite similar to the one we use for financial corporate performance. However, recognizing the qualitative nature of the performance indicators that measure organizational capabilities, the great challenge is to produce metrics that could meaningfully describe achievements in those areas.

Figures 16–7 and 16–8 present the examples of P&G and NKK respectively. Notice that, in these cases, it is difficult to assign specific numbers to measure the performance of each indicator. The challenge imposed by the need to have

FIGURE 16–6. Corporate Performance Objectives for Centralized Functions

PERFORMANCE INDICATORS		Past Years			Current Year	Objective Targets	
		19x1	19x2	19x3	19x4	Short Term	Long Term
Human Resources Management	Job satisfaction Job performance Turnover Absenteeism Motivation Job security Career prospects Psychological stress Safety health conditions Income						
Technology	Rate of technological innovation R&D productivity Rate of return on R&D investment Resources allocated to R&D Rate of new products introduction Technology-based diversification Royalties or sales of technology Cycle time of product development						
Procurement	Cost Service Quality Vendor relationships						
Manufacturing	Cost Delivery Quality Flexibility New products introduction						
Marketing	Product strategy Distribution Price strategy Promotion and advertising						

This table suggests performance criteria for each function. Specific quantitative indicators must be defined to fit the particulars of a firm.

a management control is to continue monitoring and assessing nonfinancial performance in as objective a way as possible. Financial indicators often give us an understanding of the historical performance of the firm. Nonfinancial indicators, on the other hand, can address the issue of future sustainability of the firm's performance.

The issue of managerial performance has been hotly debated in the recent past. Quite a number of path-breaking new approaches have been

FIGURE 16–7. Corporate Nonfinancial Performance Objectives—The Case of P&G

PERFORMANCE INDICATORS	OBJECTIVES/METRICS
R&D Spending/Sales	Maintain at 3%
R&D Productivity	Number of R&D driven innovations
Product Development Time	Average of 3 months
Job Satisfaction	Turnover, Employee Surveys
Procurement Costs	Decrease 10% cost of materials
Procurement Quality	Quality control report on purchases
Supplier Relationships	Percentage of supplier's sales to P&G
New Product Introductions	Number of introductions
Manufacturing Costs	Decrease 10% production costs
Manufacturing Quality	Number of defects (or defective runs)
Environmental Protection	Number of environmentally safe products
Geographical Expansion	Percentage of sales in different regions

NOTE: This is not an official document. It is an illustration drawn from public sources.

proposed to enhance the ability of managers to measure performance in the short term and in the long run, and from an operational and strategic perspective. Some of these new approaches have produced the best business practices. Paramount among them are competitive benchmarking, created at Xerox Corporation; and activity-based costing and the balance scorecard, both pioneered by Robert Kaplan and some of his associates.[3]

FIGURE 16–8. Corporate Nonfinancial Performance Objectives—The Case of NKK

Performance Indicators	Current	Objectives		
	1992	1993	1994	1995
HRM & IR				
Turnover ration of new employees (%)	5	5	4	3
# of Serious injuries (# of Deaths)	1	0	0	0
Technology				
Ratio of patents that receive public notice (%)	52.1	55	60	65
Sales of new products per total sales (%)	–	3	5	7

*Current shows recent average figures.
**Figures are not publicly available for these items.

SOURCE: Tada (1993). This is not an official document of NKK Corporation.

Notes

1. The two pioneering books on the subject of business reengineering are: Michael Hammer and James Champy, *Reengineering the Corporation: A Manifesto for Business Revolution* (New York: Harper Business, 1993); and Thomas H. Davenport, *Process Innovation: Reengineering Work through Information Technology* (Boston, MA: Harvard Business School Press, 1993). For a more recent publication on this subject, see James Champy, *Reengineering Management: The Mandate for New Leadership* (New York: Harper Business, 1994).

2. The issue of the soundness of the performance metrics used by the firm has received a great deal of attention recently. For some broad discussion of the subject, see: H. Thomas Johnson and Robert S. Kaplan, *Relevance Lost: The Rise and Fall of Management Accounting* (Boston, MA: Harvard Business School Press, 1987); John K. Shank and Vijay Govindarajan, *Strategic Cost Management: The New Tool for Competitive Advantage* (New York: Free Press, 1993); and Robert S. Kaplan, (Ed.), *Measures for Manufacturing Excellence* (Boston, MA: Harvard Business School Press, 1990).

3. The pioneering reference for benchmarking is Robert C. Camp, *Benchmarking: The Search for Industry Best Practices that Lead to Superior Performance* (Milwaukee, WI: Quality Press, 1989). The original references for the Balanced Scorecard are: Robert S. Kaplan and David P. Norton, "The Balanced Scorecard—Measures that Drive Performance," *Harvard Business Review* (January–February, 1992) 71–79; and Robert S. Kaplan and David P. Norton, "Putting the Balanced Scorecard to Work," *Harvard Business Review* (September–October, 1993) 134–142. The original reference for Activity-Based Costing is Robin Cooper and Robert S. Kaplan, "Measures the Costs Right: Make the Right Decisions," *Harvard Business Review* (September–October, 1988).

17

Resource Allocation and Portfolio Management

After all the proposals related to corporate, business, and functional programs are completed, a major task that inevitably resides at the corporate level is the allocation of limited resources to attend the wide array of requests coming from the lower levels of the firm. In most organizations, top managers face the difficult decision of having to discriminate among the proposals that are finally submitted because the financial, technological, and human resources available to the firm are not sufficient to support every proposed initiative. This fact of life is the fundamental reason why resource allocation is a truly centralized decision that cannot be delegated to lower echelons of the firm. Besides, this calls for the identification of criteria to allow the organization to make the best possible use of the available restricted resources.

In business firms, the bottom line for resource allocation is *value creation*. In financial terms, it means that the profitability enjoyed by the economic entity—the firm, the business, or a project—should exceed its cost of capital.

The cost of capital is a concept that has involved technical ramifications. However, from a simple point of view, it represents the required rate of return of a given investment, and it consists of two components. One is the risk-free rate, namely, an opportunity available to any investor that guarantees without any uncertainty a return. In the United States, the normal measures of the risk-free rate are Treasury Bills and Government Bonds. Having been assured of that level of profitability, a rational investor would only consider additional investment alternatives if they could generate a higher level of return. This additional level of profitability fundamentally depends on the inherent risk of the financial investment option, and it is called risk premium. Thus, the cost of capital is simply the risk-free rate of return plus a risk premium. Figure 17–1 presents a procedure to estimate the cost of equity capital by using the capital-assets pricing model.

FIGURE 17–1. Estimate of the Cost of Capital Using the Capital-Asset Pricing Model

The cost of equity capital may be estimated as:

$$k_E = \text{risk-free rate} + \text{risk premium} = r_f + \beta_E \times (r_m - r_f)$$

1. *Risk-free rate* $= r_f$

   The risk-free rate corresponds to the return on an investment that offers a sure return. Normally, it is estimated as the return on goverment-backed Treasury bills.

2. *Risk premium* $= \beta_E \times (r_m - r_f)$

   The risk premium may be estimated as the product of two terms:

   Risk premium =

   {Volatility of the equity cash flow} x {Average risk premium for the capital markets}

   2.1 *Average risk premium* $= (r_m - r_f)$

   The average risk premium for the capital markets has been estimated to be about 9%. The term r_m represents the average return of the market.

   2.2 *Volatility* $= \beta_E$

   The volatility is a coefficient that measures the inherent risk of an equity cash flow. When the volatility is 1, the risk is equivalent to the average in the market. The volatility coefficient for a given business can be estimated from historical market returns for the firm or for other firms in the same industry. Volatility estimates for specific companies are provided by Merrill Lynch, and other financial firms. In the following table we present a summary of the relative riskiness of different industries as measured through their β-coefficients.

   The β-Coefficient of Different Industries*

Industry	Beta
Electronic components	1.49
Crude petroleum and natural gas	1.07
Retail department store	0.95
Petroleum refining	0.95
Motor vehicle parts	0.89
Chemicals	0.88
Metal mining	0.87
Food	0.84
Trucking	0.83
Textile mill products	0.82
Paper and allied products	0.82
Retail grocery stores	0.76
Airlines	0.75
Steel	0.66
Railroads	0.61
Natural gas transmission	0.52
Telephone companies	0.50
Electric utilities	0.46

*These are asset betas. The effect of financial leverage has been removed.
SOURCE: Richard A. Brealey and Stewart C. Myers, *Principles of Corporate Finance*, 3rd ed. (New York: McGraw-Hill, 1988), p. 182.

Although this is a simple economic concept, we often find that managers do not recognize the significance of economic profitability as a yardstick for measuring the financial performance of every individual unit of the firm. Obviously, accounting profitability—meaning that the businesses are in the black—is not enough. Economic value is only created when the businesses of the firm, and the firm as a whole, enjoy profitability levels which exceed that of their respective cost of capital.

If we consider the definition of return on equity:

$$ROE = \frac{Profit\ after\ interests\ and\ taxes}{Equity}$$

we can assert that: *Accounting profitability* results when ROE is positive (ROE > 0); *Economic profitability* results when ROE exceeds the cost of equity capital (ROE > k_E), in which case, the spread—defined as (ROE - k_E)—is positive. The spread is the number of percentage points that ROE enjoys above the cost of equity capital.

Sources of Value Creation

When economists talk about perfect competitive markets, there always seems to be a tendency to emphasize the long-term equilibrium conditions that result from perfect competition. In this world of perfect balance of supply and demand, there are no real sources of economic returns that can legitimately exceed the cost of capital. When perceived from that dimension, the true objective of a strategy is to break the economic equilibrium law. The objective is to search for windows of opportunity that might position the firm with a unique competitive advantage that can legitimately allow it to claim economic rents beyond those resulting from perfect competition. Rather than living in this long-term equilibrium condition, the central purpose of a strategy is, first, to identify opportunities to create disequilibrium, and then to protect and sustain those conditions as long as possible. This is the essence of a long-term sustainable competitive advantage.

Throughout this book, we have been addressing the sources of competitive advantage—which we are now labeling sources of value creation—and the mechanisms to exploit them. The winning formula is very simple. It consists of understanding the opportunities available in the industries in which we participate, and then developing internally—primarily through value-chain mechanisms—the necessary competencies to allow us to achieve a unique competitive position.

Alan Shapiro, a finance professor, when reflecting about corporate strategy and capital budgeting decisions, concludes that there are five basic lessons that must be learned if one is to achieve excess return:[1]

1. Investments structured to fully exploit economies of scale are more likely to be successful than those that are not.

2. Investments designed to create a position at the high end of anything, including the high end of the low end, differentiated by quality or service, will generally be profitable.

3. Investments aimed at achieving the lowest delivered cost position in the industry, coupled with a pricing policy to expand market share, are likely to succeed, especially if the cost reductions are proprietary.

4. Investments devoted to gaining better product distribution often lead to higher profitability.

5. Investments in projects protected from competition by government regulation can lead to extraordinary profitability. However, what the government gives, the government can take away.

These are indeed sobering lessons that emphasize important sources for competitive advantage, such as economies of scale, product differentiation, cost advantage due to learning curve, proprietary technology, and monopoly control of low-cost raw materials; advantages of new entrants in deregulated industries mainly when a new technology becomes available, access to distribution channels, and government protection.

Measuring the Contribution to Value Creation

There are a wide number of methodologies available to assess the attractiveness of any form of economic activity at the level of the firm, the business unit, or a project.[2] We review briefly the most important ones.

THE DISCOUNTED CASH-FLOW MODEL

There is no question that the best methodology available to assess the economic value of the firm, a business unit belonging to the firm, or a project within an individual business unit is to compute the net present value (NPV) of the expected future cash flows generated, discounted at an appropriate rate, and adjusted for inflation and risk. The discount rate is, in fact, the cost of capital associated to the entity.[3]

The advantages and disadvantages of discounted cash-flow models and the mechanics of calculation are well known and have received wide attention. We assume that the reader is familiar with this basic concept. Because of the orientation of the book, we concentrate on methodologies more directly applicable to strategic assessment of businesses within the context of the firm's overall portfolio.

THE MARKET-TO-BOOK VALUE MODEL (M/B)

A meaningful proxy for the value of the equity of the firm in a country with an efficient capital market, such as the one prevailing in the United States, is given by the market value of the common stock. The assumption is that the market price of common shares represents a consensus of the present value assigned by investors to the expected cash flow streaming from the assets the firm already has in place, as well as from investments the firm will have the opportunity to make at some time in the future, once the interest payments to debtholders have been subtracted.

The market value of a firm's common shares is an indicator that can assist managers both in assessing the shareholders' wealth, as well as in measuring its economic and financial performance vis-a-vis other firms in its industry. It is not surprising, therefore, that managers carefully observe long-term trends in the capital market as an ultimate guide for the managerial success of business firms. On the other hand, excessive concern about day-to-day movements of stock market indicators has been repeatedly stated as one of the most negative forces pressuring American managers to inappropriate short-term orientation. Therefore, there seems to be a paradox in the capital-market messages to the manager. But this is not so. There is plenty of evidence that the market does reward long-term performance, and penalizes erratic behavior intended to hide unfavorable developments in the short run.

The preceding considerations make highly desirable the use of evaluation methodologies in which the market price of the common shares plays an essential role, while retaining the legitimacy of the NPV approach. The M/B model represents such a tool.

The M/B model is a blend of two different perspectives of the firm. In the denominator, the book value of the firm's shares provides the accountant's perspective, which corresponds to the historical measurements of resources contributed by shareholders. In the numerator, the market value of the firm's shares gives the investor's perspective, which corresponds to an assessment of future payments generated from the assets the firm already has in place and from the investments the firm would have the opportunity to make at some time in the future. Therefore, the M/B ratio can be equated to:

$$\frac{\textit{Expected future payments}}{\textit{Past resources committed}}$$

The basic message of the M/B model can be summarized as follows:

- If M/B is equal to 1, the future payments are expected to yield a fair return on the resources committed. The firm is neither creating nor destroying value.
- If M/B is greater than 1, there is an excess return. The firm is creating value for the shareholders.
- If M/B is less than 1, the return is under the benchmark provided by the market. The firm is destroying value for its shareholders.

When we refer to book value, we assume that all distortions induced by accounting rules have been corrected, mainly the ones produced by inflation and the charges of certain investments as expenditures in one period (most notably R&D and advertising).[4]

The Relationship Between Profitability and Growth

Two of the most relevant measures of corporate performance are growth and profitability. Although there are strong interactions between these two concepts, very often growth and profitability goals are set up completely independent of one another. This is a major logical flaw. There is a close association between profitability and growth as measured by spread (ROE - k_E), market-to-book value (M/B), and net present value (NPV). The relationships are exhibited in Figure 17–2.

When a business is profitable, it means that its return on equity exceeds its cost of equity capital (spread is positive), which implies that the business is creating value (therefore, M/B is greater than 1) and the corresponding discounted cash flow produces a positive net present value (NPV positive). Under those conditions, growth will significantly contribute to create value at a compounding rate, and the greater the growth, the greater the value created. Exactly the opposite is true when the business is unprofitable, in which case the spread is negative, M/B is less than one, net present value is also negative, and growth is a damaging contribution that helps to accelerate the value destruction process. The optimal strategy for ongoing businesses that are generating a

FIGURE 17–2. Relationship Between Profitability and Growth

	Profitability of the Firm or Business		
	Profitable	Break Even	Unprofitable
Spread = ROE – k_E	positive	0	negative
M/B	greater than 1	1	less than 1
NPV	positive	0	negative
Contribution of growth to value creation	growth creates value	growth does not create nor destroy value	growth destroys value

return on equity below the cost of capital is to minimize growth, or even better, to disinvest and have a negative growth. In that way, market value is maximized. Eventually, the best strategy could be liquidation, particularly if the permissible disinvestment rates are very small. Finally, when the business is at break-even (spread is zero, M/B equals 1, and net present value is also zero) growth does not help nor hinder value creation.

Factors Affecting the Market Value of the Firm

Previously, we have reflected on the sources behind the acquisition of a competitive advantage, which, in turn, should be translated into an increased market value of the firm. From a financial point of view, these sources can be explained in terms of three critical factors that determine market value: the size of spread, the rate of reinvestment of the firm's profits, and the number of years during which a firm will enjoy a favorable spread. We comment on them now.

The Size of the Spread = ROE - k_E.
Economic profitability is achieved when the return on equity enjoyed by the firm exceeds its cost of equity capital. This concept can be captured in a single measurement, which is the spread. Obviously, the greater the spread, the greater the economic profitability and, therefore, the greater the market value.

The value of k_E represents the cost of equity capital of the firm. This is a fundamental parameter that is unique to each business unit. It depends on the general condition of the economy, the situation of the industry in which the business operates, and the particular policies used by the firm in managing the business. A procedure for estimating the cost of equity capital is based on the so-called capital-asset pricing model (CAPM), which was outlined in Figure 17–1.

The Rate of Reinvestment of the Firm's Profits = p.
The profits of the firm can be assigned either as dividends to its shareholders or reinvested in profitable opportunities available within the firm. The reinvestment rate (p) is one of the critical determinants for the growth of the firm. Let us define growth as the fraction of reinvested profits to the existing equity base of the firm:

$$growth = \frac{profits\ reinvested}{equity}$$

In order to get the relationship between growth and profitability, we can simply multiply and divide the right-hand side of this expression by the profits:

$$growth = \frac{profits\ reinvested}{profits} \cdot \frac{profits}{equity}$$

This leads us to the relationship that links growth with the reinvestment rate and profitability:

$$g = p \cdot ROE$$

where

$$
\begin{aligned}
g &= \ growth\ in\ equity \\
p &= \ profit\ reinvestment\ rate \\
ROE &= \ return\ on\ equity
\end{aligned}
$$

In turn, ROE can be expressed as a function of ROA as follows (see appendix at the end of the chapter).

$$ROE = ROA + \frac{D}{E}[ROA - k_D (1 - T_C)]$$

where

$$
\begin{aligned}
D &= \ total\ debt \\
E &= \ total\ equity \\
k_D &= \ debt\ interest\ rate\ before\ tax \\
T_C &= \ corporate\ tax\ rate
\end{aligned}
$$

The term $[k_D (1 - T_C)]$ is the after-tax cost of debt, since interests are deducted from tax in the U.S. Notice that ROE is greater than ROA. The term $\frac{D}{E}[ROA - k_D (1 - T_C)]$ is called *financing contribution*, because it represents the addition to the return on assets (ROA) that will determine the value of the return on equity (ROE). Notice that the return on equity will be greater than the return on assets only if the financing contribution is positive. In turn, the financing contribution is positive only when the return on assets exceeds the after-tax cost of debt. Does leverage $(\frac{D}{E})$ help? In other words, is it beneficial for the firm to acquire debt? The answer is positive only if debt is allocated in assets whose return exceeds the cost of debt.

From the above expression for ROE, growth can be expressed as:

$$g = p \cdot \left(ROA + \frac{D}{E}[ROA - k_D (1 - T_C)] \right)$$

This expression represents a first cut of the *maximum-sustainable growth*[5] that assumes a stable debt-equity ratio and dividend-payout policy, as well as a fixed overall rate of return on assets and cost of debt. Although a coarse approximation, this number might represent a guide for corporate growth that should be considered at the corporate level.

There are many variations of alternative expressions for the maximum sustainable growth. Our aim has been to present the simplest of those expressions in order to stress the underlying concept that a firm faces an upper bound in its objectives for future growth when the financing policy does not consider other sources of capital, such as issuing new shares, and divesting underperforming assets.

The Number of Years During Which a Firm Will Enjoy a Favorable Spread = n.

As we indicated when discussing the sources of value creation, a positive spread is an anomaly for a firm operating in conditions of perfect competition because, in the long run, the market conditions will make the spread nil. The reason, however, for finding economic opportunities with positive profitability is because of the ability of the firm to sustain a form of competitive advantage that gives access to excess returns. This is what we refer to as the window of a profitable investment opportunity, and its duration is measured by the value n. Obviously, the larger this value, the more the firm will enjoy large abnormal returns, and the greater the impact on value creation.

The three factors contributing to value creation—spread, growth, and duration—as well as the second-order determinants of these factors are graphically displayed in Figure 17–3. The relationships displayed in the figure have enormous implications for strategic planning and management control. From a planning point of view, we can reflect on the levers that are subject to some degree of control, and could contribute to the increase of the market value of the firm. This relationship allows us to go all the way to some key indicators such as sales margin, assets turnover, leverage, cost of debt, corporate tax rate, and profit reinvestment rate with the purpose of diagnosing where additional opportunities for value creation might reside. Subsequently, having decided on the proper courses of action to take, we can use the targets set for every indicator as an important base for management control.

Throughout this discussion, we have identified the firm as the focus of analysis; however, the same logic can be used to describe the factors that affect value added at the level of the business unit.

Once again, we are confronted with the fundamental question of the options available to the firm to create value based on the development of unique competencies vis-a-vis the firm's competitors. Considering the factors that contribute to value creation that we have recently presented, William Fruhan proposes the following basic options.[6]

- "*Increase revenues,* for example by pricing the product higher than what had been possible without the existence of some entry barrier. The barrier could be the existence of patents or some form of successful product differentiation. The barrier might also result from the simple exercise of market forces such as that enjoyed by a monopolist.

FIGURE 17–3. Factors Affecting the Market Value of the Firm Under Stationary Growth for a Finite Period

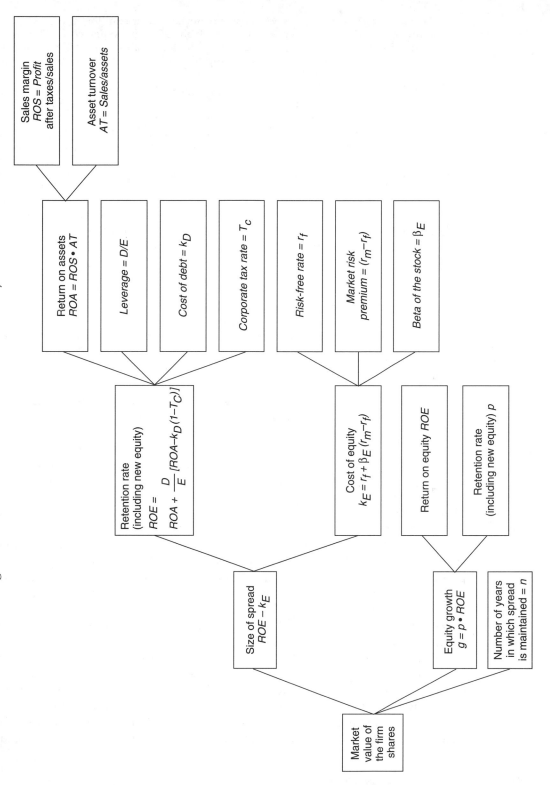

- *Reduce costs below that of competitors,* again perhaps as a result of the existence of some barrier that prevents all competitors from achieving equal costs. The barrier in this instance could be, for example, scale economies achievable by only the largest firm in a market, or the ownership of captive sources of low-cost raw materials.
- *Reduce the cost of equity capital,* for example, through the design of an equity security that appeals to a special niche in the capital markets and thereby attracts funds at a cost lower than the free-market rate for equivalent risk investments, or simply by reducing the business risk below the level enjoyed by competitors.
- *Maximize the financial contribution to the market value* of the firm by increasing the tax shield from debt and reducing the cost of debt capital. This can be done by designing a debt security that is suited for a special group investors in the market."

This message reinforces many of the issues that we have been addressing so far, such as barriers to entry, economies of scale, and differentiation. But it adds an additional component of a financial type, which, although harder to capture, could still be the foundation for competitive advantages.

The Market-to-Book Value versus Spread

One of the important uses of the M/B model is strictly as a diagnostic tool intending to position the firm against its competitors in terms of economic and financial performance. This task is greatly facilitated due to the considerable amount of public information regarding the variables included in the M/B model. The Compustat files, Value Line reports, annual reports, and financial analysts' studies all can be used to produce estimates for the firm's current market value, book value, return on equity, equity growth rate, and cost of equity capital.

A simple way of contrasting the profitability position of various firms is plotting the group of firms under consideration in an M/B-versus-spread diagram. Figures 17–4 ,17–5, and 17–6 on the following pages show this diagram for the firms included in the thirty Dow Jones Industrials, for the years 1980, 1987, and 1992 respectively.

A first glance at the figures tends to confirm that there is a positive association between M/B and spread. In the upper-right quadrant of Figure 17–4, perhaps the most striking deviation from that perceived association is the position of both Standard Oil of California (SD) and Exxon (XON). Those were companies that in the late 1970s were making extraordinarily high profits, reflected in a large spread. However, the future expectations regarding the ability of these firms to maintain those profit levels were not as high. This was reflected by an M/B ratio which, although greater than 1, did not correspond to the historical values of the spread. The measurement of spread is anchored on past performance, while the M/B ratio contains the future expectations regarding the profitability of the firm on the part of the shareholders.

There is an interesting contrast in the overall comparison of the three figures. In 1980, we had a very depressed economy in the United States, and

FIGURE 17–4. An M/B-versus-Spread Graph for the Thirty Dow Jones Industrials (1980)

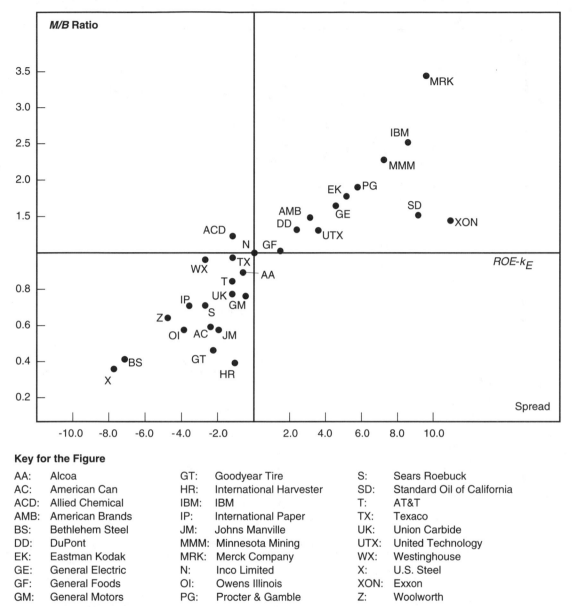

Key for the Figure

AA:	Alcoa	GT:	Goodyear Tire	S:	Sears Roebuck
AC:	American Can	HR:	International Harvester	SD:	Standard Oil of California
ACD:	Allied Chemical	IBM:	IBM	T:	AT&T
AMB:	American Brands	IP:	International Paper	TX:	Texaco
BS:	Bethlehem Steel	JM:	Johns Manville	UK:	Union Carbide
DD:	DuPont	MMM:	Minnesota Mining	UTX:	United Technology
EK:	Eastman Kodak	MRK:	Merck Company	WX:	Westinghouse
GE:	General Electric	N:	Inco Limited	X:	U.S. Steel
GF:	General Foods	OI:	Owens Illinois	XON:	Exxon
GM:	General Motors	PG:	Procter & Gamble	Z:	Woolworth

SOURCE: Marakon Associates, "Criteria for Determining an Optimum Business Portfolio," 1981. Reprinted by permission of Marakon Associates, San Francisco, CA.

Figure 17–4 shows it. More than half of the Dow Jones Industrials were having negative spreads and M/B ratios less than 1. Also, the largest levels of spread were about 10, and Merck, the best performer, enjoyed an M/B ratio of 3.5. The 1987 graph, admittedly built with data just before the October Wall Street crash

FIGURE 17–5. An *M/B*–versus–Spread Graph for the Thirty Dow Jones Industrials (1987)

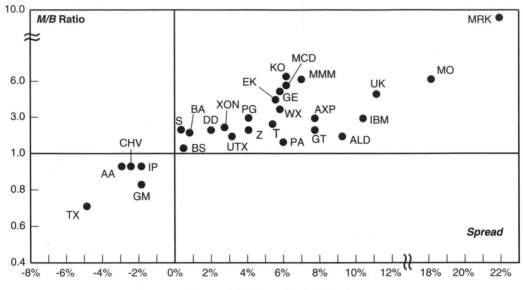

Forecast *ROE* less Cost of Equity

Key for the Figure

ALD:	Allied Signal	MCD:	McDonald's
AA:	Alcoa	MMM:	Minnesota Mining
AXP:	American Express	MRK:	Merck
BS:	Bethlehem Steel	MO:	Philip Morris
BA:	Boeing	PA:	Primerica
CHV:	Chevron	PG:	Procter & Gamble
DD:	DuPont	S:	Sears Roebuck
EK:	Eastman Kodak	T:	AT&T
GE:	General Electric	TX:	Texaco
GM:	General Motors	UK:	Union Carbide
GT:	Goodyear Tire	UTX:	United Technologies
IBM:	IBM	WX:	Westinghouse
IP:	International Paper	XON:	Exxon
KO:	Coca-Cola	Z:	Woolworth

SOURCE: James M. McTaggart, "The Ultimate Takeover Defense: Closing the Value Gap," *Planning Review,* (January–February 1988), pp. 27–32. Reprinted by permission of *Planning Review,* a publication of The Planning Forum, Oxford, Ohio.

of that year, reflects an extraordinarily bull market. Only five of the Dow Jones Industrials are found in the lower left quadrant. Merck continues to be the leading performer, but this time it exhibits a 22 percent spread and an M/B value of 10. Both market expectations and historical spread were significantly higher for all the players.

FIGURE 17–6. An M/B–versus–Spread Graph of the Thirty Dow Jones Industrials (1992)

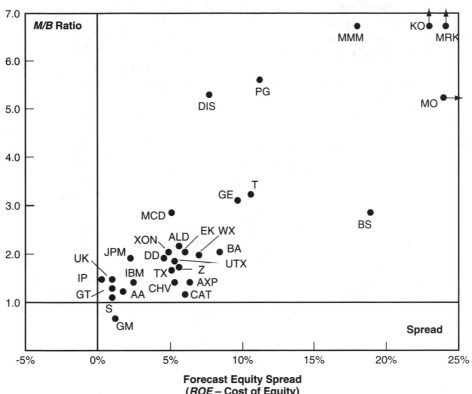

Key for the Figure

ALD:	Allied Corp.	IP:	International Paper
AA:	Aluminum Co. of America	JPM:	J.P. Morgan
AXP:	American Express	KO:	Coca-Cola
BA:	Boeing	MCD:	McDonald's
BS:	Bethlehem Steel	MRK:	Merck & Co.
CAT:	Caterpillar	MMM:	3M
CHV:	Chevron	MO:	Philip Morris
DD:	duPont	PG:	Procter & Gamble
DIS:	Walt Disney	S:	Sears, Roebuck
EK:	Eastman Kodak	T:	AT&T
XON:	Exxon	TX:	Texaco
GE:	General Electric	UK:	Union Carbide
GM:	General Motors	UTX:	United Technologies
GT:	Goodyear Tire	WS:	Westinghouse
IBM:	International Business Machines	Z:	Woolworth

SOURCE: Value Line Investment Survey (1992); Marakon Associates analysis, in James M. McTaggart, Peter W. Kontes, and Michael Mankins, *The Value Imperative: Managing for Superior Sherholder Returns*, New York: The Free Press, 1994.

The chart in Figure 17–6 shows the M/B ratio at the end of 1992. The market is enjoying record-low interest rates and economic forecasts expecting a strong turnaround in the economy. Only General Motors is having a market-to-book value of less than one. It is still intriguing to look at the different treatment the market gives to companies with similar spreads, such as 3M and Bethlehem Steel. The fact that 3M more than doubles the M/B of Bethlehem Steel is entirely due to different expectations regarding future growth. Similar comments can be made about the other companies located in the upper side of the graph, such as Merck, Coca-Cola, Procter and Gamble, and Walt Disney.

The same kind of analysis can be carried out at different levels, with different focuses of attention. Figure 17–7 presents the M/B-Versus-Spread graph for fourteen United States industries. The drug industry is the leading performer, while the most depressed one is the oil field services. Figure 17–8 on page 291 analyzes the key firms in the United States paper and forest products industry. We observe great differences in spread among those companies, yet the M/B ratio is relatively flat and does not necessarily reward the higher performers. Finally, Figure 17–9 on page 292 corresponds to an application of the M/B-versus-spread graph to the portfolio of a business of a given firm. In order to do so, we have to compute directly the market value of each individual business unit by projecting its equity cash flow and then discounting it back using the equity cost of capital as the discount rate. This is not needed in the case of a firm because the market value can he obtained directly from the price of its common shares.

Equity cash flows are determined as follows:

> Business profits after tax
> — After tax interest payments corresponding to the SBU
> — Retained earnings for further investments in the SBU
> Equity cash flow contributed by the SBU

Normally the cash flows are projected through a limited time horizon, say five years, at the end of which a terminal value has to be attached. The actual number for the terminal value depends on the assumptions being made with regard to the nature of the cash flows after the planning horizon. If the business unit is going to have an ROE equal to its cost of capital, the terminal value should be the equity book value at the end of the planning horizon. If this results in a fairly conservative assumption, a more realistic estimate of the terminal value should be attached.

Figure 17–9 allows us to distinguish clearly which are the businesses within the company portfolio that are adding value (those placed in the upper-right quadrant) and which are those that are destroying value (those placed in the lower-left quadrant).

FIGURE 17-7. Profitability of Fifteen U.S. Industries (September 1987)

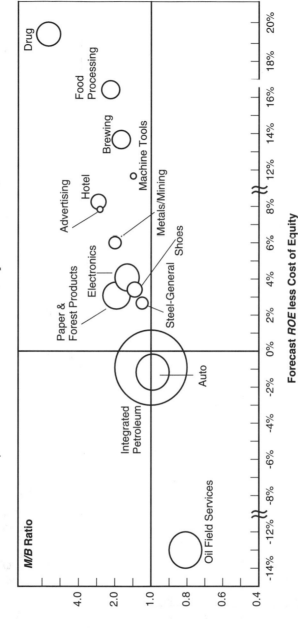

SOURCE: McTaggart (1988).

FIGURE 17–8. Profitability of Paper and Forest Products Companies (Spring 1987)

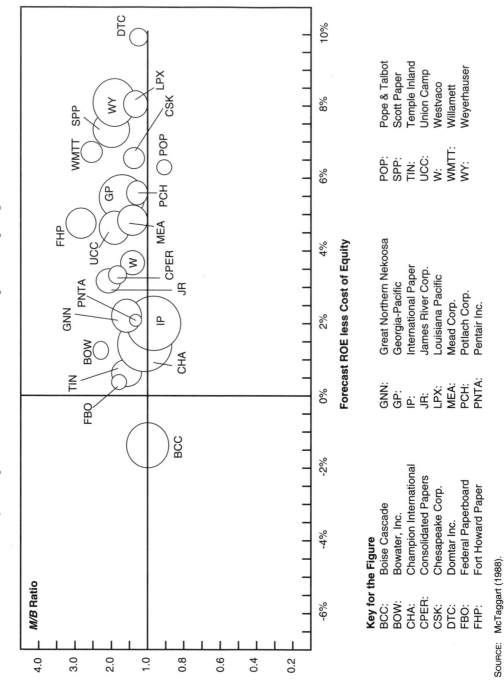

SOURCE: McTaggart (1988).

FIGURE 17–9. Profitability of Company Portfolio

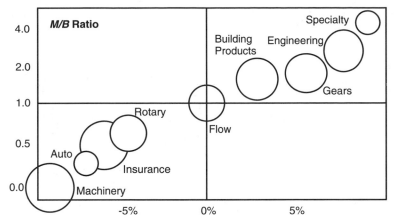

SOURCE: McTaggart (1988).

The Market-to-Book Value Ratio versus Economic-to-Book Value Ratio (M/B vs. E/B)

In order to contrast the discrepancy between the market value and the historical performance of the firm, McKinsey and Co. uses a different way of examining the economic performance of a group of firms competing in a given industry. They plot the M/B ratio against an indicator they call economic-to-book value ratio. The economic value calculation is based on historical performance projected into the future. That is, a company that has earned a positive spread of 3 percentage points, has sustained a 5 percent dividend payout to investors, and has grown its equity base at 10 percent annually in the recent past, is assumed to do so for the next five years in the economic value calculation. Any significant discrepancy between these two values raises a diagnostic flag that would have to be examined carefully.

Figure 17–10 depicts M/B versus E/B plots for a group of companies in the publishing industry and in the oil industry. Those companies below the diagonal are expected to have a poorer performance in the future than they have accomplished in the past. The opposite is true for a firm above the diagonal. Those firms having M/B and E/B ratios below 1 are in a more difficult position. Also, we can observe an industry standard—the regression line in the graph—that attempts to capture average industry performance. In the two examples displayed in the figure, we see that the expectations are for industry performance in the future to be above past performance. Therefore, we

FIGURE 17–10. The *M/B* versus *E/B* Graph

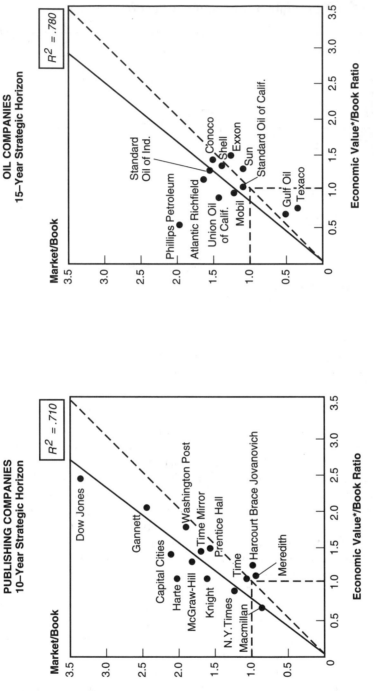

PUBLISHING COMPANIES
10–Year Strategic Horizon

$R^2 = .710$

Market/Book

Dow Jones

Gannett

Washington Post

Capital Cities

Time Mirror

Harte

Prentice Hall

McGraw-Hill

Knight

Harcourt Brace Jovanovich

N.Y.Times

Time

Macmillan

Meredith

Economic Value*/Book Ratio

OIL COMPANIES
15–Year Strategic Horizon

$R^2 = .780$

Market/Book

Phillips Petroleum

Standard Oil of Ind.

Conoco
Shell
Exxon

Atlantic Richfield

Sun

Standard Oil of Calif.

Union Oil of Calif.

Mobil

Gulf Oil

Texaco

Economic Value*/Book Ratio

SOURCE: Compustat, McKinsey analysis. Source: Lily K. Lai, "Corporate Strategic Planning for a Diversified Company," 1983. Reprinted by permission of Lily K. Lai.
* Based on historic (five-year average) values.

encounter another yardstick to separate high and low performer firms with regard to the industry standard. Finally, the chart is able to display those firms that have been in a difficult economic position in the past and are expected to stay in that situation in the near future. Those are the firms falling inside the lower-left quadrant, with both M/B and E/B ratios less than one.

The Profitability Matrix

Marakon Associates developed a very useful scheme to portray the economic contribution of each business unit of a firm in terms of what they refer to as *the profitability matrix*.

There are several ways of constructing such a matrix. The initial form proposed by Marakon is exhibited in Figure 17–11, in which the business ROE

FIGURE 17-11 The Profitability Matrix

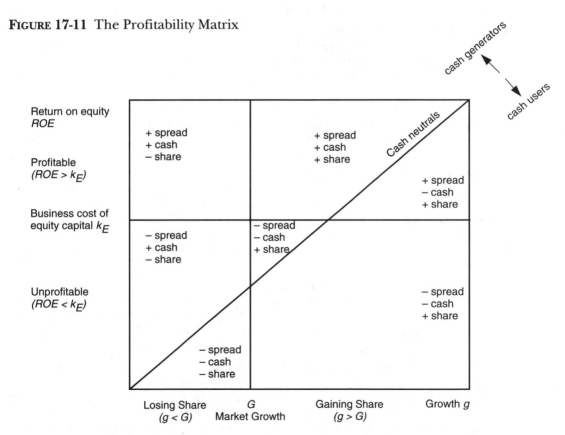

SOURCE: Adapted from Marakon Associates, "The Marakon Profitability Matrix," Commentary No. 7, 1981. Reprinted by permission of Marakon Associates, San Francisco, CA.

is plotted against its corresponding growth. There are two significant cut-off points to separate the status of each business. The ROE axis is divided by the cost of equity capital (k_E) into businesses that are profitable $(ROE > k_E)$ versus unprofitable $(ROE < k_E)$. The cut-off line for the growth axis corresponds to the total market growth (G) for the industry in which a business is competing. Thus, businesses where growth is greater than G are building market share, and those with a growth lower than G are losing market share, perhaps from being positioned in a harvest strategic mode. Finally, the diagonal separates those businesses that are generating cash from those that are absorbing cash. This can easily be seen by realizing that a business that falls exactly on the diagonal has a profitability equal to its growth rate. Since the business growth is given by $g = p \cdot ROE$, businesses on the diagonal have p equal to 1, which means that they reinvest all their profits. That is, they are cash neutral; they neither require cash from, nor deliver cash to the corporation. Businesses that are above the diagonal have a profitability greater than their growth. Therefore, p is less than 1, and they are cash generators. For opposite reasons, businesses below the diagonal are cash users.

An impacting message is derived from this matrix because it has an ability to capture in a simple and clear way the three central strategic objectives constituting the essence of managing the portfolio of businesses from a resource allocation perspective: profitability, market share, and cash flow implications.

Looking at the profitability matrix, it seems that the best of all worlds is to be in a position where one enjoys positive spread, increasing share, and cash generation. But very often the relationship among these variables is more complex than that. If we demand profitability from a business at a too-early stage of development, we may endanger its full potential. If we push for share too aggressively, we might erode our profitability positioning. If we deny the necessary cash to a business by targeting it inappropriately as a cash cow, we might significantly impair its chances of success. Therefore, there is no easy mechanistic way to read the strength of a business in terms of its positioning in the portfolio matrix; but yet the matrix portrays a wealth of relevant information with regard to profitability.

We can think only of three cases where we can tolerate unprofitable businesses. One is when we are dealing with a temporary situation, such as a new start up, where we are investing in the future and have clear expectations of long-run healthy profitability. The second is when the cost of exit far exceeds the cost of staying in business. This often occurs when a business is generating cash and enjoys an accounting profitability below the cost of equity capital, but the nature of its assets is such that their liquidation value is lower than the value that the business is contributing to the firm. The third situation arises when we have a losing business that has a significant strategic importance to the firm. This could happen for a number of reasons. The business could be a subproduct of another dominant activity, or it could add to the product breadth in an essential way for the firm to establish a competitive position, or it could simply have a role as a competitive harasser, intended to neutralize or diminish the strength of a key adversary.

With regard to market share, the matrix serves to reemphasize the previous comments that profitability and growth are intimately intertwined. You do not grow for growth's sake. Growth is only acceptable when it reinforces a profitable position, in which case it helps to compound the rate of return on investment. Growth is also acceptable because it could be used as a preemptive strategic measure that, however costly as an initial move, will produce significant gains in the long run.

Finally, with regard to cash flow, the matrix states quite clearly that cash generation alone is not a meaningful attribute; it clearly depends on whether the business is profitable or not.

The inherent limitations of the matrix, as presented so far, reside in the representation of the two cut-off points. Since different businesses have normally different costs of capital as well as total market growth rates, it is not possible to identify single cut-off points applicable to all businesses of a corporation. Therefore, a slight modification is needed, as illustrated in Figure 17–12,

FIGURE 17–12. An Alternative Profitability Matrix

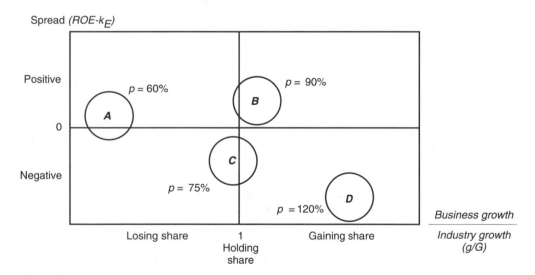

p = Reinvestment rate

SOURCE: Adapted from Marakon Associates, "The Marakon Profitability Matrix," Commentary No. 7, 1981. Reprinted by permission of Marakon Associates, San Francisco, CA.

where spread $(ROE - k_E)$ is used in the vertical axis, and relative growth (business growth/industry growth = g/G) is used in the horizontal axis. Unfortunately, we lose in this characterization the ability to identify what is the cash position of a business; that is, whether it is a cash generator, cash neutral, or cash user. In order to overcome this deficiency, each business unit has attached its corresponding value of the reinvestment rate (p). Obviously, if $p < 100\%$, the business is a cash generator, while if $p > 100\%$, it is a cash user. Finally, the area of each circle is proportional to total sales.

VALUE CREATION AT THE BUSINESS LEVEL

We have addressed previously the question of how to apply some of the value creation methodologies at the level of the business through the M/B-versus spread graph and the profitability matrix. However, there are additional issues still worth raising. First is the question of the contribution of each individual business to the total value of the firm. A compact way of summarizing the value contribution by each individual business of the corporation is presented in Figure 17–13 where market value is plotted against book value. As can be seen from that graph, the company as a whole has a market value lower than its book value, which might suggest that it is an organization in trouble. However, a more careful look indicates that its basic businesses, A and B, are pretty healthy, and business C is earning its cost of capital. Business D is adding value, but its profitability is below its cost of capital. It should be a candidate for divestment if its liquidation value L exceeds the value contributed by the business. Finally, business E should be divested as soon as possible, since it is subtracting value from the firm. Businesses of this sort are referred to as *cash traps*, involving a permanent negative cash flow that is diminishing the contribution of other businesses having positive cash flows. Under such conditions, divestiture might be the most logical decision for a firm to consider. The central question pertaining to that issue is whether or not the liquidation alternative is better than holding onto that unprofitable business.

After all of those rearrangements of the firm's portfolio, the company situation should improve markedly because market value can only increase as a result of the decision to drop unprofitable businesses.

Another issue to be raised at the business level is the proper evaluation of business strategies in terms of their overall contribution to the value of the firm. Certainly, we would like to have a process whereby true options are presented to the top managers of the organization. In practice, this process does not happen. Instead, top managers are confronted with a single monolithic proposal that they either have to accept or reject. It is a typical case of reversed authority. When top managers are asked to cast a judgment on the benefits of an investment alternative, the decisions have already been made because the alternatives have already been screened out, leaving no real ground for decision making.

FIGURE 17–13. Example of Contribution to Market Value of Each Business of a Hypothetical Firm

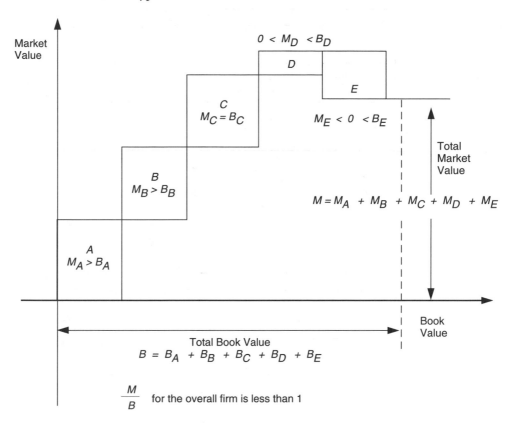

To overcome this limitation, Marakon proposes requiring from each business unit a number of distinct strategic alternatives based on different sets of competitive strategies. In terms of market share, we could characterize them as build, hold, harvest, and divest. Each one of these central thrusts should generate different scenarios for cash-flow projections that, in turn, produce different market-to-book value results. The collective analysis is then presented to top managers for final consideration, where they can legitimately exercise their decision-making rights. On the surface, this might not seem to be a major deviation from common practice. In reality, it truly enforces a discipline of reflecting on the economic consequences of very different strategic options. The full economic implication of these options is brought into the open with a realistic set of alternatives that otherwise might never arise in a bottom-up resource allocation process. Figure 17–14 on page 300 attempts to capture the essence of this proposal.

FIGURE 17–14.
Selecting the Best Strategy for a Business Unit: Evaluation of Alternative Strategic Thrust Options

For each business unit, characterize the strategic options in terms of market share thrust as:
- Build (aggressively, gradually, or selectively)
- Maintain (aggressively or selectively)
- Harvest
- Divest

Project the equity cash flow associated with each strategic option, and compute the corresponding M/B ratio.
M represents the present value of cash flow and B the existing book value of the equity base.

Summarize the M/B values for the different strategic options, for all of the business units of the firm.

Business Unit	Build	Hold	Harvest	Divest
1	1.0	**1.6**	1.4	1.2
2	**2.1**	1.5	0.9	1.8
3	0.8	1.2	**1.4**	1.1
4	0.3	0.5	0.7	**0.8**
5	2.2	**2.5**	1.8	1.9
6	0.5	**0.7**	0.6	0.5

Shaded values represent the M/B ratios under the optimum strategy for each business unit.

Select, for each business unit, the alternative that takes into account the optimum economic performance, as well as the host of additional impacts that the business positioning might have on the overall competitive standing of the firm.

Portfolio Matrices

During the 1970s and early 1980s, a number of leading consulting firms developed the concept of portfolio matrices to help managers in reaching a better understanding of the competitive position of the overall portfolio of businesses, to suggest strategic alternatives for each of the businesses, and to develop priorities for resource allocation. There has been an undeniable influence of these matrices on the practice of strategic management. Several studies have reported on their widespread use among American firms.

Portfolio matrices have several elements in common. First, they constitute graphical displays of the overall competitive standing of the portfolio of businesses of the firm. As such, they indeed constitute a powerful communication vehicle because in one single picture we are able to apprehend the overall strength or weakness of the portfolio. In order to avoid visualizing the portfolio as a static snapshot, it is also possible to follow its chronological evolution, including a future projection. In that case, the message has an additional dynamic quality attached to it.

Second, each matrix positions the business unit of the firm according to two dimensions. One is an external dimension that attempts to capture the overall attractiveness of the industry in which the business participates. The other is an internal dimension, relating to the strength of the business within its industry. The factors that describe industry attractiveness are normally uncontrollable by the firm; those that contribute to business strength are largely under the control of the firm.

The most popular portfolio matrices are:

- the growth-share matrix developed by the Boston Consulting Group, which pioneered this concept;
- the industry attractiveness-business strength matrix, conceived jointly by General Electric and McKinsey and Company. The latter organization was the first to introduce multidimensional criteria in the external and internal dimensions;
- the life-cycle matrix developed by Arthur D. Little, Inc., which contains a fairly comprehensive methodology that leads to a wide array of broad action programs to support the desired strategic thrust of each business;
- the alternative Boston Consulting Group matrix, which enriches the original BCG matrix by bringing in broader descriptions of industry structure; and
- the profitability matrix proposed by Marakon, which captures the three most central strategic objectives of each business: profitability, growth, and cash-generation capabilities.

Figure 17–15 briefly summarizes the characteristics of external and internal dimensions used by each one of the portfolio matrices.

Third, the positioning of each business unit in the corresponding portfolio matrix is associated with a strategy that fits the competitive strength enjoyed by the business, and the degree of attractiveness of its industry. This is

FIGURE 17–15. The Most Important Portfolio Matrices and Their External and Internal Factors

MATRICES	EXTERNAL FACTORS	INTERNAL FACTORS
Growth-Share Matrix	Market growth	Relative market share
Industry Attractiveness-Business Strength Matrix	Overall industry attractiveness • Critical structural factors • Five-forces model	Sources of competitive advantage • Critical success factors • Value chain
Life-Cycle Matrix	Industry maturity	Overall measurement of business position
Alternative BCG Matrix	Ways to compete (opportunities for differentiation)	Size (sustainability) of competitive advantage
Profitability Matrix	Market growth potential Cost of capital	Profitability Cash generation

what has been referred to as generic strategy or natural strategy, which serves as a useful initial reflection in the process of designing the overall strategy for the business unit.

Finally, and most importantly, this methodology contains a suggestion for allocating resources to each business in accordance with the priorities that can be identified by its position in the corresponding matrix. To facilitate this purpose, it might be useful to display not just the position of the business units of the firm within a given matrix, but also to attach some key financial information—such as sales, net income, assets, and return on net assets—in accordance to the contribution generated by the businesses in each one of the cells of the matrix. Figure 17–16 provides an example of such a display for the industry attractiveness-business strength matrix. By examining that information, we can analyze the degree of expected performance of a business, due to its position in the matrix, and the actual results. Whenever corrections are needed, the resource allocation process can be instrumental in eliminating the sources of distortion.

Portfolio matrices have received wide attention in the literature.[7] For this reason, we are providing highly compact summaries with only their essential features. Figures 17–17 through 17–20 provide this basic information related to the growth-share matrix, the industry attractiveness-business strength matrix, the life-cycle matrix, and the alternative BCG matrix respectively. The profitability matrix was already discussed in a previous section of this chapter.

(Figures 17-16 through 17-20 follow on pages 303–311)

FIGURE 17–16. Selected Set of Performance Measurements to Describe the Portfolio of Businesses in the Industry Attractiveness–Business Strength Matrix

Positioning of Businesses*

Industry Attractiveness (IA)

		H	M	L	Total
	H	2,9,17 18,19	7,12	16	8
Business Strength (BS)	M	1,3,4,14	8,10,13	11,15	9
	L	5,6	—	—	2
	Total	11	5	3	19

Distribution of Corporate Sales (%)

IA

		H	M	L	Total
	H	49.2	4.4	6.7	60.3
BS	M	25.5	0.6	1.1	27.2
	L	12.5	—	—	12.5
	Total	87.2	5.0	7.8	100

Distribution of Corporate Net Income (%)

IA

		H	M	L	Total
	H	80.2	6.1	16.3	102.6
BS	M	9.9	(1.2)	1.7	10.4
	L	(13.0)	—	—	(13.0)
	Total	77.1	4.9	18.0	100

Distribution of Corporate Assets (%)

IA

		H	M	L	Total
	H	42.1	3.4	5.7	51.2
BS	M	32.1	0.5	1.1	33.7
	L	15.1	—	—	15.1
	Total	89.3	3.9	6.8	100

Return on Net Assets (%)

IA

		H	M	L	Total
	H	12.8	12.2	19.1	13.5
BS	M	2.1	(19.5)	12.1	2.0
	L	(5.8)	—	—	(5.8)
	Total	5.8	8.7	17.8	100

* There are 19 businesses, each one characterized by a number 1 through 19.

FIGURE 17–17. The Growth–Share Matrix

Matrix

Relative Market Share

		High	Low
Market Growth	High	Star	Question Mark
	Low	Cash Cow	Dog

Dimensions of the Matrix

• External: Market growth rate (%)
(year 19x1)

$$= \frac{\text{Total market } 19x1 - \text{Total market } 19x0}{\text{Total market } 19 \times 0} \times 100$$

• Internal: Relative market share
(year 19x1)

$$= \frac{\text{Business sales } 19x1}{\text{Leading competitor's sales } 19x1}$$

Cut-off points

• Horizontal: Industry growth rate, or GNP growth rate, or weighted average of industries growth rate, or managerial objective for overall growth.

• Vertical: Relative market share equal to 1 for separating leadership from followership, or equal to 1.5 to indicate strong leadership or dominance.

Generic Strategies

Business Category	Market Share Thrust	Business Profitability	Investment Required	Net Cash Flow
Stars	Hold/Increase	High	High	Around zero or slightly negative
Cash Cows	Hold	High	Low	Highly positive
Question Marks	* Increase / Harvest/ Divest	None or negative / Low or negative	Very high / Disinvest	Highly negative / Positive
Dogs	Harvest/ Divest	Low or negative	Disinvest	Positive

* There is a selective application of the strategy depending on the decision made with regard to the business: either to enter aggressively or withdraw.

FIGURE 17–18. The Industry Attractiveness–Business Strength Matrix

Matrix

Industry Attractiveness

Business Strength	High	Medium	Low
High	Investment and growth	Selective growth	Selectivity
Medium	Selective growth	Selectivity	Harvest/Divest
Low	Selectivity	Harvest/Divest	Harvest/Divest

Dimensions of the Matrix

- Industry Attractiveness — Subjective assessment based on external factors, noncontrollable by the firm, that are intended to capture the industry and competitive structure in which the business operates.

- Business Strength — Subjective assessment based on the critical success factors, largely controllable by the firm, that define the competitive position of a business within its industry.

For an illustration of the use of this matrix, see Chapter 7.

Generic Strategies

Industry Attractivess

Business Strength	High	Medium	Low
High	Grow Seek dominance Maximize investment	Identify growth segments Invest strongly Maintain position elsewhere	Maintain overall position Seek cash flow Invest at maintenance level
Medium	Evaluate potential for leadership via segmentation Identify weaknesses Build strengths	Identify growth segments Specialize Investment selectively	Prune lines Minimize investment Position to divest
Low	Specialize Seek niches Consider acquisitions	Specialize Seek niches Consider exit	Trust leader's statesmanship Sic on competitor's cash generators Time exit and divest

SOURCE: Reproduced by permission of A. T. Kearney Inc., Chicago, Ill.

FIGURE 17–19. The Life-Cycle Portfolio Matrix

MATRIX

Wide range of strategic options

Caution: selective development

Danger: withdraw to market niche, divest or liquidate

DIMENSIONS OF THE MATRIX

• External: Stages of industry maturity judgementally assessed based on the following eight external factors and their corresponding description.

Descriptors	Development Stage			
	Embryonic	Growth	Mature	Aging
Market Growth Rate	Accelerating; meaningful rate cannot be calculated because the base is too small	Faster than GNP, but constant or decelerating	Equal to or slower than GNP, cyclical	Industry volume cycles but declines over long term
Industry Potential	Usually difficult to determine	Substantially exceeds the industry volume, but is subject to unforeseen developments	Well-known; primary markets approach saturation industry volume	Saturation is reached; no potential remains
Breadth of Product Lines	Basic product line established	Rapid proliferation as product line are extended	Product turnover, but little or no change in breadth	Shrinking
Number of Competitors	Increasingly rapid	Increasing to peak; followed by shake-out and consolidation	Stable	Declines; but business may break up into many small regional suppliers
Market Share Stability	Volatile	A few firms have major shares; rankings can change, but those with minor shares are unlikely to gain major shares	Firms with major shares are entrenched	Concentration increases as marginal firms drop out; or shares are dispersed among small local firms
Purchasing Patterns	Little or none	Some; buyers are aggressive	Suppliers are well known; buying patterns are established	Strong; number of alternatives decreases
Ease of Entry	Usually easy, but opportunity may not be apparent	Usually easy, the presence of competitors is offset by vigorous growth	Difficult; competitors are entrenched, and growth is slowing	Difficult; little incentive
Technology	Concept development and product engineering	Product line refinement and extension	Process and materials refinement; new product line development to renew growth	Role is minimal

FIGURE 17–19. The Life-Cycle Portfolio Matrix (continued)

• Internal: Competitive position of the business arrived at judgementally, based on the following six competitive categories:

Criteria for Classification of Competitive Position

1. *Dominant:* Dominant competitors are very rare. Dominance often results from a quasimonopoly or from a strongly protected technological leadership.

2. *Strong:* Not all industries have dominant or strong competitors. Strong competitors can usually follow strategies of their choice, irrespective of their competitors' moves.

3. *Favorable:* When industries are fragmented, with no competitor clearly standing out, the leaders tend to be in a favorable position.

4. *Tenable:* A tenable position can usually be maintained profitably through specialization in a narrow or protected market niche. This can be a geographic specialization or a product specialization.

5. *Weak:* Weak competitors can be intrinsically too small to survive independently and profitably in the long term, given the competitive economics of their industry, or they can be larger and potentially stronger competitors, but suffering from costly past mistakes or from a critical weakness.

6. *Nonviable:* Represents the final recognition that the firm really has no strength whatsover, now or in the future, in that particular business. Therefore, exiting is the only strategic response.

GENERIC STRATEGIES

A. *Market share thrust*

	Embryonic	Growth	Mature	Aging
Dominant	All-out push for share Hold position	Hold position Hold share	Hold position Grow with industry	Hold position
Strong	Attempt to improve position All-out push for share	Attempt to improve position Push for share	Hold position Grow with industry	Hold position or Harvest
Favorable	Selective or all-out push for share Selectively attempt to improve position	Attempt to improve position Selective push for share	Custodial or maintenance Find niche and attempt to protect	Harvest or Phased withdrawal
Tenable	Selectively push for position	Find niche and protect it	Find niche and hang on or Phased withdrawal	Phased withdrawal or Abandon
Weak	Up or Out	Turnaround or Abandon	Turnaround or Phased withdrawal	Abandon

FIGURE 17–19. The Life-Cycle Portfolio Matrix (continued)

B. *Investment requirements*

	Embryonic	Growth	Mature	Aging
Dominant	Invest slightly faster than market dictates	Invest to sustain growth rate (and preempt new [?] competitors)	Reinvest as necessary	Reinvest as necessary
Strong	Invest as fast as market dictates	Invest to increase growth rate (and improve position)	Reinvest as necessary	Minimum reinvestment or maintenance
Favorable	Invest selectively	Selective investment to improve position	Minimum and/or selective reinvestment	Minimum maintenance Investment or disinvest
Tenable	Invest (very) selectively	Selective investment	Minimum reinvestment or disinvest	Disinvest
Weak	Invest or divest	Invest or divest	Invest selectively or disinvest	Divest

The terms invest and divest are used in the broadest sense and are not restricted to property, plant, and equipment.

C. *Profitability and cash flow*

	Embryonic	Growth	Mature	Aging
Dominant	Probably profitable but not necessary Net cash borrower	Profitable Probably net cash producer (but not necessary)	Profitable Net cash producer	Profitable Net cash producer
Strong	May be unprofitable Net cash borrower	Probably profitable Probably net cash borrower	Profitable Net cash producer	Profitable Net cash producer
Favorable	Probably unprofitable Net cash borrower	Marginally profitable Net cash borrower	Profitable Net cash producer	Moderately profitable Cash flow balance
Tenable	Unprofitable Net cash borrower	Unprofitable Net cash borrower or cash flow balance	Minimally profitable Cash flow balance	Minimally profitable Cash flow balance
Weak	Unprofitable Net cash borrower	Unprofitable Net cash borrower or cash flow balance	Unprofitable Possibly net cash borrower or net cash producer	Unprofitable (Write-off)

In addition to cash throw-off or use, each unit may use or throw-off managerial resources.
Note: In some cases, the tax shield value of a unit should be taken into account in evaluating unit performance.

FIGURE 17–19. The Life-Cycle Portfolio Matrix (continued)

In addition to the previously prescribed generic strategies, the ADL methodology recommends broad action programs depending on the position of the business unit in its matrix. The strategies of business units are categorized according to four different families: natural development, selective development, prove viability, and out, which are broadly characterized in the following display.

Stages of Industry Maturity / Competitive Position	Embryonic	Growth	Mature	Aging
Dominant				
Strong				
Favorable				
Tenable				
Weak				Out

Natural development — *Selective development* — *Prove viability*

Each family of businesses has the following options regarding the definition of its strategic thrusts:

Natural Development	**Selective Development**	**Prove Viability**	**Out**
Start-up	Find niche	Catch-up	Withdraw
Growth with industry	Exploit niche	Renew	Divest
Gain position gradually	Hold niche	Turnaround	Abandon
Gain position aggressively		Prolong existence	
Defend position			
Harvest			

Once having selected the appropriate strategic thrust from among the ones available for each family, you are offered the following menu of broad action programs:

A	Backward integration	M	Market rationalization
B	Development of overseas business	N	Methods and functions efficiency
C	Developent of overseas facilities	O	New products/New markets
D	Distribution rationalization	P	New products/Same market
E	Excess capacity	Q	Production rationalization
F	Export/Same product	R	Product line rationalization
G	Forward integration	S	Pure survival
H	Hestitation	T	Same products/New markets
I	Initial market development	U	Same products/Same markets
J	Licensing abroad	V	Techology efficiency
K	Complete rationalization	W	Traditional cost-cutting efficiency
L	Market penetration	X	Unit abandonment

FIGURE 17–19. The Life-Cycle Portfolio Matrix (continued)

The ADL methodology suggests the following mapping among families, strategic thrusts, and broad action programs:

Generic Strategies

Strategic Thrust \ Strategies	A	B	C	D	E	F	G	H	I	J	K	L	M	N	O	P	Q	R	S	T	U	V	W	X
Natural Development																								
Start-up					E				I			L												
Growth with industry	A	B	C			F	G			J				N		P				T	U			
Gain position gradually							G					L								T				
Gain position aggressively		B	C		E		G					L		N	O	P				T		V		
Defend position	A		C											N							U	V	W	
Harvest				D				H			K		M				Q	R			U		W	
Selective Development																								
Find niche	A						G		I			L	M					R		T				
Exploit niche		B	C		E							L		N		P					U	V		
Hold niche			C	D										N			Q				U			
Prove Viability																								
Catch-up				D	E							L	M			P	Q	R						
Renew				D									M		O	P	Q	R			U			
Turn around				D								L	M	N			Q	R				V	W	
Prolong existence	A			D		F				J	K		M	N			Q	R	S	T			W	
Out																								
Withdraw				D									M				Q	R					W	
Divest				D							K						Q	R	S					
Abandon																								X

(Left margin label: Strategic Thrusts)

SOURCE: Arthur D. Little, Inc.

310

FIGURE 17–20. The Alternative Boston Consulting Group Matrix

Matrix

Size of Competitive Advantage

	Small	Large
Many	Fragmented	Specialization
Few	Stalemate	Volume

(Left axis label: Ways to Compete (Opportunities for differentiation))

(Top axis label: Size of Competitive Advantage — Small, Large)

Dimensions of the Matrix

- Ways to Compete: Assess judgmentally whether there are many or few ways to achieve competitive advantage. This is greatly determined by the capabilities or differentiation within the industry.

- Size of Competitive Advantage: Assess judgmentally whether the extent and sustainability of the advantage is small or large. This is largely dependent on the size of barriers to entry into the industry.

Generic Strategies

Category of Business	Generic Strategy
Volume	• Lowest cost position, sales leadership
Specialization	• Either niche in a segment of the market or cover the entire market with differentiated products
	• Do not get stuck in the middle
Fragmented	• Many ways to compete. Look at your relative strengths and unique competencies
Stalemate	• Survive, reduce costs, maximize productivity

Contribution of Portfolio Approaches to Strategic Planning

Portfolio approaches have made important contributions to the improvement of strategic planning. Some of the most significant among them follow.

1. They represent simple and effective ways to facilitate the decomposition of the firm's activities into a set of well-defined businesses. Moreover, while conducting the necessary analysis to position the businesses in the two-dimensional matrix, ample opportunities exist to reassess the merits of the proposed segmentation. By permitting a clear differentiation of the nature of each business in terms of industry attractiveness and competitive position, portfolio approaches allow top managers to set appropriate and distinct strategies for each business in accordance with its inherent potential and developmental needs.

2. Portfolio approaches represent a pragmatic way to capture the essence of strategic analysis. By means of a simple visual display of the portfolio of businesses, they provide a useful device to understand and communicate important characteristics of the strategic options confronted by the firm.

3. The application of portfolio approaches at the corporate level provides useful guidelines for top managers to address the question of business strategy evaluation and resource allocation.

   a. It allows the establishment of an orderly set of priorities for investment depending on the business potential for growth and profitability derived from its position in the portfolio matrix.

   b. It provides a mechanism for checking the consistency between business requests of financial and human resources and their inherent needs obtained from their position in the portfolio matrix.

   c. It facilitates the proper balancing of cash requirements and cash supplies among businesses of the corporation.

   d. It permits the establishment of management control mechanisms suitable for monitoring the performance of each business using key variables consistent with their current and future potential.

4. Portfolio approaches can also be applied in the process of strategy formulation at the business level, but the focus of attention changes from the entire business to the more detailed collection of product-market segments.

5. By representing the complete collection of businesses of the firm, portfolio approaches provide a useful mechanism to consider potential acquisitions and divestitures.

6. Portfolio approaches were most significant in raising the strategic alertness of most managers. To a great extent, the use of portfolio matrices was responsible for accelerating the adoption of formal competitive analyses and for increasing the competitive awareness in American firms. This was accomplished because the implementation of the portfolio approach requires the formal collection and processing of some information regarding competitors. This constitutes a useful first step in improving competitive intelligence. Also, portfolio matrices can be constructed for major competitors, generating valuable insights with regard to their overall strengths and ability to anticipate their potential responses and moves. At the very least, this judgmental call would put in evidence the need to improve the firm's understanding of its major competitors.

In spite of the legitimate contributions attached to the methodology introduced by portfolio matrices, they are not without criticism. In fact, in the recent past, the whole area of strategic planning has been the target of strong attacks, to a great extent due to the legacy that portfolio matrices left to strategic planning in the last decade. The most common complaints have been that matrices tend to trivialize strategic thinking by converting it into simplistic and mechanistic exercises, whose final message is dubious at best. Also, the matrix methodology has tended to take strategic analysis and, subsequently, strategic thinking, away from managers and into the realm of planning departments.

There is a clear element of truth in these criticisms, but what they fail to capture is that matrices are simple tools and not the final output of a properly designed strategic planning process. As with any tool, its final value depends on the craftsmanship of its users. It is our experience that portfolio matrices can assist in bringing intelligent and appropriate communicational opportunities to the hard issue of portfolio management. Every single one of the matrices is a grossly oversimplified model of a complex problem. As is the case with any model, portfolio matrices are simple abstractions that attempt to capture a partial but critical element pertaining to resource allocation in a portfolio setting. Since each one of them adopts a single biased orientation, individually they could be judged as being too narrow in scope, ignoring important additional perspectives. However, collectively, they can produce, from various angles, a combined picture that begins to capture in a much more forceful way the broader complexities of the resource allocation problem. This is the reason why we strongly advise, whenever they are applied, that all of them be used in conjunction.

The Process of Resource Allocation

From a strict financial theory point of view, one could argue, as we did at the beginning of this chapter, that the only legitimate evaluation tool for resource allocation is the net present value (NPV) of future cash flows to be generated by a business, discounted at a proper cost of capital rate, which includes adjustments for risk and inflation. Without reducing the significance of NPV in judging the quality of investment decisions, we can say that it does not necessarily address all of the central issues present in resource allocation.

First, the decision-making process is not necessarily a cold, analytical, rational activity. Instead, it is loaded with emotions, self-centered interests, and biased positions that are at the heart of a complex bargaining and power game. In a rather humorous way, Brealey and Myers have stated what they have declared to be their "second law," which indicates that the proportion of prepared projects having a positive estimated NPV is independent of top management's estimate of the opportunity cost of capital.[8] It simply means that business managers can actually "prove" to their top counterparts that their investment proposals are acceptable regardless of the hurdle imposed on them.

Second, there is a major difference between project evaluation and project generation. NPV is an important tool for evaluating projects, but by no means does it serve as a stimulus to make business managers generate the right kind of projects to support their businesses according to their strategic positioning. This is probably the most important role that can be played by portfolio matrices, because they rank businesses according to the attractiveness of their industry and the intrinsic strength that the firm can achieve. Thus, prior to undertaking numerical calculations that might not add significantly to supporting the strategic role of a business unit, we might want to communicate to business managers the expectations that corporate officers have with regard to their degree of aggressiveness to be shown by each business in their requests for resource allocation.

The financial theory and the strategic positioning point of view are at the core of an important controversy in resource allocation. We feel that both points of view are legitimate and have important merits on their own. Rather than being alternative procedures for analyzing investment proposals, they truly complement each other.

SOME PRINCIPLES FOR RESOURCE ALLOCATION.

James MacTaggart and his colleagues at Marakon argue, in their recent book "The Value Imperative,"[9] that many companies cannot provide a clear description of the process they follow to determine and allocate resources. In their book they make the rather startling observation they have collected from their consulting practice that 100 percent of the value created is concentrated in less than 50 percent of the capital employed. This implies that significant portions of resources are committed to activities that destroy rather than create value. They propose four basic principles to remedy this situation :

The Principle of Zero-Based Resource Allocation.
Companies tend to focus the resource allocation on incremental new capital investments and additional people. This incrementalism has a bias towards constantly growing, rather than establishing the right commitment of people and capital to value-creating businesses. A zero-based resource allocation process evaluates the use of all resources, sunk as well as incremental, to assure that they are contributing to value creation.

The Principle of Funding Strategies, Not Projects.
A business strategy can be regarded as a bundle of projects. The resource allocation process should concentrate on the value created by this entire bundle, rather than looking at individual projects in isolation. This is exactly what our business strategy methodology recommends. It leads us from the desired competitive position to the explicit statement of the action programs required to achieve that position. These programs are subsequently priced as part of the business budget, which is approved when one fully recognizes the value created by the complete business strategy. In Chapter 7 we discussed the details of the formulation of the business strategy, leading to the strategic and operational budgets; and in Chapter 8 we reviewed and illustrated the methodology for the strategic and economic evaluation of the merits of a business strategy.

Principle of No Capital Rationing.

Typically, the assumption imbedded in most processes of resource allocation is that capital is scarce but free. Exactly the opposite is true: capital is plentifully available, but it is expensive. There are internal as well as external sources of capital available for value-creating strategies. When allocating this capital to individual businesses, they should be charged their corresponding cost of capital.

The Principle of Zero Tolerance for Bad Growth.

It is unavoidable that managers will end up making mistakes in allocating resources to new investments. What is essential, however, is that these mistakes are not perpetuated. The principle of zero tolerance for bad growth makes the redeployment of those resources from unprofitable or bad-growth businesses to value-creating ones. Therefore, the principle not only helps to minimize bad growth, but also maximizes good growth.

In conclusion, business strategies and resource-allocation should be intimately linked. This is accomplished when resources are allocated through business strategies. While retaining the business focus as one of the central dimensions of resource allocation, we should also be conscious of the other corporate and functional dimensions, which will generate new demands for resource allocation. These requests typically affect more than one business, and are often congruent with the horizontal strategies of the firm.

DIAGNOSING THE VALUE GAP

This chapter has concentrated on describing the concepts and methodologies that allow managers to understand the process of value creation, enhance their diagnostic capabilities on the current status of the business portfolio, and suggest ways in which resources could be allocated to assure a superior competitive advantage for each business. This is in accordance with the effectiveness of the industry and the firm's ability to mobilize unique capabilities. We would expect that, at this stage, both corporate and business managers would have thoroughly prepared all the necessary supporting information and analysis that would allow them to have a clear picture of the strength of the overall portfolio. The major question to be asked at this point is whether we could detect a *value gap* between the current standing of the firm and its future potential.

McTaggart offers the following questions to guide an organization in detecting possible opportunities for additional creation of value:[10]

- Are there any businesses in the portfolio that significantly underperform competitors?
- Are there any businesses that are out of their start-up phase and still losing money?
- Are there any businesses that would clearly be worth more to someone else due to synergy or operating economies?
- Are resources allocated to businesses in a way that reflects their profitability potential, or do you tend to overfund losers and underfund winners?
- Is performance measured by using average cost asset and debt allocations, and an arbitrary corporate hurdle rate?

- Are any of your long-term incentives tied directly to relative stock performance or indirectly to the drivers of shareholder value?
- Is capital spending driven mostly by capital budgeting rather than the strategic planning process?
- Is the company underleveraged? Could the company be taken private in an LBO at today's stock price?
- If the company did go private in an LBO, which assets would be sold to repay debt? How much overhead could be cut without damaging the long-term health of the company?

We feel that this is an important set of questions that could trigger the recognition of possible opportunities for value creation.

SOME FURTHER ISSUES IN THE PROCESS OF RESOURCE ALLOCATION

There are three additional issues we would like to comment upon regarding the process of resource allocation.

Defining the Availability of Strategic Funds, the Debt Policy, and the Maximum Sustainable Growth.

Another task that is important at this step is the determination of total strategic funds available at the corporate level to support investment in fixed assets, and in increases in working capital and developmental expenses. A sound way of calculating these funds is first to forecast the sources of funds forthcoming to the firm. The primary components of the sources of funds are:

- earnings
- depreciation
- new debt issuing
- new equity issuing
- divestitures

Notice that earnings contain, as part of the cost of goods sold, the normal levels of developmental expenses that are assigned to the various functions of the organization, in particular R&D.

The second part of the computation requires the forecast of uses of funds. The most important items are:

- dividends
- debt repayment (principal)
- strategic funds
- new fixed assets and acquisitions
- increases in working capital
- increases in development expenses

Therefore the total strategic funds available can be estimated as:

$$\text{Total strategic funds availability} =$$
$$\text{Total sources of funds} - \text{Dividends payments} - \text{Debt repayment}$$

It is apparent from this relation that the firm's debt capacity and financial leverage policies have a significant impact on the ability of the firm to increase its growth. Establishing a sound debt policy congruent with the company's financing requirements is another issue to be addressed at this point.

Another useful guide to address the question of corporate growth is the calculation of the *maximum sustainable growth* of the firm, which we have already described in a previous section of this chapter.

Figure 17–21 provides the calculation of strategic funds debt policy and maximum sustainable growth for AMAX, Inc.

FIGURE 17–21. Availability of Strategic Funds, Debt Policy, and Maximum Sustainable Growth for AMAX, Inc.

Availability of Strategic Funds

Sources		Uses	
Earnings	93	Dividends	40
Depreciation	210	Debt repayments	140
New debt issues	—	Strategic funds*	268
New equity issues	40		
Divestitures	75		
Other (deferred taxes)	30		
Total	448	Total	448

* Strategic funds: 448 - 40 - 140 = 268

Debt Policy

Lower the debt-to-total-capital ratio 25% (or a D/E of approximately 35%) from its actual level of 44%.

Maximum Sustainable Growth

$$g = p \left[ROA + \frac{D}{E} (ROA - i) \right]$$

where:

g	=	maximum sustainable growth
p	=	fraction of retained eanings = 0.50
D/E	=	debt-to-equity ratio = 0.35
ROA	=	after-tax return on assets = 12%
i	=	after-tax interest on debt = 6%
g	=	0.50 [12 + 0.35(12 - 6)] = 7%

SOURCE: Adapted from Gray (1984)

Once the total strategic funds have been determined, we have to deduct from them the funds appropriated for investments that are required to fulfill legal obligations or correspond to previous commitments to ongoing projects.

The calculation of the total availability of strategic funds that we have just proposed could generate a proper baseline for assessing the financial resources originating from internal and external sources. This should not appear as a contradiction of the principle of capital rationing that we cited before. When calculating the available resources, we should make an effort to identify all the relevant internal as well as external sources; in particular, this includes the funds that could be provided by restructuring unprofitable and bad growth investments.

Evaluation of Proposed Action Programs and Assignment of Priorities for Resource Allocation.

The previous considerations have allowed us to assess the affordable growth of the corporation and the total funds available for its future development. Having that information in mind, we should now turn our attention to the assignment of priorities to be given to each business unit in terms of resource allocation. This will allow realistic programs to be formulated, which not only respond properly to the desired strategic direction of each business unit, but are also consistent with the financial and human resources in place.

There are various ways to establish such priorities. We recommend using the following categories of strategic growth: build aggressively, build gradually, build selectively, maintain aggressively, maintain selectively, prove viability, divest-liquidate, and competitive harasser.[11] A detailed description of these categories is shown in Figure 17–22.

A form that we have found useful for deciding on priorities for resource allocation among existing as well as new business is presented in Figure 17–23 on page 320. Although resource allocation is clearly a controversial subject, we have found that concentrating on the decisions that are embedded in that figure helps the group of top managers of the organization to open up a thorough discussion of the central issues leading toward the generation of a wide consensus.

We have been stressing throughout only the assignment of financial resources among business units. Often financial resources are the easiest to transfer and the most plentiful available; human resources are frequently the most constrained ones. This is the case faced by many high technology firms that find themselves restricted in their growth not because of the lack of availability of financial resources, but rather because of the unavailablity of scarce technical talent. Therefore, resources should be interpreted here in its broadest sense.

Resource Allocation and Definition of Performance Measurements for Management Control.

Having identified the total funds available for resource allocation and the priorities assigned to each individual business unit, we are faced with the following tasks pertaining to the specific assignment of resources:

FIGURE 17–22. Business Strategic Priorities Emerging from the Portfolio Approach to Strategic Planning

Build aggressively: The business is in a strong position in a highly attractive, fast-growing industry, and management wants to build share as rapidly as possible. This role is usually assigned to an SBU early in the life cycle, especially when there is little doubt as to whether this rapid growth will be sustained.

Build gradually: The business is in a strong position in a very attractive, moderate-growth industry, and management wants to build share, or there is rapid growth but doubt as to where this rapid growth will be sustained.

Build selectively: The business has good position in a highly attractive industry and wants to build share whether it feels it has strength, or can develop strength, to do so.

Maintain aggressively: The business is in a strong position in a currently attractive industry, and management is determined to aggressively maintain that position.

Maintain selectively: Either the business is in a strong position in an industry that is getting less attractive, or the business is in a moderate position in a highly attractive industry. Management wishes to exploit the situation by maximizing the profitability benefits of selectively serving where it best can do so, but with minimum additional resource deployments.

Prove viability: The business is in a less-than-satisfactory position in a less attractive industry. If the business can provide resources for use elsewhere, management may decide to retain it, but without additional resource support. The onus is on the business to justify retention.

Divest-Liquidate: Neither the business nor the industry has any redeeming features. Barring major exit barriers, the business should be divested.

Competitive harasser: This is a business with a poor position in either an attractive or highly attractive industry, and where competitors with a good position in the industry also compete with the company in another industry. The role of competitive harasser is to attack sporadically or continuously the competitor's position, not necessarily with the intention of long-run success. The objective is to distract the competition from other areas, deny them from revenue business, or use the business to cross-parry when the competition attacks an important sister business of the strategic aggressor.

SOURCE: Adapted from Ian C. MacMillan, "Seizing Competitive Initiative." Reprinted by permission of *The Journal of Business Strategy*, Spring 1982. Copyright © Warren, Gorham, & Lamont, Inc., Boston, MA. All rights reserved.

- Collection and classification of all the information submitted by SBUs and functional units
- Analysis of the coherence between the strategic role assigned to SBUs and functional units, and the requests for funds
- Analysis of economic indicators and value-creation potential of proposed programs
- Final allocation of resources for the coming year
- Development of performance measurements to facilitate the controlling and monitoring of the broad and specific action programs supporting business and functional strategies, both in the short run and over an extended planning horizon.

When resources are allocated among SBUs at this stage, we should only be concerned about checking for final consistency between the priorities assigned to each SBU and the final requests for funds.

FIGURE 17–23. Priorities for Resource Allocation

Existing Businesses	Build			Maintain		Prove Viability	Divest/Liquidate
	Aggressively	Gradually	Selectively	Aggressively	Selectively		
1							
2							
3							
4							
5							
6							
7							
8							
9							
10							

New Businesses	Build			Prove Viability	How to Build		
	Aggressively	Gradually	Selectively		Internal Growth	Acquisition	Joint Venture
1							
2							
3							

Notes

1. Alan C. Shapiro, "Corporate Strategy and the Capital Budgeting Decision," *Midland Corporate Finance Journal*, 3, no. 1 (Spring 1985), 22–36.

2. Good references for value creation are: Tom Copeland, Tim Koller, and Jack Murrin, *Valuation: Measuring and Managing the Value of Companies* (New York: John Wiley, 1990); James M. McTaggart, Peter W. Kontes, and Michael C. Mankins, *The Value Imperative: Managing for Superior Shareholder Returns* (New York: Free Press, 1994); and G. Bennett Stewart, III, *The Quest for Value: A Guide for Senior Managers* (New York: Harper Business, 1991). For a novel treatment of investment and competitive sustainability, see Pankaj Ghemawat, *Commitment: The Dynamic of Strategy* (New York: Free Press, 1991). For an application of this methodology, see Chapter 8.

3. The NPV computation can be expressed as:

$$NPV = -I + \sum_{t=1}^{t=T} \frac{C_t}{(1+r)^t}$$

   For a thorough treatment of the NPV model, the reader is referred to Richard A. Brealey and Stewart C. Myers, *Principles of Corporate Finance*, 4th ed. (New York: McGraw-Hill, 1992). For a valuable discussion of the gap between financial theory and financial strategy, see: Stewart C. Myers. "Finance Theory and Financial Strategy,"

Interfaces, 14, no. 1 (January–February 1984), 126–137.

4. For a comprehensive analysis of the M/B model, the reader is referred to Arnoldo C. Hax and Nicolas S. Majluf, *Strategic Management: An Integrative Perspective* (Englewood Cliffs, NJ: Prentice Hall, 1984), Chapter 10; William E. Fruhan, *Financial Strategy* (Homewood, IL: Richard D. Irwin, Inc., 1979); and James M. McTaggart, et al. (1994) op. cit.

5. Alan J. Zakon, "Capital Structure Optimization," in J. F. Weston and M. B. Goudzwaard, eds., *The Treasurer's Handbook* (Homewood, IL: Dow Jones-Irwin, 1976).

6. Fruhan, *Financial Strategy*, (1979).

7. For a comprehensive analysis of portfolio matrices, see Hax and Majluf, *Strategic Management*, (1984), Chapters 6 through 10.

8. Brealey and Myers, Principles of Corporate Finance, (1992).

9. James M. McTaggart, et al., (1994) op. cit.

10. James M. McTaggart, "The Ultimate Takeover Defense: Closing the Value Gap," Planning Review (January–February 1988), 27–32.

11. The categories of strategic growth were originally proposed by Ian C. Macmillan, "Seizing Competitive Advantage," The Journal of Business Strategy (Spring 1982), 43–57.

Appendix: The Relationship Between ROE and ROA

The fundamental managerial objectives are growth and profitability. Therefore, it is appropriate to ask ourselves how to execute a proper measure of these two dimensions. First with regard to profitability, the most commonly used indicators are return on equity (ROE) and return on assets (ROA). These two indicators are fractions that differ both in the content of the numerator as well as the denominator

ROE is defined as follows:

$$ROE = \frac{Profit\ after\ interest\ and\ after\ taxes}{Equity}$$

The numerator is the true bottom line. It represents the net profit of the firm from operations after we pay taxes and interest over the loan. The denominator also has a similar bottom-line characteristic. It measures the equity that belongs to the shareholders of the firm. Therefore, ROE is bottom-line profits as allocated to the owners of the firm. This measure of profitability is commonly used to assess the overall financial performance of the firm.

In contrast, ROA is defined as:

$$ROA = \frac{Profit\ after\ taxes\ but\ before\ interest}{Assets}$$

Now the distinction between the two measures of profitability is clear. ROA measures profits after taxes but before interest. Since it is normally applied at the level of the business unit, we do not want to make the manager accountable for the means of financing the assets that have been entrusted to him or her. Similarly, the denominator measures total assets as opposed to equity because we are interested in examining the profitability of the business itself without regard to its sources of financing (remember that assets are equal to debt plus equity). There is an important relationship that links ROE and ROA, which can be easily developed:

$$\{Profit\ after\ interest\ and\ after\ taxes\} =$$
$$\{Profit\ before\ interest\ and\ after\ taxes\} - \{Interest\ after\ taxes\}$$

$$\{E\ x\ ROE\ \} = \{(D + E)\ x\ ROA\} - \{k_D(1 - T_C)\ x\ D\}$$

$$ROE = ROA + \frac{D}{E}\ \{ROA - k_D(1 - T_C)\}$$

where

$$
\begin{aligned}
D &= total\ debt \\
E &= total\ equity \\
k_D &= debt\ interest\ rate\ before\ tax \\
T_C &= corporate\ tax\ rate
\end{aligned}
$$

18

Functional Strategy: The Core Concepts

Out of the three levels of strategy formulation—corporate, business, and functional—the functional dimension has been the most neglected in America. We believe that this neglect has been one of the central causes of the decline of global competitiveness during the 1970s and 1980s in this country.

Functional Benchmarking

Dealing with functions strategically means being aware of what competitors are doing to develop unique capabilities and being able to match or exceed their competencies. From a strategic point of view, we are not interested in simply knowing our cost base, or our productivity rate, or the rate of product innovation, or the advances we are making in adopting new technologies and refining our manufacturing processes, or the state of utilization or modernization of our physical facilities, or the degree to which information technology is changing our operational and administrative skills. None of that is relevant unless we contrast it with similar kinds of skills being developed by competitors. It is not our cost that matters; it is our cost relative to our key competitors. It is not our productivity, but our ability to match our competitors' productivity; and so on. Therefore, dealing with managerial functions strategically requires being fully aware of competitors and of the firm's internal capabilities in relation to them.

What we have just stated is the need to have a strong base of functional intelligence to establish the yardsticks that can be used as standards of excellence for functional capabilities. The proper identification of these standards has generated a new challenging and relevant business practice commonly referred to as benchmarking.[1]

There are three ways of conducting a relevant benchmarking. One is internal; that is, to compare your performance against yourself. The most straightforward comparison is to analyze your evolution through time. Another alternative is to contrast the performance of different functional units that belong to a broad-based corporation. In this latter case, a widely diversified global organization might develop standardized measures of performance that could allow examining the efficiency of, say, different manufacturing facilities across the world. Asea Brown Boveri's ABACUS (Asea Brown Boveri Accounting and Communication System) system is celebrated for doing this with remarkable effectiveness.

The second way of establishing a benchmarking comparison is to contrast your functional capabilities with those of the leading competitors in your industry. One could argue that this is the most relevant form of comparison, because it is the one that identifies the sources of sustainable competitive advantage. However, the most demanding yardstick is to compare your capabilities, function-by-function, against the so called "best in class". In this last case, we examine what is truly required to achieve superior competencies by contrasting our performance in each functional category against the "masters." Surprisingly, it is easier to have access to the information required to perform this benchmarking than to the information you need in order to contrast yourself against your competitors. The best-in-class players, particularly if they are your suppliers or customers, have strong incentives to assist you in improving your competitive capabilities, while competitors will rarely cooperate in helping you gather the appropriate information.

Functional Capabilities and Business Process Reengineering

In 1993, Michael Hammer and James Champy published their book, *Reengineering the Corporation: A Manifesto for Business Revolution*.[2] It sold more than two million copies and produced an extraordinary impact on the business world. In fact, it redirected the entire range of business consulting services in America. The central idea behind this crusade was relatively simple: businesses should be viewed not in terms of functions, divisions, or products, but as processes. This processes—such as developing new products, delivering products to customers, and managing customer relationships—cut across the standard organizational units of the firm, primarily, when the organizational structure is functionally driven. By recognizing these business processes, for which, in the conventional organizational structure, no one has responsibility, we could open up enormous opportunities to achieve dramatic improvements in cost, quality, service, and speed. Moreover, by recognizing the activities that are part of the business processes, we will be able to identify those activities that do not add value: those that may have crept up inadvertently through time without receiving any proper attention. The removal of these nonvalue-added activities are the sources of the radical improvements that are at the heart of business reengineering.

There is a lot of wisdom and pragmatic value about this new approach. It directs attention to an area were, indeed, significant improvements could be realized. However, as often happens with these new exciting ideas, they tend to be overstated and overemphasized. Suddenly, business processes are in, and functions are depicted as "silos" that narrowly separated the business activities of the firm. In this scenario, functions are viewed as walls that prevent a proper business integration. Business *processes* are suddenly in fashion, while *functions* are out of fashion.

We believe that there is a dangerous message in this quick conclusion. As often happens, it is not an either/or proposition that is relevant. Both effective business processes and, equally important, functional capabilities, are needed for attaining a healthy competitive position. Obviously, we need to address in relevant terms the responsibilities to generate effective business processes; but, at the same time, we should retain functional excellence.

Functional Segmentation: Selecting the Relevant Focuses of Analysis

The guiding framework for identifying the relevant focuses of analysis in the development of functional strategy is the value chain. In Figure 18–1 we have grouped the firm's activities in a way that generates six major areas for strategic functional analysis:

- financial strategy
- human resources strategy
- technology strategy
- procurement strategy
- manufacturing strategy
- marketing strategy

These are the central areas of functional strategic concern treated in this part of the book. We have purposely left aside the ones that we refer to as central administrative functions, not because they lack strategic significance, but because of our inability to deal with them effectively within the scope of this book.

The specific perspectives to be used when dealing with each functional strategy are:

For Financial Srategy the Focus of Analysis is the Entire Business Firm. Finance is the most centralized functional area. Final accountability unavoidably resides with the CEO. Key decisions—such as obtaining and allocating financial resources, and balancing the portfolio of businesses—can only be made from the perspective of the firm as a whole.

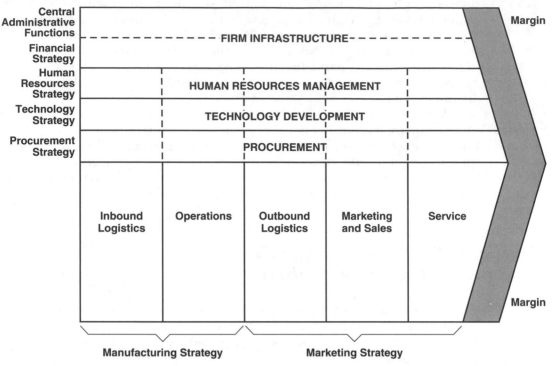

SOURCE: Michael E. Porter, *Competitive Advantage: Creating and Sustaining Superior Performance*, New York: The Free Press, 1985. A Division of Macmillan, Inc. Reprinted by permission.

For Human Resources Strategy, There Are Two Relevant Foci of Analysis: The Segmentation of Labor Markets and the SBU.

Typical categories in the labor market are: managers, professionals, clerical workers, and hourly paid workers; but the recognition of more specialized segments may be desirable for some firms. The SBU perspective is added to distinguish among the different business units in terms of the human resources they need from a strategic viewpoint. The development of human resources strategy is covered in Chapter 19.

For Technology Strategy, the Focus of Analysis Is the Strategic Technology Unit (STU).

An STU includes the skills or disciplines that are applied to a particular product, service, or process addressing a specific market need. Identifying all the relevant STUs of the firm is a critical task in the development of technology strategies. It produces the full portfolio of the key technologies the firm needs to embody in its products and processes in order to achieve competitive advantage. This leads to a critical question: which technologies do we possess, and which ones should we acquire in order to protect and enhance our competitive capabilities? Defining all of the relevant technologies is the core of the STU segmentation. Next, we have to analyze the strengths of the resulting technology portfolio. The methodology for conducting this assessment is reviewed in Chapter 20.

For Manufacturing Strategy, the Focus of Analysis Is the Strategic Manufacturing Unit (SMU).

An SMU is a group of products sharing the same manufacturing strategic objectives expressed in terms of cost, quality, dependability, flexibility, and innovativeness. Ever since Wickham Skinner wrote his classic paper on the focused factory,[3] manufacturing managers have paid attention to this important and simple concept: A plant cannot do a large variety of very different tasks exceptionally well. A factory with a clear competitive objective that focuses on a narrow product mix for a well-defined market will outperform a conventional plant with an inconsistent set of manufacturing objectives. The key to understanding the degree of focus of a plant is the SMU. Manufacturing strategy is the subject of Chapter 21.

For Procurement Strategy, There Are Two Relevant Foci of Analysis: the SMU and the SBU.

The SMU is important when dealing with make-vs.-buy decisions and other procurement issues related to the degree of vertical integration of the firm. The SBU becomes the central concern when procurement is viewed as a basic function to support the strategic development of the business.

For Marketing Strategy the Focus of Analysis Is the SBU.

SBUs are defined from a market perspective, in terms of the products or services offered to a given group of clients and confronting a specified set of competitors, which is precisely the perspective required to address marketing strategy.

The Fundamental Elements of the Definition of a Functional Strategy

The basic elements in an overall framework for the definition of a functional strategy are portrayed in Figure 18–2. The central tasks required in the development of a functional strategy follow a close parallel to those indicated at the business level. However, there are differences worth noting.

First, the corporate strategy provides a most important initial input. It defines basic requirements to which the functional strategy has to attend; it specifies targets and scope for the functional strategy. At the corporate level, the major inputs emerge from the statement of the mission of the firm and, particularly, that portion that addresses the central ways to compete. Corporate managers have to define, as part of the mission statement of the firm, the strategic significance of developing various functional capabilities. It is often in that statement where top managers identify the critical roles played by each

FIGURE 18–2. The Fundamental Elements of the Definition of a Functional Strategy

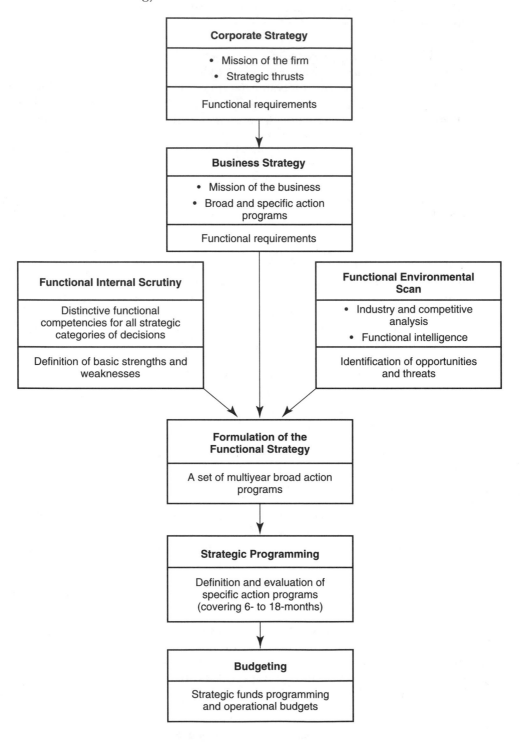

function in developing a unique competitive advantage. Moreover, the full set of strategic thrusts carries implications for functional challenges that are passed on from the corporate level.

Likewise, the businesses strategies carry an enormous functional impact. The statement of business mission has a similar relevance as the mission of the firm, except that the functional implications tend now to be sharper and more detailed, having as a central objective to support the desired competitive position of the business unit. The implications of the business challenges for each individual function are also clearly spelled out in the full set of broad and specific action programs developed at the business level.

A business strategy contains, primarily, a set of well-coordinated multi-functional programs aimed at creating or reinforcing the competitive standing of the business. Therefore, during the process of business strategy formulation, we need to identify all the necessary functional support, thus producing the most critical set of functional requirements. A functional strategy cannot be generated independently of the businesses it is intending to support.

The functional environmental scan and internal scrutiny tasks are specific for each function. In particular, the relevant analysis for the formulation of a technology strategy has the STU as a focus of attention; and similarly, the SMU is the unit of analysis for the manufacturing strategy. As is the case with business strategy, the environmental scanning process is aimed at obtaining an understanding of the critical industrial trends, and the present and future standings of key competitors. But in this case of the functional environmental scan, we stress a new dimension, which we have labeled *functional intelligence*, that we addressed already in the introduction to this chapter.

With regard to the functional internal scrutiny, besides the recognition of overall strengths and weaknesses typical of the analysis at the business level, we need to determine the specific skills that we could build for each individual function in order to gain competitive advantage. We group these as *strategic categories of decisions* linked to functional strategies.

Each function must respond to corporate and business demands, and to the requirements arising from its own external and internal characteristics. Even when the SBUs of a firm are completely autonomous and decentralized, the functional managers should participate actively and directly in formulating business strategies, because the competitive position of the various functions is defined at the business level. In addition, whenever functions are shared by two or more SBUs, the managers of these functions must formulate a horizontal strategy by identifying and exploiting whatever synergism is present.

Finally, we must *define broad and specific programs, budgets,* and *measures of performance*. We thus spell out in very concrete terms the strategic commitments of the functions and merge all of the relevant inputs into a coherent expression of functional responsibilities consistent with corporate and business long-term objectives. It is particularly important to identify ways to measure the performance of each function. This is not a trivial task; if properly done, it raises the level of strategic awareness at the functional level and provides meaningful yardsticks for functional effectiveness.

Functional Interactions and the Need
for Better Coordination Across Functions

It is important to point out some elements of commonalty in the development of functional strategies. First, functional strategy formulation depends heavily on the guidelines provided at the corporate and business levels. There is a shared set of characteristics from the firm and each one of the businesses, which provide a pattern and a common basis to all functions. As a result of this, all of the functions interact greatly with one another.

Second, a number of central strategic decisions cut across several of the functions. For example, a decision such as the degree of vertical integration has ingredients that affect all functions: manufacturing, to analyze the capabilities of the firm to make rather than buy a given product; procurement, to explore the detailed purchasing alternatives and cost; technology, to examine the design capabilities and the resulting manufacturability of the product; finance, to consider the economic and financial consequences of the decision; marketing, to assess the demand implications; and human resources, to assure the availability of the necessary labor and managerial skills. It is not surprising, therefore, that several strategic decision categories attributed primarily to one function are also considered an important matter of concern for another function.

Third, as is the case with strategic objectives at every level, functional strategies attempt to capture the challenges generated from the external environment in a way that contributes to competitive advantage. Therefore, we need to understand how each function has to deal with all the major external markets—financial, labor, technology, products, and other factors of production—in order to improve the strategic functional position. It is worth noticing that all of these external markets are naturally lined up with a given functional area. One could argue that financial markets are the province of the finance function; labor markets of human resources management; technology markets of the technology function; product markets of the marketing function; and other factors of production of the procurement function. Curiously, the only function that does not seem "to own" any specific external market is manufacturing; perhaps this can explain why manufacturing tends to have an inward orientation—unless this is purposely avoided. Figure 18–3 depicts this situation. We can observe that, to deal with an external market, we must line up the mediation of the specific function. This is another important reason for heavy interdependence among functions.

These observations have, in turn, two important practical implications for the development and implementation of functional strategies. One, a proper formulation of each functional strategy has to be done through a careful interaction among key functional managers. This allows for the adequate recognition of the impact that the external markets have on each function, and it also leads to the formulation of broad and specific action programs with the needed interfunctional flavor. Two, in order to facilitate the functional interactions, the firm has to put in place the necessary coordinating mechanisms—committees,

FIGURE 18–3. Main Functional Relations with External Markets

task forces, integrating managers, and the like—for attaining the proper alignment of all functions when formulating and executing the key strategic tasks.

Functional Strategic Decisions and Performance Measurements

Although there are a number of common elements in the development of a functional strategy, there are also specific knowledge, skills, and capabilities that apply to each individual function. The thorough understanding of that know-how constitutes the substance of a given functional strategy. Obviously, it is outside the scope of this book to examine in depth the host of methodological frameworks that apply to each managerial function. However, it is meaningful to address two seemingly straightforward central issues in developing a functional strategy. One is the identification of the key *strategic decision-making categories* that are linked to each one of the major functions, and that lead to the identification of the sources of competitive advantages that reside at the functional level. No attempt is made here to perform a detailed description of the endless tasks associated with the operations of a function. The second issue is the definition of *strategic measures of functional performance.* By that we mean an attempt to capture the quality of the final outputs of a functional strategy, in terms of their ability to achieve competitive advantage.

For reasons of conciseness, we are presenting the key strategic decision categories and performance measures of the six central functions in a figure format. We urge the readers to reflect on the lists we are putting forward and to expand and modify them according to the circumstances of their own particular settings. The proposed lists must be continuously adjusted to reflect different times, circumstances, country, and firm idiosyncrasies. The figures that we present should be taken merely as an initial suggestion in a complex and formidable task.

Figures 18–4 through 18–15 provide the information on major strategic decision categories and strategic performance measures for each one of the six functions. There are just two common categories of strategic decisions for all functions: the capturing of external intelligence, and the development of the appropriate managerial infrastructure. The first deals with the understanding of the external environment, and the second with the mechanisms to be put in place for the proper implementation of selected strategies. Also, horizontal strategy is an option that should be kept in mind for all functions because there is always the possibility of special economies of scale or scope, or of a unique form of interrelationship among functions (Chapter 13). We have chosen to stress horizontal strategy only within the realm of technology, but there are additional horizontal opportunities in all of the other functions. Now, we comment briefly on each one of the six functions.

Finance is the most centralized of functions. Its strategic categories are mostly in the sphere of corporate decision making, and its performance measures are closely watched by external audiences and embody the economic results of the firm as a whole. The major categories of decisions linked to finance strategy are presented in Figure 18–4, and the performance measures in Figure 18–5.

Human resources management is the most decentralized and pervasive of functions. The strategic decisions cannot be realized without the full participation and responsibility of managers and supervisors at all hierarchical levels. Think, for example, of selection or appraisal; only at the work place resides all the information necessary for a proper assessment of an individual. The measures of performance are oriented at detecting the attitudes and behavior of individuals in the firm through a broad array of approaches, in order to produce an indication of the healthiness of the organizational climate. The major categories of decisions linked to human resources management strategy

FIGURE 18–4. Major Categories of Decisions Linked to Finance

Financial intelligence, oriented at understanding the current characteristics and future trends of financial and capital markets around the world, such as: the enormous array of financial opportunities, changes in legislation, fluctuations of exchange rates, and the alternative options for risk management through financial transactions.

Capital budgeting, mainly: criteria for deciding on the goodness of investments, requests for capital appropriation by type of investment, and the budget for total capital expenditures.

Mergers, acquisitions, and divestments, including: identification and evaluation of opportunities, ownership alternatives, joint ventures, international expansions, and, in general, guidelines for addressing these issues with a corporate perspective.

Equity management and dividends policy, integrating: retained earnings as source of financing, share repurchasing, new equity issues and preferred stocks, stock splits and stock consolidations, and policies concerning leveraged buyouts.

Long-term debt financing, which is central for determining the capital structure of the firm and the debt rating, and is mainly geared at: opening new sources of long-term debt, establishing the most convenient debt terms, and managing the debt portfolio.

Working capital management, dealing with all decisions linked to the short-term financing of the firm; basically: cash management, credit management, and inventory management.

Pension fund management, encompassing all decisions pertaining to the management of funds contributed by the firm and its employees for retirement purposes.

Tax management, involving a number of financial and legal issues that determine the total tax payments of a corporation to a variety of governmental institutions, both domestic and abroad. They include interactions with: investment, acquisition, and divestment decisions; financing and dividend policies; and international ventures.

Risk management, to help the firm protect its operations from unanticipated events that may cause financial hardship or even default in extreme situations. Among available alternatives may be counted: hedging by means of options, futures, forwards, swaps, or other alternatives to protect the firm from risks originated in inflation, interest, and exchange rates, commodity prices, and stock instability; investment strategy by trading off fixed vs. current assets, long-vs.-short-lived assets, and business, industry, and international diversification practices; alliances and partnerships; financing strategies; governmental protection and concessions; and a variety of operational policies related to make vs. buy decisions, long- vs. short-term contracts, and fixed vs. variable cost options.

Managing the relationship with the financial community, including: commercial and investment banking, international organizations, industry analysts, and rating agencies.

Financial organization and managerial infrastructure, including the role of the finance function within the firm's organizational structure and the design of managerial systems dealing with: accounting procedures, responsibility centers, measures of financial performance, the scope of the treasury and comptroller functions, and the information systems support.

Source: See Note 4.

are presented in Figure 18–6, and the performance measures in Figure 18–7. We expand on the treatment of this function in Chapter 19.

Technology is currently considered to be one of the central functions for achieving competitive advantage, because we are living through a period of fast-paced technological transformations. Technology intelligence is a must in

FIGURE 18–5. Measures of Performance Related to the Financial Strategy

Capital market indices, oriented at representing an external assessment of the economic performance of the firm in relation to key competitors, through a variety of popular and widely watched indicators such as: price-earnings ratio (P/E), dividend yield (dividend-price ratio), earnings per share (EPS), market-to-book value (M/B), and many others.

Profitability measures, being the most widely used: return on assets (ROA), return on equity (ROE), return on investments (ROI), and sales margin. It is important to observe the capability of the firm to earn a profitability above its cost of capital. These measures can be contrasted with the firm's competitors to judge the firm's performance against its industry.

Risk, measured in terms of beta leverage (debt/equity) or bond rating, for example.

Cost of capital, for both debt and equity, and other meaningful weighted average combinations of them.

Growth, of assets, earnings, sales, investment opportunities, and whatever is considered relevant for the firm.

SOURCE: See Note 4.

order to gather information on the dynamics of technological markets; but the laborious and delicate process of internal management of technology must also be carefully addressed. The major categories of decisions linked to technology strategy are presented in Figure 18–8, and the performance measures in Figure 18–9. We expand on the treatment of this function in Chapter 20.

Procurement participates, as expected, in supplying all the needs of raw materials, goods, and services for a smooth operation of the firm businesses, at minimum cost, and with a high level of service and quality. In addition, procurement management requires creating a special base of suppliers, developing relationships with them, participating in the design of processes and products, and contributing to the resolution of the make-vs.-buy decisions, this last subject being at the heart of the vertical integration issue. The major categories of decisions linked to procurement strategy are presented in Figure 18–10, and the performance measures in Figure 18–11.

Manufacturing is a very special function, due to the fact that all relationships with external markets are mediated through other functions. This requires a certain reiteration of issues that may well be considered in the realm of other functions, but are also central for manufacturing. Therefore, it is worthwhile to include them in the major categories of strategic decisions affecting manufacturing. The issues that are most clearly interfaced with other functions are: one, vertical integration, with procurement for backward integration, and with marketing for forward integration; two, process technologies with the technology function; three, product scope and introduction of new products with marketing; four, human resources with the human resources management function; and five, suppliers' relations with the procurement function. The major categories of decisions linked to manufacturing strategy are presented in Figure 18–12, and the performance measures in Figure 18–13.

FIGURE 18–6. Major Categories of Decisions Linked to Human Resources Management

---

Human resources management intelligence, oriented at understanding the practices of management prevailing in human resources markets, and the expected changes in them. Important issues are: reward structures, levels or compensations for different positions and jobs, alternatives for training and capacities development, changes in legislation related to human resources management, trends in unionization, external focuses of attraction of key specialists, obsolescence of skills in lower level personnel, and retraining practices.

Selection, promotion and placement, for managing the flow of people in, through, and out of the organization, and matching available human resources to jobs in the organization.

Appraisal, for evaluating the performance of people within the organization, thus enabling the proper allocation of rewards, the design of effective management development programs, the maintenance of current inventory of talent, and the proper promotion and placement of personnel.

Rewards, providing compensation in different forms, such as: monetary, promotion, management praise, career opportunities, appreciation from customers, personal sense of well-being, opportunities to learn, security, responsibility, respect and friendship with coworkers.

Management development, creating mechanisms to enhance skills, promotional opportunities, and career paths.

Labor/employee relations and voice, aimed at establishing a cooperative climate between managers and employees.

Human resources management organization and managerial infrastructure, focused on defining the location of human resources management in the organizational structure, and the procedures and systems required for its smooth administration, mainly the responsibilities that fall in a centralized human resources unit, and the participation required from other units of the firm.

SOURCE: See Note 5.

This subject is further expanded in Chapter 21, which is fully devoted to the development of the manufacturing strategy.

Marketing is oriented toward the satisfaction of consumer needs, and includes all the logistics of distribution and after-sales services. This function is characterized by being preferentially decentralized at the level of the SBU, and by the largely external nature of its main focuses of attention. The key is the understanding of consumers' needs, the inducement of new necessities, and the triggering of purchasing behavior. The major categories of decisions linked to marketing strategy are presented in Figure 18–14, and the performance measures in Figure 18–15.

Let us close this section with a caveat. The categories of decision making represent our own biases in the selection of central areas of strategic attention in each function. We have borrowed heavily from the references. Likewise, the performance measurements are intended to possess only a strategic orientation. The ability to follow-up on the quality of execution of action programs supporting each strategic category is not relevant, since that is the domain of conventional management control systems design. What is relevant is the

- Job satisfaction

- Job performance

- Personnel turnover

- Absenteeism

- Motivation

- Job security

- Career prospects

- Psychological stress

- Safety/health conditions

- Income

These attributes are subject to measure through the collection of statistics, personal communication between supervisors and supervised, commitments generated by management-by-objectives type of systems, employee reaction surveys, and job diagnostic surveys.

In essence, we have to mobilize a wide array of mechanisms to detect the degree of health of human resources climate. Moreover, the proposed list can be easily expanded or modified to fit more closely the strategic position of the firm and its individual circumstances.

SOURCE: See Note 5.

capturing of the competitive strength resulting from the overall functional strategy. These are not easy tasks, so every effort must be made to complete them in a comprehensive and consistent way.

A Methodology for the Development of Functional Strategies

In this section we make explicit some of the steps that may be followed to develop a functional strategy in accordance with the general framework presented in Figure 18–2. We limit ourselves to presenting the content of some forms that we have used to help practicing managers in the construction of functional strategies. These forms should not be interpreted as a set of structured and mechanistic instructions, but rather as conceptual frameworks to lead us in a more systematic way toward the analysis of the central issues that affect the formulation of functional strategies. In the next three chapters we provide a full illustration of this procedure for the cases of the human resources, technology, and manufacturing functions. A summary of the methodology is shown in Figure 18–16.

FIGURE 18–8. Major Categories of Decisions Linked to Technology Strategy

Technology intelligence, basically oriented at: gathering information concerning the current and future state of technology development, identifying the strategic technical units (STU) of the firm, evaluating the technical strength by STU in relation to key competitive firms, and detecting the locus of innovation by key product area (users, manufacturers, suppliers, others).

Selection of technologies, in which the firm will concentrate its efforts, to innovate in processes and products, in each stage of the business life-cycle.

Timing of new technology introduction, mainly decisions as to whether to lead or to lag competitors in process and product innovations, identifying the benefits and risks associated with a leadership and followership strategy, and assuring the congruency of the selected technology strategy with the business strategies of the firm.

Modes of technology acquisition, by relying on its own internal efforts or resorting to external sources. Options available are: internal development, acquisition, licensing, internal ventures, joint ventures or alliances, venture capital, and education acquisitions.

Technology horizontal strategy, identifying and exploiting technological interrelationships that exist across distinct but related businesses, to enhance the competitive advantage of the firm through: common product technologies, common process technologies, common technologies in other value added activities, one product incorporated into another, and interface among products.

Project selection, evaluation, resource allocation, and control, including: criteria for resource allocation, project-oriented resources versus loosely controlled funds to support and plan projects, the degree of fluctuation in technology funding, and the magnitude in the profit gap to be filled by new products.

Technology organization and managerial infrastructure, focused on: the definition of the organizational structure of the technology function, the identification of the horizontal coordinating mechanisms needed to exploit the technological interrelationships among the various business units and the activities of the value chain, the development of career paths for scientists and technical professionals, the design of motivational and reward systems for scientists and technical professionals, degree of involvement of top managers in technological decisions, the decision-making process for resource allocation to technological projects, and the protection of the technological know-how through patents policies and publication policies.

SOURCE: See Note 6.

FIGURE 18–9. Measures of Performance Related to the Technology Strategy

---

Rate of technological innovation, selecting one or more measures of technological performance for key products and processes (the S-curve is a good graphical portrayal of the rate of technological innovations).

R&D productivity, measured by the improvement in the performance of product or processes divided by the incremental investment in R&D.

Rate of return in R&D investment, measures the profit generated by the amount of R&D investment.

Resources allocated to R&D, monitors the level of expenditures allocated to the various projects, businesses, and the firm as a whole.

Rate of new product introduction, measured by the number of new products introduced by year, the number of patents obtained, or the percentage of sales derived from new products.

Technology-based diversification, measures the degree of success in achieving diversification through technological competencies, such as the percentage of sales resulting from technology-driven diversification initiatives.

Other appropriate measures, such as: royalties or sales of technologies, training time of people in new technologies, cycle time of new product development, developmental cost per stage, and level of technological competencies.

SOURCE: See Note 6.

FIGURE 18–10. Major Categories of Decisions Linked to Procurement Strategy

---

Procurement intelligence, geared at understanding the common practices prevailing in markets that are factors of production for the firm, and trying to anticipate transformations that may affect the performance of the procurement function. Important issues are: alternative sources of supply from around the world, legislative changes, cartelization of suppliers, general health and competitive standing of key suppliers, technological changes that may affect procurement, distribution patterns, and material management practices and innovations.

Selection, evaluation, and development of suppliers, for: finding, selecting, evaluating, developing, administering and motivating suppliers able and willing to provide consistent quality, service, and competitive prices; maintaining a healthy relationship with suppliers, subcontracting, buying inside the company, and make vs. buy decisions.

Quality management of purchased goods, which includes: defining the proper quality specifications of the procured goods, inspection of the purchased items to ensure conformance with the stated specification, and even establishing a quality control process at the suppliers plant.

Materials management of purchased goods, dealing with the flow of all of the purchased goods into the organization, mainly: materials planning and control, order processing, incoming traffic, inventory control, receiving, in-plant materials movements, and scraps and surplus disposal.

338

FIGURE 18-10 *Continued*

Value analysis, price/cost analysis, and standardization, to confront with ample information the difficult trade-offs among price, quality, design, manufacturability, standardization, and cost. Value analysis is a systematic effort directed at analyzing the functional requirements for achieving the lowest attainable cost, consistent with the needed performance, reliability, quality, and maintainability of a product.

Procurement organization and managerial infrastructure.

a) Organization. The decisions regarding the way to structure the procurement function should address two central issues: the degree of centralization vs. decentralization of purchasing, and the need to coordinate the procurement activities with the other managerial functions—most importantly: manufacturing, technology, marketing, distribution, quality control, and finance. Four prerogatives should reside with the procurement function: selection of the sources of supplies, contact with suppliers, auditing the purchase request against the need, and managing the commercial aspects of the function—including the manner of purchase, price, terms and conditions of the order, and packaging and shipping instructions.

b) Procurement System. A key element of the managerial infrastructure support is the development of a comprehensive procurement logistic system including, among others, the following elements: checking requisitions, securing quotations, scheduling purchases and deliveries, issuing purchase orders, checking legal conditions of contracts, following up for delivery, checking receipt of materials, and verifying invoices. Moreover, the system should be capable of maintaining and updating all records and required information for a proper handling of the procurement issues.

SOURCE: See Note 7.

FIGURE 18–11. Measures of Performance Related to Procurement Strategy

An effective measurement for procurement performance is hard to define because of the many factors that have to be traded off to provide a steady flow of materials as needed, at lowest ultimate cost. The desired objectives for procurement are to obtain: optimum quality, minimum final cost, effective supplier service, continuity of supply, a solid supplier know-how, and good and permanent supplier relations. Some examples of performance measurements are:

Indicators of cost performance, costs of procured goods vs. standard costs, administrative costs of the purchasing department as a fraction of total purchases, total value added of purchased goods as a fraction of total cost, inventory turnover ratios, and cost savings.

Indicators for services performance, percentage of orders on time, and average delay on delinquent orders.

Indicators for quality performance, percentage of orders meeting specifications, reliability of purchased goods, and vendor quality.

Indicators for vendor relationships.

SOURCE: See Note 7.

FIGURE 18–12. Major Categories of Decisions Linked to Manufacturing Strategy

Manufacturing intelligence, to observe the practices and trends of manufacturing in the industry, such as: changes in competitors' facilities, technological developments in process technologies, new raw materials or components, standardization, capital investment practices, and environmental legislation.

Facilities, mainly the number of plants, their sites and location, and most importantly, how specialized or focused facilities are and the degree of flexibility they possess.

Capacity, as determined by: the plant equipment and human resources available, the slack in the use of capacity with regard to demand, the ability to handle demand peaks, and the decisions pertaining to the sequences of capacity expansion.

Vertical integration, addressing among other issues: the definition of the boundaries of the firm with regard to its value chain (the questions of make vs. buy), the management of the relationship among the firm and its external constituencies (primarily suppliers, distributors, and customers), and the conditions under which those characteristics should be altered to gain competitive advantage and to increase the appropriation of value by the firm.

Process technologies, involving decisions as to: the degree of the technology and process equipment used (from general to specific purposes), the labor skills required, the degree of automation, and the flexibility for scope and volume, as well as the rate of new product introductions.

Product scope and introduction of new products, including issues such as: the definition of the breadth of product lines, the rate and mode of new product introductions, and the desirable length of the product life-cycle.

Human resources, addressing questions such as: recruitment, selection, promotion and placement; appraisal; rewards, incentives, and job security; skills development and adjustment to changing technological demands; and labor/employee relations, and voice.

Quality management, dealing with: the definition of the desirable product quality, quality improvement program, assignment of responsibilities for quality, training, quality control, prevention, and testing.

Suppliers relations, including issues such as: suppliers' selection, qualification, degree of partnership, manufacturer/supplier strategies, list of competitive bidding, and supplier controls. This has been another area receiving close attention because of the different kind of practices existing in Japan among manufacturers and suppliers, based primarily on close partnership and trust as opposed to the arm-length attitudes prevailing until recently among American firms.

Manufacturing organization and managerial infrastructure, most importantly: the design of the proper organizational structure (including the degree of centralization of responsibilities), the design of planning and scheduling systems, control and information systems, and forecasting and inventory management. This area has attracted significant attention due to the revolutionary innovation of Japanese manufacturing management represented particularly by Just-in-Time (JIT) and Total-Quality-Management (TQM) systems.

SOURCE: See Note 8.

Cost, which can be measured in a variety of ways, the most relevant ones being: variable unit cost and total unit cost (from the point of view of the manufacturer), and total life-cycle cost (from the point of view of the user).

Delivery, measured in terms of: percentage of on-time shipments, predictability of delivery dates, and response time to demand changes.

Quality, measured in terms of the adherence of products to the various dimensions of quality (performance, features, reliability, conformance, durability, serviceability, aesthetics, and perceived quality), rejection rates, return rates, cost and rates of field repair, and cost of quality.

Flexibility to volume changes and new product introduction, measured as: response to products or volume changes, product substitutability, and product options or variants.

Normally, cost and delivery represent a different way to compete from quality and flexibility. If a firm wants to establish itself as a low-cost producer, it might adopt a strategy that prevents delivering highly customized products and simultaneously being able to absorb significant changes both in volume and in product innovation.

SOURCE: See Note 8.

Continued

FIGURE 18–14. Major Categories of Decisions Linked to Marketing Strategy

Marketing intelligence, corresponding to the effort conducted by the firm to decipher competitors' standing and to anticipate their future moves. Important issues are product introductions, marketing approaches, changes in segmentation practices, price policies, product liabilities, new distribution channels, and improved services approaches.

Defining and analyzing markets, for generating inputs to guide the product positioning of the firm, through an appropriate market segmentation and a finer definition of product-market segments, so as to capture the different preferences and needs of customers. In each of those segments, an analysis of the behavior of consumers and organizational buyers is conducted, as well as of the overall strategic competitive situation.

Product strategy, including decisions on: product offering, breadth of product lines, mix, bundling, target markets, establishing strategic objectives for products (market share, profit contribution), and selecting a branding strategy.

New products development and introduction, mainly: ideas generation, screening and evaluation of ideas, business analysis, development of a prototype and testing, formulation of a marketing approach, market testing in pilot regions, adjustment of administrative and support systems, and new products introduction.

Distribution strategy, involving selection of a distribution channel (whether direct or via retailers, wholesalers, or agents), design and management of the physical distribution system (including customer service, demand forecasting, inventory control, materials handling, order processing, parts and service support, warehousing and storage, procurement, packaging, returned goods handling, and traffic and transportation), and push vs. pull mode of operation of the distribution and sales systems.

Price strategy, considering: the product competitive positioning, its product mix, brand strategy, product quality and features, and distribution, advertising and sales force strategies.

Promotion and advertising strategies, based on: advertising, presentation and promotion of ideas, goods, or services by an identified sponsor; personal selling, sales promotion, and publicity.

Marketing organization and managerial infrastructure, considering: the development of an organizational structure; planning, control and information systems; and rewards and incentives systems in accordance with the culture of the firm and the marketing strategy.

SOURCE: See Note 9.

FIGURE 18–15. Measures of Performance Related to Marketing Strategy

Product strategy, measured by: sales growth rate, market share, relative market share, breadth of product line, market coverage, degree of differentiation, rate of successful new product introductions, and product bundling.

Distribution strategy, measured by: efficiency of distribution channels, customer service levels, distribution costs per channel, and distribution and sales force productivity.

Price strategy, measured by: price sensitivity and pricing of marketing mix.

Promotion and advertising strategy, measured by: product segmentation, brand acceptance, and marketing intelligence (ability to anticipate customer needs and to detect changes in marketing trends).

SOURCE: See Note 9.

FIGURE 18–16. A Methodological Approach for the Development of a Functional Strategy

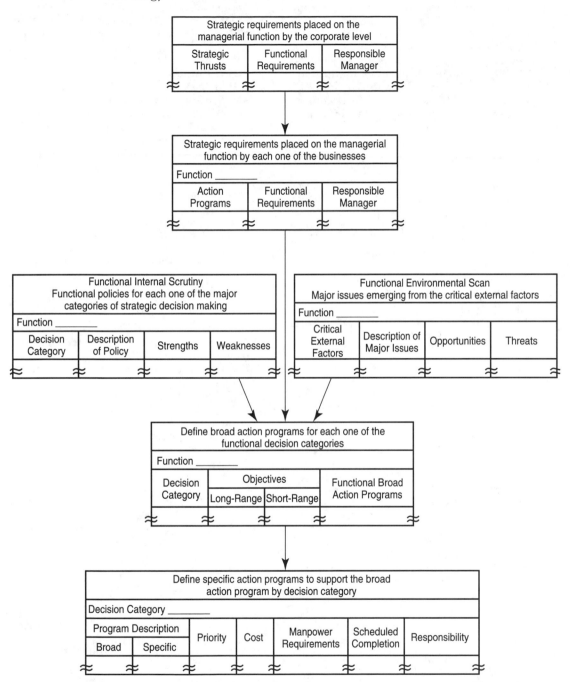

Notes

1. Xerox Corporation was the pioneer in the benchmarking field. For the classical reference in this area, see Robert C. Camp, *Benchmarking: The Search for Industries' Best Practices that Lead to Superior Performance* (New York: Quality Press, 1989). Another useful reference is Kathleen H.J. Leibfried and C.J. McNair, *Benchmarking: A Tool for Continuous Improvement* (New York: HarperCollins, 1992).

2. The first comprehensive review of business process reengineering is reported in: Michael Hammer and James Champy, *Reengineering the Corporation: A Manifesto for Business Revolution* (New York: Harper Collins, 1993). Subsequently, James Champy published *Reengineering Management: The Mandate for New Leadership* (New York: Harper Business, 1995). For an additional reference, see Thomas A. Davenport, *Process Innovation* (Boston, MA: Harvard Business School Press, 1993).

3. Wickham Skinner, *Manufacturing: The Formidable Competitive Weapon* (New York: John Wiley & Sons, 1985).

4. For references to finance see: Harold Bierman, Jr., *Strategic Financial Planning* (New York: The Free Press, 1980); Richard A. Brealey, and Stewart C. Myers, *Principles of Corporate Finance*, 4th ed. (New York: McGraw-Hill Book Co., 1991); T. Copeland, T. Koller, and J. Murrin, *Valuation: Measuring and Managing the Value of Companies* (New York: Wiley, 1990); Pankaj Ghemawat, *Commitment: The Dynamic of Strategy* (New York: The Free Press, 1991); Philippe C. Haspeslagh and David B. Jemison, *Managing Acquisitions: Creating Value Through Corporate Renewal* (New York: The Free Press, 1991); James McTaggart, Peter Kontes, and M. Mankins, *The Value Imperative: Managing for Superior Shareholder Returns* (New York: The Free Press, 1994); Bennett Stewart, *The Quest for Value: A Guide for Senior Managers* (New York: Harper, 1991).

5. For references to human resources see: Thomas A. Barocci and Thomas A. Kochan, *Human Resources Management and Industrial Relations* (Boston, MA: Little, Brown and Co., 1985); M. Beer, B. Spector, P.R. Lawrence, D.Q. Mills, and R.E. Walton, *Managing Human Assets*, (New York: The Free Press, 1984); Robert Eccles, Nitin Nohria, and James Berkley, *Beyond the Hype: Rediscovering the Essence of Management* (Boston, MA: Harvard Business School Press, 1992); C. J. Fombrum, N.M. Tichy, and M.A. Devanna, *Strategic Human Resource Management* (New York: John Wiley, 1984); Jay R. Galbraith, Edward E. Lawler III, & Associates, *Organizing for the Future: The New Logic for Managing Complex Organizations* (San Francisco: Jossey-Bass, 1993); Arnoldo C. Hax, "A New Competitive Weapon: The Human Resources Strategy," *Training and Development Journal*, 39, no. 5 (May 1985), 76–82; Jon Katzenbach and Douglas Smith, *The Wisdom of Teams: Creating the High-Performance Organization* (Boston, MA: Harvard Business School Press, 1993); Thomas Kochan and Michael Useem (eds.), *Transforming Organizations* (New York: Oxford University Press, 1992); John P. Kotter, *A Force for Change: How Leadership Differs from Management* (New York: Free Press, 1990); Edward E. Lawler III, *The Ultimate Advantage: Creating the High-Involvement Organization* (San Francisco, CA: Jossey-Bass, 1992); David Nadler, Marc Gerstein, Robert Shaw, and Associates, *Organizational Architecture: Designs for Changing Organizations* (San Francisco, CA: Jossey Bass, 1992); Glenn M. Parker, *Team Players and Teamwork: The New Competitive Business Strategy* (San Francisco, CA: Jossey-Bass, 1990); Jeffrey Pfeffer, *Managing with Power* (Boston, MA: Harvard Business School Press, 1992); Edgar S. Schein, *Career Dynamics* (Part 3) (Reading, MA: Addison-Wesley, 1978) 189–256; Edgar S. Schein, *Organizational Culture and Leadership* (San Francisco, CA: Jossey-Bass, 1992); Peter Senge, *The Fifth Discipline: The Art and Practice of the Learning Organization* (New York: Doubleday, 1990).

6. For references to technology, see: Stephen Bradley, Jerry Hausman, and Richard Nolan (eds.), *Globalization, Technology, and Competition: The Fusion of Computers and Telecommunications in the 1990s,* (Boston, MA: Harvard Business School Press, 1993); Robert A. Burgelman and Modesto A. Maidique, *Strategic Management of Technology and Innovation* (Homewood, IL: Richard D. Irwin

Press, 1988); Kim Clark and Takahiro Fujimoto, *Product Development Performance: Strategy, Organization, and Management in the World Auto Industry* (Boston, MA: Harvard Business School Press, 1991); Richard N. Foster, *Innovation: The Attacker's Advantage* (Summit Books, 1986); Mel Horwitch (ed.), *Technology in the Modern Corporation: A Strategic Perspective* (New York: Pergamon Press, 1986); Hamid Noori, *Managing the Dynamics of New Technology,* (Englewood Cliffs, NJ: Prentice Hall, 1990); Michael E. Porter, *Competitive Advantage: Creating and Sustaining Superior Performance* (New York: The Free Press, 1985), Chapter 5; Edward B. Roberts (ed.), *Generating Technological Innovation,* (New York: Oxford University Press, 1987); Philip A. Roussel, Kamal N. Saad, and Tamara J. Erickson, *Third Generation R&D* (Boston, MA: Harvard Business School Press, 1991); David J. Teece, (ed.), *The Competitive Challenge: Strategies for Industrial Innovation and Renewal* (Cambridge, MA: Ballinger Publishing Co., 1987); Brian Twiss, *Managing Technological Innovation* (London: Longman Group, 1982); James M. Utterback, *Mastering the Dynamics of Innovation* (Boston, MA: Harvard Business School Press, 1994); Eric Von Hippel, *The Sources of Innovation* (New York: Oxford, 1988); Steven C. Wheelwright and Kim B. Clark, *Revolutionizing Product Development,* (New York: The Free Press, 1992)

7. For reference to procurement see: Stuart F. Heinritz, Paul V. Farrell, and Clifton L. Smith, *Purchasing: Principles and Applications,* 7th ed., (Englewood Cliffs, NJ: Prentice Hall, 1986).

8. For references to manufacturing see: Elwood S. Buffa, *Meeting the Competitive Challenge: Manufacturing Strategy for U.S. Companies* (Homewood, IL: Richard D. Irwin, 1984); Kim Clark, and Takahiro Fujimoto, *Product Development Performance: Strategy, Organization, and Management in the World Auto Industry* (Boston, MA: Harvard Business School Press, 1991); Bill Creech, *The Five Pillars of TQM: How to Make Total Quality Management Work for You,* (New York: Dutton Truman Tulley Books, 1994); W. Edwards Deming, *Out of the Crisis* (Cambridge, MA: Massachusetts Institute of Technology, Center for Advanced Engineering Studies, 1986); Peter F. Drucker, "The Emerging

Theory of Manufacturing," *Harvard Business Review,* 68, no. 3 (May–June 1990), 94–102; Charles Fine and Arnoldo C. Hax, "Manufacturing Strategy: A Methodology and an Illustration," *Interfaces,* 15, no. 6, (November–December 1985), 28–46; David A. Garvin, *Managing Quality: The Strategic and Competitive Edge* (New York: The Free Press, 1988); Thomas G. Gunn, *21st Century Manufacturing: Creating Winning Business Performance* (New York: Harper Business, 1992); Kathryn Rudie Harrigan, *Strategic Flexibility: A Management Guide for Changing Times* (Lexington, MA: Lexington Books, 1985); Robert J. Hayes and Steven C. Wheelwright, *Restoring Our Competitive Edge: Competing Through Manufacturing* (New York: John Wiley, 1984); Robert J. Hayes, Steven C. Wheelwright, and Kim B. Clark, *Dynamic Manufacturing: Creating the Learning Organization,* (New York: Free Press, 1988); Masaaki Imai, *Kaizen* (New York: McGraw-Hill Publishing, 1986); J.M. Juran, *Juran on Quality by Design* (New York: The Free Press, 1992); John P. MacDuffie and John F. Krafcik, "Integrating Technology and Human Resources for High-Performance Manufacturing: Evidence from the International Auto Industry," in Thomas A. Kochan and Michael Useem (eds.), *Transforming Organizations* (New York: Oxford University Press, 1992); *Manufacturing 21 Report—The Future of Japanese Manufacturing* (Whealing, IL: Association for Manufacturing Excellence, 1990); Patricia E. Moody, *Strategic Manufacturing: Dynamic New Directions for the 1990s* (Homewood, IL: Dow-Jones Irwin, 1990); B. Joseph Pine, II, *Mass Customization: The New Frontier in Business Competition* (Boston, MA: Harvard Business School Press, 1993); Rakesh K. Sarin (ed.), *Perspectives in Operations Management: Essays in Honor of Elwood S. Buffa* (Kluwer Academic Publishers, 1993); Richard J. Schonberger, *Japanese Manufacturing Techniques* (New York: The Free Press, 1982); Richard J. Schonberger, *World Class Manufacturing: The Lessons of Simplicity Applied* (New York: The Free Press, 1987); Wickham Skinner, *Manufacturing: The Formidable Competitive Weapon* (New York: John Wiley & Sons, 1985); Kiyoshi Suzaki, *The Manufacturing Challenge: Techniques for Continuous Improvements* (New York: The Free Press, 1987); Steven C. Wheelwright and Kim B. Clark, *Revolution-*

izing Product Development (New York: The Free Press, 1992); James P. Womack, Daniel T. Jones, and Daniel Roos, *The Machine that Changed the World* (New York: Rawson Associates, 1990).

9. For references to marketing see: David A. Aaker, *Managing Brand Equity* (New York: The Free Press, 1991); David W. Cravens, *Strategic Marketing* (Homewood, IL: Richard D. Irwin, 1987); George S. Day, *Market Driven Strategy: Processes for Creating Value* (New York: The Free Press, 1990); George S. Day, *Strategic Market Planning* (St. Paul, MN: West Publishing, 1984); John R. Hauser, and Don Clausing, "The House of Quality," *Harvard Business Review*, 66, no. 3 (May–June 1988), 63–73; James Heskett, W. Earl Sasser, and Christopher Hart, *Service Breakthroughs: Changing the Rules of the Game* (New York: The Free Press, 1990); Steven P. Schannaars, *Marketing Strategy: A Customer Driven Approach* (New York: The Free Press, 1991); Richard Schonberger, *Building a Chain of Customers* (New York: The Free Press, 1990); Richard C. Whiteley, *The Customer Driven Company* (Reading, MA: Addison Wesley, 1991).

CHAPTER **19**

Human Resources Strategy

The central priority of most managers requiring the greatest amount of time and attention is the proper identification, development, promotion, and reward of key personnel. According to General Electric's chairman, Jack Welsch, if you define the right tasks, put the appropriate persons in charge of them, and back them up with the right kind of reward system, you do not need to be a good manager to obtain excellent results.[1]

The undeniable importance of human resources for every organization has been intensified in American firms due to the presence of a number of forces requiring a broader, strategy-oriented treatment of this subject. Recent pressures that have raised the level of concern on human resources management can be summarized as follows:[2]

- increasing international competition, particularly from the Far East
- increasing complexity and size of organizations
- slower growth or declining markets in a great many industries
- greater government involvement in human resources practices
- increasing education of the work force
- changing values of the work force
- more concern with career and life satisfaction
- changes in work-force demographics.

These concerns have drawn attention to the problem of managing human resources in a strategic manner; that is, in a way that allows firms to establish and sustain a long-term advantage over their competitors. However, in spite of growing interest, the strategic management of human resources is far from a reality in most American enterprises. The formulation of corporate and busi-

347

ness strategies is becoming commonplace, but the issue of human resources is not being addressed with a proper sense of priorities. Rather, the personnel requirements embedded in those strategies are identified after the fact and passed only to personnel managers so they can supply the necessary managers, workers, and administrative staff at the various skill levels demanded by the strategic plans.

This practice not only diminishes the strategic role of human resources, but also fails to recognize that the effective use and development of human resources involve *every* line manager in the organization. It is not a staff activity to be relegated exclusively to the personnel function.

Strategic Decision Categories Linked to Human Resources Management

We recognize that any methodology to support the development of a human resources strategy should be tailor-made to accommodate for the idiosyncrasies of a given firm, the characteristics of its industry and its competitive environment, and the managerial style and culture of the organization. However, we find that there are enough common issues in the formulation of a human resources strategy to allow us to generate a useful, general-purpose process to guide managerial thinking in this area.

A human resources strategy must be comprehensive, in the sense of addressing all of the diverse personnel and human resource activities central to the long-term development of the businesses of the firm. Its foundation lies in the proper recognition of the major categories of human resource strategic decision making:[3]

- selection, promotion, and placement managing the flow of people in, through, and out of the organization
- appraisal to evaluate the performance of people within the organization
- rewards providing adequate compensation, fringe benefits, and motivational support to employees at all levels
- management development creating mechanisms to enhance skills, promotional opportunities, and career
- Labor/employee relations and voice to establish a cooperative climate among managers and employees

These categories of decisions are further defined in Figure 19–1. That figure also describes the central strategic issues related to each category, as well as the corresponding strategic choices. The alternatives available as strategic options for each category are responsible for defining the human resources policy and the resulting quality of the organization as a working place. It is, therefore, useful to reflect briefly on the nature of these options.

FIGURE 19-1. The Major Strategic Decision-Making Categories Linked to Human Resources Management

	Selection, Promotion, and Placement	Appraisal	Rewards	Management Development	Labor/Employee Relations and Voice
Definition	Includes all those activities related to the internal movement of people across positions and to the external hiring into the organization. The essential process is one of matching available human resources to jobs in the organization.	Perhaps the least liked managerial activity. It contributes to three essential processes: • Rewards can be allocated in relation to performance. • Human resources planning and development of current inventory of talent. • Development process.	Pays in various forms: promotion, management praise, career opportunities, appreciation from customers and clients, personal sense of well-being, opportunities to learn, security, responsibility, respect from coworkers, friendship with coworkers.	Activities designed to ensure that individuals are properly equipped with skills and knowledge to carry out their jobs.	Activities oriented toward establishing a degree of collaboration between management and labor/employee focus.
Strategic Issues	• Devising an organization-wide selection and promotion system to support corporate and business strategies. • Creating internal flows of people that match the business strategies. • Matching key executives to the business strategies.	Designing an appraisal system supportive of the corporate and business strategies.	Designing a reward system to reverse the tendency of short-sighted management, providing balanced support to short-term and long-term strategic goals.	• Job improvement: the development of specific job skills. • Career planning: a longitudinal form of individual growth. • Succession planning ensuring an adequate supply of human resource talent by projected needs.	Developing a policy regarding the amount of influence employees have with regard to matters such as business goals, pay, working conditions, career progression, employment security, etc.
Strategic Choices	• Make vs. buy • Little recruiting above entry level vs. sophisticated recruiting at all levels. • Selection based on weeding out undesirable employees vs. careful initial screening.	• Process-oriented vs. result-oriented system. • Identification of training needs vs. staffing needs. • Individual/group vs. division/corporate performance evaluation. • Time-series vs. cross-section comparisons.	• Compensation oriented toward position in the organizational hierarchy vs. toward performance. • Internal consistency vs. external competitiveness. • Total compensation driven by cash vs. non-cash incentives.	• Formal vs. informal development programs. • Extensive vs. limited development programs. • Skills building vs. skills identification and acquisition.	• Unionization vs. non-unionization. • Minimize vs. share power and influence of labor force. • Autocratic vs. participatory management systems. • Development of employee-influence mechanisms such as soil-management groups, task forces, quality of work-life committees, ombudsmen, etc.

SELECTION, PROMOTION, AND PLACEMENT: STRATEGIC CHOICES

Make versus Buy.

A pure-make human resources strategy only allows hiring at the entry level, counting on promotion, placement, and development processes for building necessary skills for individuals to do their job effectively. On the contrary, a pure-buy strategy permits acquiring human resources as needed at any level in the organizational hierarchy. In practice, business firms may locate themselves anywhere in the spectrum between these two extremes.

Little Recruiting above Entry Level versus Sophisticated Recruiting at All Levels.

Firms that embrace the pure-make strategic option in human resources tend to concentrate on recruiting exclusively at the entry level; and only in the most exceptional circumstances will they recruit at higher levels in the organization. The converse also follows with a pure-buy strategy.

Selection Based on Weeding Out Undesirable Employees versus Careful Initial Screening.

Firms engaged in a practice of adhering to life-long employment would be required to exercise a great amount of care in the initial screening process. Some financial institutions regard the hiring decision of key personnel to carry with it a life-long $5 million price tag. This clearly conveys the economic significance of such a decision.

APPRAISAL: STRATEGIC CHOICES

Process-Oriented versus Result-Oriented System.

In a pure result-oriented appraisal system, we are only concerned about the ability of the individual to meet a prearranged set of performance indicators, without paying much attention to the conditions that facilitate or deter the realization of those indicators. On the contrary, a pure process-oriented appraisal system tries to penetrate into the circumstances that are part of the process of achieving the desired results, both of an internal and external nature.

Identification of Training Needs versus Staffing Needs.

In a pure-make system, identification of training needs is mandatory, so that we develop the necessary skills and knowledge of our existing work force. In a purely buy system, identification of staffing needs replaces the training requirement.

Individual-Group versus Division-Corporate Performance Evaluation.

This taxonomy serves to discriminate the scope within which performance is evaluated. On one end of the spectrum, only individual performance matters;

on the other extreme, the individual disappears, and only corporate goals are measured. A critical choice to be made in most appraisal and reward systems is what weight to give to individual, group, and corporate performance, in such a way as to stimulate both the recognition of employee efforts and the development of a constructive group attitude.

Time-Series versus Cross-Section Comparisons.
A time-series appraisal system has memory. It judges how performance has evolved through a relevant historical time frame. On the contrary, a cross-section comparison appraises performance at a single point in time. The only relative meaningful comparison could be against peers in the organization or in other institutions.

REWARDS: STRATEGIC CHOICES

Compensation Oriented Toward Position versus Compensation Oriented Toward Performance in the Organizational Hierarchy.
At the one extreme of this dichotomy, we have a system where compensation is dictated by the nature of the work itself. Jobs tend to have a specific rank, depending on where they are in the organizational hierarchy, which carries with it a compensation figure. At the other extreme, we encounter firms that pay almost no attention to structure but compensate entirely based on performance.

Internal Consistency versus External Competitiveness.
This choice points to the degree to which compensation is driven by a sense of internal fairness or by responses generated from the external labor market.

Total Compensation Driven by Cash versus Noncash Incentives.
Pay could come in various forms, one of which is monetary. The question posed by this taxonomy is the extent to which compensation includes other forms of incentives, such as employment stability, career development, appreciation, respect from the various constituencies of the enterprise, and an overall sense of well-being. Particularly in the higher echelons of the firm, the development, retention, and exercise of power could be an important noncash incentive.

MANAGEMENT DEVELOPMENT: STRATEGIC CHOICES

Formal versus Informal Development Programs; Extensive versus Limited Development Programs; and Skills Building versus Skills Identification and Acquisitions.
These three types of choices signal the degree of commitment that the firm has to management development. Companies that regard management development as the core activity in human resources management opt for formal and

extensive development programs aimed at building and constantly updating the skills and knowledge required for managers to perform their jobs effectively. To the contrary, companies that resort to buying human resources tend to have informal and sporadic development programs and use them to identify the skills that should be acquired from the external marketplace.

LABOR/EMPLOYEE RELATIONS AND VOICE: STRATEGIC CHOICES

Unionization versus Nonunionization; Minimize versus Share Power and Influence of Labor Force; Autocratic versus Participatory Management System; Development of Employee-influence Mechanisms, such as Self-management Groups, Task Forces, Quality of Work-life Committees, Ombudsmen, and So On.
All of these strategic choices finally determine the degree, quality, and collaboration prevailing among management, employees, and the labor force.

Congruency of the Human Resources Management Strategy

The strategic choices we have just commented on define the character and quality of the human resources environment. The strategic choices of each of the five decision categories have to be consistent with one another; otherwise, the human resources strategy lacks coherence, and it may fail to operate as intended. The significance of this deficiency could be overwhelming. It is unthinkable that the firm will successfully deploy and sustain a winning strategy without having an effective human resources strategy, particularly with regard to its key personnel. We present this as the last strategic task residing at the corporate level, because it does indeed provide the glue that allows all of the previous activities to be properly executed.

It is easy to see how the five human resources strategic categories of decision are linked. Selection, promotion, and placement identify the best available talent to perform the critical job of the enterprise. These alone will not be enough in a world where knowledge and skills have to be continuously updated in order for the human resources to remain competent. Thus, management development is a key strategic activity. Furthermore, a skillful and properly developed work force must be wholeheartedly committed to the organization. This brings into focus the importance of the rewards and motivational activities, as well as a careful management of the labor/employee relations and voice. And finally, none of these tasks can be properly done if an effective appraisal system is not in place. This system should allow for the proper matching of the available human resources to the necessary jobs in the organization, the planning and execution of management development efforts, the design and operation of an intelligent rewards system,

FIGURE 19–2. The Major Human Resources Strategic Categories and the Business Life Cycle

Business Life Cycle

Human Resource Strategic Decision Category	Embryonic	Growth	Maturity	Decline
Selection, Promotion, and Placement	Recruit best technical/professional talent. Entrepreneurial style.	Recruit adequate mix of qualified workers. Management succession planning. Manage rapid internal labor market movements.	Encourage sufficient turnover to minimize layoffs and provide new openings. Encourage mobility as reorganizations shift jobs around.	Plan and implement work force reductions and reallocations. Transfers to different businesses. Early retirement.
Appraisal	Appraise milestones linked to plans for the business, flexible.	Linked to growth criteria, e.g., market share, volume unit cost reduction.	Evaluate efficiency and profit margin performance.	Evaluate cost savings.
Rewards	Salary plus large equity position.	Salary plus bonus for growth targets, plus equity for key people.	Incentive plan linked to efficiency and high-profit margins.	Incentive plan linked to cost savings.
Management Development	Minimum until a critical mass of people in business, then job related.	Good orientation programs for fast start-ups. Job skills. Middle-management development.	Emphasis on job training. Good supervisory and management development programs.	Career planning and support services for transferring people.
Labor/Employee Relations and Voice	Set basic employee relation philosophy and organization.	Maintain labor peace, employee motivation and morale.	Control labor costs and maintain labor peace. Improve productivity.	Improve productivity. Achieve flexibility in work rules. Negotiate job security and employment adjustment policies.

353

and the detection of the necessary activities to establish the kind of participatory environment needed for the success of the enterprise.

Besides the need for the five decision categories to be consistent with one another, the resulting human resources strategy has to be congruent with the corporate and business strategies it intends to support. A common way of recognizing this fact is to reflect on the necessary changes he made in the human resources strategy as a business travels through the various stages of its business life cycle. Figure 19–2 tries to capture how the management of human resources is modified through the four major life-cycle stages of embryonic, growth, maturity, and decline.

A Framework for Strategic Decision Making in Human Resources Management: An Illustration

We propose a simple conceptual framework to organize the thought process regarding strategic decision making for the management of key personnel. Using the five major categories of decisions linked to human resources management as the focus of primary attention, we suggest a three-step approach involving:

1. Diagnosis to characterize the state of present policies regarding the major strategic decision categories in human resources management, and to define the performance measurements to describe the existing quality of human resources management in the organization.
2. Profile of strategic choices to represent current policies and select the desired options to define the future policies of human resources management.
3. Definition of a strategic broad action program to specify the key tasks to he undertaken by the major strategic decision categories in human resources management.

We illustrate the framework with a hypothetical case adapted from a real application to a major firm.

DIAGNOSIS OF EXISTING HUMAN RESOURCES MANAGEMENT PRACTICES

We have found it useful to start the process of defining human resources strategies of key personnel by requesting the top management team to provide a brief description of the current policies by each of the five strategic decision categories. Also included should be an evaluation of their current strengths and weaknesses. Figure 19–3 summarizes the outcome of such a task. In spite of its brevity, the figure eloquently portrays the enormous complexity of human resources management. It is clear that this organization has a strong character

FIGURE 19–3. Diagnosis of Existing Human Resources Management Practices: An Illustration

Decision Category	Description of Policy	Strengths	Weaknesses
Selection, Promotion, and Placement	Strongly promote from within, and purely on merits. Heavy recruiting at entry level, through highly selected screening.	High retention rate. Thorough knowledge of business. Continuity with regard to customer. Development of strong culture.	Stagnation. Some lack of objectivity. Short-term focus on business goals conflict with human resource development needs.
Appraisal	Appraise individuals in a very objective manner using specific MBOs (for both officers and clerks). Narrative appraisal format vs. check-off list. Connection of appraisal directly to development needs via negotiated and signed commitments between supervisors.	Clarity and objectivity. No surprises. Benchmark oriented. Direct connection between weaknesses and development.	Too rigid goals. Not focused on coaching but appraisal. Friction. Overly competitive environment. Short-term orientation.
Rewards	Merits driven with differentiation based on performance ranking. MBO oriented.	Clarity. Bottom-line oriented. Motivates aggressive people. Discriminates outstanding, average, and below average performers.	Creates an elitist environment. Short-term oriented. Demotivates the average performer.
Development	To supply managers with both pragmatic and conceptual skills, to enable them to manage both people and businesses.	Evolution of a well-rounded manager. Development of a sense of ownership and professionalism.	Creation of conflict between financial goals and people development goals. Too many activities competing for people's time.
Labor/Employee Relations, Voice	The full and complete participation of all staff based upon the belief that those closest to the work and/or customer are best equipped to come out with the best solutions.	Obtain the best information. Create a sense of ownership down to the lowest levels. Reduction of cost and increase service.	Weakening the authority of the manager. Lengthening of the decision-making process.

and well-defined human resources policies, which result in impressive strengths; however, invariably the achievement of some strengths tends to generate a counterpart of weaknesses. The resulting trade-offs are hard to resolve, and often it is impossible to correct the weaknesses without losing substantial advantage .

It is also a helpful diagnostic instrument to measure the overall quality of human resources by a set of properly designed performance indicators. A set of such indicators and relevant measurements are presented in Figure 19–4. As it shows, some indicators are highly qualitative and need to be measured by personal communications. management by objectives, and different types of surveys. Altogether, they could give us a good description of the existing quality of human resources management, as well as providing goals for improving performance in that area.

PROFILE OF STRATEGIC CHOICES IN HUMAN RESOURCES MANAGEMENT

We have already discussed the available strategic choices in each of the major categories in human resources management. At this stage of the process, it is recommended to prepare a profile of those choices as illustrated in Figure 19–5. The case presented in the figure denotes an organization that tends to favor extreme positions: a pure-make strategy as far as selection, promotion, and placement; an appraisal system characterized by a purely result orientation, individual and cross-sectional performance; a reward system seeking internal consistency with compensation depending on performance; a management

FIGURE 19–4. Strategic Peformance Measurements for Human Resources Management

INDICATORS	ASSOCIATED MEASUREMENTS
Job Satisfaction	Personal communications Employees retention rate Continuous employee reaction survey (CERS)
Job Performance	Management by objectives (MBO)
Turnover	Statistics
Absenteeism	Statistics
Motivation	CERS Job diagnostic service (JDS)
Job Security	CERS
Career Projects	JDS
Psychological Stress	JDS
Safety/Health	JDS
Income	Comparison with external surveys

FIGURE 19–5. Profile of Strategic Choices Linked to Human Resources Management

Selection, Promotion, and Placement

Left	1	2	3	4	5	Right
Make	X					Buy
Little recruiting above entry level	X					Sophisticated recruiting at all levels
Selection based on weeding out undesirable employees					X	Careful initial screening

Appraisal

Left	1	2	3	4	5	Right
Process-oriented system					X	Result-oriented system
Identification of training needs	X					Identification of staffing needs
Individual performance evaluation	X					Corporate performance evaluation
Time-series comparisons					X	Cross-section comparisons

Rewards

Left	1	2	3	4	5	Right
Compensation depending on position in hierarchy					X	Compensation depending on performance
Internal consistency	X					External competitiveness
Total compensation driven by cash			X			Total compensation driven by noncash incentives

Management Development

Left	1	2	3	4	5	Right
Formal development programs	X					Informal development programs
Extensive development programs	X					Limited development programs
Skills building	X					Skills identification and acquisition

Labor-Employee Relations and Voice

Left	1	2	3	4	5	Right
Unionization					X	Nonunionization
Minimize power and influence of labor force			X			Share power and influence of labor force
Autocratic management systems				X		Participatory management systems
High user of employee-influence mechanisms			X			Low use of employee-influence mechanisms

development activity based on extensive and formal development programs aimed at skills building; and a labor/employee relation marked by strong nonunionization policies with an intermediate participatory climate. The overall pattern of decision tends to be quite consistent, and it also serves to reaffirm the recognition of strengths and weaknesses described in the previous step.

DEFINITION OF STRATEGIC BROAD ACTION PROGRAMS

Based on the information collected in the diagnostic stages and the profiling of the strategic choices previously performed, we can now establish long- and short-range objectives and broad action programs for each of the human resources strategic decision-making categories. This step is illustrated in Figure 19–6. The programs proposed in the figure are intended to correct the weaknesses uncovered in the diagnostic phase. Notice the overabundance of training and development activities to overcome limitations present in all the decision categories. This is not necessarily a general trend in human resources management, but it is one that is widely adopted by the institution in this case study.

Notes

1. For further references on the subject of human resources management, see Thomas A. Barocci and Thomas A. Kochan, *Human Resources Management and Industrial Relations* (Boston, MA: Little Brown and Company, 1985); Michael Beer, Bert Spector, Paul R. Lawrence, D. Quinn Mills, and Richard E. Walton, *Managing Human Assets* (New York: The Free Press, 1984); Robert Eccles, Nitin Nohria, and James Berkley, *Beyond the Hype: Rediscovering the Essence of Management,* (Boston, MA: Harvard Business School Press, 1992); Charles J. Fombrum. Noel M. Tichy, and Mary Ann Devanna, *Strategic Human Resources Management* (New York: John Wiley, 1984); Jay R. Galbraith, Edward E. Lawler, III & Associates, *Organizing for the Future: The New Logic for Managing Complex Organizations* (San Francisco: Jossey-Bass, 1993); Arnoldo C. Hax, "A New Competitive Weapon: The Human Resources Strategy," *Training and Development Journal,* 9, no. 5 (May 1985), 76–82; Jon Katzenbach and Douglas Smith, *The Wisdom of Teams: Creating the High-Performance Organization* (Boston, MA: Harvard Business School Press, 1993); Thomas Kochan and Michael Useem (eds.), *Transforming Organizations* (New York: Oxford University Press, 1992); John P. Kotter, *A Force for Change: How Leadership Differs from Management* (New York: Free Press, 1990); Edward E. Lawler III, *The Ultimate Advantage: Creating the High-Involvement Organization* (San Francisco, CA: Jossey-Bass, 1992); David Nadler, Marc Gerstein, Robert Shaw, and associates, *Organizational Architecture: Designs for Changing Organizations,* (San Francisco, CA: Jossey-Bass, 1992); Glenn M. Parker, *Team Players and Teamwork: The New Competitive Business Strategy* (San Francisco, CA: Jossey-Bass, 1990); Jeffrey Pfeffer, *Managing with Power* (Boston, MA: Harvard Business School Press, 1992); Edgar S. Schein, *Career Dynamics* (Part 3) (Reading, MA: Addison-Wesley, 1978), 189–256; Edgar Schein, *Organizational Culture and Leadership* (San Francisco, CA: Jossey-Bass, 1992); Peter Senge, *The Fifth Discipline: The Art and Practice of the Learning Organization* (New York: Doubleday, 1990).

2. Beer et al., *Managing Human Assets,* (1984), op. cit.

3. See Barocci and Kochan, *Human Resources Management and Industrial Relations,* (1984); Beer et al., *Managing Human Assets,* (1984); Fombrum et al., *Strategic Human Resources Management,* (1984), op. cit.

FIGURE 19–6. Definition of Broad-Action Programs for Each Strategic Decision-Making Category

Decision Category	Objectives		Broad Action Programs
	Long Range	Short Range	
Selection, Promotion, and Placement	Develop the present staff via cross-training and retraining to occupy future positions.	Development of individual manpower plan for all staff.	Manpower plan. Massive training. Analysis of future required skills. Management trainee program at entry level.
Appraisal	Change appraisal into a coaching system.	To make managers more comfortable with the appraisal system.	Performance appraisal career awareness workshop with joint participation of supervisors and subordinates. Corrective action workshop (how to deal with poor performance). Staff relations workshop. Development management skills workshop.
Rewards	To continue differentiating without alienating the average performer.	To reinforce the differentiation among performers.	Compensation workshop for supervisors, connecting appraisal and rewards. Ongoing coaching to managers by compensation unit of human resources. Quality service award. Trying smarter awards. Perfect attendance awards. Global account management/global account profitability awards. Bonus programs and stock options.
Development	To increase market share, service, quality, and productivity.	To prepare managers for the changing environment of the industry.	Executive development program. Management resource planning reviews at corporate level. Managing people series. Organizational growth project. Zero defect process.
Labor/Employee Relations, Voice	Nonunionization. Increase profits and market share.	Motivation of staff at all levels.	Weekly breakfast and lunch programs with staff and supervisors. Variety of formal communication programs at all levels with great frequency (all monitored and tracked).

20

Technology Strategy

Linking technology and business strategies is a demanding task that has central importance in strategy formation. Now that technology is a critical source to achieve and sustain competitive advantage, the ability to incorporate technology into a business strategy can make the difference between a winning or a losing strategic alternative. This chapter discusses a methodology that can be used to explore systematically the way to link business and technology strategies, and presents an application of the suggested methodology in a real-life setting.[1]

The role of technology has become so pervasive in the business world that it is appropriate to say there is hardly any significant industry that can be classified as low-tech. In fact, technological forces are restructuring industries and defining new ways to compete. Managers are confronted with the demanding task of accelerating the speed at which innovations in new products and processes are translated into profitable commercial ventures.

Though there are many studies that analyze the process and sources of innovation,[2] the disruptions introduced by new technologies,[3] the concept of core competencies,[4] the strategic management of technology,[5] or the human issues related to technology,[6] there is less documentation on how to develop a strategic plan that integrates technology into the business strategy of a firm. This paper suggests a methodology to accomplish this task. The methodology is consistent with the strategic planning framework proposed in Chapter 18, and is further illustrated by applying it to a start-up company in the massive parallel computer (MPC) industry. A brief description of the company, Masscalc, is provided in the Appendix to this chapter.[7]

A Framework for the Development of Technology Strategy

The formation of technology strategy takes place at all the key hierarchical levels of the firm: corporate, business, and functional. Figure 20–1 illustrates the primary tasks that we identify as relevant in the development of technology

FIGURE 20–1. A Framework for the Development of Technology Strategy

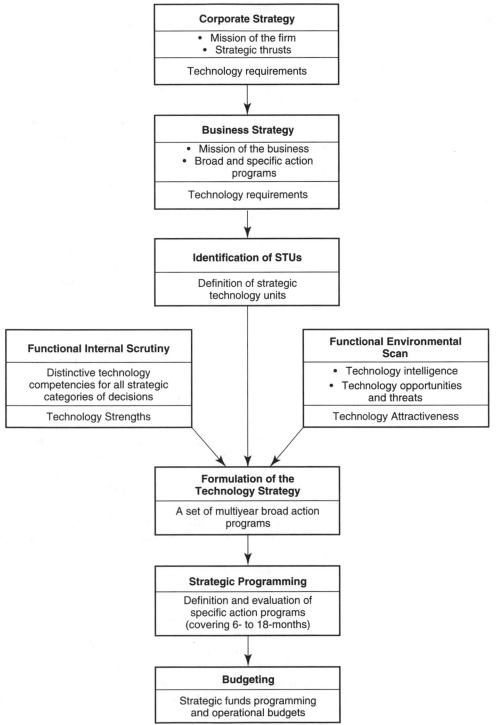

361

strategy. Notice that the only difference that exists between this framework and the one proposed in Figure 18–2 is that we have added here the identification of strategic technology units (STUs) as a task to be performed prior to the development of the environmental scan and the internal scrutiny.

First, top managers have to decide, as part of the corporate strategy of the firm, what role is to be played by technology in advancing the firm's competitive capabilities, the amount of resources to be allocated to technology, and the aggressiveness the firm will use in the innovative process and in imbedding technology into the firm's products and processes. Corporate attention is required since frequently a given technology is shared by several businesses and affects various managerial functions. Therefore, its strategic development cannot be totally decentralized at the business and functional levels. The elements of corporate strategy that communicate more pointedly to the technological requirements are the mission of the firm—particularly the statement of unique competencies—and the corporate strategic thrusts—an expression of the primary issues the firm has to address in order to establish a strong competitive position.

Next, technology strategies are formulated at the business level. During the process of business strategy formation we need to define the technological support required to create or reinforce the competitive advantage sustained by each business unit. This is supplied by the mission of the businesses and their respective strategic action programs. Obviously, a technology strategy cannot be created in isolation from the corporate objectives and the businesses it is intended to support.

Finally, at the technology level resides the task of interpreting all the requirements emerging from corporate and business levels, which will become the critical inputs for shaping the technology strategy of the firm. At this stage it is also necessary to identify the portfolio of specific technologies the firm will be using in supporting its business strategies. This leads to the definition of the strategic technology units (STUs), the central focus of attention in the development of technology strategy. The STU identifies the skills or disciplines that are applied to a particular product or process in order to gain technological advantage. The STUs should contain all the core technologies used now or needed in the future across the whole organization.

The STUs are critical to the execution of the technology environmental scan and internal scrutiny, the next tasks in the planning process. The environmental scan is aimed at obtaining an understanding of the key technology trends, assessing the attractiveness of each STU, and identifying technological opportunities and threats. This form of analysis we refer to as *technology intelligence*. Its purpose is to generate all the relevant information concerning the current and future state of development of the technology function. It is not only the existing managerial practice and state of technological progress that are important to detect. Even more critical is the recognition of future trends, state-of-the-art developments, and their embodiment in actions by competitors.

With regard to the internal scrutiny, besides the recognition of strengths and weaknesses associated with each STU, we need to determine the specific technological competencies we should build to gain competitive advantage. We conduct this analysis by examining the *strategic categories of decisions* linked to the technology function. A detailed listing of the decisions is given in Figure 18–8.

Finally, we have the remaining tasks of defining broad and specific action programs, and preparing budgets. These tasks represent the final output of the technology strategy formation process. They should respond to the corporate and business requirements as well as the challenges emerging from the environmental scan and internal scrutiny activities.

TECHNOLOGICAL REQUIREMENTS

As shown in Figure 20–1, the first step in developing the technology strategy is to derive a clear, unified statement of coherent strategic requirements that the company places over the technology function. The identification of these requirements helps to create a common understanding among top management of the horizontal nature of the technology function allowing them to identify and exploit potential synergy among distinct but related business units. More importantly, this step provides a mechanism that establishes an effective linkage between corporate, business, and technology strategies.

Figure 20–2 shows some of the technological requirements put onto Masscalc's technology function. Although we list those requirements by corporate and business strategies, this distinction is rather blurry in this case since Masscalc is, at this time, only in one business, the massive parallel computer (MPC) business.

FIGURE 20–2. Technology Requirements*

IMPLIED BY	TECHNOLOGICAL REQUIREMENTS
Corporate Strategy	• Acquire and develop those technologies and procedures required to ensure high quality and reliability in large scale production of existing Massive Parallel Computer (MPC) product line. (Period of accomplishment: 12 months) • Develop the technological capabilities needed to design and bring to the market a new generation of MPC. (Time period: 3 years) • Enhance existing product line with minor innovations every six months.
Business Strategy	• Reduce board and system manufacturing cost by 10% every six months by better use of available technologies. • Acquire technical capabilities (human and equipment) in the area of demonstration technologies to serve actual market needs. • Bring to the market high speed input/output and video devices in 9 months.

* This is a selected subset of technological requirements. In real applications the list should be collectively exhaustive.

THE DEFINITION OF STRATEGIC TECHNOLOGY UNITS (STUS)

The strategic technological units are a planning tool used to shape the strategic response to the aforementioned technological requirements. Thus, the proper selection of STUs is one of the most critical elements of the proposed methodology.

An STU refers to a discrete technology or group of technologies that are used by the company. The cluster of STUs should encompass any technology that has impact on the company's overall competitive position in the marketplace. To be effective, any STU should:

- Be broad enough not to leave out potential innovations, yet specific enough to allow a clear understanding of the technological position of the company.
- Have continuity, i.e., the STU will exist over a relatively long period of time in order to develop expertise and management control. This does not preclude the underlying product and process technologies included in a given STU from evolving through time.
- Be critical to the product or service. It is recognized as a potential source of competitive advantage.
- Require a set of distinctive technical capabilities. Each STU will represent a unique contribution.

FIGURE 20–3. Identification of All Relevant STUs to Support Competitive Advantage

1. **System architecture:** Technologies related to the definition of the basic architecture of the computer.
2. **Chip design and engineering:** Technologies related to chip design and manufacturing. It includes alternative technologies to the one used right now.
3. **Board and system design and engineering:** Board and system design and manufacturing.
4. **Support software:** Includes microcodes, compilers, and basic libraries.
5. **Application software:** Technologies to support companies that develop software to run in Masscalc machines.
6. **Management of information systems:** Information systems to support all activities of the company, including marketing, sales, and service.
7. **Process technologies:** Procurement and control of suppliers' production processes as well as in-house assembly.
8. **Testing technology:** Technologies used to test subassemblies and the whole system.
9. **Demonstration technologies:** Includes video and communications vehicles to help in preparing and delivering shows, demonstrations, etc.
10. **Peripherals:** Technologies required to design or subcontract the design of high-speed peripherals for visualization and image processing.
11. **Service:** Technologies and methodologies for delivering service to the computer industry (e.g., remote diagnosis, education of technicians, etc.)

Figure 20–3 shows the STUs identified at Masscalc. Note that some of the STUs cut across organization units (STUs 1 and 2 encompass activities of the R&D and the Engineering Divisions). Also, some of them do not relate directly to the core business, but have a strategic relevance in supporting the corporate and business strategies. This is the case of "demonstration technologies" or "service," two supporting technologies with an important strategic role in Masscalc.

ENVIRONMENTAL SCAN

Only a deep knowledge of the intrinsic characteristics of the technologies used by a firm can generate the high-quality strategic thinking required for the healthy, long-term development of technology-based competitive advantages. The objective of the environmental scan is to gain this knowledge and to derive from it the degree of attractiveness of each technology as well as the opportunities and threats that technology presents to the firm. This analysis is done based on the STUs previously identified.

Developing strategic advantages from technology requires recognizing the trends followed by each specific technology, deciding which innovations the firm is going to incorporate, and setting up the internal means to take advantage of those innovations.

An important first step to facilitate this task is to identify the potential *sources of innovation* for each STU. Eric von Hippel[2] has generated seminal work in this field. By conducting a large number of empirical studies, he has been able to pinpoint the sources of innovation in a large variety of industrial developments. The source of innovation varies greatly depending on whom is expected to receive the benefits from the innovation efforts. Primary sources are users, manufacturers, and suppliers. Of special interest is the ability to identify *lead users,* if they are relevant to the innovation process. Lead users combine two characteristics: they have a need which is in advance of the general market, and they expect high benefits from a solution to that need. Whenever lead users do exist, it is of paramount importance to follow their innovation progress closely since they could be ahead of the market in their innovation capabilities. Figure 20–4 shows the sources of innovation for each of the STUs of Masscalc.

The second task of the environmental scanning process is to assess the degree of attractiveness of each of the technologies the firm is using or is considering using in its products and processes. A technology with a high degree of attractiveness is one that, when applied, will enhance significantly the competitive position of the businesses it supports. To assess the attractiveness of the technologies, we have to define those factors, normally external to the firm, which allow us to analyze the impact of each technology. The factors that we have used in our case are illustrated in Figure 20–5, which shows the current and future profile for the STU number 3, board and systems design.

A similar assessment should be conducted for each of the STUs, leading toward a reflection of the overall opportunities and threats the portfolio of technologies presents to the firm.

FIGURE 20–4. Sources of Innovation by STU

STU	POTENTIAL SOURCE OF INNOVATION
1. Systems architecture	Competitors, universities
2. Chip design and engineering	Suppliers, competitors, and other computer companies
3. Board and system design and engineering	Suppliers, and electronic and computer companies
4. Support software	Lead users, suppliers, competitors
5. Application software	Lead users, suppliers, competitors
6. Management of information systems	Suppliers, industry in general
7. Process technologies	Suppliers and companies with analogous production processes
8. Testing technologies	Electronic companies and suppliers
9. Demonstration technologies	Lead users, competitors, and other computer companies
10. Peripherals	Lead users, and electronic and peripherals companies
11. Service	Lead users and competitors

INTERNAL SCRUTINY

The internal scrutiny process is a disciplined approach to assessing the technological strengths and weaknesses of the firm against its most relevant competitors. The process starts with the identification of the critical success factors associated with each STU. Those factors represent capabilities controllable by the firm in which it has to excel to achieve a competitive superiority in each STU. Once the factors are identified, we conduct a competitive profile, measuring the position of the firm now and in the future. In the internal scrutiny phase the future profile does not represent a trend forecast, as was done in the environmental scan, but a desirable position the firm would like to achieve against its leading competitors.

Figure 20–6 shows the analysis as performed on the STU 3 of Masscalc, the board and system design. Notice that there are two categories of evaluation factors: those that measure the technological capabilities of the firm (knowledge, equipment, patents, etc.) and those that measure its efficiency in embodying this knowledge into products and processes.

A second element of the technology internal scrutiny that we have found particularly useful is to analyze the strengths and weaknesses of the existing

FIGURE 20–5. Technology Attractiveness

| | | | | | | X: 1992 |
| | | | | | | O: 1994–95 |

STU 3: Board and system design

FACTORS	=	–	E	+	++	COMMENTS
Potential for enhancing competitive advantage in						Most of the innovations are incremental, so a small group of people can keep up with them
• products				XO		
• process				XO		
Rate of technological change			O	X		
Potential for long-term value added			XO			
Impact on:						It is a key technology in terms of cost, performance, and quality.
• cost					XO	It drives most of the manufacturing
• performance					XO	and assembling processes and
• quality					XO	has strong implications in procurement
• differentiation			XO			
Impact on entry barriers			XO			The technology has a moderate impact on changing the industry
Impact on setting industry standards			XO			structure, the barriers to entry, and the industry standards.
Impact on improving industry			XO			

Key: = The STU is not relevant as a source of competitive advantage.
    – Potential for minor support.
    E Even—The STU supports average performance.
    + Potential for mild competitive advantage.
    ++ Potential for strong competitive advantage.

policies the firm follows in each of the critical categories of decision making. The taxonomy of decisions that are relevant to technology strategy was presented in Figure 18-8, and consists of seven key categories of decisions: technology intelligence; technology selection; timing of new technology introduction; modes of technology acquisition; technology horizontal strategy; project selection, evaluation, and resource allocation; and technology organization and managerial infrastructure.

Figure 20–7 shows the description of the policies adopted by Messcalc in each technology decision-making category and their corresponding strengths and weaknesses. The high degree of informality the firm has in its technology strategy emerges from these descriptions. This behavior is quite common in start-up entrepreneurial firms.

FIGURE 20–6. Technology Strength

						X: 1992 O: 1994–95
STU 3: Board and system design—Major Competitor ABC						
FACTORS	=	–	E	+	++	**COMMENTS**
Technology Capabilities						Masscalc has low level of human resources in this area. Its
Human resources		X		O		intentions are to change that due
Equipment and laboratories		X		O		to the technology importance in
Access to external sources			XO			cost reduction and reliability of
Recent patents			O	X		the final product.
Technology Embodiment						The company is selecting technologies that do not optimize cost and that increase risk,
Cost reduction in design		X		O		focusing only on higher performance,
Effective use of manufacturing standards			X	O		contrary to the business strategic focus.
Procurement eagerness		X				
Quality of product			XO			

Key: = The STU is not relevant as a source of competitive advantage.
  – Potential for minor support.
  E Even—The STU supports average performance.
  + Potential for mild competitive advantage.
  ++ Potential for strong competitive advantage.

THE TECHNOLOGY-ATTRACTIVENESS/ TECHNOLOGY-STRENGTH PORTFOLIO MATRIX

Portfolio matrices have been used for over twenty years in American industry.[8] The concept of business portfolio matrices can be extended easily to address the strength of the overall portfolio of technologies available to the firm. The technology portfolio matrix graphically displays all of the STUs of the firm according to two dimensions: technology attractiveness and technology strength. These two dimensions were already assessed in our study on the environmental scan and internal scrutiny processes, respectively. Recall that Figure 20–5 illustrated how to evaluate current and future attractiveness of STU 3, board and system design; while Figure 20–6 showed how to specify the current and future strengths of that same STU. Those tables evaluated attractiveness and strength through the use of several relevant factors. It is now required, either subjectively or by assigning different weights to each factor, to translate these multifactor profiles into a single measure of technology attractiveness and strength.

Figure 20–8 shows the technology portfolio matrix for Masscalc. The circles identify the existing position of each STU, the dots the future position. Ideally we would like to have all the STUs in the high-attractiveness, high-strength cell of the matrix, such as STU 1. What is critical is to reflect on the competitive moves that have to be made in order to gain competitive strength

FIGURE 20–7. Characterization of Present Technology Policies Regarding the Major Categories of Decision Making

Decision Category	Description of Policy	Strengths	Weaknesses
Technology intelligence	There is no action plan to capture external innovations nor any measure of how much information is coming in and how it is disseminated through the company.	The informal policy may be very adequate now that the company is small.	It is very dangerous because many important innovations, requirements, or problems with the product will probably not be captured on time.
Technology selection	With the exception of STUs 1 and 2, technologies are selected without consideration of the business mission.	None.	Cost ineffective. May endanger some of the key business objectives.
Timing of new technology introduction	Incorporate advanced versions of the technology once less sophisticated, safer ones are already in the product.	Low technological risk. Leverage of experience.	By not defining the policy in terms of STUs and its support to the business, there is a risk of missing the right time for technology introduction.
Modes of technology acquisition	Basically internal, with very few exceptions.	Easier coordination of proper development and use of technologies	Suboptimization of resources. Very unlikely to be able to excel in all areas.
Technology horizontal strategy	Relies basically on informal communications.	Better disposition to share technology.	Requires a strong culture to maintain this approach as the company grows.
Project selection, evaluation, and resource allocation	Projects selected based on market inputs.	Supports the company market driven approach.	Potential for losing long term innovations.
Technology organizational and managerial infrastructure	Most of the responsibilities for long and short term rely on the same people.	Gives control over what is going on, and facilitates coordination of previous policies.	May generate large decision problems as the company and the breadth of products grow.

369

FIGURE 20–8.   Technology Portfolio Matrix

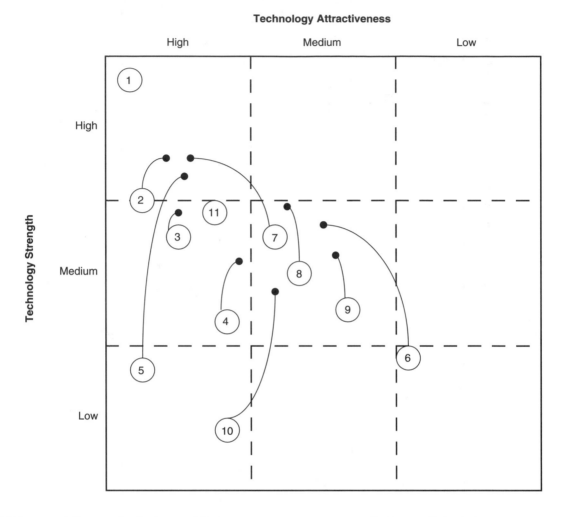

STU Representation: 1. Systems architecture   7. Process technologies
                       2. Chip design and engineering   8. Testing technologies
                       3. Board and system design and engineering   9. Demonstration technologies
                       4. Support software   10. Peripherals
                       5. Application software   11. Service
                       6. Management of information systems

in highly attractive STUs such as 2, 11, 3, 4, 5, and 10. The amount of effort and resources to be allocated to each STU depends both on our ability to gain competitive advantage, and the projection of future attractiveness of a given STU. In our example, STU 6 seems to be in a very precarious current position, but since its attractiveness is projected to be improved significantly, it makes sense to intend to raise the firm's competitive strength in it.

It is important to separate the current portfolio representation from its future projection. The current position should be the result of an objective, factual diagnosis of existing technology attractiveness and the firm's technological competencies. The future is more speculative, and needs to be critically examined in terms of the degree of confidence in the future technological trends, and the firm's capacity to improve its competitive standing. We have found the technology portfolio matrix to be a powerful diagnostic tool.

FORMULATION OF STRATEGIC ACTION PROGRAMS AND BUDGETS

Having identified the technological requirements generated from corporate and business strategies, and completed the environmental scan and internal scrutiny processes, we are ready to address the last stage of technology strategy formation: the development of broad and specific action programs, as well as the budgets, which translate into financial terms the strategic and operational commitments implicit in the technology decisions.

To be consistent with the framework we propose, the strategic action programs should:

- Respond to the technological requirements emanating from corporate and business strategies.
- Seize the opportunities and neutralize the threats identified in the environmental scanning process.
- Reinforce the strengths and eliminate the weaknesses detected in the internal scrutiny process.
- Address all the issues linked to the strengthening of the portfolio of technologies of the firm.

Figure 20–9 provides a rather incomplete representation of the technology broad action programs of Masscalc. In a real-life situation, a higher degree of specification and comprehensiveness will be required.

TECHNOLOGY POLICIES

When the strategic analysis uncovers some serious deficiencies in the technology policies of the firm, it might be necessary to reevaluate them. Technology policies tend to be broad guidelines that define the scope in which technology decisions are to be made. These policies have some inherent stability and, therefore, are not supposed to be redefined at the end of every planning cycle. In the case of Masscalc, managers opted for issuing a simple statement of technology policies that group the seven categories of decision making we used for policy evaluation under three headings: *innovation policies,* including technology intelligence, technology selection, timing of new technology introduction, and modes of technology acquisition; *technology dissemination and resource allocation,* including technology horizontal strategy, and project selection, evaluation, resource allocation, and control; and *technology organization and managerial infrastructure.* Figure 20–10 describes Masscalc's technology policy statement.

FIGURE 20–9. Technology Broad Action Programs

Action Program	Responds To*	1st Milestone
Define the specific needs of people in engineering and procurement for complying with short product cycles and incremental innovations.	TR, IS	June 1992: the specification of needs.
Define the specific technologies to be used in board design according to the established innovation policies.	TR, ES	September 1992: critical analysis of available technologies rated by cost, performance, and riskiness.
Develop and launch a program to acquire the next generation of board design and manufacturing techniques with special focus on cost reduction and quality.	ES, TR	September 1992: critical analysis of new developing technologies.
Create a unit fully responsible for board design and manufacturing.	IS	December 1992: description of needs to be covered by this unit and means needed to achieve it.
Set up review meetings for chip and architectural design each six months. The purpose of these review meetings should be to track and evaluate external upcoming innovations.	IS	First review meeting in September 1992.
Introduce demonstration technologies in accordance with technology policies and marketing requirements.	TR, IS	In two months there should be a specification of what the company needs in the near future and which companies can provide the service.
Establish a program to develop a new generation of chip and architecture within three years.	IS	Define project by June 1992.

*   This column identifies the appropriate state of the technology planning process a particular action program is responding to, according to the following convention:
TR = Technology requirements generated by corporate or business strategies
ES = Environmental scanning process
IS = Internal scrutiny process.

FIGURE 20–10. Technology Policies

INNOVATION POLICIES

- Be leaders in introducing incremental concepts in system architecture and chip design.

- Be followers in major innovations in chip manufacturing and board design and manufacturing technologies.

- Select those technologies that lead the company toward standards, mainly in those technologies that are not the core of the business.

- Select standard hardware and software available in the market or that can be designed and manufactured outside without interfering with company's proprietary knowledge.

- Acquire from outside all the support software that is not crucial for the proprietary technology or expertise of the company.

- With regard to demonstration technologies and other non-crucial activities, look for an agreement with some external company and an internal coordinator.

TECHNOLOGY DISSEMINATION AND RESOURCE ALLOCATION

- Set a program for temporal rotation of people. It should include:

  - Interchange between people at R&D center and engineering.

  - People working at the R&D center should be allocated one month every three years as marketing support personnel, in a rotational basis.

- Maintain policies regarding resource allocation.

TECHNOLOGY ORGANIZATION AND MANAGERIAL INFRASTRUCTURE

- Establish a program for evaluation of new changes in current designs, to ensure that each new innovation included is appropriate in terms of factors such as market needs, cost reduction, better service to either final customer or software companies, etc. Establish priorities among these factors.

- The R&D organization will be under the Engineering and Manufacturing department. But, R&D will be seated at all the top-management committees to ensure that its long term objectives are pursued.

- Lower the organizational level at which technological decisions are made.

- Set up, within the evaluation program, an analysis of technological decisions made and its agreement with satisfaction of technological requirements and technology policies.

Appendix:
Masscalc—A High-Performance Computer Company

The company that is used to illustrate the application of the methodology recommended to link technology and strategy is briefly described in this appendix. In order to protect the confidential nature of the strategic audit we conducted, we have slightly modified its content and used the fictitious name

Masscalc. High-performance computers are devoted to applications that require very large computing capabilities. The whole size of the high performance computers market accounted in 1990 for $10 billion and is growing at 20 percent. There are about twenty companies that serve most of the world market. The technological environment of the industry is very volatile, with incremental innovations being announced every few months. Also, the cycle of major innovations in the technologies used is short, requiring a sustained effort to improve actual models while working in the development of the technology of the next series of products.

Massive parallel computers (MPC) are a new family of high performance computers representing one of the most recent and significant technological breakthroughs of the industry. Most of the companies manufacturing MPCs are new companies, and none of them sell any other type of computers. Nowadays, MPCs compete in the market arena with two much more mature technologies (supercomputers and array processors), and though MPCs still account for a very small share of the market, most experts predict a very impressive market share increase.

Masscalc is a start up company committed to designing, producing, and selling MPCs. Its primary target is to provide computers to support the production rather than the R&D function of its customers, as most high-performance computer companies do. Masscalc's challenge is to be able to produce large volumes of MPCs that are affordable, user friendly, and able to operate with commercially available software. This will transform the company from a design-focused organization into a massive producer of MPCs.

At the time of this study, Masscalc had successfully introduced its first model, which received an excellent review by the industry experts. All the computer parts were subcontracted and manually assembled in-house. A well-conceived and well-implemented technology strategy is critical to Masscalc's success.

Notes

1. The presentation follows Arnoldo Hax and Manuel No, "Linking Technology and Business Strategy: A Methodological Approach and an Illustration," in Rakesh K. Sarin (ed.), *Perspectives in Operations Management: Essays in Honor of Elwood S. Buffa* (Boston, MA: Kluwer Academic Publishers, 1993), 133–155.

2. Eric von Hippel, *The Sources of Innovation* (New York: Oxford University Press, 1988).

3. W. J. Abernathy and J.M. Utterback, "Patterns of Industrial Innovation," *Technology Review*, 80, no. 7 (1978), 40–47; J.M. Utterback and L. Kim, "Invasion of an Estab-lished Business by Radical Innovation," Proceedings from *The Management of Productivity and Technology in Manufacturing*, 113–151, edited by P. R. Kleindorfer (New York: Plenum Press, 1986); P. Anderson and M. L. Tushman, "Technological Discontinuities and Dominant Designs: A Cyclical Model of Technology Change," *Administrative Science Quarterly*, 35, (1990) 604-633.

4. C. K. Prahalad and G. Hamel, "The Core Competence of the Corporation," *Harvard Business Review*, 90, no. 3, (1990), 79–91.

5. C. K. Prahalad, and G. Hamel, "The Core Competence of the Corporation," *Harvard*

Business Review, 90, no. 3 (1990), 79–91; B. L. White, *The Technology Assessment Process. A Strategic Framework for Managing Technical Innovation* (Westport, CT: Quorum Books, 1988).

6. U. E. Gattiker, and L. Larwood, *Managing Technological Development: Strategic and Human Resources Issues* (Hawthorne, NY: Walter de Gruyter, 1988); B. Twiss and M. Goodridge, *Managing Technology for Competitive Advantage: Integrating Technological and Organizational Development: From Strategy to Action* (Aulander, NC: Pitman, 1989).

7. For a more detailed account of this case the reader is referred to Manuel No, "Developing a Methodology for Technology Strategy: An Application in the High Technology Industry," unpublished masters thesis, Sloan School of Management, MIT, (1991).

8. In Chapter 17 we provide a brief review of the most important portfolio business matrices. For a more detailed discussion, see Chapters 7 through 10 in A. C. Hax and N. S. Majluf, *Strategic Management: An Integrative Perspective* (Englewood Cliffs, NJ: Prentice Hall, 1984).

CHAPTER 21

Manufacturing Strategy

This chapter provides another example of the development of a functional strategy using manufacturing as the illustrative case.[1]

For most industrial companies, the manufacturing operation is the largest, the most complex, and the most difficult-to-manage component of the firm. The formation of a comprehensive manufacturing strategy affects, and is affected by, many organizational groups inside and outside the firm. These are mainly business units, other functions, competitors, and the various external markets represented in Figure 21–1. It can be observed that in developing the strategy, manufacturing has to interact with all the remaining managerial functions of the firm: finance, marketing, technology, human resources management, and procurement. Cooperation and consistency of overall objectives is the key to success in these interactions. Also, the definition of the manufacturing strategy must be based on careful monitoring by manufacturing specialists of the firm's basic external markets, along with the other functional groups. For example, manufacturing managers, in conjunction with the technology group, may monitor developments in the electronics industry to be aware of new applications to process technology. Similarly, manufacturing, in conjunction with marketing, monitors the product markets in which they compete to maintain alertness with regard to their competitors' improvements and new product introductions.

Manufacturing Strategic Performance Measures

Normally, manufacturing objectives are expressed in terms of the four major dimensions of performance measurement used in formulating manufacturing strategy: cost, quality, delivery, and flexibility. Important trade-offs must be

FIGURE 21–1. Interaction of Manufacturing with Basic External Markets Through the Mediation of Other Functions

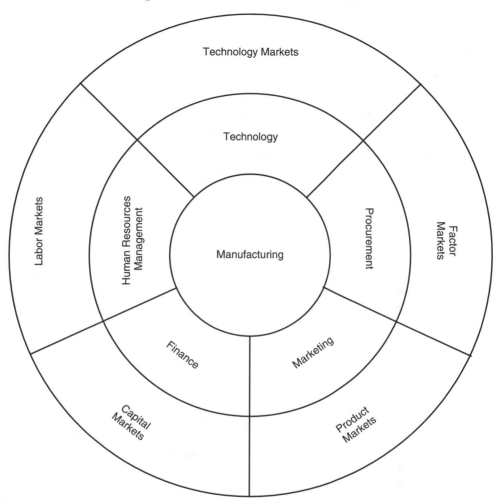

made among these objectives; it is impossible to excel in all of them simultaneously. Defining the central manufacturing competitive thrusts, the tasks to accomplish these goals, and a performance measurement system are central to designing manufacturing strategy.[2]

Cost objectives are frequently measured using labor, materials, and capital productivity, inventory turnover, and unit costs. *Quality* measures include percent defective or rejected, the frequency of failure in the field, cost of quality, and mean time between failures. To measure *delivery* performance, percentage of on-time shipments, average delay, and expediting response time may he used. *Flexibility* may be measured with respect to product mix, volume, and lead time for new products. Matching performance measures to corporate and business objectives can be difficult because changes in short-term operating policies often have uncertain long-term effects.

Strategic Decision Categories in Manufacturing

A manufacturing strategy must be comprehensive, but at the same time the complex web of decisions required must be broken down into analyzable pieces. We use nine strategic decision categories: facilities, capacity, vertical integration, process technologies, product scope and introduction of new products, human resources, quality management, manufacturing organization and managerial infrastructure, and supplier relations. This is shown in Figure 21–2. The outer ring displays the basic strategic manufacturing decision categories. The figure further suggests which other functional departments in the firm are the main contributors in each decision category. For instance, manufacturing has to interact with both marketing and sales, and finance in making capacity decisions. However, in human resources decisions, it is enough for manufacturing to interact solely with personnel. Vertical integration deals with make-versus-buy decisions and, therefore, requires a joint manufacturing and procurement involvement.

We now comment on the nine categories of strategic decisions.

Facilities

Facilities decisions are classic, long-term, "cast-in-concrete" manufacturing decisions. A key step in devising policies for a multifacility organization is choosing how to specialize or focus each facility.[3] Facilities may be focused by geography, product group, process type, volume, or stage in the product life cycle.

In any industry, decisions on the focus of facilities usually depend on the economics of production and distribution. For example, because of the economies of scale in refining and the high cost of transportation, oil companies tend to locate process-focused plants near crude oil sources (oil wells or ports). Consumer-product companies have large, centralized plants where they can achieve significant economies of scale in manufacturing and delivery time is not critical (for example, nonperishable food manufacturers). Firms have small plants focused on a product or location if scale economies are not significant or proximity to the customers is important (for example, furniture manufacturers). Firms in rapidly changing industries, such as semiconductor firms, often focus plants by stages in the product life cycle. They may have low-volume, high-flexibility facilities for manufacturing prototypes and high-volume, dedicated plants for maturing products in high demand.

Developing a well-thought-out strategy for facility focus automatically guides the firm in determining the size, location, and capabilities of each facility.

FIGURE 21–2. Major Categories of Strategic Decisions Linked to Manufacturing and Their Relationship with Basic External Markets

Capacity

Capacity decisions are highly interconnected with facility decisions. Capacity is determined by the plant, equipment, and human capital of the firm. Important decisions include how to deal with cyclical demand (for example, by holding "excess" capacity, by holding seasonal inventories, by peak-load pricing, or by subcontracting); whether to add capacity in anticipation of future demand (aggressive, flexible approach) or in response to existing demand (conservative, low-cost approach); and how to use capacity decisions to affect the capacity decisions of competitors.

Vertical Integration

Operations managers are directly affected by decisions to integrate vertically because they are responsible for coordinating the larger and more complex system that usually results. Such decisions involve replacing a market mechanism, over which the operations managers have limited control, with an internal mechanism, which is their sole responsibility. Before making such a decision, a firm must be sure that it can design and control an internal mechanism that will be more efficient than the market it replaces.

Important issues related to vertical integration include the cost of the business to be acquired or entered, the degree of supplier reliability, whether the product or process to be brought in house is proprietary to the firm, and the transaction costs of contracting through a market, compared to nonmarket, mechanism.[4] Other important issues are the impact of integration on the risk, product quality, cost structure, and degree of focus of the firm.

Legal ownership of the series of productive processes may not itself produce the benefits of integration. Toyota Motor Company in Japan plays a large role in directing the operations of its legally independent suppliers. Toyota benefits from lower transaction costs because they coordinate the production of independently owned suppliers with the just-in-time system. The success of this system points out that the crucial element for success of integrated operations is not *ownership* but *management and coordination* of the series of processes.

Process Technologies

The traditional approach has been to choose among the principal generic process types (project, job shop, batch, assembly line, continuous flow) by matching product characteristics with process characteristics.[5] Although crude, this framework is quite useful for conceptualizing important trade-offs in process choice. Compared to assembly lines, job shops use more general purpose machines and more highly skilled labor, provide more product flexibility, and yield higher unit production costs.

Recent innovations in computer-aided design (CAD), computer-aided manufacturing (CAM), robotics, and flexible manufacturing systems have made decisions on technology more complex. New, highly automated factories can be extremely expensive. In many cases, such advanced technology can drastically change the manufacturing cost structure, capital intensity, unskilled labor usage, and ability to deliver high-quality products rapidly at low cost.

Many firms decide to invest in these new technologies because they believe their survival depends on it. Traditional financial and accounting evaluation tools are often unable to capture all of the benefits that can be derived from these systems. Therefore, thorough strategic analysis is necessary in order to properly evaluate them.

Product Scope and Introduction of New Products

The degree of difficulty of the manufacturing management task is strongly influenced by the range of products and processes, and the rate of new product introductions. In well-run organizations, manufacturing management has signficant input into decisions about product scope and new products. Firms with rapid and frequent product introductions or broad product lines must design flexible, responsive, efficient manufacturing organizations.Product designers must understand what demands product design will place on manufacturing. Design, marketing, and manufacturing must be in close communication to prevent excessive diversification and lack of focus in the products manufactured in a given plant.

Human Resources Management

The principal issues in human resources management are selection, promotion, and placement of personnel, appraisal of employee performance, rewards and motivational support, management development, and employee relations. Human resources managers must design policies to motivate employees to work as a team to achieve the firm's goals.[6]

Designing such policies can be quite complex. For example, a firm must decide whether to compensate its people as a function of hours worked, quantity or quality of output, seniority, skill levels, effort expended, or loyalty. Asymmetries in information about skill levels or effort levels complicate the matter because the firm can base compensation only on observable measures. Aside from pecuniary compensation, employees are often rewarded with perquisites (such as cars or loans), training (human capital investments by the firm), employment guarantee, recognition for achievement, promotions to better jobs, and so forth. A well-thought-out incentive system will combine these elements to promote quality, efficiency, and employee satisfaction.

Quality Management

Managing quality improvement is a crucial and extremely challenging task in most U.S. firms today. A strategy for quality improvement requires zealous support from top management, a well-articulated philosophy, and concrete objectives. It must specify how responsibilities are to be allocated, what decision tools and measurement systems are to be used, and what training programs will be instituted. To be successful, a quality improvement program must be a permanent and ongoing process applied throughout the organization, and its chief objective must be the constant quest for improvement.

Quality can be categorized as design quality and conformance quality. Although manufacturing managers should be somewhat involved with design quality (especially regarding manufacturability), their most crucial role is with conformance quality.

Three important issues related to conformance quality are quality measurement, economic justification of quality improvements, and allocation of responsibility for quality. The principal tool of quality measurement is statistical quality control.

Economic justification of quality improvements is difficult and controversial. Cost of quality accounting (COQ), the only economic tool widely used to evaluate quality projects and programs, has two severe drawbacks. First, COQ ignores revenue effects of quality such as market-share benefits and price premiums for high-quality products. Second, it emphasizes short-term cost effects without considering long-term consequences. A system that measures the revenue effects of quality as well as the cost effects is needed for sound decision making. We know of no instances where measurement of the revenue effects of conformance quality has been attempted.

Responsibility for product quality has traditionally resided in the quality assurance or quality control unit in the firm. Recently, the viewpoint has been advanced that each worker should be responsible for the quality of his or her work. Implementing this proposal would require a significant change in many companies where hourly workers are not expected to exercise judgment. Where implemented successfully, this corporate cultural regime has proven to be very efficient.[7]

Manufacturing Organization and Managerial Infrastructure

A solid organizational infrastructure is essential to support decision making and implementation and requires planning and control systems, operating policies, and well-understood lines of authority and responsibility. A corporate culture that reinforces the manufacturing strategy is also crucial.

Manufacturing management must also make decisions on materials management, production planning, scheduling, and control. In managing materials, firms should consider the relative merits of classical production and inventory systems, materials requirements planning (MRP), and just-in-time (JIT) systems.

Production planning and scheduling decisions are typically thought of as tactical rather than strategic. However, aggregate production planning and delivery system design include strategic considerations. In aggregate planning, the firm must decide how to match productive capacity to variable demand over the medium-term planning horizon (12 to 18 months). The choices are usually to hire or lay off workers, schedule overtime or undertime, increase or reduce the number of work shifts, or build up or run down seasonal inventories.

In designing the delivery system, the principal decision is whether the system should produce to stock or to order. In a make-to-order shop where flexibility is crucial, scheduling is difficult, but the system responds readily to varying customer requirements. Make-to-stock shops are generally "under the gun" less often because they have finished goods inventories to buffer the production operation from customer demand; however, they have significant holding costs. In many machine shops, where the number of possible products is extremely high, a make-to-stock system is not feasible.

Supplier Relations

There are two popular but diametrically opposed views on purchasing and supplier-relations strategy: the competitive approach and the cooperative or

Japanese approach. The competitive approach recommends developing multiple sources for materials inputs, so that a number of firms compete to retain supply contracts. Buyer-supplier relationships resemble spot contracting more than long-term contracting because suppliers can be dropped on short, or no, notice. Tapered integration is recommended as an additional threat to take business away from errant suppliers. Tapered integration was used by some major automobile producers (such as General Motors and Ford). They used to produce some components in house and purchase the rest; this making a threat of backward integration credible and also giving them detailed knowledge of manufacturing costs. All contracts formally account for many contingencies. Dependence on a supplier is to be avoided.

The cooperative approach recommends developing long-term relationships based on mutual dependence and trust. Suppliers are given advice and training if their performance is unsatisfactory. Contracts are informal and contingencies are dealt with as they occur. Single sourcing is common.

The contrast between these two views is quite sharp. The prevailing trend in the United States is to move towards the cooperative approach, establishing long-term relationships with a reduced number of suppliers.

Although we recognize that a methodology should be tailor-made to a given firm, we find enough common issues in the formulation of a manufacturing strategy to recommend the following useful general-purpose process to guide managerial thinking:

1. Provide a framework for strategic decision making in manufacturing.
2. Assure that business strategies and manufacturing strategy are linked.
3. Conduct an initial manufacturing strategic audit to detect strengths and weaknesses in the current manufacturing strategy by each decision category and to assess the relative standing of each product line against those of the most relevant competitors.
4. Address the issue of product grouping by positioning the product lines in the product or process life cycle and by assessing commonality of performance objectives and product family missions,
5. Examine the degree of focus existing at each plant or manufacturing unit.
6. Develop manufacturing strategies and suggest allocation of product lines to plants or manufacturing units.

We review now each step in the process, occasionally presenting the forms we use for reporting results. To illustrate the process, we describe an application of the methodology to Packard Electric, a component division of General Motors. We concentrate on Packard's wire and cable SBU, which has four plants: three located near division headquarters in Warren, Ohio, and one in Clinton, Mississippi. A vast majority of Packard's sales are to General Motors. Recently Packard has been pressured to reduce costs, improve quality, and improve product development.[8]

A FRAMEWORK FOR STRATEGIC DECISION MAKING IN MANUFACTURING

The framework we present in this chapter identifies the nine major categories of manufacturing strategic decision making just discussed and the four performance measures presented at the outset to address the objectives of the manufacturing strategy:

- Cost (unit cost, total cost, life-cycle cost)
- Delivery (percentage of on-time shipments, predictability of delivery dates, response time to demand changes)
- Quality (return rate, product reliability, cost and rate of field repairs, cost of quality)
- Flexibility (product substitutability, product options or variants, response to product or volume changes)

LINKING MANUFACTURING STRATEGY TO BUSINESS STRATEGIES

The strategic planning process is hierarchical. First, the corporate level articulates the vision of the firm and its strategic posture; next, the business managers develop business strategies in consonance with the corporate thrusts and challenges; and, finally, the functional managers provide the necessary functional strategic support.

It is important, therefore, to assure that the business strategies and the resulting manufacturing strategy are properly linked. To accomplish this, we start by identifying the manufacturing requirements imposed by the broad action programs of each strategic business unit (SBU). Figure 21–3 shows the requirements placed on manufacturing by the wire and cable businesss unit's broad action programs at Packard Electric Division of General Motors. Out of all the action programs that are part of the wire and cable business strategy, we have identified the three that involve the manufacturing function. For these three programs, we have identified more specifically the manufacturing requirements.

Occasionally, business and manufacturing managers may disagree as to the effectiveness or feasibility of some of these manufacturing requirements. If they cannot agree through direct negotiation on some issues, those issues may be referred to higher levels of the organization for resolution.

INITIAL MANUFACTURING STRATEGIC AUDIT

Early in the planning process, a strategic audit should be performed on the current manufacturing strategy. Although later analysis provides a more thorough diagnosis, it is useful at the outset to extract the participating managers' feelings about the status of their manufacturing function.

FIGURE 21–3. Linking Manufacturing Strategy to Business Strategy

SMU Wire and Cable SBU, Packard Electric

SBU	Broad Action Programs	Manufacturing Requirements
Wire and Cable	Identify GM requirements not being supplied	Assure capacity and technology for new demand
	Study impact of silicon chips on cable substitution	Plan for eventual electronics changeover
	Design packaging for new customers	Develop new packaging capability

This initial audit has two objectives: to assess the strengths and weaknesses of existing policies in each of the nine manufacturing categories, and to establish the competitive standing of each major product line according to the four measures of manufacturing performance. Figure 21–4 presents an analysis of existing manufacturing policies at the wire and cable business unit of Packard Electric. The major policies pertaining to each manufacturing strategic decision category are broadly described, and the corresponding strengths and weaknesses compared with those of the leading competitor are assessed. Figure 21–5 provides an evaluation of the relative importance and performance of the product lines of the wire and cable business unit of Packard Electric.

ADDRESSING THE ISSUE OF PRODUCT GROUPING

One of the most difficult problems in manufacturing planning revolves around the product grouping. Even in small firms, manufactured items proliferate. Since it is impossible to deal with each item separately, they must be aggregated into sensible product groups sharing common attributes.

Two analytical devices are helpful. The first is the product-process life cycle matrix.[9] This matrix positions each product line in a two-dimensional grid (Figure 21–6). The horizontal axis represents the stages in the product life cycle, which has long been recognized as a valuable tool for analyzing the dynamic evolution of products and industries. This evolution is a four-phase process initiated by low-volume, one-of-a-kind products and culminating in highly standardized commodity products. Similarly, the vertical axis captures the production processes, which evolve from highly flexible but costly job-shop processes to special-purpose, highly automated manufacturing processes.

The matrix captures the interaction between product and process life cycles. For our analysis it provides two useful insights. First, it can show which of the firm's product lines are similarly positioned within their product-process cycles and are therefore candidates for homogeneous strategic groups. Second, and more important, it is useful for detecting the degree of congruency

FIGURE 21–4. Strategic Audit of Manufacturing: Assessment of Strengths and Weaknesses of Existing Policies in Each of the Nine Categories of Strategic Decision Making

SMU Wire and Cable SBU, Packard Electric

Decision Category	Description of Policy	Strengths	Weaknesses
Facilities	Process focus	Economies of scale	Long physical supply distances
Capacity	Use overtime, third shift, and inventories to respond to cyclicalities	Flexibility	Layoffs and overtime are costly
Vertical Integration	Significant backward integration—all the way to wire rod	Good control over cost and quality	Less focus, transfer complications
Process Technologies	Cable and copper in automated, continuous processes Printed circuits in job shop process	State-of-the-art in cable and copper	Automation in printed circuits could reduce costs
Product Scope and Introduction of New Products	Respond to GM in principal lines	Low risk	Reactive rather than anticipatory Focus concept ignored
Human Resources Management	Strong quality-of-work-life programs	Employee participation in decisions, good communications	Compensation system does not consider quality of output
Quality Management	Heavy use of statistical process Control and cost of quality tools	Integrated approach Top management support	Quality lags relative to Japanese competition
Manufacturing Organization and Managerial Infrastructure	Control system with short-term tactical orientation	Good control orientation	Short-sighted system
Supplier Relations	Cost-oriented competitive bidding Multiple sources	Keeps costs down	Hurts quality, and cooperative ventures

between a product structure and its "natural" process structure. The natural congruency exists when product lines fall in the diagonal of the product-process matrix. A product line outside the diagonal could either be explained by inadequate managerial attention or by concerted strategic actions seeking to depart from conventional competitive moves. Figure 21–7 provides a sharp description of the matching characteristics of product and process as they evolve from a "fluid" to a more "specific" state.

FIGURE 21–5. Strategic Audit of Manufacturing: Establishing the Competitive Standing of Each Product Line by Each of the Four Measures of Manufacturing Performance

SMU Wire and Cable SBU, Packard Electric

Product Line	External Performance Measures							
	Cost		Quality		Delivery		Flexibility	
	Importance	Performance	Importance	Performance	Importance	Performance	Importance	Performance
1. Cable	30	++	40	–	20	E	10	–
2. Printed Circuits	20	–	50	E	20	+	10	+
3. Copper	20	+	40	+	30	++	10	–

Special forms are used to collect data to establish product-line grouping by product and market characteristics, and to map these groupings onto the product-process life-cycle matrix. Figure 21–8 shows the assessment of the stage of the product life cycle for the product lines of the wire and cable business unit of Packard Electric. Breadth of product line, market volume, market growth rate, product standardization, and pace of product introduction are used to determine the product life-cycle stage of each product line. Figure 21-9 portrays the positioning of each product line of the wire and cable business unit of Packard Electric in the product-process life-cycle matrix. The location of copper rod manufacturing appears anomolous in this matrix because low-volume products are being manufactured on a continuous-flow process. Historically, this came about because the copper rod is produced in the cable factory, which has always been solely a continuous-flow operation.

Another way to arrive at product groupings is to identify families of product lines sharing similar competitive success requirements and product family missions. Carrying out this task after the product-process life-cycle matrix exercise tends to produce additional insights for grouping products.

ASSESSING THE DEGREE OF FOCUS AT EACH PLANT

Ever since Wickham Skinner wrote his classic paper on the focused factory, manufacturing managers in the United States have paid attention to this important but simple concept: A plant cannot do a large variety of very different tasks exceptionally well. A factory with a clear competitive objective that focuses on a narrow product mix for a well-defined market will outperform a conventional plant with an inconsistent set of manufacturing policies that attempts to do too many conflicting tasks.

FIGURE 21-6. The Product-Process Life-Cycle Matrix

PROCESS STRUCTURE PROCESS LIFE-CYCLE STAGE	PRODUCT STRUCTURE PRODUCT LIFE-CYCLE STAGE				Key management tasks:
	I LOW VOLUME-LOW STANDARDIZATION, ONE OF A KIND	II MULTIPLE PRODUCT, LOW VOLUME	III FEW MAJOR PRODUCTS, HIGHER VOLUME	IV HIGHER VOLUME-HIGH STANDARDIZATION, COMMODITY PRODUCTS	Flexibility-quality
I JUMBLED FLOW (Job Shop)					Fast reaction / Loading plant, estimating capacity / Estimating costs and delivery times / Breaking bottlenecks / Order tracking and expediting
II DISCONNECTED LINE FLOW (Batch)					Systematizing diverse elements / Developing standards and methods, improvement / Balancing process stages / Managing large, specialized, and complex operations
III CONNECTED LINE FLOW (Assembly Line)					Meeting material requirements / Running equipment at peak efficiency / Timing expansion and technological change / Raising required capital
IV CONTINUOUS FLOW				Dependability-cost	Dependability-cost
	Flexibility-quality			Dependability-cost	
Dominant competitive mode:	Custom design / General purpose / High margins	Custom design / Quality control / Service / High margins	Standardized design / Volume manufacturing / Finished goods inventory / Distribution / Backup suppliers	Vertical integration / Long runs / Specialized equipment and processes / Economies of scale / Standardized material	

NOTE: The margin of the matrix indicate the trade-offs to be made among the four external performance measurements (flexibility, quality, dependability, and cost), and the changing nature of the managerial tasks and competitive modes in different stages of the product-process life-cycle matrix.
SOURCE: Adapted and reprinted by permission of *Harvard Business Review*. An exhibit from, "Link Manufacturing Process and Product Life Cycles," by Robert H. Hayes and Steven C. Wheelwright, January-February 1979. Copyright © 1978 by the President and Fellows of Harvard College; all rights reserved.

FIGURE 21-7. The Relationship of Product Innovation and Production Process Characteristics

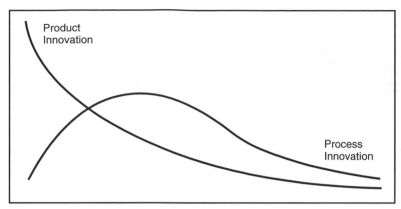

Fluid Pattern

Product Innovation
- Emphasis on maximizing product performance
- Stimulated by information on user needs
- Novelty of radicalness high
- Frequency of product innovation is rapid
- Predominant type is product rather than process

Production Process
- Flexible and inefficient
- Small size or scale
- General purpose equipment used
- Available materials used as inputs
- Product is frequently changed or custom designed

Transitional Pattern

Product Innovation
- Emphasis on product variation
- Increasingly stimulated by opportunities created through an expanding technical capability
- Predominant type is process required by rising volume
- Demands placed on suppliers for specialized components, materials and equipment

Production Process
- Some sub-processes are automated, creating "islands of automation"
- Production tasks and control become more specialized
- Process changes tend to be major and discontinuous, involving new methods of organization and changed product design
- At least one product design is stable enough to have significant production volume

Specific Pattern

Product Innovation
- Emphasizes cost reduction
- Predominant mode is incremental for product and process
- Effect is cumulative
- Novel or radical innovations occur infrequently and originate outside productive unit
- Stimulation arises from disruptive external forces

Production Process
- Efficient, system-like, capital-intensive
- Cost of change is high
- Scale and facility market share is large
- Special purpose process equipment used
- Specialized input materials or extensive vertical integration
- Products are commodity-like and largely undifferentiated

SOURCE: James Utterback, "Management of Technology," in *Studies in Operations Management* , edited by Arnoldo C. Hax (New York: North Holland Publishing, 1978).

FIGURE 21–8. Assessment of the Stage of Product Life Cycle

<u>**SMU** Wire and Cable SBU, Packard Electric</u>

Product Line	Product /Market Characteristics					Product Life-Cycle Stage*
	Breadth of Product	Market Volume Line	Market Growth	Product Standardization	Pace of Product Introduction	
1. Cable	High	High	Medium	Low	Medium	III
2. Copper Rod	Medium	Low	Medium	High	Low	I
3. Printed Circuits	Medium	High	High	Low	High	II

*Key: I: Low volume, low standardization, one of a kind
       II: Multiple products, low volume
       III: Few major products, higher volume
       IV: High volume, high standardization, commodity products

To detect the degree of focus at each plant of a firm, we once again use the product-process matrix. This time we prepare one matrix for each plant, positioning within the matrix every product line manufactured at that plant. The resulting plot allows us to judge the plant's degree of focus and to examine the degree of consistency between the products and the processes employed to manufacture them.

The final diagnosis can be summarized in a form such as that exhibited in Figure 21–10. This form is used to diagnose the degree of focus of each of the plants making the product lines of the wire and cable business unit of Packard Electric. Plant 10 is the most focused of the three plants. Plant 3 has the highest degree of diversity.

DEVELOPMENT OF MANUFACTURING STRATEGIES

After this analysis, the next step is to state strategic objectives to be articulated through broad action programs for each of the nine manufacturing strategic decision categories. Action programs may be targeted at one or more product groups. Figure 21–11 establishes the definition of broad action programs pertaining to the wire and cable business of Packard Electric for each manufacturing decision category. Each broad action program has to be more thoroughly defined by a set of specific action programs that can be monitored easily, and whose contributions are measurable. We spell out the specific action programs corresponding to the quality management decision category in Figure 21–12.

Finally, we consider the reallocation of products to plants, if the previous analysis of products and plants suggests such a change.

FIGURE 21–9. Positioning of Each Product Line in the Product-Process Life-Cycle Matrix

SMU Wire and Cable SBU, Packard Electric

PRODUCT STRUCTURE PRODUCT LIFE-CYCLE STAGE	I LOW VOLUME-LOW STANDARDIZATION, ONE OF A KIND	II MULTIPLE PRODUCT, LOW VOLUME	III FEW MAJOR PRODUCTS, HIGHER VOLUME	IV HIGHER VOLUME-HIGH STANDARDIZATION, COMMODITY PRODUCTS
PROCESS STRUCTURE PROCESS LIFE-CYCLE STAGE				
JOB SHOP		Printed Circuits		
BATCH				
ASSEMBLY LINE				
CONTINUOUS FLOW	Copper Rod		Cable	

CONCLUSION

The manufacturing function can be a formidable weapon to achieve competitive superiority. After painful experiences in a wide range of industries, most American managers today clearly understand this. We have attempted to provide a conceptual framework and a set of pragmatic guidelines for designing a manufacturing strategy.

We recognize that different companies will pursue different paths to manufacturing strategy design. However, we have tried to capture in the proposed framework and methodology the essential elements that must be considered by any firm attempting to design a manufacturing strategy.

FIGURE 21–10. Assessing the Degree of Focus at Each Plant

SMU Wire and Cable SBU, Packard Electric

Plant	Existing Lines Manufactured in Each Plant or Operating Unit	Strategy for Product Line	Stage of Product-Life Cycle	Process Technology Currently Used
10	Cable Copper rod	Grow with industry Grow with industry	Mature Mature	Continuous flow Continuous flow
22	Cable Metal stamping Molding	Grow with industry Hold position Hold position	Mature Aging Aging	Continuous flow Job shop Job shop
3	Printed circuits Plastic molding Ignition cable Neoprene	Up or out Hold position Improve position Find niche and protect	Embryonic Aging Mature Mature	Job shop Job shop Assembly line Job shop

FIGURE 21–11. Definition of Broad Action Programs

SMU Wire and Cable SBU, Packard Electric

| Decision Category | Objectives | | Broad Action Programs |
	Long Range	Short Range	
Facilities	Rationalize plant focus	Study focus issue	Consider separating stamping and molding options
Capacity	Respond better to fluctuations	Meet recent demand upturn	Design a model to simulate the impact of product substitution in cable capacity
Vertical integration	Integrate only when strategically justified	Standardize make-or-buy decision process	Reduce backward integration for increased flexibility
Process technologies	Maintain state-of-the-art	Install more automation	Increase automation where possible
Product scope and introduction of new products	Anticipate customer needs	Upgrade customer contact	Become involved in GM decision process
Human resources management	Utilize fully employee resources	Upgrade personnel function	Improve compensation system
Quality management	Institutionalize improvement	Improve training	Increase self-inspection by operators
Manufacturing organization and managerial infrastructure	Develop central system to support new automated manufacturing technologies	Improve performance measurement system	Design new performance measures
Supplier relations	Develop closer ties	Propose joint projects	Identify supplier candidates for joint projects

FIGURE 21–12. Definition of Specific Action Programs

Decision Category Quality Management   **SMU** Wire and Cable SBU, Packard Electric

Program Description	Priority	Cost	Manpower Requirements	Scheduled Completion	Responsibility
Improve quality training	A	$150K	2 man-yrs	August '86	Quality VP
Develop cost-of-quality system	B	$700K	10 man-yrs	1987	Controller and Quality VP
Implement experimental design concepts	C	$25K	1/2 man-yr	1986	SQC Experts and Design Engineers
Fit quality into incentive	B	$75K	1 man-yr	1986	Personnel and Quality VP

Categories as follows:
A = Absolute first priority: Postponement will significantly hurt our position.
B = Highly desirable: Postponement will adversely affect our position in the market.
C = Desirable: If funds were to be available to enhance our position.

Notes

1. The presentation follows Charles Fine and Arnoldo Hax, "Manufacturing Strategy: A Methodology and an Illustration," *Interfaces*, 15, no. 6 (November–December 1985), 28–46.

2. On manufacturing performance measures, see Steven C. Wheelwright, "Japan, Where Operations Really Are Strategic," *Harvard Business Review*, 59, no. 4 (July–August 1981), 67–74; and Robert H. Hayes, Steven C. Wheelwright, and Kim B. Clark, *Dynamic Manufacturing: Creating the Learning Organization* (New York: Free Press, 1988). On matching performance measures with business objectives, see Robert S. Kaplan, "Measuring Manufacturing Performance: A New Challenge for Managerial Accounting, Research," *The Accounting Review*, 58, no. 4 (October 1983), 686–705; and Robert S. Kaplan, *Measures for Manufacturing Excellence* (Boston, MA: Harvard Business School Press, 1990).

3. The concept of focused factory is a central one in facilities management. It was pioneered by Wickham Skinner, who first published it in his highly influential paper: "The Focused Factory," *Harvard Business Review*, 52, no. 3 (May–June 1974),

113–121. For a more complete reference, see: Wickham Skinner, *Manufacturing: The Formidable Competitive Weapon*, (New York: John Wiley & Sons, 1985).

4. Oliver E. Williamson has worked extensively on the costs and benefits of internalizing in the firm the transaction costs incurred by the operation of market mechanisms. See Oliver E. Williamson, *Market and Hierarchies* (New York: The Free Press, 1975), *Markets and Hierarchies: Analysis and Antitrust Implications* (New York: Free Press, 1975), and *The Economic Institutions of Capitalism* (New York: Free Press, 1985).

5. The framework for matching product and process characteristics has been proposed by among others, Paul W. Marshall, et al., *Operations Management: Text and Cases* (Homewood, IL: Richard D. Irwin, 1975); and Robert H. Hayes and Steven C. Wheelwright, "Link Manufacturing Process and Product Life Cycles," *Harvard Business Review*, 57, no. 2 (January–February 1979), 133–140.

6. We have dealt with the issue of human resources management in Chapters 18 and 19. See also Arnoldo C. Hax, "A New

Competitive Weapon: The Human Resource Strategy," *Training and Development Journal,* 39, no. 5 (May 1985), 76–82.

7. Further references on the important topic of quality management are: Bill Creech, *The Five Pillars of TQM: How to Make Total Quality Management Work for You* (New York: Truman Tulley Books, Dutton, 1994); W. Edwards Deming, *Out of the Crisis* (Cambridge, MA: MIT, Center for Advanced Engineering Studies, 1986); William E. Deming, *Quality, Productivity, and Competitive Position* (Cambridge, MA: MIT CAES, 1983); David A. Garvin, , *Managing Quality: The Strategic and Competitive Edge* (New York: The Free Press, 1988); Eugene L. Grant and Richard S. Leavenworth, *Statistical Quality Control* (New York: McGraw-Hill, 1980); Joseph M. Juran, *Juran on Quality by Design* (New York: The Free Press, 1992); Joseph M. Juran, ed., *Quality Control Handbook,* 3rd ed. (New York: McGraw-Hill, 1974); Joseph M. Juran and Frank M. Gryna, *Quality Planning and Analysis* (New York: McGraw-Hill, 1980); Richard J. Schonberger, *Japanese Manufacturing Techniques* (New York: The Free Press, 1982).

8. This illustration has been adapted from Luis A. Ortega, "Analysis of the Development of a Strategic Planning System," unpublished masters thesis, Sloan School of Management, MIT, (1985).

9. The product-process life-cycle matrix was originally proposed by Robert H. Hayes and Steven C. Wheelwright, "Link Manufacturing Process and Product Life Cycles," (1979), op cit.

Glossary

An *italicized term* in the glossary text has its own heading that can be referenced to get its precise definition.

Action programs. Action programs are well-defined activities that emanate from broader definitions of strategy (at business and functional levels). They correspond to a pragmatic expression of strategy. Action programs should respond to the desired changes in the mission, address properly the opportunities and threats revealed by the environmental scanning process, and reinforce the strengths as well as neutralize the weaknesses uncovered in the internal scrutiny. The action programs are defined at two different levels of specificity: broad action programs typically covering a multiyear planning horizon, normally understood to represent long-term strategic objectives; and specific action programs, covering six to eighteen months, which represent the necessary tactical support to realize strategic objectives.

Activity-based costing. A procedure to allocate overheads to the various outputs of the firm (e.g. products, services, projects, and the like) in a three-step process to avoid distortions induced by old practices. First, identification of the activities the firm is engaged in; second, the allocation of overhead to these activities; and third, the allocation of overheads to the final products and services generated by these activities. (The activities alluded to here can be identified and redefined by a *business process reengineering* effort.)

Administrative systems. (See *integration approaches.*)

Alternative Boston Consulting Group matrix. (See *portfolio matrices.*)

Appropriability. The ability to retain inside the firm the value created by a strategy that is both unique and sustainable. Value may be diverted to non-owners who might control complementary and specialized factors (*holdup*); or it may be dissipated by inefficiencies or the granting of unwarranted benefits (*slack*). (See *resource-based view of the firm.*)

Balance. The process of establishing congruency between the chosen organizational structure and the managerial processes that go with it: planning, management control, communication and information, and human resources management and reward systems. This process amounts to a search for a proper fit among all the formal-analytical managerial systems in the strategic management framework. The full-fledged operation of these systems provides a background of integrative relationships that the simple organizational structure fails to represent. Moreover, these systems must be designed both to reinforce the primary foci chosen by the organization, and to support those activities relegated to a secondary level in the definition of the organizational structure. (See *integration approaches.*)

Balanced scorecard. A comprehensive measure of business performance based on four basic dimensions:

1. The financial perspective, which responds to the question—"How do we look to our shareholders?"
2. The customer perspective—"How do our customers see us?"
3. The internal business perspective—"What should we excel at?"
4. The innovation and learning perspective—"Can we continue to improve and create value?"

Basic organizational structure. The basic structure represents the major segmentation of the businesses the firm is engaged in through a hierarchical order that reveals the priorities managers assign to the firm's central activities. The definition of a basic structure requires the full recognition of the businesses of the firm and their further segmentation into manageable units. Only the primary echelons of the organizational chart that are intimately linked to the strategic positioning of the firm are recognized in this definition.

Benchmarking. The comparison of selected performance measurements against some challenging yardsticks. These can be generated by internal-historical comparisons; by comparing ourselves against the key competitors in our industry or by measuring ourselves against the "best-in-class" performers in every functional activity.

Breadth of vertical integration. The breadth of vertical integration measures how broadly or narrowly the firm depends on its own internal sources for all of its important inputs and outputs. Breadth can be measured as the fraction of value provided by the internal inputs or outputs of the firm with regard to the total value of its internal and external transactions, for a given organizational unit.

Broad action programs. (See *action programs.*)

Broad corporate objectives. (See *corporate philosophy.*)

Budgeting. The final task of strategy that captures the financial implication of broad and special *action programs.* The corporation will evaluate those programs, allocate resources, make a formal commitment through the agreed-upon budget figures, and define the performance measurements needed to carry out an intelligent strategic *management control.*

Budgets. They represent projections of financial data normally covering one or more years.

Business process reengineering. The radical redesign of those business processes that cut across different organizational units of the firm, and which no one is given full responsibility for their effectiveness. Through the passage of time, all kind of inefficiencies could be generated, creating significant opportunities for major improvements. The processes are broken down into a set of specific activities, and these activities are analyzed to detect if they are adding value or not.

Business scope. A definition of the overall portfolio of businesses of the firm, indicating the businesses the firm will enter or exit, as well as the discretionary allocation of tangible and intangible resources assigned to them. Pragmatically, it means identifying the products and services generated, the markets served, and the geographical reach covered; and assigning priorities for resource allocation.

Business segmentation. It is the identification of the businesses the firm is in or intends to be in. It requires grouping the firm activities into coherent categories that will allow a most effective management of the firm resources. (See *business scope; strategic business unit.*)

Business strategy. A well-coordinated set of *action programs* aimed at securing a sustainable *competitive advantage.* Business managers are supposed to formulate and implement strategic actions congruent with the general corporate directions, and constrained by the overall resources assigned to the particular business unit.

Business strength. It is the result derived from the *internal scrutiny* at the business level expressed in terms of major strengths and weaknesses in the current and future standing of the business, in relation to its most relevant competitors. A common procedure to perform this scrutiny is based on the *value chain.* (See *internal scrutiny at the business level.*)

Calendar-driven planning process. A formal planning process that stipulates the completion of major tasks and steps in the planning cycle by well-defined dates.

Capabilities. *Resources* are converted into capabilities when the firm develops the necessary organizational routines to use them effectively.

Commitment. The result of investments in the development of unique resources and capabilities inside the firm, which are scarce, durable, specialized, and untradable; and, consequently, hard to imitate or substitute by other players in the industry. The resources could be both tangible—such as financial and physical assets—and intangible—such as reputation, brand power, product innovation, and superior customer orientation. Resources of this kind require investments in the so-called "sticky factors," which are enduring in nature, and thus maintained through a rather long period of time. From an economic point of view, they are largely "sunk costs." Resources are converted into capabilities which the firm develops the necessary organizational routines to use them effectively.

Commitment is also the result of a disinvestment decision, which represents the determination to forego a host of strategic opportunities that otherwise would be open.

Commitment, either by a major investment or disinvestment, represents an irreversible repositioning of the firm's strategy.

Common-size financial statements. A technique for carrying out the financial statement analysis of firms of different size that starts with the standardization of their financial figures to a common base (usually, total assets and total sales revenues are defined as 100 percent for balance sheet and income statement respectively).

Communication system. It is an activity that allows managers to transmit the messages they think should be given to interested parties at all organizational levels, as well as the relevant external stakeholders. (See *information system.*)

Competitive advantage. It is the distinct way a business or a firm is positioned in the market in order to obtain an advantage over competitors, which means an ability to maintain sustained levels of profitability above the industry average. At the heart of achieving a long-term sustainable competitive advantage is the identification of opportunities to create conditions of disequilibrium which can legitimately allow a firm to claim economic rents beyond those resulting from perfect competition, and then to protect and sustain those conditions for as long as possible. (See *unique competencies; generic competitive strategies; resource-based view of the firm.*)

Competitive positioning. The relevant standing the firm has against its most relevant competitors. The *value-chain* is a guiding framework to assess the uniqueness of the competitive standing of a business. (See *unique competencies.*)

Competitor interrelationships. (See *horizontal strategy.*)

Concept of strategy. Strategy is a coherent, unifying, and integrative pattern of decisions that determines and reveals the organizational purpose in terms of long-term objectives, action programs, and resource allocation priorities. A firm's strategy selects the businesses the organization is in or is to be in, attempts to achieve a long-term sustainable advantage in each of its businesses by responding properly to the opportunities and threats in the firm's environment and the strengths and weaknesses of the organization. The strategic concept engages all the hierarchical levels of the firm (corporate, business. functional) and defines the nature of the economic and noneconomic contributions it intends to make to its stakeholders. Strategy is also an expression of the *strategic intent* of the organization, which is intended to develop and nurture the *core competencies* of the firm. Finally, the strategy provides a means to invest selectively in tangible and intangible *resources* to develop *capabilities* that assure a sustainable *competitive advantage.*

Configuration. It refers to the location of each one of the activities of the *value chain* across the different areas of the firm's operation. It is particularly relevant for global firms with different operations in many countries.

Control and motivational systems. (See *management control.*)

Coordination. It refers to the design of the organizational and administrative systems put in place to achieve a state of adequate coordination among the different activities of the *value chain,* mainly when their *configuration* is dispersed among many different countries. (See *integration approaches.*)

Core competencies. The consolidation of corporate-wide technologies and production skills that empower business units to adapt quickly to changing opportunities. A core competency provides access to a wide variety of markets; it makes a significant contribution to the perceived customer benefits of the end product; and it should be difficult for competitors to imitate.

Core products. Intermediate products that embody the *core competencies* of the firm and that are used in the final assembly or manufacturing of end-products.

Corporate culture. (See *organizational culture.*)

Corporate environmental scan. (See *environmental scan that the corporate level.*)

Corporate internal scrutiny. (See *internal scrutiny at the corporate level.*)

Corporate performance objectives. Corporate performance objectives are quantitative indicators of the overall strategic and operational performance of the firm. Typically, companies choose to express corporate objectives via a very selective number of indices. Although there is no universal set of such indices, we can classify them into two major categories. The first includes quantitative financial measures that relate to size, growth, profitability, capital markets, and a host of other financial variables. The second is oriented at measuring the overall efficiency of the managerial functions of the firm; in particular human resources, technology, procurement, manufacturing, and marketing. Incorporating these functional measures at the corporate level is relevant whenever we deal with centralized functions. Otherwise, the functional measure should become part of either divisional or business performance indicators, depending on where the function resides within the organization.

Corporate philosophy. Corporate philosophy is a rather permanent statement, articulated primarily by the chief executive officer, addressing the following issues: (1) the relationship between the firm and its primary "stakeholders"—employees, customers, shareholders, suppliers, and the communities in which the firm operates; (2) a statement of "broad corporate objectives" of the firm's expected performance, primarily expressed in terms of growth and profitability; (3) a definition of basic "corporate policies" with regard to issues such as management style, organizational policies, human resources management, financial policies, marketing, and technology, and (4) a statement of "corporate values" pertaining to ethics, beliefs, and rules of personal and corporate behavior. The corporate philosophy has to provide a unifying theme and a vital challenge to all organizational units, communicate a sense of achievable ideals, serve as a source of inspiration for confronting the daily activities, and become a contagious, motivating, and guiding force congruent with the corporate ethic and values.

Corporate policies. (See *corporate philosophy.*)

Corporate strategic tasks. At the corporate level reside the decisions which, by their nature, should be addressed with full corporate scope. These are decisions that cannot be decentralized without running the risks of committing severe suboptimization errors. The central issue behind the strategic corporate tasks is how to add value at the corporate level. The corporate tasks respond to economic and managerial imperatives. There are eight corporate tasks associated with the "economic imperative" of corporate strategy: (1) *environmental scan at the corporate level*—understanding the external forces impacting the firm; (2) *Mission of the firm*—choosing competitive domain and the way to compete; (3) *Business segmentation*—selecting planning and organizational focuses; (4) *Horizontal strategy*—pursuing synergistic linkages across business units; (5) *Vertical integration*—defining the boundaries of the firm; (6) *Corporate philosophy*—defining the relationship between the firm and its stakeholders; (7) *Strategic posture of the firm*—identifying strategic thrusts; and corporate performance objectives; (8) *Portfolio management*—assigning priorities for resource allocation and identifying opportunities for diversification and divestment; there are two additional tasks associated with the "managerial imperative;" (9) *Organization* and *managerial infrastructure*—defining and adjusting the organizational structure, managerial processes, and systems in consonance with the culture of the firm to facilitate the implementation of strategy; and (10) *Human resources management of key personnel*—selection, development, appraisal, reward, and promotion.

Corporate strategic thrusts. Strategic thrusts are the primary issues the firm has to address during the next three to five years to establish a healthy competitive position in the key markets in which it participates. They are a powerful expression of all the key issues that need to be addressed to consolidate an integrative strategy for the overall firm. The corporate strategic thrusts translate the broad sense of directions the organization wants to follow into a practical set of instructions to all key managers involved in the strategic process. There are three dimensions on defining the strategic thrusts of the firm:

1. The agenda, that must be comprehensive (responding to the statement of opportunities and threats resulting from the *corporate environmental scan;* and to the collective set of issues that emerge from the *corporate internal scrutiny*) and stretch the organization. (See *stretching the organization.*)

2. The assignment of responsibilities and accountability, which calls for the identification of all key organizational units and specific individuals in charge of defining the action programs which respond to each thrust and monitoring their subsequent implementation.

3. The measures of control, that deal with developing the necessary metrics to monitor the progress being made by the firm to live up to the challenges of the strategic thrusts. This is the linkage between planning and *management control,* and the true basis for the development of the executive *information systems* of the firm.

Corporate strategy. (See *corporate strategic tasks.*)

Corporate tasks. (See *corporate strategic tasks.*)

Corporate values. (See *corporate philosophy.*)

Cost center. (See *responsibility center.*)

Cost leadership. (See *generic competitive strategies.*)

Cost of capital. It is a benchmark defining the minimum rate of return that must be required of an investment, if it must generate a positive contribution to the *economic profitability* of a firm. The cost of capital is estimated by adding two components: a risk-free rate of return, and a positive risk premium to compensate for the inherent risk in the investment.

Critical success factors. The limited number of areas in which satisfactory results will ensure a successful competitive performance for a business unit. These indicators are specific to each business, and they reflect managerial preferences with regard to key variables at a given point in time. Therefore, they must he constantly adapted to reflect changes taking place in the organization or its environment. (See *key performance indicators.*)

Cultural audit. A systematic process to uncover the basic underlying principles at the core of an *organizational culture.*

Cultural risk. A measure of the compatibility between the strategy being considered for a firm and the *organizational culture.*

Cultural risk assessment. A methodology to determine the *cultural risk* of the different *action programs* of a strategy, and to suggest a way to go when a high-risk situation is detected.

Culture. (See *organizational culture.*)

Detailed organizational structure. The process of fleshing out the *basic organizational structure* with numerous specific details that pertain to the operational domain of the firm. The definition of a detailed organizational structure has two objectives: to identify all the major *business processes* and operational tasks the organization should undertake in the pursuit of its daily activities, and to assign them to the organizational segments identified in the basic structure previously defined.

Differentiation. (See *generic competitive strategies.*)

Direction of vertical integration. The direction of vertical integration recognizes two different ways of adding value to the inputs and outputs of the firm: backward—which means getting closer to suppliers by incorporating into the firm a given input to the current core, and forward—which involves a greater proximity to customers by putting a given output of the core under the firm's umbrella. These two forms of vertical integration are sometimes referred to as upstream and downstream extensions, respectively.

Discretionary cost center. It is a *cost center* characterized by the inability to measure delivered outputs in a strict financial way, or by the lack of a clear association between inputs and outputs. Such is the case with most of the administrative activities of a firm (for example, legal, human resources, accounting departments), the research and development function, and marketing activities such as promotion and advertising.

Divisional organization. The divisional form is structured according to the outputs generated by the organization. The most common distinction of the outputs is in the terms of the products delivered. However, other types of outputs could serve as a basis for divisionalization, such as services, programs, and projects. Markets, clients, and geographical locations also could serve as criteria for divisionalization. This is a decentralized form of organization because many conflicts and decisions can be resolved at the divisional manager's level, preventing an overburdened top hierarchy.

Distinctive competencies. (See *unique competencies.*)

Economic imperative. (See *corporate strategic tasks.*)

Economic profitability. A measure of profitability that includes, among the cost of resources, the total cost of the capital used (including equity capital, which is normally omitted in the commonly used measures of accounting profitability).

Economic-to-book value model (E/B). It is equivalent to the *market-to-book value model,* in which the assessment of market value is done as a direct projection into the future of past trends for all financial indicators.

Environmental scan at the business level. The environmental scan at the business level attempts to identify the degree of attractiveness of the *industry* in which the business belongs, in terms of its potential for a sustainable long-term profitability.

Environmental scan at the corporate level. It attempts to diagnose the general health of the industrial sectors relevant to the businesses in which the corporation is engaged. It concentrates on assessing the overall economic, political, technological, and social climates that affect the corporation as a whole. This assessment has to be conducted, initially, from a historical perspective to determine how well the corporation has mobilized its resources to meet the challenges presented by the external environment. Then, with a futuristic view in mind, future trends in the environment must be predicted and a repositioning of the internal resources sought to adapt the organization to those environmental trends. The main components of this scan are the "economic overview"; the analysis in the "primary industrial sectors" or markets in which the firm competes; and the "basic external factors" analysis which encompasses the study of favorable and unfavorable impacts from technological trends, supply of human resources, political factors, social factors, and legal factors. This analysis becomes much more laborious when the firm competes in a global setting, because these dimensions are completely different in the regions and countries in which the firm operates.

Executive information system (EIS). (See *information system.*)

Extended performance evaluation approach. A system of *managerial compensation* that rewards managers for achieving certain performance levels over a multiyear period, by awarding them with deferred stock or stock options according to each one's ability to fulfill various strategic goals over the agreed-upon planning horizon.

Extent of integration. The extent of integration refers to the length of the *value chain* housed by the firm; whether it is limited to just a few stages or covers the whole array. One way of measuring the extent of integration is through the fraction of the final value of a product or service that is added by the firm.

External-factors analysis. A methodology to perform the environmental scan at the business level based on the identification of those critical external factors considered to be the central determinants of *industry attractiveness* in the opinion of key managers of the business. Managers are required to engage in an exercise for probing the identification of those issues which are considered truly significant, and to concentrate their efforts in assessing their influence on industry attractiveness.

Financial performance. Broadly understood, it refers to the performance of a firm or business unit in terms of the different dimensions included in the *financial ratio analysis.* Narrowly understood, it refers exclusively to the firm profitability, which can be measured in a score of different indicators, particularly return on assets, return on equity, return on investment, margin of sales, and *spread.*

Financial ratio analysis. The financial ratio analysis is aimed at characterizing the firm in a few basic dimensions considered fundamental to the financial health of a company. They are usually categorized in five types: (1) liquidity ratios (ability to meet short-term financial obligations); (2) leverage/capital structure ratios (ability to fulfill long-term commitments with debtholders); (3) profitability ratios (ability to generate profits); (4) turnover ratios (efficiency or productivity ratios); and (5) common stock security ratios (performance from the point of view of shareholders).

Financial statement analysis. A technique that makes use of public financial information (balance sheet, income statement, statement of changes in the financial position, and 10K reports) for gaining an understanding of the relative financial standing of different firms. In this book it is used as a methodology for determining the competitive position of firms participating in an industry. There are two basic procedures to make financial figures more easily comparable among different competitors: define *common-size financial statements* and perform a *financial ratio analysis*.

Fit. (See *balance.*)

Five-forces model. A model proposed by Michael Porter to determine *industry attractiveness* by performing an analysis of the industry structure. The five forces that typically shape the industry structure are intensity of rivalry among competitors, threat of new entrants, threat of substitutes, bargaining power of buyers, and bargaining power of suppliers. These five forces delimit prices, costs, and investment requirements which are the basic factors that explain long-term profitability prospects and industry attractiveness. The generic structure of an industry is represented by the main players (competitors, buyers, suppliers, substitutes. and new entrants), their interrelationships (the five forces), and the factors behind those forces accounting for industry attractiveness.(See Figure 5-l.)

Flexibility. The ability of the firm to adapt its strategy and change its course of action if confronted with unexpected events.

Flexible budgets. They are *budgets* that allow for the modification of the parameters used to define them, when the actual level of operations changes.

Focus. (See *generic competitive strategies.*)

Formal-analytical approaches. (See *integration approaches.*)

Formal planning process. (See *strategic planning process.*)

Free cash flow. The cash coming from operations after the addition of depreciation and the deduction of interest, taxes, and all *strategic funds* committed. The free cash flow is what has to be discounted to obtain the net present value of the business, which is a measure of the wealth created to shareholders.

Full integration. A firm that is fully integrated backward on a given input satisfies all the needs for that particular input from internal sources. Likewise, when a firm is fully integrated forward for a given output, it is self-sufficient in providing internally the demand for that product or source. Fully integrated companies have complete ownership of their assets.

Functional environmental scanning process. This is a process aimed at obtaining an understanding of critical industrial trends and the present and future standing of key competitors. A critical component in this process is functional intelligence, whose purpose is to generate all the relevant information concerning the current and future states of development of each individual function. It is not only the existing managerial practice and state of technological progress that are important to detect, but even more critical is the recognition of future trends and state-of-the-art developments, and their embodiment in actions by competitors.

Functional intelligence. (See *functional environmental scanning process.*)

Functional internal scrutiny. It is an effort aimed at the recognition of overall strengths and weaknesses typical of the analysis at the business level, and the determination of specific skills that could be built for each individual function in order to gain *competitive advantage*.

Functional organization. The functional form is structured around the inputs required to perform the tasks of the organization. Typically, these inputs are functions or specialties such as finance, marketing, production, engineering, research and development, and personnel. It is a centralized form of organization because only at the top is there a confluence of all the inputs required for conflict resolution and final decision making.

Functional strategy. Functional strategies are sets of well-defined *action programs* aimed at consolidating the functional requirements demanded by the composite of businesses of the firm, and also at developing unique competencies to exceed or at least match competitors' unique capabilities. The six major foci for strategic functional analysis are financial strategy, human resources strategy, technology strategy, procurement strategy, manufacturing strategy, and marketing strategy.

Generic competitive strategies. The general approach a business follows to compete in an industry to attain a sustainable level of profitability above the industry average. Michael Porter suggests three generic strategies: (1) Overall cost leadership requires aggressive construction of efficient-scale facilities, vigorous pursuit of cost reductions from experience, tight costs and overhead control, avoidance of marginal customer accounts, and cost minimization in areas such as R&D, service, sales force, advertising, and so on. (2) Differentiation calls for creating something that is perceived industry-wide as being unique. Approaches to differentiation can take many forms: design of brand image, technology, features, customer service, dealer network, or other dimensions. (3) Focus consists of concentrating on a particular buyer group, segment of the product line, or geographic market. As with differentiation, focus may take many forms. Although the low-cost and differentiation strategies are aimed at achieving those objectives industry-wide, the entire focus strategy is built around servicing a particular market target very well, and each functional policy is developed with this in mind.

Generic strategy. (See *generic competitive strategies.*)

Growth-share matrix. (See *portfolio matrices.*)

Growth strategies (for the firm). (See Figure 11-1.)

Growth strategies (product-market segments). There are four major alternatives for growth strategies: (1) market penetration, when based on existing products and existing markets (like expansion in sales volume, geographical extensions, and market-share improvements), (2) product development, when based on the introduction of new product lines into existing markets, (3) market development. when based on the introduction of existing products into new markets, and (4) diversification, when based on the introduction of new products into new markets, which amounts to an entry into a new business. (See Figure 4-7).

Hierarchical levels of planning. There are three basic conceptual hierarchical levels that have been recognized as the essential layers of any formal planning process: corporate, business, and functional. (See *strategic corporate tasks; business strategy; functional strategy.*)

Holdup. (See *appropriability.*)

Horizontal strategy. Horizontal strategy is a set of coherent long-term objectives and action programs aimed at identifying and exploiting interrelationships across distinct but related business units. The types of possible interrelationships are: tangible interrelationships, arising from opportunities to share activities in the value chain; intangible interrelationships, involving the transference of management know-how among separate value chains; and competitor interrelationships, stemming from the existence of rivals that actually or potentially compete with the firm in more than one business unit.

Human resources management of key personnel. (See *management of key personnel.*)

Hybrid organization. An organizational structure that does not follow a unique set of criteria to segment activities, as in the case of a *functional organization* or a *divisional organization,* but mixes these two models, though a dominant pattern can be traced back to one of them. For example, most divisional organizations have a number of functional specialties centralized at the corporate level.

Imprinting the vision of the firm. The process of internalizing the *vision* in the organization via a number of formal-analytical approaches (appealing to the rational self to generate calculated reactions), and power-behavioral approaches (appealing to the affective self to generate intuitive reactions) in a way that is congruent with the culture of the firm. This process is at the heart of *strategic management.*

Industry. A group of firms offering products or services that are close substitutes for each other. Thus, the boundaries of the industry are determined from a user's point of view. Close substitutes are products that, in the eye of the individual, perform approximately the same function. Technically speaking, this means that they have high cross-elasticities of demand.

Industry and competitive analysis. An orderly process which attempts to capture the structural factors that define the long-term profitability prospects of an industry, and to identify and characterize the behavior of the most significant competitors. Four methodologies to perform this analysis are: the *five-forces model*, the *external-factors analysis*, the *strategic groups analysis*, and the *financial statements analysis*.

Industry attractiveness. It is the result derived from the *environmental scan at the business level* and is expressed in terms of opportunities (factors that affect favorably) and threats (factors that constitute adverse impacts) to long-term profitability prospects in the industry. A common procedure to perform this scan is the structural analysis of the industry based on the use of the *five-forces model*. Another useful procedure is the *external-factors analysis*.

Industry-attractiveness/business strength matrix. (See *portfolio matrices*.)

Informal organization. (See *power-behavioral approaches*.)

Informal managerial processes. (See *power-behavioral approaches*.)

Information system. The formal process and administrative system of gathering, digesting, filtering, and distributing the information relevant to managers at all hierarchical levels. (See *communication system*.)

Intangible interrelationships. (See *horizontal strategy*.)

Integration approaches. A number of different managerial processes that are designed to provide incentives so that all individuals within the organization work in a harmonious way while seeking the achievement of the organizational vision. There are two major categories of integration approaches that we have recognized in the *strategic management framework*. The first one results from the formal-analytical approaches and is represented by the lateral coordinating mechanisms (mainly the creation of liaison roles, task forces, committees, integrating managers, and matrix relations), and by the central administrative systems of the firm (planning, control, communications and information, and human resources management and reward systems). The character of these formal-analytical mechanisms is dependent on the kind of strategy they are intended to support. The second one is generated from power-behavioral approaches to management; and they are basically informal, political, and psychological mechanisms intended to affect behavior in the desired strategic direction.

Intelligent budgets. They are *budgets* that are not a mere extrapolation of the past into the future but are instead instruments that contain both strategic and operational commitments.

Internal scrutiny at the business level. A systematic and disciplined approach to guide a manager through all the necessary steps to perform the *internal scrutiny* at the business level. The process attempts to identify the major strengths and weaknesses of the firm against its most relevant competitors *(business strengths)*. The internal scrutiny is supported by the following tasks: identification of the most relevant *SBU's* competitors; determination of critical success factors, (that is, those capabilities controllable by the firm in which it has to excel for the SBU to achieve a long-term sustainable competitive advantage and a profitability level above industry standards); development of a competitive profile for the SBU, by measuring the business strengths and weaknesses against each of the most relevant competitors; and preparation of the summary assessment and identification of overall strengths and weaknesses associated with the SBU.

Internal scrutiny at the corporate level. The key actions and decisions the corporation has to address to gain a *competitive positioning* that is in line with the *strategic challenges* generated by the external environment and conducive to the development of a sustainable corporate advantage, which is transferable to the various businesses of the firm and enhances its *resources* and *capabilities*. The tasks which are part of the internal scrutiny are: *mission of the firm, business segmentation, horizontal strategy, vertical integration,* and *corporate philosophy*. The internal scrutiny concludes with an overall statement of corporate strengths—that the firm wishes to maintain and reinforce - as well as a statement of corporate weaknesses—that the firm wishes to correct or eliminate. (See *environmental scan at the business level; competitive advantage; unique competencies; sustainability*.)

Investment center. (See *responsibility center*.)

Issue escalation. The formal process by which critical disagreement among members of a firm located at similar hierarchical levels in the organizational structure of a firm is moved to the next higher level in the managerial hierarchy for final sanctioning.

Key performance indicators. A stable set of indicators, considered to be key to follow up the operation and performance of a business unit, which allow managers to detect and monitor the competitive position of all businesses the firm is engaged in. These indicators tend to be permanent and uniformly applied to all business units of a firm. (See *critical success factors*.)

Leadership imperative. The vision and sense of purpose provided by the CEO, which poses a significant but yet attainable challenge to the entire organization, motivating people and generating a spirit of success.

Life-cycle matrix. (See *portfolio matrices*.)

Linking-pin. An integrating role aimed at coordinating the activities of two different units of the firm.

Logical incrementalism. A strategy formation process proactively guided by managers that builds strategy at disaggregated levels, later integrating these subsystem strategies step by step in order to produce the strategy for the overall firm. This process of strategy formation is fragmented, evolutionary, and largely intuitive.

Major tasks of a planning cycle. Tasks that need to be updated and revised at every planning cycle: *strategy formulation* and *strategic and operational budgeting*. Each one of these major tasks is composed of a number of steps that progressively defines the different levels of the strategy of a firm (corporate, business, and functional) in terms of a hierarchy of objectives that moves from broad to very specific.

Management accounting approach. A system of *managerial compensation* based on the adjustment of the financial accounting model, in order to reflect both strategic and operational results of the firm. One way of achieving this is by breaking down expenses into strategic and operational, and maintaining a *strategic funds* accountability.

Management control. Management control is a structured process, quantitatively oriented, which is based on the definition of performance standards for the entire firm and each one of its units, and on the comparisons of planned with actual results obtained from operations. In this way, top managers can derive an opinion on the effectiveness of the implementation of strategic directions and the efficiency achieved in the use of its primary resources and then act accordingly, taking corrective action whenever needed. Management control is a major system for managing day-to-day operational and strategic activities with a unitary sense of direction imprinted in the quantitative benchmarks selected as standards for comparison. Finally, management control, mainly when coupled with the compensation and reward system, becomes a driver of individual behavior in the organizational setting. (See *activity-based costing; balanced scorecard;* and *benchmarking.*)

Management of key personnel. One of the key corporate tasks that calls for the management of human resources in a strategic manner; that is, in a way that allows firms to establish and sustain a long-term advantage over competitors. A human resources strategy must be comprehensive in the sense of addressing all the diverse personnel and human resource activities central to the long-term development of the businesses of the firm. Its foundation lies in the proper recognition of the major categories of human resource strategic decision making: (1) selection, promotion, and placement—managing the flow of people in, through, and out of the organization; (2) appraisal—evaluation of the performance of people within the organization; (3) rewards—providing adequate compensation, fringe benefits, and motivational support to employees at all levels; (4) management development—creating mechanisms to enhance skills, promotional opportunities. and career paths; and (5) labor/employee relations and voice—establishing a cooperative climate among managers and employees.

Managerial compensation. The monetary reward received by managers for their individual and group performance as judged from their contribution to short-term and long-term results. (See *rewards systems.*)

Managerial imperative. (See *corporate strategic tasks.*)

Managerial infrastructure. A set of corporate tasks more directly related to the implementation of strategy: the design of the *organizational structure* and *administrative systems,* and the *management of key personnel.*

Managing by strategy. (See *strategic management; balance.*)

Market attractiveness-business strength matrix. (See *portfolio matrices.*)

Market-to-book value model (M/B). The M/B model is a blend of two different perspectives of the firm. In the denominator, the book value of the firm's shares provides the accountant's perspective, which corresponds to the historical measurements of resources contributed by shareholders. In the numerator, the market value of the firm's shares gives the investor's perspective, which corresponds to an assessment of future payments generated from the assets the firm already has in place and from the investments the firm would have the opportunity to make at some time in the future. Therefore, the M/B ratio can be equated to:

$$\frac{Expected\ future\ payments}{Past\ resources\ committed}$$

Master budget. It is a collection of *budgets* that includes all those activities whose monitoring is judged to be important for a healthy development of the firm's businesses. Among them are sales, manufacturing, administrative activities, investment, and cash management.

Matrix organization. Matrix organizations are structured around two (or more) design concepts. *Functional organizations* are structured around inputs and *divisional organizations* around outputs. Matrix organizations are a fundamental departure from this unitary notion because both inputs and outputs are considered equally important as criteria for segmentation of the organizational activities.

Maximum sustainable growth. The maximum growth of the assets of a firm that can be financed by maintaining a stable debt-equity ratio and dividend-payout policy.

Mission of the business. It is a statement of the current and future expected business scope and a definition of the way to attain *competitive advantage.* Business scope is expressed as a broad description of products, markets, and geographical coverage of the business today, and within a reasonably short time frame, commonly three to five years. For some businesses, technology is added as another dimension of its scope. (See *competitive advantage.*)

Mission of the firm. A statement of the current and future expected *business scope,* and of the *unique competencies* that the firm has developed and will continue to promote into the future. The declaration made explicit in the mission statement contains an inherent definition of priorities for the strategic agenda of the firm and identifies the major opportunities for growth and the capabilities that have to be enhanced to achieve a superior competitive advantage. As such, it provides basic guiding principles and a set of expectations that are going to condition the rest of the strategic activities at all managerial levels of the firm.

Mobility barriers. An assessment of the degree of difficulty that a *strategic group* within an industry has to penetrate into an adjacent strategic group.

Motivational and rewards system. (See *rewards system.*)

Natural strategy. The normal course of action suggested by the positioning of a business in *portfolio matrices,* commonly expressed in terms of a thrust for market share, using categories such as the following: build aggressively, build gradually, build selectively, maintain aggressively, maintain selectively, prove viability, and divest-liquidate.

Nonconcurrence. A vote cast by functional managers when they do not agree with a proposed business plan because it is judged to contain inadequate or unrealistic commitment in a functional area. The conflict thus generated is solved by *issue escalation.*

Nonintegration. A firm that decides not to integrate on a given input or output and depends completely on external providers for its necessary support. The commitments that facilitate the reliance on those external parties are normally drafted in terms of contracts that represent joint responsibilities but no internal integration. Common forms of contracts are competitive bids, long-term contracting, and rent of assets.

Operational funds. They are expense items required to maintain the business in its present position (funds to keep up the momentum).

Opportunism and timing. The cost incurred in acquiring the resources and capabilities that generate economic value is lower than the value thus generated. (See *resource-based view of the firm.*)

Opportunistic planning. A flexible form of planning to meet unexpected events not properly anticipated in the formal planning process. It is normally concentrated in a more narrow segment of corporate activities, and prompt answer rests on the provision of financial and organizational slack to absorb additional duties without experiencing a severe organizational constraint.

Organization. Organizations are groups of people seeking the achievement of a common purpose via division of labor, integrated through formal-analytical administrative systems and power-behavioral managerial approaches congruent with its *organizational culture* continuously through time.

Organizational archetypes. Different templates to guide the designs of the organizational structure. They are the *functional organization, divisional organization,* and *matrix organization.* A combination of these is the *hybrid organization.*

Organizational architecture. A term including the formal *organizational structure,* the design of work practices (*business processes*), the nature of the informal organization or operating style (*power-behavioral approaches*), and the process of selection, socialization, and development of people (*management of key personnel*).

Organizational culture. Organizational culture is a complex set of basic underlying assumptions and deeply held beliefs shared by all members of the group that operate at a preconscious level and drive in important ways the behavior of individuals in the organizational context.

Organizational structure. (See *basic organizational structure; detailed organizational structure; balance.*)

Overall cost leadership. (See *generic competitive strategies.*)

Performance measurements. They are quantitative indicators of the performance of the firm defined at different hierarchical levels: corporate, business, and functional. They are basically oriented at measuring the financial soundness of a firm or a business, and the overall efficiency of each one of the managerial functions of a firm, in particular: human resources, technology, procurement, manufacturing, and marketing. (See Figure 16-3 and 16-6, *corporate performance objectives; financial statement analysis; financial performance; key performance indicators; critical success factors; strategic measures of functional performance.*)

Perspectives of strategy. There are three basic perspectives which have been recognized as the essential components of any formal planning process: corporate, business, and functional. These perspectives are different both in terms of the nature of the decisions they address, as well as the organizational units and managers involved in formulating and implementing the corresponding *action programs* generated. (See *corporate strategic tasks; business strategy; functional strategy.*)

Planning cycle. A formal strategic planning process that is periodically conducted in a firm. (See *major tasks of a planning cycle.*)

Planning guidelines. They specify the different steps and responsibilities in the formal planning process through time and define the basic parameters, mainly economic assumptions, to be used by all the managers involved in this effort.

Planning tasks. (See *corporate strategic tasks; strategic planning process.*)

Portfolio management. Portfolio management is a major responsibility of the corporate level geared at the analysis of the basic characteristics of the portfolio of businesses of a firm, in order to assign priorities for *resource allocation. Portfolio matrices* can be used toward this end.

Portfolio matrices. A set of graphic displays developed by leading consulting firms to help managers in reaching a better understanding of the competitive position of the overall portfolio of businesses, to suggest strategic alternatives for each of the businesses, and to develop priorities for resource allocation. Each matrix positions the business units of the firm in accordance with two dimensions: one is an external dimension that attempts to capture the overall attractiveness of the industry in which the business participates; the other is an internal dimension that relates to the strength of the business within its industry. The factors that describe industry attractiveness are normally uncontrollable by the firm; those that contribute to business strength are largely under the control of the firm. The most popular portfolio matrices are: (1) the growth-share matrix, developed by the Boston Consulting Group, which pioneered this concept; (2) the industry attractiveness-business strength matrix, conceived jointly by General Electric and McKinsey and Company, which was the first one to introduce multidimensional criteria in the external and internal dimensions; (3) the life-cycle matrix developed by Arthur D. Little, Inc., which contains a fairly comprehensive methodology that leads to a wide array of broad action programs to support the desired strategic thrust of each business; (4) the alternative Boston Consulting Group matrix that enriches the original BCG matrix by bringing in broader descriptions of industry structure; and (5) the profitability matrix proposed by Marakon, which captures the three most central strategic objectives of each business—profitability, growth, and cash-generation capabilities. The position of a business in a matrix suggests a strategic course of action, called generic or natural strategy, and a priority for resource allocation.

Positioning. (See *competitive positioning*.)

Power-behavioral approaches. (See *integration approaches*.)

Primary structure. (See *basic organizational structure*.)

Principle of integration. Managers should create the conditions that will allow the members of an organization to achieve their own goals best by directing their efforts to the success of the enterprise.

Priority assessment. The effort and resources that will be allocated to address changes in the mission statement.

Process of strategy. (See *strategy formation process*.)

Process reengineering. (See *business process reengineering*.)

Profit center. (See *responsibility center*.)

Profitability matrix. (See *portfolio matrices*.)

Program-period planning process. A formal planning process that allows for program initiatives to be generated at any time during the year (as opposed to a calendar-driven planning process that prescribes a timing for it). But at a given point in time, all programs are consolidated through a formal process called period planning.

Quasi-integration. Quasi-integrated firms do not have full ownership of all assets in the value chain related to a given input or output. Rather, they resort to several mechanisms to assure steady relationships with external constituencies. These reside somewhere in between long-term contracts and full ownership. Prevalent terms of quasi-integrations are joint ventures or alliances, minority equity investments, loans, loan guarantees, licensing agreements, franchises, R&D, partnerships, and exclusivity contracts.

Reengineering. (See *business process reengineering.*)

Resource allocation. A corporate task that requires discrimination among the wide array of requests for funding of the corporate, business, and functional programs defined in the strategic planning process. This is necessary because the financial, technological, and human resources available to the firm are not sufficient to support every proposed activity.

Resource-based view of the firm. A model that explains the competitive advantage of a firm in terms of the factors of production, thus departing significantly from the strategic approach that is based on market-driven considerations. According to this model, the central sources of competitive advantage depend on the development of unique *resources* and *capabilities* on the part of the firm (*unique competencies*) which are hard to imitate or substitute by competitors (*sustainability*) leaving aside industry conditions as the cause of superior profitability. Furthermore, it is required that the benefits derived from these advantages are retained inside the firm (*appropriability*) and that the timing of the acquisition of the necessary resources and capabilities is so opportune that their cost will not offset the resulting benefits (*opportunism and timing*). If all these conditions are met, the competitive advantage that is created will generate an incremental economic value of the firm.

Resources. The basic factors of production, which could be both tangible (such as financial resources and physical assets) and intangible (such as reputation, customer orientation, production innovation, technology superiority, etc.). (See *capabilities; unique competencies; resource-based view of the firm.*)

Responsibility center. A responsibility center is an organizational unit with a clearly identified scope of activities that has been entrusted to a responsible manager. It may be pictured in terms of three main factors: its inputs, such as materials, parts, components, and labor; its outputs, such as the different kinds of products and services generated by the unit; and the fixed resources assigned to the manager as total assets or net investment. Depending on the nature of managerial control, the responsibility center may be defined as: cost centers where managers are accountable for expenses generated from the input streams; revenue centers where accountability stems from revenues generated from the output streams as well as expenses from the input streams; profit centers where accountability is judged by ability to generate profits (revenues minus expenses); and investment centers where accountability is measured in terms of profit as percentage of the total investment base.

Revenue center. (See *responsibility center.*)

Rewards system. It is a formal definition of the different components considered in the performance evaluation of managers and the assignment of monetary and nonmonetary rewards to them.

SBU. (See *strategic business unit.*)

Scarcity. The difficulty to imitate or substitute the *resources* and *capabilities* which are the sources of *competitive advantage.* (See *sustainability.*)

Segmentation. The process of conceptualizing the purpose of an organization and translating it in terms of a variety of specific tasks, whose execution is located in different units of the organization.

SFU. (See *strategic functional unit.*)

Shared common resources (among business units). *Horizontal strategy* defined for resources shared among business units, such as manufacturing facilities, distribution channels, technology, or other functions support.

Shared concerns (among business units). *Horizontal strategy* defined for concerns shared among business units, including common geographical areas and key customer accounts.

Slack. (See *appropriability.*)

SMU. (See *Strategic Manufacturing Unit.*)

Sources of value creation. Sources of value creation are the different mechanisms a firm uses to create *competitive advantages* and the ways to exploit them.

Special strategic issues. One of the strategic corporate tasks that calls for managers to transform the traditional ways of conducting businesses in a given industry. Among them, globalization, technological innovations, and the requirement of a new form of executive leadership are issues that are having a profound impact on business practices.

Specific action programs. (See *action programs.*)

Stakeholders. Individuals or groups who directly or indirectly receive the benefits or sustain the costs derived from the action of the firm: shareholders, employees, managers, customers, suppliers, debtholders, communities, government, and so forth. (See *corporate philosophy.*)

Standard cost center. It is a *cost center* characterized by having well-defined output measures and clean relationships between the required inputs and the resulting outputs. Such is the case with manufacturing operations where standards can be computed to the amount of inputs—labor, raw materials, supplies, and additional supporting services—needed to produce a unit of a specific product.

Sticky factors. (See *commitment.*)

Strategic and operational budgeting. One of the major tasks of the planning cycle, which includes the formulation and consolidation of *budgets* at the business and functional levels, and the approval of *strategic funds* and *operational funds.* (See *budgeting.*)

Strategic business unit (SBU). An SBU is an operating unit or a planning focus that groups a distinct set of products or services, which are sold to a uniform set of customers, facing a well-defined set of competitors. The external (market) dimension of a business is the relevant perspective for the proper identification of an SBU. Therefore, an SBU should have a set of external customers and not just serve as an internal supplier.

Strategic categories of decisions (linked to functional strategies). The set of specific skills related to each managerial function of a firm that could be built in order to gain *competitive advantage*.

Strategic challenges. An expression of the critical changes to be addressed in the definition of the mission statement at the business and corporate levels. Challenges should be specific and explain exactly what will be done to bring about the desired change in business scope and unique competencies. Broad and specific *action programs* defined later in the planning process should respond to these challenges

Strategic factors approach. A system of *managerial compensation* that involves the identification of the critical success factors governing the future profitability of the business, and the assignment of proper weights depending on the inherent characteristics of the business unit and its agreed-upon strategy. This approach allows for establishing congruency in terms of the performance measurements to be used and the position of the business within the corporate portfolio.

Strategic functional unit. It is the focus of attention that drives all functional strategic analysis for all key functional areas.

Strategic funds. They are expense items required for the implementation of strategic action programs whose benefits are expected to be accrued in the long term beyond the current budget period. There are three major components of strategic funds: (1) investment in tangible assets, such as new production capacity, new machinery and tools, new vehicles for distribution, new office space, new warehouse space, and new acquisitions; (2) increases (or decreases) in working capital generated from strategic commitments—such as the impact of increases in inventories and receivables resulting from an increase in sales, the need to accumulate larger inventories to provide better services, increasing receivables resulting from a change in the policy of loans to customers, and so on; and (3) developmental expenses that are over and above the needs of existing business—such as advertising to introduce a new product or to reposition an existing one—R&D expenses of new products, major cost-reduction programs for existing products, introductory discounts, sales promotions, and free samples to stimulate first purchases, development of management systems—such as planning, control, and compensation—certain engineering studies, and so on.

Strategic group analysis. A procedure to define *strategic groups* within an industry and the different degrees of *industry attractiveness* of each one of these groups. For the definition of strategic groups, Michael Porter suggests the following dimensions to identify differences in firm strategies within an industry: specialization, brand identification, push-versus-pull marketing approach, channel selection, product quality, technological leadership, vertical integration, cost position, service, price policy, financial and operating leverage, relationship with parent company, and relationship to home and host government. The industry attractiveness at the group level may be assessed using the *five-forces model,* in a process referred to as industry analysis within an industry.

Strategic groups. They correspond to aggregations of firms within an industry that include, in a unique set, competitors that follow a common or similar strategy along well-defined dimensions. Groups collect firms that are relatively homogeneous according to the way they compete. (See *strategic group analysis.*)

Strategic intent. An active management process that creates a sense of urgency, focuses the organization on the essence of winning, and motivates people through actions like: developing a competitor focus, providing employees with the skills they need, leaving room for individual and team contribution, giving the organization time to digest and challenge before launching another, establishing clear milestones and review mechanisms to track progress and ensure that internal recognition and reward reinforce desired behavior. (See *stretching the organization.*)

Strategic mapping. A useful tool that can guide the separation of *strategic groups* in an industry. It is a two-dimensional display that helps to explain the different strategies of firms. Those dimensions should not be interdependent because otherwise the map would show an inherent correlation. The two most common dimensions used for a strategic mapping purpose are the breadth of the product line and the degree of vertical integration. They allow us to separate firms which, on the one extreme, have a full coverage of product lines and, at the same time, are fully self-reliant from those firms that are focusing on a very narrow line and concentrating in a short range of the value-added chain. Other dimensions are brand identification, product leadership, *configuration* of activities (geographical dispersion), and *coordination* of activities (degree of centralization).

Strategic management. Strategic management is a way of conducting the firm that has as an ultimate objective the development of corporate values, managerial capabilities, organizational responsibilities, and administrative systems that link strategic and operational decision making, at all hierarchical levels, and across all businesses and functional lines of authority in a firm. Institutions that have reached this stage of management development have eliminated the conflicts between long-term development and short-term profitability. Strategies and operations are not in conflict with one another, but they are inherently coupled in the definition of the managerial tasks at each level in the organization. This form of conducting a firm is deeply anchored in managerial style, beliefs, values, ethics, and accepted forms of behavior in the organization, which makes strategic thinking congruent with the *organizational culture.*

Strategic Manufacturing Unit (SMU). The proper focus for analyzing manufacturing strategy. An SMU is a group of products sharing the same manufacturing strategic objectives expressed in terms of cost, quality, dependability, flexibility, and innovativeness.

Strategic measures of functional performance. A collection of categories of variables that can be used as measures of performance to assess the quality of the final outputs of a functional strategy, in terms of the ability to achieve *competitive advantage*.

Strategic planning process. The strategic planning process is a disciplined and well-defined organizational effort aimed at the complete specification of a firm's strategy and the assignment of responsibilities for its execution. A formal planning process should recognize the different roles to be played by the various managers within the business organization in the formulation and execution of the firm's strategies.

Strategic posture. The strategic posture of the firm is a set of pragmatic requirements developed at the corporate level to guide the formulation of corporate, business, and functional strategies. It is expressed primarily through *corporate strategic thrusts* and *corporate performance objectives.*

Strategic programming. Definition and evaluation of specific *action programs* at the business and functional levels.

Strategic Technology Unit (STU). The proper focus for analyzing the technology strategy. It includes the skills or disciplines that are applied to a particular production, service, or process addressing a specific market need. Identifying all the relevant STUs produces the full portfolio of key technologies the firm needs to embody in its products and processes to achieve *competitive advantage.*

Strategic thrusts. (See *corporate strategic thrusts.*)

Strategy. (See *concept of strategy; strategy formation process; corporate strategic tasks; business strategy; functional strategy.*)

Strategy formation process. The relevant dimensions that should be considered in delineating a strategy formation process responsive to the firm's needs are:

Explicit versus implicit strategy:

1. The openness and breadth to communicate strategy both internally in the organization and to all relevant external constituencies
2. The degree to which different organizational levels participate
3. The amount of consensus built around intended courses of action, especially the depth of CEO involvement in this effort.

Formal-analytical process versus power-behavioral approach:

4. The extent to which formal processes are used to specify corporate, business, and functional strategies
5. The incentives provided for key players to negotiate a strategy for the firm

Pattern of past actions versus forward-looking plan:
6. The linkage of strategy to the pattern of action in the past

7. The use of strategy as a force for change and as a vehicle for new courses of action

Deliberate versus emergent strategy:
8. The degree to which strategy is either purely deliberate or purely emergent.

Strategy formulation. One of the major tasks of the planning cycle, including all the steps required for the formulation of strategy at the corporate, business, and functional levels; and for their consolidation at the corporate level. (See Figure 2–4.)

Strengths and weaknesses of a business. A summary of the *internal scrutiny at the business level.*

Strengths and weaknesses of the firm. A summary of the *internal scrutiny at the corporate level.*

Stretching the organization. The organizational search for seemingly unattainable goals, rather than mere matching industry opportunities with available resources. Instead of searching for advantages that are inherently sustainable, it strives to accelerate organizational learning that will enable the firm to develop new rules that eliminate the incumbent's advantages.

Structural analysis of industries. A procedure for environmental scanning at the business level based on the tenet that an attractive industry is one that has a favorable structure that enhances long-term profitability projects. (See *five-forces model; industry attractiveness.*)

STU. (See *Strategic Technology Unit.*)

Sunk costs. (See *commitment.*)

Sustainability. The ability to sustain the economic value generated by the *unique competencies* of the firm, from either imitation or substitution by competitors. (See *resource-based view of the firm.*)

Tangible interrelationships. (See *horizontal strategy.*)

Tapered integration. Tapered integration represents a partial integration, backward or forward, that makes the firm dependent on external sources for the supply of a portion of a given input or for the delivery of a portion of a given output. For the fraction of the input or output that the firm handles internally, it can resort to either a full integration or a quasi-integration mode of ownership.

Transfer prices. The internal prices set by a firm to determine the cash value of transfers of goods and services among its units. The most common criteria to establish transfer prices are: market prices; cost measured either as total cost, marginal cost, or standard cost; cost plus a profit margin where cost is measured according to the same alternatives just stated; and negotiated prices, either directly by the parties involved, via a mediator designated by both parties, or determined by top managers.

Unique competencies. The *resources* and *capabilities* owned by the firm which are unmatched by competitors and explain the origin of the economic value generated by a firm. (See *core competencies* and *resource-based view of the firm*.)

Valuation. An assessment of the economic value generated by a strategy under different scenarios.

Value chain. A framework proposed by Michael Porter to conduct an *internal scrutiny at the business level* in order to assess the *business strength*. The tasks performed by the business are classified into nine broad categories. Five of them are the so-called primary activities, and the other four are support activities. The primary activities are those involved in the physical movement of raw materials and finished products, in the production of goods and services, and in the marketing, sales, and subsequent services of the outputs of the business firm. The support activities are much more pervasive. As the name indicates. their essential role is to provide support not only to the primary activities but to each other. They are composed by the managerial infrastructure of the firm—which includes all processes and systems to assure proper coordination and accountability—human resource management, technology development, and procurement. (See Figures 6–1 and 6–2.)

Value creation. A financial concept that expresses in quantitative terms the ability of an economic entity (a firm, business unit, or project) to create value; that is, to generate a profitability that exceeds its *cost of capital*.

Value gap. A diagnostic tool to determine if a business or firm is making adequate use of all available opportunities to create value. (See *value creation*.)

Vertical integration. Vertical integration involves a set of decisions that, by the nature of their scope, reside at the corporate level of the organization. These decisions are threefold: (1) defining the boundaries a firm should establish over its generic activities on the value chain (the question of make versus buy or integrate versus contract); (2) establishing the relationship of the firm with its constituencies outside its boundaries, primarily its suppliers, distributors, and customers; and (3) identifying the circumstances under which those boundaries and relationships should be changed to enhance and protect the firm's competitive advantage. This set of decisions is of critical importance in defining what the firm is and is not, what critical assets and capabilities should reside irrevocably within the firm, and what type of contracts the firm should establish to deal with its external constituencies. (See *direction of vertical integration; full integration; quasi-integration; tapered integration; nonintegration; breadth of vertical integration; extent of integration*.)

Zero-base budgeting (ZBB). It is a budgeting process that establishes a set of comprehensive rules to force managers to justify their budgetary allocations from ground zero, rather than defining the new budget in an incremental way. (See *budgets*.)

References

AAKER, David A., *Managing Brand Equity* (New York: The Free Press, 1991).

ABERNATHY, W. J., and J.M. Utterback, "Patterns of Industrial Innovation," *Technology Review*, 80, no. 7, (1978), 40–47.

ADAMS, Walter, *The Structure of American Industry,* 7th ed. (New York: Macmillan, 1986).

ANDERSON, Philip, and Michael L. Tushman, "Technological Discontinuities and Dominant Designs: A Cyclical Model of Technology Change," *Administrative Science Quarterly*, 35, (1990), 604–633.

ANDREWS, Kenneth R., *The Concept of Strategy* (Homewood, IL: Richard D. Irwin, 1980).

_____, "Corporate Strategy as a Vital Function of the Board," *Harvard Business Review,* 59, no. 6 (November–December 1981), 174–184.

ANSOFF, H. Igor, *Corporate Strategy* (New York: McGraw-Hill, 1965).

_____, *Implanting Strategic Management* (Englewood Cliffs, NJ: Prentice Hall, 1984).

ARTHUR D. LITTLE, INC., *Discovering the Fountain of Youth: An Approach to Corporate Growth and Development* (San Francisco, CA: 1979).

_____, *A Management System for the 1980s* (San Francisco, CA: 1980).

_____, A *System for Managing Diversity* (Cambridge, MA: December 1974).

BADEN-FULLER, Charles, and John M. Stopford, *Rejuvenating the Mature Business: The Competitive Challenge* (London: Routledge, 1992) .

BARNEY, Jay, "Firm Resources and Sustained Competitive Advantage," *Journal of Management*, 17, no. 1 (1991), 99–120.

BAROCCI, Thomas A., and Thomas A. Kochan, *Human Resources Management and Industrial Relations*, (Boston, MA: Little Brown and Co., 1985).

BEER, Michael , Bert Spector, Paul R. Lawrence, D. Quinn Mills, and Richard E. Walton, *Managing Human Assets* (New York: The Free Press, 1984).

BIERMAN, Harold Jr., *Strategic Financial Planning* (New York: The Free Press, 1980).

BOWER, Joseph L., and Yves Doz, "Strategy Formulation: A Social and Political Process," in *Strategic Management: A New View of Business Policy and Planning*, edited by C. W. Hofer and Dan Schendel (Boston, MA: Little Brown and Co., 1979).

BRADLEY, Stephen, Jerry Hausman, and Richard Nolan (eds.), *Globalization, Technology, and Competition: The Fusion of Computers and Telecommunications in the*

1990s, (Boston, MA: Harvard Business School Press, 1993).

BREALEY, Richard A., and Stewart C. Myers, *Principles of Corporate Finance*, 4th ed. (New York: McGraw-Hill Book Co.,1991).

BUFFA, Elwood S., *Meeting the Competitive Challenge: Manufacturing Strategy for U.S. Companies* (Homewood, IL: Richard D. Irwin, 1984).

BURGELMAN, Robert A., and Modesto A. Maidique, *Strategic Management of Technology and Innovation* (Homewood, IL: Richard D. Irwin Press, 1988).

CAMP, Robert C., *Benchmarking: The Search for Industry Best Practices that Lead to Superior Performance* (Milwaukee, WI: Quality Press, 1989).

CAVES, Richard E., *American Industry: Structure, Conduct, Performance*, 6th ed. (Englewood Cliffs, NJ: Prentice Hall, 1987).

CHAMPY, James, *Reengineering Management: The Mandate for New Leadership* (New York: Harper Business, 1995).

CHANDLER, Alfred D., Jr., *Strategy and Structure: Chapters in the History of American Industrial Enterprise* (Cambridge, MA: The MIT Press, 1962).

CHARLES, Dexter H., *International Commercial Banks Take on Wall Street, An Analysis and Evaluation*, unpublished masters thesis, Sloan School of Management, MIT, 1986.

CLARK, Kim, and Takahiro Fujimoto, *Product Development Performance: Strategy, Organization, and Management in the World Auto Industry* (Boston, MA: Harvard Business School Press, 1991).

COKINS, Gary, Alan Stratton, and Jack Helbling, *The ABC Manager's Primer* (Montvale, NJ: The Institute of Management Accountants, 1992).

COOPER, Robin, and Robert S. Kaplan, "Measure the Costs Right: Make the Right Decisions," *Harvard Business Review* (September–October, 1988).

COOPER, Robin, Robert S. Kaplan, Lawrence S. Maisel, Eileen Morrissey, and Ronald M. Oehm, *Implementing Activity-Based Cost Management: Moving from Analysis to Action* (Montvale, NJ: Institute of Management Accountants, 1992).

COPELAND, Tom, Tim Koller, and Jack Murrin, *Valuation: Measuring and Managing the Value of Companies* (New York, NY: John Wiley, 1990).

CRAVENS, David W., *Strategic Marketing* (Homewood, IL: Richard D. Irwin, 1987).

CREECH, Bill, *The Five Pillars of TQM: How to Make Total Quality Management Work for You* (New York: Truman Tulley Books, Dutton, 1994).

CYERT, Richard M., and James G. March, *A Behavioral Theory of the Firm* (Englewood Cliffs, NJ: Prentice Hall, 1963).

DAVENPORT, Thomas H., *Process Innovation: Reengineering Work Through Information Technology* (Boston, MA: Harvard Business School Press, 1993).

DAY, George S., *Market Driven Strategy: Processes for Creating Value* (New York: The Free Press, 1990).

_____, *Strategic Market Planning*, (St. Paul, MN: West Publishing, 1984).

DEMING, W. Edwards, *Out of the Crisis* (Cambridge, MA: Massachusetts Institute of Technology, Center for Advanced Engineering Studies, 1986)

_____, *Quality, Productivity, and Competitive Position* (Cambridge, MA: MIT CAES, 1983).

DiSANO, Daniel, *Strategic Implications of the Merck-Medco Acquisition*, unpublished student paper, Sloan School of Management, MIT, December 1994.

DONALDSON, Gordon, *Corporate Restructuring: Managing the Change Process from Within* (Boston, MA: Harvard Business School Press, 1994).

DRUCKER, Peter F., "The Emerging Theory of Manufacturing," *Harvard Business Review*, 68, no. 3 (May–June 1990), 94–102.

ECCLES, Robert , Nitin Nohria, and James Berkley, *Beyond the Hype: Rediscovering the Essence of Management* (Boston, MA: Harvard Business School Press, 1992.

FINE, Charles, and Arnoldo Hax, "Manufacturing Strategy: A Methodology and an Illustration," *Interfaces*, 15, no. 6 (November–December 1985), 28–46.

FOMBRUM, Charles J., Noel M. Tichy, and Mary Ann Devanna, *Strategic Human Resources Management* (New York: John Wiley, 1984).

FOSTER, George, *Financial Statement Analysis*, 2nd ed. (Englewood Cliffs, NJ: Prentice Hall, 1986).

FOSTER, Richard N., *Innovation: The Attacker's Advantage* (Summit Books, 1986).

FRUHAN, William E., *Financial Strategy* (Homewood, IL: Richard D. Irwin, Inc., 1979).

GALBRAITH, Jay R., Edward E. Lawler III & Associates, *Organizing for the Future: The New Logic for Managing Complex Organizations* (San Francisco: Jossey-Bass, 1993).

GARVIN, David A., *Managing Quality: The Strategic and Competitive Edge* (New York: The Free Press, 1988).

GATTIKER, U. E., and L. Larwood, *Managing Technological Development: Strategic and Human Resources Issues* (Hawthorne, NY: Walter de Gruyter, 1988).

GENERAL ELECTRIC COMPANY, "Background Note on Management Systems: 1981," Case #181-111 (Boston, MA: Harvard Business School, 1981) .

GHEMAWAT, Pankaj, *Commitment: The Dynamics of Strategy* (New York, The Free Press, 1991).

GOMES-CASSERES, Benjamin, "Computers: Alliances and Industry Evolution," in David B. Yoffie (Ed.), *Beyond Free Trade* (Cambridge, MA: Harvard University Press, 1993), 79–128.

GRANT, Eugene L., and Richard S. Leavenworth, *Statistical Quality Control* (New York: McGraw-Hill, 1980).

GRAY, John C., *The Strategic Planning Process Applied to a Natural Resource-Based Firm*, unpublished masters thesis, Sloan School of Management, MIT, 1984.

GUNN, Thomas G., *21st Century Manufacturing: Creating Winning Business Performance* (New York: Harper Business, 1992).

HAMEL, Gary, and C.K. Prahalad, *Competing for the Future* (Boston, MA: Harvard Business School Press, 1994).

_____, Gary, and C.K. Prahalad, "Strategic Intent," *Harvard Business Review* (May–June 1989), 63–76.

HAMMER, Michael, and James Champy, *Reengineering the Corporation: A Manifesto for Business Revolution* (New York: Harper Collins, 1993).

HARRIGAN, Kathryn Rudie, *Strategic Flexibility: A Management Guide for Changing Times* (Lexington, MA: Lexington Books, 1985).

HASPESLAGH, Philippe C., and David B. Jemison, *Managing Acquisitions: Creating Value Through Corporate Renewal* (New York: The Free Press, 1991).

HAUSER, John, and Don Clausing, "The House of Quality," *Harvard Business Review*, 66, no. 3 (May–June 1988), 63–73.

HAX, Arnoldo C., "A New Competitive Weapon: The Human Resource Strategy," *Training and Development Journal*, 39, no. 5 (May 1985), 76–82.

_____, and Nicolas S. Majluf, "The Corporate Strategic Planning Process," *Interfaces*, 14, no. 1 (January–February 1984b), 47–60.

_____, and Nicolas S. Majluf, *Strategic Management: An Integrative Perspective* (Englewood Cliffs, NJ: Prentice Hall, 1984).

_____, and Manuel No, "Linking Technology and Business Strategy: A Methodological Approach and an Illustration," in Rakesh K. Sarin (Ed.), *Perspectives in Operations Management: Essays in Honor of Elwood S. Buffa* (Boston, MA: Kluwer Academic Publishers, 1993), 133–155.

HAYES, Robert H., and Steven C. Wheelwright, "Link Manufacturing Process and Product Life Cycles," *Harvard Business Review*, 57, no. 2 (January–February 1979), 133–140.

_____, and Steven C. Wheelwright, *Restoring Our Competitive Edge: Competing Through*

Manufacturing (New York: John Wiley, 1984).

_____, Steven C. Wheelwright, and Kim B. Clark, *Dynamic Manufacturing: Creating the Learning Organization* (New York: Free Press, 1988).

HEINRITZ, Stuart F., Paul V. Farrell, and Clifton L. Smith, *Purchasing: Principles and Applications*, 7th edition (Englewood Cliffs, NJ: Prentice Hall, 1986).

HESKETT, James, W. Earl Sasser, and Christopher Hart, *Service Breakthroughs: Changing the Rules of the Game* (New York: The Free Press, 1990).

HORWITCH, Mel (ed.), *Technology in the Modern Corporation: A Strategic Perspective*, (New York: Pergamon Press, 1986).

IMAI, Masaaki, *Kaizen* (New York: McGraw-Hill Publishing, 1986).

JOHNSON, H. Thomas, and Robert S. Kaplan, Relevance Lost: *The Rise and Fall of Management Accounting* (Boston, MA: Harvard Business School Press, 1987).

JURAN, Joseph M., *Juran on Quality by Design* (New York: The Free Press, 1992).

_____, (Editor), *Quality Control Handbook*. 3rd ed. (New York: McGraw-Hill, 1974).

_____, and Frank M. Gryna. *Quality Planning and Analysis* (New York: McGraw-Hill, 1980).

KAPLAN, Robert S., *Measures for Manufacturing Excellence* (Boston, MA: Harvard Business School Press, 1990).

_____, "Measuring Manufacturing Performance: A New Challenge for Managerial Accounting Research," *The Accounting Review*, 58, no. 4 (October 1983), 686–705.

_____, and David P. Norton, "The Balanced Scorecard—Measures that Drive Performance," *Harvard Business Review* (January–February, 1992) 71–79.

_____, and David P. Norton, "Putting the Balanced Scorecard to Work," *Harvard Business Review* (September–October, 1993) 134–142.

KATZENBACH, Jon, and Douglas Smith, *The Wisdom of Teams: Creating the High-Perfor-*

mance Organization (Boston, MA: Harvard Business School Press, 1993).

KOCHAN, Thomas, and Michael Useem (eds.), *Transforming Organizations* (New York: Oxford University Press, 1992).

KOH, Lynnet, *Strategic Analysis of the Worldwide Telecommunications Equipment Industry*, unpublished masters thesis, Sloan School of Management, MIT (1986).

KOTTER, John P., *A Force for Change: How Leadership Differs from Management* (New York: Free Press, 1990).

_____, *The Leadership Factor* (New York: Free Press, 1988).

LAWLER, Edward E. III, *The Ultimate Advantage: Creating the High-Involvement Organization* (San Francisco, CA: Jossey-Bass, 1992).

LEARNED, Edmund P., C. Roland Christensen, Kenneth R. Andrews, and William D. Guth, *Business Policy: Text and Cases* (Homewood, IL: Richard D. Irwin, 1965).

LEE, Kung-Shih, *A Business Strategy for a Life-Insurance Company*, unpublished masters thesis, MIT, Sloan School of Management, 1993.

LEIBFRIED, Kathleen H.J., and C.J. McNair, *Benchmarking: A Tool for Continuous Improvement* (New York: HarperCollins, 1992).

LEWIS, Jordan D., *Partnerships for Profit: Structuring and Managing Strategic Alliances* (New York: Free Press, 1990).

LINDBLOM, Charles E., "The Science of Muddling Through," *Public Administration Review* (Spring 1959), 79–88.

LORANGE, Peter, *Corporate Planning: An Executive Viewpoint* (Englewood Cliffs, NJ: Prentice Hall, 1980).

LORANGE, Peter, and Johan Roos, *Strategic Alliances: Formation, Implementation and Evolution* (Cambridge, MA: Blackwell, 1992).

MacDUFFIE, John P., and John F. Krafcik, "Integrating Technology and Human Resources for High-Performance Manufacturing: Evidence from the International Auto Industry," in Thomas A. Kochan, and Michael Useem (eds.), *Transforming Organi-*

zations (New York: Oxford University Press, 1992).

MACEDA, Emmanuel P., *Strategic Analysis: Du Pont Company, Engineering Polymers Division,* unpublished student paper, Sloan School of Management, MIT, 1988.

MACMILLAN, Ian C., "Seizing Competitive Advantage," *The Journal of Business Strategy* (Spring 1982), 43–57.

MALONE, Thomas W., and John F. Rockart, "Computers, Networks, and the Corporation," *Scientific American,* (September 1991),121–136.

_____, and Stephen A. Smith, "Modeling the Performance of Organizational Structures," *Operations Research,* 36, no. 3 (May–June 1988), 421–436.

_____, JoAnne Yates, and Robert I. Benjamin, "Elcctronic Markcts and Elcctronic Hierarchies," *Communications of the ACM,* 30 (1987), 484–497.

Manufacturing 21 Report —The Future of Japanese Manufacturing, (Whealing, IL: Association for Manufacturing Excellence, 1990).

MARSHALL, Paul W., et al., *Operations Management: Text and Cases* (Homewood, IL: Richard D. Irwin, 1975).

McTAGGART, James M., "The Ultimate Takeover Defense: Closing the Value Gap," *Planning Review* (January–February 1988), 27–32.

_____, Peter W. Kontes, and Michael C. Mankis, *The Value Imperative: Managing for Superior Shareholder Returns* (New York: Free Press, 1994).

MINTZBERG, Henry, "Crafting Strategy," *Harvard Business Review,* 65, no. 1 (July–August 1987), 66–75.

_____, "Patterns in Strategy Formation," *Management Science* (1976), 934–948.

_____, and James A. Waters, "Of Strategy Delivered and Emergent," *Strategic Management Journal,* 6, no. 3 (July–September 1985), 257–272.

MOODY, Patricia E., *Strategic Manufacturing: Dynamic New Directions for the 1990s* (Homewood, IL: Dow-Jones Irwin, 1990).

MUIRHEAD, Greg, "The ABC's of PBMs: Pharmacy Benefit Managers Control Pharmacy Industry," Drug Topics, 138, no.17 (September 5, 1994), 76.

MYERS, Stewart C., "Finance Theory and Financial Strategy" *Interfaces,* 14, no. 1 (January–February 1984), 126–137.

NADLER, David, Marc Gerstein, Robert Shaw, and Associates, *Organizational Architecture: Designs for Changing Organizations* (San Francisco, CA: Jossey-Bass, 1992).

NELSON, Richard, "Recent Writing on Competitiveness: Boxing the Compass," *California Management Review,* 34, no 2 (Winter 1992), 127–137.

_____, "Why Do Firm Differ, and How Does It Matter?", in Richard Rumelt, Dan E. Schendel, and David J. Teece (eds.) *Fundamental Issues in Strategy* (Boston, MA: Harvard Business School Press, 1994), 247–269.

NICHOLS, Nancy A., "Medicine, Management, and Mergers," *Harvard Business Review,* (November–December 1994), 110.

NO, Manuel, *Developing a Methodology for Technology Strategy: An Application in the High Technology Industry,* masters thesis, Sloan School of Management, MIT (1991).

NOORI, Hamid, *Managing the Dynamics of New Technology* (Englewood Cliffs, NJ: Prentice Hall, 1990).

ORTEGA, Luis A., *Analysis of the Development of a Strategic Planning System,* unpublished masters thesis, Sloan School of Management (Cambridge, MA: MIT, 1985).

OSTER, Sharon M., *Modern Competitive Analysis,* 2nd ed.(New York: Oxford University Press, 1994).

PARKER, Glenn M., *Team Players and Teamwork: The New Competitive Business Strategy* (San Francisco, CA: Jossey-Bass, 1990).

PETERAF, Margaret A., "The Cornerstones of Competitive Advantage: A Resource-Based View," *Strategic Management Journal,* 14, no. 3 (March 1993) 179–192.

PFEFFER, Jeffrey, *Competitive Advantage through People* (Boston, MA: Harvard Business School Press, 1994).

_____, *Managing with Power: Politics and Influence in Organizations* (Boston, MA: Harvard Business School Press, 1992).

PINE, B. Joseph, II, *Mass Customization: The New Frontier in Business Competition* (Boston, MA: Harvard Business School Press, 1993).

PORTER, Michael E, *Competition in Global Industries* (Boston, MA: Harvard Business School Press, 1986).

_____, *Competitive Advantage: Creating and Sustaining Superior Performance* (New York: The Free Press, 1985).

_____, *Competitive Strategy: Techniques for Analyzing Industries and Competitors* (New York: The Free Press, 1980).

_____, "From Competitive Advantage to Corporate Strategy," *Harvard Business Review* 65, no. 3 (May–June 1987) 43–59.

_____, "Towards a Dynamic Theory of Strategy," Strategic Management Journal, 12 (Winter 1991), 95–117.

PRAHALAD, C.K., and Gary Hamel, "The Core Competence of the Corporation," *Harvard Business Review* (May–June 1990), 71–91.

QUINN, James Brian, "Formulating Strategy One Step at a Time," *The Journal of Business Strategy*, 1, no. 3 (Winter 1981), 42–63.

_____, *Strategy for Changes—Logical Incrementalism* (Homewood, IL: Richard D. Irwin, 1980).

_____, Henry Mintzberg, and Robert M. James, *The Strategy Process: Concepts, Context, and Cases* (Englewood Cliffs, NJ: Prentice Hall, 1988).

ROBERTS, Edward B. (ed.), *Generating Technological Innovation* (New York: Oxford University Press, 1987).

ROTHSCHILD, William E., "How to Insure the Continuous Growth of Strategic Planning," *The Journal of Business Strategy*, 1, no. 1 (Summer 1980), 11–18.

ROUSSEL, Philip A., Kamal N. Saad, Tamara J. Erickson, *Third Generation R&D*, (Boston, MA: Harvard Business School Press, 1991).

RUMELT, Richard P., "How Much Does Industry Matter?", *Strategic Management Journal*, 12 (1991), 167–185.

SARIN, Rakesh K., (ed.), *Perspectives in Operations Management: Essays in Honor of Elwood S. Buffa* (Boston, MA: Kluwer Academic Publishers, 1993).

SCHANNAARS, Steven P., *Marketing Strategy: A Customer Driven Approach* (New York: The Free Press, 1991).

SCHEIN, Edgar S., *Career Dynamics* (Reading, MA: Addison-Wesley, 1978), 189–256.

_____, *Organizational Culture and Leadership* (San Francisco, CA: Jossey-Bass, 1992).

SCHERER, F. M., *Industrial Market Structure and Economic Performance*, 2nd ed. (Boston: Houghton Mifflin, 1980).

SCHMALENSEE, Richard, "Do Markets Differ Much?", *The American Economic Review*, 75 (June 1985), 341–351.

SCHONBERGER, Richard, *Building a Chain of Customers* (New York: The Free Press, 1990).

_____, *Japanese Manufacturing Techniques* (New York: The Free Press, 1982).

_____, *World Class Manufacturing: The Lessons of Simplicity Applied* (New York: The Free Press, 1987).

SENGE, Peter, *The Fifth Discipline: The Art and Practice of the Learning Organization* (New York: Doubleday, 1990).

SHANK, John K., and Vijay Govindarajan, *Strategic Cost Management: The New Tool for Competitive Advantage* (New York: Free Press, 1993).

SHAPIRO, Alan C., "Corporate Strategy and the Capital Budgeting Decision," *Midland Corporate Finance Journal*, 3, no. 1 (Spring 1985), 22–36.

SHOEMAKER, Paul J.H., "Scenario Planning: A Tool for Strategic Thinking," *Sloan Management Review*, 36, no. 2 (Winter 1995), 25–40.

_____, "When and How to Use Scenario Planning: A Heuristic Approach with Illustrations," *Journal of Forecasting* 10 (1991) 549–564.

_____, and Cornelius A.J.M. van der Heijden, "Strategic Planning at the Royal Dutch/Shell," *Journal of Strategic Change*, 2 (1993) 157–171.

SIMON, Herbert A., *Administrative Behavior: A Study of Decision-Making Processes in Administrative Organizations* (New York: The Free Press, 1976).

SKINNER, Wickham, "The Focused Factory," *Harvard Business Review*, 52, no. 3 (May–June 1974), 113–121.

_____, *Manufacturing: The Formidable Competitive Weapon*, (New York: John Wiley & Sons (1985).

STEINER, George A., and John B. Miner, *Management Policy and Strategy* (New York: Macmillan, 1977).

STEWART, G. Bennett, III, *The Quest for Value: A Guide for Senior Managers* (New York: Harper Business, 1991).

STONICH, Paul J., "How to Use Strategic Funds Programming," *The Journal of Business Strategy*, no. 2 (Fall 1980), 35–50.

STUCKEY, John, and David White, "When and When Not to Vertically Integrate," *Sloan Management Review*, 34, no 3 (Spring 1993), 71–83.

SUZAKI, Kiyoshi, *The Manufacturing Challenge: Techniques for Continuous Improvements* (New York: The Free Press, 1987).

TADA, Masayuki, *Corporate Strategy for a Japanese Steel Manufacturing Company*, unpublished masters thesis, Sloan School of Management, MIT, 1993.

TAYLOR, William, "The Logic of Global Business: An Interview with ABB's Percy Barnevik," *Harvard Business Review*, 69, no. 2 (March–April 1991), 91–105.

TEECE, David J. (ed.), *The Competitive Challenge: Strategies for Industrial Innovation and Renewal* (Cambridge, MA: Ballinger Publishing Co., 1987).

_____, "Profiting from Technological Innovations: Implications for Integration, Collaboration, Licensing, and Public Policy," in David J. Teece, ed., *The Competitive Challenge: Strategies for Industrial Innovations and Renewal*, (Cambridge, MA: Ballinger Publishing Co., 1987).

TULLY, Shawn, "America's Best Wealth Creators," *Fortune* (November 28, 1994) 143–162.

TWISS, Brian, *Managing Technological Innovation* (London: Longman Group, 1982).

TWISS, B., and M. Goodridge, *Managing Technology for Competitive Advantage: Integrating Technological and Organizational Development: From Strategy to Action* (Aulander, NC: Pitman, 1989).

UTTERBACK, James M., *Mastering the Dynamics of Innovation* (Boston, MA: Harvard Business School Press, 1994).

_____, and L. Kim, "Invasion of an Established Business by Radical Innovation," *Proceedings from The Management of Productivity and Technology in Manufacturing*, 113–151, edited by P. R. Kleindorfer (New York: Plenum Press, 1986).

VANCIL, Richard F., "Better Management of Corporate Development," *Harvard Business Review*, 50. no. 5 (September–October 1972), 53–62.

VANCIL, Richard F., and Peter Lorange, "Strategic Planning in Diversified Companies," *Harvard Business Review*, 53, no. 1 (January–February 1975), 81–90.

VON HIPPEL, Eric, *The Sources of Innovation* (New York: Oxford, 1988).

WACK, P., "Scenarios: Shooting the Rapids," *Harvard Business Review* (November–December 1985) 139–150.

_____, "Scenarios: Uncharted Waters Ahead," *Harvard Business Review* (September–October 1985) 73–89.

WALKER, Gordon, "Strategic Sourcing, Vertical Integration and Transaction Costs," *Interfaces*, 19, (May–June 1988), 62–73.

WERNERFELT, Birger, "A Resource-Based View of the Firm," *Strategic Management Journal*, 5 (1984), 171–180.

_____, and Cynthia Montgomery, "Tobin's q and the Importance of Focus in Firm Performance," *The American Economic Review*, 78, no 1, 246–250.

WHEELWRIGHT, Steven C., "Japan, Where Operations Really Are Strategic," *Harvard Business Review*, 59, no. 4 (July–August 1981), 67–74.

_____, and Kim B. Clark, *Revolutionizing Product Development* (New York: The Free Press, 1992).

WHITE, B. L., *The Technology Assessment Process. A Strategic Framework for Managing Technical Innovation* (Westport, CT: Quorum Books, 1988).

WHITELEY, Richard C., *The Customer Driven Company* (Reading, MA: Addison-Wesley, 1991).

WILLIAMSON, Oliver E., *The Economic Institutions of Capitalism* (New York: Free Press, 1985).

_____, *Markets and Hierarchies: Analysis and Antitrust Implications* (New York: Free Press, 1975).

WOMACK, James P., Daniel T. Jones, and Daniel Roos, *The Machine that Changed the World*, (New York: Rawson Associates, 1990).

WRAPP, H. Edward, "Good Managers Don't Make Policy Decisions," *Harvard Business Review*, 62, no. 4 (July–August 1984), 8–21.

YAVITZ, Boris, and William H. Newman, *Strategy in Action. The Execution, Politics and Payoff of Business Planning* (New York: The Free Press, 1982).

ZAKON, Alan J., "Capital Structure Optimization," in J. F. Weston and M. B. Goudzwaard, eds., *The Treasurer's Handbook* (Homewood, IL: Dow Jones-Irwin, 1976).

Index